owed by malic acid at slightly lower concentration, with trace amounts of citric

n thereafter has been taken. **alcohol**, the common name for ethanol, is variously

gn, '°'. Since the latter part of the 1990s, the alcohol content in wine has become

nd red wines other than pinot noir. **alternative varieties** is a strictly non-scientific

itis vinifera varieties. **antioxidant** is a term that is frequently found on labels of

ulphite (223) or ascorbic acid (300), these numbers simply substituting for the

anuary 2009. The change was necessitated by the terms of the Wine Agreement

ll of a wine early in its life, when the varietal expression of the grape or grapes is

es with young wines (especially cabernet sauvignon) it is not a fault if there is

tween the different components of wine, including alcohol, acidity, sweetness,

ass a barrique (225 l) or a hogshead (300 l). The latter was once the most widely

ons (500 l). **barrel maturation** is used for all quality red wines, and for some white

tringency, and is detectable on the back of the tongue (rather than the gums or

th, principally deriving from alcohol and tannin. **bouquet** is the smell of the wine

ers present in any wine. **breathing** results from the removal of the seal from the

g wine, but can, on occasion, remove the so-called bottle-stink from old wines.

ak-matured, but which can also develop from long bottle age. It is typically found

stralia, first making the statistical records in the middle of the 1980s. At that time

ated. **cabernet sauvignon**, a spontaneous crossing of interplanted cabernet franc

hose besotted by pinot noir would strongly disagree. **carbonic maceration** is the

her than yeast. It is a complex process, but suffice it to say that once the alcohol

ally linked to a given grape variety (that is, varietal character), or terroir (regional

nd will likely always be so, although there is a gulf between Australia's chardonnay

a wine conforming exactly to style and of ver   but it does have

oreign or 'off ' odour or flav   a wine of quality.

actor in determining w   to second place.

oying describes the pa   ficient acidity to

ly tannins, and which   ring the making

taint. **corks**, obviously e   rk tree, *Quercus*

ed hexagonal cells per   has proved very

our a bottle of wine int   s, a specifically

hite, it will separate the   ent at the bottom of the bottle.

e is old and may have developed reduced or other similar characteristics. **dry** is

nt absence of sweetness, with a normal technical cut-off of 7 grams per litre of

a trio (the other two being fruity and savoury), which has as much to do with

t the least unpleasant, ranging from fresh earth to the smell of litter on a forest

ntation, the most common in fermenting or recently fermented wines being ethyl

tion, at its most simple, is the process of converting grape sugar to ethanol (ethyl

omplex, and is best found in technical wine books or manuals. **finish** is the flavour

a critical factor in determining the quality of a wine. **firm** is a term usually applied

wine is made by the addition of grape-derived spirit to partly fermented juice

nd leaves the wine with not less than 18% alc/vol. **fruity** describes the aroma and

rapes in Australia until 1969, when the first machine harvester arrived after its

een continually improved; in the early decades, the removal of the bunches was

eld of vines, regardless of the impact on quality; or to increase quality, but not

growing season. **jammy** is a tasting term describing excessively ripe and heavy

s which fall to the bottom of the barrel or tank at the end of primary fermentation.

or white wine vinification. It takes place while the juice of the grape remains in

unstoppable over the 25 years from 1980. By 2005 it was promiscuously planted

play varietal character. **metallic** is the taste of metal, sometimes encountered in

sult of Bretannomyces remaining after attempts to remove it with sulphur dioxide.

bviously alcohol, acid and tannins, but also extending to the interaction of those

e, largely used by winemakers to describe their approach to creating their wine(s).

bottled. **nose** is an all-encompassing term embracing both aroma and bouquet.

THE INVENTORS OF THE MODERN WINE GLASS

Halliday

POCKET WINE COMPANION

The 2023 guide to Australia's best value wines

Hardie Grant

BOOKS

The *Pocket Wine Companion 2023* presents the best value wines from Australia's definitive wine guide. While value can be difficult to define with wine, it's a big part of the decision when it comes to choosing a bottle. Here we've put it front and centre by only featuring the wineries and wines with value rosettes from the *Wine Companion 2023*.

This guide is divided into states, so that you can find a value drop wherever you are in Australia – whether you're looking to visit a winery, buy local, or learn which areas are able to produce which wine varieties at great-value pricepoints. Wineries are listed alphabetically within their zone or region, there's a map on the next page to help you navigate these. Where the winery sources grapes from a number of regions, they will appear at the beginning of their state.

SA p.36

VIC p.98

WA p.148

TAS p.178

Wine zones and regions

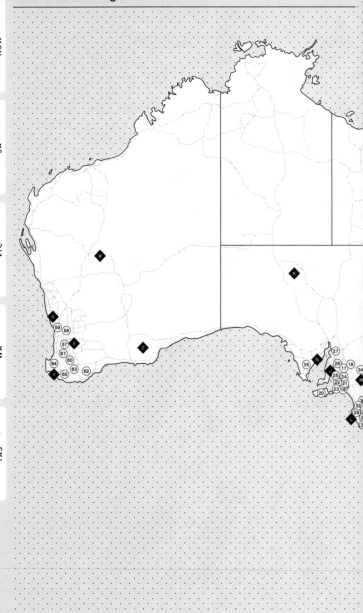

ZONE		REGION
New South Wales		
A Big Rivers	1	Murray Darling
	2	Perricoota
	3	Riverina
	4	Swan Hill
B Central Ranges	5	Cowra
	6	Mudgee
	7	Orange
C Hunter Valley	8	Hunter
D Northern Rivers	9	Hastings River
E Northern Slopes	10	New England Australia
F South Coast	11	Shoalhaven Coast
	12	Southern Highlands
G Southern New South Wales	13	Canberra District
	14	Gundagai
	15	Hilltops
	16	Tumbarumba
H Western Plains		
South Australia		
J* Barossa	17	Barossa Valley
	18	Eden Valley
Fleurieu	19	Currency Creek
	20	Kangaroo Island
	21	Langhorne Creek
	22	McLaren Vale
	23	Southern Fleurieu
Mount Lofty Ranges	24	Adelaide Hills
	25	Adelaide Plains
	26	Clare Valley
K Far North	27	Southern Flinders Ranges
L Limestone Coast	28	Coonawarra
	29	Mount Benson
	30	Mount Gambier
	31	Padthaway
	32	Robe
	33	Wrattonbully
M Lower Murray	34	Riverland
N The Peninsulas	35	Southern Eyre Peninsula
Victoria		
P Central Victoria	36	Bendigo
	37	Goulburn Valley
	38	Heathcote
	39	Strathbogie Ranges
	40	Upper Goulburn
Q Gippsland		
R North East Victoria	41	Alpine Valleys
	42	Beechworth
	43	Glenrowan
	44	King Valley
	45	Rutherglen
S North West Victoria	46	Murray Darling
	47	Swan Hill
T Port Phillip	48	Geelong
	49	Macedon Ranges
	50	Mornington Peninsula
	51	Sunbury
	52	Yarra Valley
U Western Victoria	53	Ballarat
	54	Grampians
	55	Henty
	56	Pyrenees
Western Australia		
V Central Western Australia		
W Eastern Plains, Inland and North of Western Australia		
X Greater Perth	57	Peel
	58	Perth Hills
	59	Swan District
Y South West Australia	60	Blackwood Valley
	61	Geographe
	62	Great Southern
	63	Manjimup
	64	Margaret River
	65	Pemberton
Z West Australian South East Coastal		
Tasmania		
	66	East Coast Tasmania
	67	Northern Tasmania
	68	Southern Tasmania
Queensland		
	69	Granite Belt
	70	South Burnett
* Adelaide Super Zone		

5

2023

Tyson Stelzer

The dynamic world of Australian wine is fast on the move, and 2021–22 certainly delivered another tumultuous and nail-biting year of instability – environmentally, economically and politically.

The lingering ramifications of China's so-called anti-dumping trade tariffs since late 2020 have shrivelled Australia's biggest wine export market by 97%. Australia's next 5 top export markets, the UK, US, Canada, Germany and New Zealand, also dropped slightly in 2021. The only Australian wine exports not to drop in value in 2021 were the over $75/bottle category.

Domestic consumption of Australian wine likewise saw a decline in volume and an even larger decline in value in 2021. The consequences on grape prices were debilitating, with the average price of shiraz falling from $650/tonne in 2020 to just $350/tonne in 2022. Meanwhile, after three lean years, the record national crush of more than 2 million tonnes in 2021 landed at precisely the wrong time. The net effect of this perfect storm has been to overload the national wine stocks to more than 2 billion litres, the highest in 15 years. Set against this backdrop, truncated yields across most regions in the 2022 harvest have perhaps proved to be a blessing in disguise.

At the time of writing, one of the most successful men in Australian wine, John Casella, has put his entire estate of 5650ha of vineyards on the market, representing more than one 25th of the nation's vineyard surface.

In retail land, the pendulum has swung back to a cycle of wine dumping, and my inbox has been bombarded with a daily parade of discounting. An unusual, and perhaps unprecedented, dynamic is increasingly emerging in which an ocean of wine is being flogged off for a song, while the great wines of the world have never been more highly sought after or more scarce. Australia's most celebrated estates have enjoyed unprecedented demand over the past two years. At the same time, Australian wine imports continue to progressively increase in both volume and value. Champagne alone smashed all records and shipped more than 10 million bottles into Australia in 2021.

The wine world is more competitive and global than ever, and in these unstable times it is vital for Australian

wine to continue to raise its game. This is a pivotal era that will set the direction for Australia's wine future.

Given this volatile environment, it has never been more important for you to distinguish the truly great wines from the ocean of ho-hum, to anticipate the top vintages, and to be ready to pounce the instant they land. This is why our expanded tasting team has assessed more than 8000 wines for this edition, and why we are releasing more reviews more often through the *Halliday* magazine and www.winecompanion.com.au.

The great 2021 vintage has landed, with most of Victoria, South Australia and Tasmania flourishing under wonderfully cool, classic conditions reminiscent of the great seasons of the 1980s and 1990s. Harvest 2022 is still underway at the time of writing, but early reports indicate similarly elegant conditions. We have much to look forward to!

Now is the time to sign up to the mailing lists of your favourite producers and to secure your allocations the moment they're unleashed. Build a relationship with a good retailer and make sure you're on their list to be alerted when new arrivals land. Armed with our selections, you'll be set to enjoy all the finest wines in Australia again this year.

NSW

97 **Isle Black Label Pinot Noir 2020, Tasmania** A very arresting and complex bouquet of dark berries and forest floor, the palate with an infusion of savoury spices, the texture and structure perfect.
Screw cap. | 13.5% alc. | Drink 2024-2035 | $90 | JH

96 **Intrigue Black Label Pinot Noir 2020, Tasmania** A stunning bouquet, with outright perfume sure to emerge in a year or 2; the palate already with spices alongside pure red and black cherry fruit.
Screw cap. | 13% alc. | Drink 2023-2033 | $70 | JH

Merriworth ★★★☆

63 Merriworth Road, Tea Tree, Tas 7017 **T** 0406 657 774 **www**.merriworth.com.au **WINEMAKER** Anna Pooley and Justin Bubb **VITICULTURIST** Mark McNamara **EST.** 2017 **DOZENS** 600 **VYDS** 2ha

It was their love of pinot noir that lured Mark McNamara and Kirralee Hatch to Tasmania after several years studying viticulture and winemaking on the Australian mainland. In 2017 they purchased the 2ha Third Child vineyard and renamed it Merriworth. The site is home to 9 clones of pinot noir and 3 of riesling, planted on river flats of cracking clay soil and shallow, eroded slopes over dolerite rock. Vibrant, young wines are made with accuracy and precision by Anna Pooley and Justin Bubb.

93 **Estate Riesling 2021, Tasmania** A cool season, pristine fruit and acute winemaking make for a delightfully precise riesling. Nuances of rose petal dance over a spine of lemon, lime and Granny Smith apple. Energetic acid drive leads a long finish, brushed with just the right touch of residual sweetness. Screw cap. | 12.5% alc. | Drink 2022-2031 | $27 | TS

Pooley Wines Winery of the Year 2023 ★★★★★

Butcher's Hill Vineyard, 1431 Richmond Road, Richmond, Tas 7025 **T** (03) 6260 2895 **www**.pooleywines.com.au **OPEN** 7 days 10-5 **WINEMAKER** Anna Pooley, Justin Bubb **VITICULTURIST** Hannah McKay **EST.** 1985 **DOZENS** 8500 **VYDS** 18ha

Pooley Wines is a glowing exemplar of a boutique Tasmanian family estate. Three generations of the family have been involved in its development, with the little hands of the fourth generation now starting to get involved. A cellar door was established in the heritage-listed sandstone barn and coach house of the distinguished 1830s convict-built Georgian home, standing in pride of place on the heritage property. Wine quality has risen to dramatic effect, no small feat while doubling production, since the return to Tasmania of Anna Pooley and husband Justin Bubb to establish the winemaking arm of the estate in 2012. Conversion to organic viticulture is currently underway, with a goal of achieving certification by the 2026 vintage. Pooley is the Wine Companion 2023 Winery of the Year. (TS)

99 **Jack Denis Pooley Pinot Noir 2020, Tasmania** This 33% whole-bunch pinot has depth beyond that of its siblings. It's full-on forest floor, full-on savoury spices, with tannins made to measure, but all bow down to the primacy of the dark berry fruit of the impossibly long finish. World class. Screw cap. | 13.1% alc. | Drink 2022-2037 | $140 | JH | ♥

97 **Butcher's Hill Pinot Noir 2020, Tasmania** Vivid crimson purple, slightly deeper than that of its siblings. The bouquet is extremely complex, with satsuma plum, dark cherry and a crescendo of spices, the palate as elegant as it is intense, and throwing in a pinch of savoury tannins.
Screw cap. | 13.1% alc. | Drink 2022-2035 | $70 | JH

Cooinda Vale Pinot Noir 2020, Tasmania Although there's only 15% whole bunches, it makes its presence felt right from the first whiff, the first sip, like a Rubik's Cube in the hands of an expert. Satisfyingly elegant. Screw cap. | 13.2% alc. | Drink 2022-2035 | $70 | JH

96 **Cooinda Vale Chardonnay 2020, Tasmania** Identical vinification to Butcher's Hill except a 20-day (not 22) ferment. This has more intensity, more length, more grapefruit, but still has the finesse and balance of its Butcher's Hill sibling. Screw cap. | 13.2% alc. | Drink 2022-2035 | $65 | JH

Pressing Matters ★★★★★

665 Middle Tea Tree Road, Tea Tree, Tas 7017 **T** 0474 380 109 **www**.pressingmatters.com.au **OPEN** Thurs-Sun 10-4 by appt **WINEMAKER** Samantha Connew **VITICULTURIST** Mark Hoey **EST.** 2002 **DOZENS** 2600 **VYDS** 7.3ha

Greg Melick wears more hats than most people manage in a lifetime. He is a major general (the highest rank in the Australian Army Reserve) a top level barrister (senior counsel) and has presided over a number of headline special commissions and enquiries into subjects as diverse as cricket match-fixing and the Beaconsfield mine collapse. Yet, if asked, he would probably nominate wine as his major focus in life. Having built up an exceptional cellar of the great wines of Europe, he has turned his attention to grape growing and winemaking. (JH)

182

Wineries

❶ Name
The name of the producer, as it appears on the front label, is used throughout the book.

❷ Opening hours
These only appear when a winery is open regularly, although many wineries may in fact be prepared to open by appointment. A telephone call will establish whether this is possible or not. For space reasons we have simplified the open hours listed; where the hours vary each day or for holidays, we simply refer the reader to the website.

❸ Winemakers
In all but the smallest producers, the winemaker is simply the head of a team; there may be many executive winemakers actually responsible for specific wines in the medium to large companies (80 000 dozens and upwards).

❹ Viticulturists
Viticulturists have long been the unsung heroes of Australian wine – you can't make great wine without great fruit. For the first time this year, we are proud to list the viticulturist for many estates.

❺ Contact details
The contact details are usually those of the winery and cellar door, but in a few instances may simply be a postal address; this occurs when the wine is made at another winery or wineries, and is sold only through the website and/or retail outlets.

❻ Website
An important reference point, normally containing material not found (for space reasons) in this book.

❼ Established
Keep in mind that some makers consider the year in which they purchased the land to be the year of establishment, others the year in which they first planted grapes, others the year they first made wine, and so on.

❽ Vineyards
Shows the hectares of vineyard(s) owned by the winery.

❾ Dozens
This figure (representing the number of 9-litre/12-bottle cases produced each year) is merely an indication of the size of the operation. Some winery entries do not feature a production figure: this is typically because the winery regards this information as confidential.

❿ Features
These symbols highlight what a winery offers as part of their cellar door experience, to help you in planning a visit.

Ⓨ **Cellar door sales.**

🍴 **Food.** From lunch platters to à la carte restaurants.

🛏 **Accommodation.** From B&B cottages to luxury vineyard apartments.

🎵 **Music events.** From monthly jazz in the vineyard to spectacular yearly concerts.

⑪ Winery ratings

★★★★★ Outstanding winery regularly producing wines of exemplary quality and typicity.

Where the winery name itself is printed in orange, it is a winery generally acknowledged to have had a long track record of excellence in the context of its region, having typically held a 5-star rating continuously for 10 years – truly the best of the best.

★★★★★ Outstanding winery capable of producing wines of very high quality, and did so this year.

★★★★☆ Excellent winery able to produce wines of high to very high quality, knocking on the door of a 5-star rating.

★★★★ Very good producer of wines with class and character.

★★★☆ A solid, usually reliable, maker of good, sometimes very good, wines.

★★★ A typically good winery, but often has a few lesser wines.

⑫ Wine ratings

97–99	**Exceptional.** Wines of major trophy standard in important wine shows.
95–96	**Outstanding.** Wines of gold medal standard, usually with a great pedigree.
94	Wines on the cusp of gold medal status.
90–93	**Highly recommended.** Wines of silver medal standard, wines of great quality, style and character, and worthy of a place in any cellar.
89	**Recommended.** Wines on the cusp of silver medal standard.
86–88	Wines of bronze medal standard; well-produced, flavoursome wines, usually not requiring cellaring.
84–85	**Acceptable.** Wines of good commercial quality, free from significant fault.

❿ Tasting notes

The tasting note opens with the vintage of the wine tasted. This tasting note will have been written within the 12 months prior to publication. Even that is a long time, and during the life of this book the wine will almost certainly change.

Ⓐ	Ⓑ	Ⓒ	Ⓓ	Ⓔ
Screw cap.	13% alc.	Drink 2022–2025	$50	JF

Ⓐ Closure
This is the closure used for this particular wine. The closures in use for the wines tasted for this year's *Wine Companion* are (in descending order): screw cap 90.7% (last year 86.8%), one-piece natural cork 4.1% (last year 6%), Diam 3.9% (last year 5.6%) and crown seal 0.7%. The remaining 0.6% (in order of importance) are Vinolok, agglomerate, Zork, synthetic and can.

Ⓑ Alcohol percentage
This information is in one sense self-explanatory. What is less obvious is the increasing concern of many Australian winemakers about the rise in alcohol levels, and much research and practical experimentation (for example, picking earlier or higher fermentation temperatures in open fermenters) is occurring. Reverse osmosis and yeast selection are two of the options available to decrease higher-than-desirable alcohol levels. Recent changes to domestic and export labelling mean the stated alcohol will be within a maximum of 0.5% difference to that obtained for analysis.

Ⓒ 'Drink-from' date
The optimal time to drink a wine is of course subjective; some of us love young wines and others old. This is as personal to the taster as their review and their score. We have proposed dates to when we would most love to drink this wine, and we commend these to you as a reference for managing your cellar and when to drink each bottle. We have long published drink-to dates, and for the first time this year, we are proud to introduce drink-from dates.

Ⓓ Price
Prices are provided by the winery. It should be regarded as a guide, particularly if purchased retail.

Ⓔ Taster
The initials DB, EL, JF, JH, JP, NG, PR and TS appearing at the end of the note signify that Dave Brookes, Erin Larkin, Jane Faulkner, James Halliday, Jeni Port, Ned Goodwin MW, Philip Rich or Tyson Stelzer tasted the wine and provided the tasting note and rating.

♥ Shortlisted for 2023 awards

Nominated by the tasting team as the best example of its variety/style in its region.

Tasting team

James Halliday

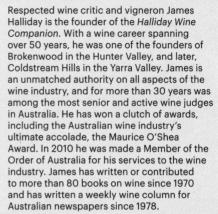

Respected wine critic and vigneron James Halliday is the founder of the *Halliday Wine Companion*. With a wine career spanning over 50 years, he was one of the founders of Brokenwood in the Hunter Valley, and later, Coldstream Hills in the Yarra Valley. James is an unmatched authority on all aspects of the wine industry, and for more than 30 years was among the most senior and active wine judges in Australia. He has won a clutch of awards, including the Australian wine industry's ultimate accolade, the Maurice O'Shea Award. In 2010 he was made a Member of the Order of Australia for his services to the wine industry. James has written or contributed to more than 80 books on wine since 1970 and has written a weekly wine column for Australian newspapers since 1978.

Regional focus: Langhorne Creek, Currency Creek, Kangaroo Island and Southern Fleurieu

Tyson Stelzer

Tyson Stelzer fell in love with wine more than 20 years ago and he is now a multi-award-winning wine writer, TV host and producer, and international speaker. Tyson is the author of 17 wine books, including six editions of *The Champagne Guide*, and a contributor to Jancis Robinson's *The Oxford Companion to Wine* (3rd edition), and regularly writes for many wine magazines. As an international speaker, Tyson has presented at wine events in 12 countries, and is also a regular judge and chair of wine shows throughout Australia. Tyson also hosts intimate Champagne tours.

Tyson is the chief editor for the *Halliday Wine Companion 2023*.

Regional focus: Tasmania and Queensland

Dave Brookes is a wine journalist with almost 30 years' experience working in the wine industry. Dave was awarded Dux of the Len Evans Tutorial in 2011 and is a sought-after wine judge and panel chair.

Regional focus: Barossa

Dave Brookes

Erin Larkin is a wine writer, judge and presenter. She is also an active consultant for retail and private clients, with a keen eye for quality and creativity in wine.

Regional focus: Western Australia, Limestone Coast, Clare Valley and Riverland

Erin Larkin

Jane Faulkner is a respected journalist. She has a special interest in Italian and alternative varieties and chairs several wine shows.

Regional focus: Southern NSW including Canberra District; Mornington Peninsula, Macedon Ranges, Sunbury and Gippsland

Jane Faulkner

Jeni Port is a wine writer and judge. She was a wine writer at *The Age* newspaper for 30 years, is deputy chair of the Wine List of the Year Awards, and was a founding board member of the Australian Women in Wine Awards.

Regional focus: Geelong and Port Philip, Central Victoria, North East Victoria, Western Victoria, North West Victoria, Mount Lofty Ranges including Adelaide Hills.

Jeni Port

Ned has worn many hats, including show judge, dux of the Len Evans Tutorial, sommelier, educator, TV host, wine buyer, consultant, critic and writer. Born in London, raised in Australia and educated in France and Japan, his international experience brings a fresh perspective to the *Wine Companion*.

Regional focus: McLaren Vale; Hunter Valley and regional New South Wales

Ned Goodwin
MW

Philip has more than 25 years' experience as a wine retailer, educator, show judge and writer. Philip co-founded Melbourne's Prince Wine Store and Bellota Wine Bar, wrote the wine column for *The Australian Financial Review* Magazine and has chaired various wine shows. Philip is general manager of wine at Karen Martini's restaurant Hero.

Regional focus: Yarra Valley

Philip Rich

Value wineries

Best Value Winery of the Year is closely tied to the awarding of rosettes for wines offering special value for money at their pricepoint. With more than 1400 rosettes awarded this year, the number of value wineries featured throughout these pages is again considerable. I prioritised not only the highest number of rosettes and the highest strike rate but also inclusion of at least two value wines under $30. When it comes to value, Western Australia leads the country, with three of our nine top contenders, including one very worthy winner!

Deep Woods Estate   MARGARET RIVER

The team, led by Julian Langworthy, has shown a thrilling disregard for accepted pricepoint quality; their entry-level wines present compelling drinking propositions, and their Reserve range frequently blitzes the competition in the quality–value stakes. (EL)

Runners up

Bleasdale Vineyards LANGHORNE CREEK

Bleasdale Vineyards breathes history. Paul Hotker, recognising that Bleasdale's larder of malbec, cabernet sauvignon and shiraz needed some balance, went to the Adelaide Hills and purchased riesling and pinot gris, with both the wines receiving value rosettes. (JH)

Bondar Wines MCLAREN VALE

A husband-and-wife team that has done everything right from the outset of Bondar Wines in 2009. Shiraz is its key, with grenache flourishing on the Blewitt Springs side. Of eight wines submitted this year, six were awarded special value rosettes. (JH)

Duke's Vineyard PORONGURUP

Duke's Magpie Hill vineyard is planted at the base of the Porongurup Range, and this site produces wines that are an ode to high-quality, cool-climate elegance. The vineyard is only so big, the production can only be so much; this limitation on quantity only adds to the excitement and the chase. (EL)

Garagiste MORNINGTON PENINSULA

The talented Barnaby Flanders focuses on Mornington Peninsula's leading varieties of chardonnay and pinot noir, turning them into exceptional wines. Le Stagiaire wines are unequivocally the best value wines on the Peninsula, matched to excellence, of course. (JF)

Hoddles Creek Estate YARRA VALLEY

This vineyard has been created by the D'Anna family with minimal assistance from outsiders. The property was purchased in 1960, the vines planted in 1997. The value for money represented across this portfolio is unparalleled. (JH)

Nick O'Leary Wines CANBERRA DISTRICT

Nick O'Leary has earned a reputation for making top-notch riesling. The White Rocks Riesling produced from the Westering vineyard is excellent value at $38, the Heywood Riesling at $34, and his regional offering crafted from several vineyards comes in at $25. Nick O'Leary represents quality and deliciousness in equal measure. (JF)

Riposte ADELAIDE HILLS

During Tim Knappstein's long winemaking history he has embraced and produced wines that everyday Australians can afford and enjoy. He and his son, Nick, continue at Riposte in the Adelaide Hills, sharing a similar philosophy. Be amazed at the quality of a host of wines – from pinot gris, sauvignon blanc and chardonnay to pinot noir priced at just $24. (JP)

Xanadu Wines MARGARET RIVER

In the hands of Glenn Goodall and Brendan Carr, wines are made to an exceptional standard at every pricepoint, showcasing their deep understanding of both the art of winemaking and the terroir of the region. While the Reserve and Stevens Road wines are undoubtedly the jewel in the Xanadu crown, the Black Label has time and again proven its quality and ageability, an astounding feat for a wine of circa $40. (EL)

WINE ZONES AND REGIONS

INTRODUCTION

HOW TO USE THIS BOOK

TASTING TEAM

2023'S BEST VALUE WINERIES

NSW

Led by Sydney and its population of more than 5 million people, New South Wales consumes more wine than any other state but it has only half the number of wineries of Victoria or South Australia. However, statistics being damned lies, NSW contributed 29% of the 2022 national crush, more than 1.7 times that of Victoria. Of its 16 regions, most are situated on the hills and foothills of the western side of the Great Dividing Range. Elevation is more important than latitude in shaping the climate of these regions.

The **Hunter Valley**, only an hour's drive north of Sydney, has truly unique, long-lived (7–20+ years) semillon and supple, medium-bodied shiraz as its foundations. Its erratic climate is hot but humid, and vintage rain a threat. It is a major tourist destination.

The Southern New South Wales zone has three regions of particular importance. The overall quality of the **Canberra District** is excellent. Its climate is strongly continental, with warm days and cold nights. Riesling and shiraz, with or without viognier, are its calling cards. **Hilltops** is adjacent, only a few kilometres from the northwestern tip of Canberra District. It is an important contract grapegrower of shiraz, cabernet sauvignon and chardonnay, plus small plantings of that most temperamental variety, nebbiolo. Finally, there is the tadpole-shaped region of **Tumbarumba**, its long western boundary the border with Victoria. Its cool elevations of 300–800m are well suited to chardonnay and pinot noir, which decorate the highest and most vertiginous slopes, with shiraz shouldering arms in the lower parts. Like Hilltops, it's a grapegrowing region with considerable potential.

The Central Ranges zone is home to **Mudgee**, at an elevation of 450m. Sturdy shiraz and cabernet sauvignon cover much of its vineyard area. The zone's other important region is **Orange**, spanning lofty altitudes between 800m and 1100m. Elevation and aspect result in an unexpectedly wide expanse of varieties, ranging from late-ripening shiraz and cabernet sauvignon to early ripening chardonnay, merlot, sauvignon blanc, pinot noir and increasingly refined sparkling, including our 2023 Sparkling Wine of the Year. **Riverina** produced 19% of the national crush in 2022. It is part of the engine room of the industry, and, coupled with the NSW share

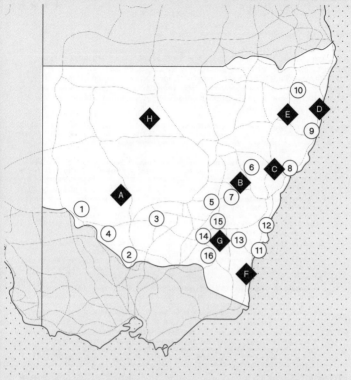

BIG RIVERS

CENTRAL RANGES

HUNTER VALLEY

NORTHERN RIVERS

NORTHEN SLOPES

SOUTH COAST

SOUTHERN NSW

WESTERN PLAINS

of the **Murray Darling/Swan Hill** output of 9% of the total, is of major economic importance.

ZONE		REGION	
A	Big Rivers	1	Murray Darling
		2	Perricoota
		3	Riverina
		4	Swan Hill
B	Central Ranges	5	Cowra
		6	Mudgee
		7	Orange
C	Hunter Valley	8	Hunter
D	Northern Rivers	9	Hastings River
E	Northern Slopes	10	New England Australia
F	South Coast	11	Shoalhaven Coast
		12	Southern Highlands
G	Southern New South Wales	13	Canberra District
		14	Gundagai
		15	Hilltops
		16	Tumbarumba
H	Western Plains		

Handpicked Wines ⓨⓜⓐ ★★★★★

50 Kensington Street, Chippendale, NSW 2008 **T** (03) 5983 0039 **www**.handpickedwines.com.au
OPEN Mon-Fri 11-10, w'ends 10-10 **WINEMAKER** Peter Dillon, Rohan Smith **EST**. 2001 **DOZENS** 100000
VYDS 83ha

Handpicked Wines is a multi-regional business with a flagship vineyard and winery on the Mornington Peninsula and vineyards in the Yarra Valley, Barossa Valley and Tasmania. They also make wines from many of Australia's leading fine wine regions. Director of winemaking Peter Dillon travels extensively to oversee quality throughout the regions; he and assistant winemaker Rohan Smith work closely with a team of viticulturists who manage the vineyards. (JH)

95   **Regional Selections Pinot Gris 2021, Mornington Peninsula** A fairly tight style with unusually racy acidity, so I'm assuming the fruit had been picked early. Oh and it's totally delicious. Light flavours of nashi pear and lemon, ginger blossom flower and fennel seeds. Screw cap. | 12.9% alc. | Drink 2022-2025 | $29 | JF

     Trial Batch Riesling 2021, Tasmania A heady aroma of lemon blossom, mandarin peel, grapefruit and ginger powder. The palate is finely tuned with tangy lemon-and-lime juice, a sherbet-powder feel to the lively acidity with a lick of sweetness on the finish, giving this some depth. It has a touch of raw-silk texture via phenolics, too. Screw cap. | 11.2% alc. | Drink 2022-2028 | $29 | JF

     Regional Selections Rosé 2021, Yarra Valley Sangiovese and nebbiolo come together to form this ultra-pale copper-hued rosé. It's delicious. Lightly aromatic, a squirt of red berries, a sprinkle of fresh basil and lemon balm with lemony freshness guaranteed. A juiciness across the palate, a mere hint of tannins to add some shape but ultimately, this is crisp, racy and seemingly thirst quenching. Screw cap. | 12.2% alc. | Drink 2022-2023 | $29 | JF

     Trial Batch Nebbiolo 2020, Pyrenees Seductive aromas of cherries and pips, tar and roses, damp earth and potpourri. The palate is far from weighty, almost lighter framed for nebbiolo, but the tannins have some give and grip on the finish, with plenty of acidity keeping it buoyant. It's neatly pitched. There's enough complexity matched to the refreshment factor to drink this now or leave for a few years. Screw cap. | 13.8% alc. | Drink 2022-2028 | $29 | JF

     Regional Selections Shiraz 2020, McLaren Vale Excellent colour, deep but bright. Clever winemaking has resulted in a wine that makes space for regional expression and varietal purity. It results in a calm, unhurried palate unfolding black fruits, notes of Asian spice and tannins that sneak up on the finish. Its overall freshness and balance are hallmarks of a very smart wine. Screw cap. | 14.4% alc. | Drink 2022-2030 | $29 | JH

94   **Trial Batch Skin-Contact Riesling 2021, Mornington Peninsula** This comes up a treat. A cloudy straw hue; ginger flower, lemon barley water, fennel and sherbet-like acidity. A burst of fruit sweetness on the palate but in essence, a savoury drink with its chewy, textural tannins. Screw cap. | 12.1% alc. | Drink 2022-2025 | $29 | JF

Woods Crampton ★★★★☆

P O Box 417, Hamilton, NSW 2303 **T** 0417 670 655 **www**.woods-crampton.com.au **WINEMAKER** Nicholas Crampton, Aaron Woods **EST**. 2010 **DOZENS** 11000

This is one of the most impressive ventures of Nicholas Crampton (his association with McWilliam's is on a consultancy basis) and winemaking friend Aaron Woods. The 2 make the wines at the Sons of Eden winery with advice from Igor Kucic. The quality of the wines and the enticing prices have seen production soar from 1500 to 11 000 dozen, with every expectation of continued success. (JH)

91   **Dry Riesling 2021, Eden Valley** Tightly bound aromatics that reveal focused lime and grapefruit characters with a little time in the glass. Hints of orange blossom, crushed quartz and lighter notes of marzipan become apparent with time. The wine shows a brisk cadence and a clean, dry finish with plenty of steely lime and citrus notes. Screw cap. | 12.2% alc. | Drink 2021-2030 | $21 | DB

90   **Shiraz 2021, Barossa** A deeply coloured, contemporary Barossa shiraz showing characters of sweet ripe plum, baking spice, salted licorice, earth and blackberry jam. Juicy and unctuous with fine tannin and a crème de cassis-like finish. Screw cap. | 14.5% alc. | Drink 2022-2027 | $21 | DB

Big Rivers

Murray Darling

Trentham Estate

★★★★

6531 Sturt Highway, Trentham Cliffs, NSW 2738 **T** (03) 5024 8888 **www**.trenthamestate.com.au
OPEN 7 days 10-5 **WINEMAKER** Anthony Murphy, Shane Kerr, Kerry Morrison **EST**. 1988 **DOZENS** 60000
VYDS 38.66ha

Remarkably consistent tasting notes across all wine styles from all vintages attest to the
expertise of ex-Mildara winemaker Tony Murphy, a well-known and highly regarded producer.
With an eye to the future, but also to broadening the range of the wines on offer, Trentham
Estate is selectively buying grapes from other regions with a track record for the chosen
varieties. In 2018 Trentham Estate celebrated its 30th anniversary. (JH)

90　　**Estate Noble Taminga 2015, Murray Darling** Trentham Estate has been a firm believer in the taminga
grape, created for Australian conditions by the CSIRO, with one parent being gewürztraminer.
Gewürz certainly pops its floral and spicy head up in this botrytised sweetie, with its distinctly
lantana, potpourri florals and lychee lifted aromatics. Honeyed spice and ginger play on the
sweet palate, which is nicely balanced by crisp acidity. 375ml.　Screw cap.　|　10.5% alc.　|
Drink 2022-2025　|　$18　|　JP

Riverina

Berton Vineyard

★★★★

55 Mirrool Avenue, Yenda, NSW 2681 **T** (02) 6968 1600 **www**.bertonvineyards.com.au **OPEN** Mon-Fri
10-4, Sat 11-4 **WINEMAKER** James Ceccato, Bill Gumbleton, Glen Snaidero **EST**. 2004 **DOZENS** 1.2 million
VYDS 104ha

The Berton Vineyards partners – Bob and Cherie Berton, James Ceccato and Jamie Bennett –
have almost 100 years' combined experience in winemaking, viticulture, finance, production
and marketing. The 30ha property in the Eden Valley was acquired in '96 and the vines
planted. Wines are released under various labels: Berton Vineyards (Reserve, Winemakers
Reserve, Metal Label), Foundstone, Outback Jack and Head Over Heels. (JH)

92　　**Reserve Botrytis 2019, Riverina** If seeking a high-quality sticky at an affordable price, look no
further. This is good. Dried mango, pineapple chunks, tangerine, ginger and candied-orange zest,
doused in honey, stream along febrile acid rails. The finish, attractively bitter with a sweetness that
lingers without being cloying.　Screw cap.　|　11% alc.　|　Drink 2021-2030　|　$20　|　NG

De Bortoli (Riverina)

★★★★☆

De Bortoli Road, Bilbul, NSW 2680 **T** (02) 6966 0100 **www**.debortoli.com.au **OPEN** Mon-Sat 9-5,
Sun 9-4 **WINEMAKER** Darren De Bortoli, Julie Mortlock, John Coughlan **VITICULTURIST** Kevin De Bortoli
EST. 1928 **VYDS** 367ha

Famous among the cognoscenti for its superb Noble One, which in fact accounts for only
a tiny part of its total production, this winery turns out low-priced varietal wines that are
invariably competently made. They come from estate vineyards, but also from contract-grown
grapes. In June '12 De Bortoli received a $4.8 million grant from the Federal Government's
Clean Technology Food and Foundries Investment Program. This grant supported an
additional investment of $11 million by the De Bortoli family in their 'Re-engineering Our
Future for a Carbon Economy' project. De Bortoli is a founding member of Australia's First
Families of Wine. (JH)

96　　**Black Noble NV, Riverina** A blend of select barrels of Noble One, fortified and aged on average
10 years. Spiritous and heady, with a waft of volatility servicing punch and a lilt of freshness across
notes of spiced dates, cinnamon, char, walnut, polished floor boards, tamarind and clove. Extremely
exotic, unctuous and resinous. Morocco revisited in liquid form. The complexity, a given. The finish,
endless.　Screw cap.　|　17.5% alc.　|　$52　|　NG

Lillypilly Estate ★★★★★

47 Lillypilly Road, Leeton, NSW 2705 **T** (02) 6953 4069 **www**.lillypilly.com **OPEN** Mon-Sat 10-5, Sun by appt **WINEMAKER** Robert Fiumara **EST.** 1982 **DOZENS** 11000 **VYDS** 27.9ha

Botrytised white wines are by far the best offering from Lillypilly, with the Noble Muscat of Alexandria unique to the winery. These wines have both style and intensity of flavour and can age well. Their table wine quality is always steady – a prime example of not fixing what is not broken. (JH)

96   **Angela Muscat NV, Riverina** A solera, resplendent with a motherlode of very old base wine hailing from 1986. The result is nothing short of exceptional. The olive rim to the hue and the pine, grape, spice, roasted walnut and varnish rancio complexities do not betray class. Here, delivered in spades. A lilt of volatility only adds to the equation. A stupid price for a fantastic wine. Screw cap. | 18% alc. | $26 | NG

95   **Noble Blend 2021, Riverina** Very fine dessert wine. Ginger-spiced complexity, as much as the full kaleidoscope of botrytis riffs: canned peach, dried mango, orange blossom and pineapple chunks. Yet it is the balletic framework of delicate weight and dutiful acidity that is so compelling, imbuing fine detail and exquisite length. Screw cap. | 11.5% alc. | Drink 2022-2035 | $29 | NG

Mino & Co Wines ★★★☆

113 Hanwood Avenue, Hanwood, NSW 2680 **T** (02) 6963 0200 **www**.minoandco.com.au **OPEN** Mon-Fri 8-4.30, w'ends by appt **WINEMAKER** Sam Trimboli **EST.** 1997 **DOZENS** 12375

The Guglielmino family, specifically father Domenic and sons Nick and Alain, founded Mino & Co in 1997. From the outset they realised that their surname could cause problems of pronunciation, so they simply took the last 4 letters for the name of their business. Mino & Co has created 2 brands: Signor Vino and A Growers Touch. Signor Vino covers wines made from Italian varieties sourced from the Adelaide Hills, Riverina and Riverland. The A Growers Touch brand covers traditional varieties, often with local growers who have been working with the family for over 2 decades. The wines are made at Hanwood Winery (established on what was once a drive-in cinema). (JH)

91   **Signor Vino Vermentino 2021, Riverina** By far the best of this range, this boasts an extra degree of mid-weighted ripeness, mid-palate weight, textural detail and fidelity to variety. A clear skein of saline freshness articulates riffs on white pepper, lemon drop, fennel and raw almond. A fine, long, mineral-driven finish. This has a 'je ne sais quoi' class that belies its affordability. Screw cap. | 13.5% alc. | Drink 2021-2024 | $18 | NG

Yarran Wines   ★★★★

178 Myall Park Road, Yenda, NSW 2681 **T** (02) 6968 1125 **www**.yarranwines.com.au **OPEN** Mon-Sat 10-5 **WINEMAKER** Sam Brewer **EST.** 2000 **DOZENS** 20000 **VYDS** 30ha

Lorraine Brewer (and late husband John) were grapegrowers for over 30 years and when son Sam completed a degree in wine science at CSU. The majority of the grapes from the estate plantings are sold but each year a little more has been made under the Yarran banner; along the way a winery with a crush capacity of 150t has been built. Sam decided to take the plunge in '09 and concentrate on the family winery. The majority of the grapes come from the family vineyard but some parcels are sourced from growers, including Lake Cooper Estate in the Heathcote region. Over the past 3 years Sam has focused on improving the quality of the estate-grown grapes, moving to organic conversion. Yarran was the Wine Companion 2021 Dark Horse of the Year. (JH)

93   **A Few Words Pétillant Naturel Montepulciano 2021, Riverina** Among the finest pet nats tasted from these shores. Made in the most authentic manner, or méthode ancestrale, as it is known, in which the first ferment simply finishes in bottle. An incantation of picked cherry, ume and shiso. A turbid, elemental beauty. A textural source of immense nourishment and pleasure. A fine amaro bitterness, marking the frothy finish. Screw cap. | 13% alc. | $25 | NG

90   **A Few Words Montepulciano Rosé 2021, Riverina** Very good rosé. Picked early. The bunches shaded by savvy vine training. pH tweaks, thus, minimal. A mid coral with copper seams. Red fruits, musk and a savoury umami note, ferrous and meaty. Fine intensity and length, here. Thoroughly impressive and worth seeking out. Screw cap. | 12.5% alc. | Drink 2021-2022 | $20 | NG

Central Ranges

BIG RIVERS

CENTRAL RANGES

HUNTER VALLEY

NORTHERN RIVERS

NORTHEN SLOPES

SOUTH COAST

SOUTHERN NSW

WESTERN PLAINS

Gilbert Family Wines ⚲Ⓜⓐ ★★★★★

137 Ulan Road, Mudgee, NSW 2850 **T** (02) 6373 1325 **www**.gilbertfamilywines.com.au **OPEN** Mon 10-2, Thurs 10-4, Fri-Sat 10-5, Sun 10-4 **WINEMAKER** Simon Gilbert, Will Gilbert **EST.** 2004 **DOZENS** 18000 **VYDS** 25.81ha

The Gilbert Family Wine Company was established in 2004 by fifth-generation winemaker Simon Gilbert; 6th-generation Will Gilbert took over the reins in '14. Will draws on extensive Old and New World winemaking experience to push boundaries with different techniques and ideas to make the Gilbert Family wines from Orange and Mudgee. Gilbert + Gilbert wines from the Eden Valley draw from the family history – Joseph Gilbert of Pewsey Vale was the first to plant grapes in the Eden Valley in 1847. (JH)

97   **Blanc de Blancs 2016, Orange** Winner of 2 awards in the Wine Companion 2023 Sparkling Wine of the Year and Sparkling White of the Year. Clearly a great deal of work has gone into the sparkling wine programme here. Intentionally tensile and bone dry, with zero dosage. The partial oak fermentation, too, endowing breadth and grip across the mid palate, while toning the fervent drive of quince, bitter almond and citrus zest. Toast, too, after 50 months on lees. Long and of such exactitude that it pulls the saliva from the mouth in readiness for the next glass.   Screw cap. | 12.2% alc. | $66 | NG | ♥

Orange

Bloodwood ⚲ ★★★★★

231 Griffin Road, Orange, NSW 2800 **T** (02) 6362 5631 **www**.bloodwood.biz **OPEN** By appt **WINEMAKER** Stephen Doyle **EST.** 1983 **DOZENS** 4000 **VYDS** 8.43ha

Rhonda and Stephen Doyle are 2 of the pioneers of the Orange district; 2024 will mark Bloodwood's 40th anniversary. The wines are sold mainly through the cellar door and by an energetic, humorous and informatively run mailing list. Bloodwood has an impressive track record across the full gamut of wine styles, especially riesling; all of the wines have a particular elegance and grace. Very much part of the high-quality reputation of Orange. (JH)

97   **Maurice 2016, Orange** Painstakingly lengthy bench-top blending sessions using the best wines in barrel worked to perfection: 90% cabernet sauvignon, 10% pressings of cabernet franc, merlot and malbec. Superb colour deep through to the crimson rim. This is positively luscious, redolent of cassis, black olive and cedar adding a dimension of flavour and texture.   Screw cap. | 14% alc. | Drink 2026-2041 | $42 | JH

96   **Riesling 2021, Orange** Such a generous and mellifluous departure from the more brittle South Australian expressions: lithe, long limbed, dry, juicy and yet driven by an effortless undercarriage of vibrant mineral force more reminiscent of great Germanic gear. Glazed quince, apricot pith, preserved lemon, fennel, white pepper and tonic. The finish, a sublime confluence of natural acidity and gentle phenolic rails pulsing very long.   Screw cap. | 13.5% alc. | Drink 2022-2032 | $30 | NG | ♥

Maurice 2018, Orange A cabernet-dominated barrel cull, with a dollop of malbec, cabernet franc and merlot. It is a pleasure to taste this release. More curvaceous than the straight-laced cab. More resinous and layered, too. Graphite, cassis, a sluice of menthol, bay leaf and assorted herbs, but best are the blazing florals that lift the wine. The oak, massaged into the fray. The length, exceptional. Lovely drinking.   Screw cap. | 13.1% alc. | Drink 2021-2032 | $40 | NG | ♥

95   **Cabernet Sauvignon 2018, Orange** This is in a nice place, although the oak bridling will meld with a little more age. Finely tuned scents of mulch, Cuban cigar, graphite, currant and a whisper of menthol. Mid weighted, immensely savoury and sleek, but for the bristle of oak around the seams. Shapely tannins make this. Finishes with a waft of sage and green olive. Sophisticated cool-climate cabernet, here. Excellent drinking now and onwards for close to a decade.   Screw cap. | 13.5% alc. | Drink 2021-2030 | $35 | NG

Cabernet Sauvignon 2017, Orange Has the presence and detail of cool-grown cabernet that has achieved phenolic ripeness and appropriate structure. Blackcurrant, bay leaf and cigar-box oak are fused with fine tannins on the long palate.   Screw cap. | 13.9% alc. | Drink 2022-2037 | $34 | JH

Colmar Estate

790 Pinnacle Road, Orange, NSW 2800 **T** 0419 977 270 **www**.colmarestate.com.au **OPEN** 7 days 11–4 **WINEMAKER** Will Rikard-Bell **VITICULTURIST** Ian 'Pearcy' Pearce **EST**. 2013 **DOZENS** 2000 **VYDS** 5.9ha

The inspiration behind the name is clear when you find that owners Bill and Jane Shrapnel have long loved the wines of Alsace: Colmar is the main town in that region. The Shrapnels realised a long-held ambition when they purchased an established, high-altitude (980m) vineyard in May '13. Everything they have done has turned to gold: notably grafting cabernet sauvignon to pinot noir, merlot to chardonnay, and shiraz to pinot gris. (JH)

96 **Block 5 Riesling 2021, Orange** This producer is becoming a tour de force of fizz and riesling. A pure, intensely flavoured expression of such filigreed structure, a testimony. It makes me want to eat schnitzel or any array of washed cheeses, so fresh and juicy is the acidity, impeccably placated with a gentle sweet wash. A kernel of lime, jasmine and quince paste skitters across the energetic finish. Impressive length and driving persistence. Very fine. Screw cap. | 12% alc. | Drink 2021–2028 | $35 | NG

95 **Le Moche Pinot Gris Traminer Riesling 2021, Orange** An Edelzwicker sort of quasi field blend that is so delicious, it feels as it were merely delivered from the vineyard – a righteous meld of variety, clonal material, handling and geology – rather than made. A little more phenolics might be nice. 980m elevation. Basalt. Courage, but and Germanic varieties. One of only 2 great blends of this mix here (the other, Tasmania's Stargazer). Rosewater, orange verbena, grape spice, lychee and tarte tatin, but pear rather than apple. A trail of cinnamon and star anise, fuelled by natural acidity, a sweep of RS (barely detectable) and moxie, lingering long. Screw cap. | 12.5% alc. | Drink 2021–2026 | $32 | NG

Patina

109 Summerhill Lane, Orange, NSW 2800 **T** 0428 662 287 **www**.patinawines.com.au **OPEN** Sat–Sun 11–5 **WINEMAKER** Gerald Naef **EST**. 1999 **DOZENS** 2500 **VYDS** 2.8ha

Gerald Naef 's home in Woodbridge in California was surrounded by the vast vineyard and winery operations of Gallo and Robert Mondavi. It would be hard to imagine a more different environment than that provided by Orange. Gerald and wife Angie left California in 1981, initially establishing an irrigation farm in northwest NSW. In '01 they moved to Orange and by '06 Gerald was a final-year student of wine science at CSU. He set up a micro-winery at the Orange Cool Stores, his first wine the trophy-winning '03 Chardonnay. (JH)

96 **Reserve Chardonnay 2018, Orange** This is a thrill ride. '18, clearly a great vintage in these parts. At least in these hands, across this most chameleonic of varieties. The longest finish. The most pixelated, juicy, complex and expansive of an impressive chardonnay suite. Nougat, as always. Hazelnut, orange blossom, honeydew melon, dried tatami and apricot. A gorgeous wine. Screw cap. | 12.7% alc. | Drink 2022–2032 | $75 | NG

Grand Tawny NV, Orange A fine, resinous blend of deeply aged wines matured oxidatively. Vinous, forceful and impressionably complex. Think Darjeeling tea-leaf, orange verbena, cinnamon, turmeric and tamarind. Long and persuasive. Screw cap. | 19.2% alc. | $55 | NG

Printhie Wines

208 Nancarrow Lane, Nashdale, NSW 2800 **T** (02) 6366 8422 **www**.printhiewines.com.au **OPEN** Fri–Sat 10–5, Sun–Thurs 11–4 **WINEMAKER** Drew Tuckwell **VITICULTURIST** Dave Swift **EST**. 1996 **DOZENS** 20000 **VYDS** 32ha

Owned by the Swift family, brothers Edward and David took over from their parents Jim and Ruth Swift in the early 2000s. Together the family have clocked up almost 20 years of commercial wine production and the vineyards are now reaching a good level of maturity at 25 years. Winemaker Drew Tuckwell has been at Printhie since 2007 and has over 20 years of winemaking experience in Australia and Europe. (JH)

94 **Topography Pinot Gris 2021, Orange** Unctuous, weighty and slippery of feel. Alsatian of styling. Light years away from the stuff picked on acidity. Marzipan, tarte tatin, spiced pear, quince and cinnamon stick. The sole caveat: could use more phenolics to bolster the structural latticework. Excellent, full-throttle gris all the same. Screw cap. | 14.3% alc. | Drink 2021–2025 | $30 | NG

Swinging Bridge

701 The Escort Way, Orange, NSW 2800 **T** 0447 416 295 **www**.swingingbridge.com.au **OPEN** Mon–Sun by appt **WINEMAKER** Tom Ward **VITICULTURIST** Tom Ward **EST**. 1995 **VYDS** 6ha

Swinging Bridge Estate was established in '95 by the Ward and Payten families. Tom and Georgie Ward took the helm in '08. The label had its founding in Canowindra with initial plantings of chardonnay and shiraz. Tom's pursuit of premium grapes resulted in a number of wines made from grapes grown on Peter and Lee Hedberg's Hill Park Vineyard (planted in 1998). Hill Park Vineyard is now the permanent home of Swinging Bridge. Tom was a Len Evans scholar in 2012 and has been president of NSW Wine since '13. (JH)

94   **by Tom Ward Eliza Riesling 2021, Orange** Light–mid weighted, the intensity of lime cordial, beeswax, blossom, green apple, camphor and quinine notes, riveting. The acidity is tingly, juicy and palpably natural. A dash of RS, the balletic balance beam that softens the acidity without detracting from perceivable dryness and vitality.   Screw cap. | 12.8% alc. | Drink 2021-2029 | $30 | NG

ZONE

Hunter Valley

REGION

Hunter

Audrey Wilkinson ⚲ 🍴 🛏

★★★★★

750 De Beyers Road, Pokolbin, NSW 2320 **T** (02) 4998 1866 **www**.audreywilkinson.com.au **OPEN** 7 days 10-5 **WINEMAKER** Xanthe Hatcher **EST.** 1866 **VYDS** 47ha

Audrey Wilkinson is one of the most historic and beautiful properties in the Hunter Valley. It was the first vineyard planted in Pokolbin, in 1866. The property was acquired in '04 by the late Brian Agnew and has been owned and operated by his family since. The wines, made predominantly from estate-grown grapes, are released in 3 tiers: Audrey Wilkinson Series, Winemakers Selection and Reserve. (JH)

96   **Marsh Vineyard Semillon 2021, Hunter Valley** Fine boned. Playing a card of greater austerity and classicism than its Ridge sibling. Real tension here, with the fruit tucked beneath a veneer of mineral, talc, juicy acidity and a verdant rub of fennel, greengage and lemongrass. This will age stupendously well, as long as one has the patience.   Screw cap. | 11.5% alc. | Drink 2021-2034 | $40 | NG

Briar Ridge Vineyard

★★★★★

593 Mount View Road, Mount View, NSW 2325 **T** (02) 4990 3670 **www**.briarridge.com.au **OPEN** 7 days 10-5 **WINEMAKER** Alex Beckett (Winemaker), Gwyn Olsen (Consultant Winemaker) **VITICULTURIST** Belinda Kelly **EST.** 1972 **DOZENS** 9500 **VYDS** 39ha

Semillon and shiraz have been the most consistent performers in the Hunter Valley. Underlying the suitability of these varieties to the region, Briar Ridge has been a model of stability, and has the comfort of substantial estate vineyards from which it is able to select the best grapes. It also has not hesitated to venture into other regions, notably Orange. Alex Beckett took over winemaking duties from Gwyn Olsen in 2017 (Gwyn remains as a consultant) and in '20 he embarked on the master of wine program. (JH)

97   **Dairy Hill Single Vineyard Semillon 2021, Hunter Valley** Wild-yeast fermented, warmer than the regional standard, and left on lees for 4 months post-ferment. I adore the sentiment behind this, but the textural build has been pushed radically. Watch the neighbours! But, I love this. A sign of the future rather than the past. A bright one! Scents of tatami, porcini, lanolin, citrus peel, glazed quince and gin and tonic. White pepper, again. Delicious. Rich for the idiom. Palate-staining finish. Thoroughly impressive.   Screw cap. | 11.8% alc. | Drink 2021-2033 | $45 | NG

95   **Albariño 2021, Hunter Valley** Wine Companion 2023 Other White of the Year 2023. Maker Alex Beckett has a good handle on this, as he does with fiano, a wine whose evolution I am following with great anticipation. Everything done right: hand picked, fermented spontaneously, with a small portion (15%) in older barriques and a brief period on skins in the press and on lees, post-fermentation. All texture-building exercises. Yet albariño's pithy stone, frangipani, saline oyster shell to white pepper riffs are not subsumed, but accentuated. Fine textural detail, energetic trajectory and succulent length, the whirl of acidity whetting the palate for the next glass.   Screw cap. | 13.1% alc. | Drink 2021-2024 | $30 | NG | ♥

Brokenwood ⚲ 🍴 🍽

★★★★★

401-427 McDonalds Road, Pokolbin, NSW 2321 **T** (02) 4998 7559 **www**.brokenwood.com.au **OPEN** Mon-Fri 11-5, Sat-Sun 10-5 **WINEMAKER** Stuart Hordern, Kate Sturgess **VITICULTURIST** Kat Barry **EST.** 1970 **DOZENS** 100000 **VYDS** 64ha

Brokenwood's big-selling Hunter Semillon provides the volume to balance the limited quantities of the flagships ILR Semillon and Graveyard Shiraz. Brokenwood purchased the Graveyard Vineyard from Hungerford Hill in '78 and has fully rehabilitated the vineyard. There is also a range of wines coming from regions including Beechworth, Orange, Central Ranges, McLaren Vale, Cowra and elsewhere. In '17 Iain Riggs celebrated his 35th vintage at the helm of Brokenwood, offering a unique mix of winemaking skills, management and a diverse business. He also contributed a great deal to various wine industry organisations. Iain retired in '20, but remains on the board of directors and consults on any issue where his experience will assist. (JH)

97   **Sunshine Vineyard Semillon 2014, Hunter Valley** Wine Companion 2023 Semillon of the Year 2023. The wine's magic has nothing to do with the winemaking and everything to do with the site and 7 years in bottle. The perfumed bouquet of lemon zest, frangipani and toast leads into a mouth-watering citrus- and honey-accented palate. The length, finish and aftertaste sing in perfect harmony.   Screw cap. | 11.5% alc. | Drink 2022-2030 | $66 | JH | ♥

96   **Lillydale Vineyard Chardonnay 2021, Yarra Valley** A wine with a marrow reminiscent of a Japanese childhood: tatami straw, dried shiitake and umami. I have segued here after tasting Hunter wines and the savoury, understated reflective state of this, impressive. Thrust of extract, parry of energy and ebb of savoury oak, nutty and fine. A bit youthful and jangly-tangy, perhaps, but this will come good.   Screw cap. | 13% alc. | Drink 2022-2030 | $66 | NG

Lillydale Vineyard Chardonnay 2020, Yarra Valley An elegant chardonnay in best Yarra style, white peach and pink grapefruit the drivers through the long palate and lingering aftertaste, its best years still to come.   Screw cap. | 12.5% alc. | Drink 2021-2030 | $66 | JH

Oakey Creek Vineyard Semillon 2019, Hunter Valley A warm year that spins palate-staining extract, yet this remains precise and intense, but so deft on its feet as to be spellbinding. Freshly cut grass, honeydew melon and lemongrass to rosemary-soused gin and tonic. Strident length. Impressive tension. Age-worthy, to be sure.   Screw cap. | 10.7% alc. | Drink 2022-2032 | $66 | NG

Oakey Creek Vineyard Semillon 2017, Hunter Valley A brilliant wine! Nascent of feel. Coiled taut, despite bottle age. Already delicious, yet the potential energy a reflection of a very fine year. Buttered toast just evident. Lime splice, orange pastille, lemon curd and pink grapefruit pulp. The acidity, juicy rather than brittle. The trail across the palate, long, a little chalky and refined.   Screw cap. | 11.5% alc. | Drink 2022-2032 | $66 | NG

Oakey Creek Vineyard Semillon 2016, Hunter Valley A lovely green glint to the straw-yellow hue. Exceptional aromas attesting to how good '17 is, particularly for whites. Dried tatami mat. Lemongrass, orange pastille, lemon balm and citrus verbena. Immensely long, tactile and juicy, with plenty in store.   Screw cap. | 11.1% alc. | Drink 2021-2032 | $66 | NG

Carillion Wines   ★★★★★

749 Mount View Road, Mount View, NSW 2325 **T** (02) 4990 7535 **www**.carillionwines.com.au
OPEN Thurs-Mon 10-5 **WINEMAKER** Andrew Ling **VITICULTURIST** Liz Riley, Tim Esson, Pete Balnaves
EST. 2000 **DOZENS** 5000 **VYDS** 148ha

In '00 the Davis family decided to select certain parcels of fruit from their 28ha Davis Family Vineyard in the Hunter Valley, along with the family's other vineyards in Orange (the 30ha Carillion Vineyard) and Wrattonbully (the 90ha Stonefields Vineyard), to make wines that are a true expression of their location. In recent years Tim Davis has taken over the reins from his father John, and brought these wines under the Carillion banner. He also launched the Lovable Rogue range of wines, which highlight his keen interest in alternative grape varieties (particularly Italian), as well as exploring innovative and experimental winemaking methods. (JH)

96   **Aged Release Stonefields Arbitrage Cabernet Merlot Shiraz 2013, Wrattonbully** Extraordinarily youthful crimson-purple hue. Cedar, cigar box and spice aromas surround a well of black fruits, tannins beating the drum on the finish. This is still evolving.   Screw cap. | 14.5% alc. | Drink 2025-2033 | $40 | JH

94   **GM198 Clone Riesling 2021, Orange** Fine, expressive and succulent riesling, verging into the stone-fruit spectrum of the greatest Germanics. Gently nudging mid weight. Apricot pith, rosewater, musk and spa salts. The finish, talcy, long and brimming with Rose's lime juice. Almost pumice-like of texture.   Screw cap. | 12% alc. | Drink 2021-2028 | $30 | NG

Colvin Wines   ★★★☆

19 Boyle Street, Mosman, NSW 2088 (postal) **T** (02) 9908 7886 **www**.colvinwines.com.au
WINEMAKER Andrew Spinaze, Mark Richardson **EST.** 1999 **DOZENS** 500 **VYDS** 5.2ha

In '90 Sydney lawyer John Colvin and wife Robyn purchased the De Beyers Vineyard, which has a history going back to the second half of the 19th century. By '67, when a syndicate bought 35ha of the original vineyard site, no vines remained. Up to '98 all the grapes were sold to Tyrrell's, but since '99 quantities have been made for the Colvin Wines label. These include Sangiovese, from a little over 1ha of vines planted by John in '96 because of his love of the wines of Tuscany. (JH)

93   **De Beyers Vineyard Semillon 2019, Hunter Valley** Archetypal: lightweight, balletic of precision and nudging the equivalent of a teenage phase, edgy and reticent, delivering talc, lanolin, lemongrass and curd without touching on the glories that come with patience and further cellaring. A warm year, handled with care. Fine length, poise and the ease of drinkability that comes with these precepts.
Screw cap. | 10.5% alc. | Drink 2021-2032 | $25 | NG

de Capel Wines ⓟ   ★★★★

101 Majors Lane, Lovedale, NSW 2320 **T** 0419 994 299 **www**.decapelwines.com.au **OPEN** By appt
WINEMAKER Daniel Binet **VITICULTURIST** Jenny Bright **EST.** 2008 **DOZENS** 400 **VYDS** 2ha

Owners David and Elisabeth Capel's love of wine and a rural life led them to the purchase of their 11ha property in '01 at which time the land (previously used for livestock) was mainly cleared, with small patches of remnant vegetation. It wasn't until '08 that they undertook major soil improvements, installed all of the vineyard infrastructure and personally planted 2.2ha of vines under the direction of viticulturist Jenny Bright. They say, 'We are very fortunate to have the support (and muscle) of our close friends and family who put in an amazing effort every vintage and help us to hand-pick every single grape that we grow'. (JH)

92   **Josephine Semillon 2021, Hunter Valley** Cool-fermented. Strong typicity of region and varietal representation. Lemon drop, tatami hay, lemongrass, raw almond and icy pole. Crunchy, fresh and long, with a welcome rail of phenolic pucker adding additional detail. Screw cap. | 10.5% alc. | Drink 2021-2033 | $25 | NG

De Iuliis ⓟ ⓦ   ★★★★★

1616 Broke Road, Pokolbin, NSW 2320 **T** (02) 4993 8000 **www**.dewine.com.au **OPEN** 7 days 10-5
WINEMAKER Michael De Iuliis **EST.** 1990 **DOZENS** 15000 **VYDS** 30ha

The Iuliis family acquired a property at Lovedale in '86 and planted 18ha of vines in '90. In '99 the land on Broke Road was purchased and a winery and cellar door were built prior to the '00 vintage. In '11 De Iuliis purchased 12ha of the long-established Steven Vineyard in Pokolbin. Winemaker Michael De Iuliis completed postgraduate studies in oenology at the Roseworthy campus of the University of Adelaide and was a Len Evans Tutorial scholar. He has lifted the quality of the wines into the highest echelon. (JH)

96   **Single Vineyard Semillon 2021, Hunter Valley** The Garden vineyard is planted on the sandy flats of central Pokolbin, the grapes hand picked on Jan '22, and whole-bunch pressed to tank for a slow cool ferment. It's a glorious semillon, unusually expressive for its age, both opulently rich and fruit-complex with Tahitian lime and Meyer lemon, backed by touches of nectarine. Screw cap. | 10.5% alc. | Drink 2022-2036 | $35 | JH

94   **Special Release Pecorino 2021, Hunter Valley** A variety from the Marche and Abruzzo regions of central Italy, the first such planted in the Hunter Valley. The dried herb and citrus-skin aromas are striking, and carry onto the palate without missing a beat. It has a similar in-your-face power to fiano, in each case increasing their textural allure – and shouting for food matches. Screw cap. | 12% alc. | Drink 2021-2026 | $25 | JH

Drayton's Family Wines ⓟ ⓦ   ★★★★☆

555 Oakey Creek Road, Pokolbin, NSW 2321 **T** (02) 4998 7513 **www**.draytonswines.com.au **OPEN** Mon-Fri 8-5, w'ends & public hols 10-5 **WINEMAKER** Mark Smith **EST.** 1853 **DOZENS** 40 **VYDS** 72ha

Six generations of the Drayton family have successively run the family business; it is now in the hands of Max Drayton, and sons John and Greg. The family has suffered more than its fair share of misfortune over the years, but has risen to the challenge. The wines come in part from blocks on the estate vineyards that are over 120 years old and in prime Hunter Valley locations. Mark Smith took over as winemaker from Edgar Vales in time for the '21 vintage. (JH)

96   **Susanne Semillon 2021, Hunter Valley** The harsh acidity that marks these wines at times is, here, a natural-feeling salve. An effortless two-step with a fine, cool vintage and restrained fruit: gooseberry, lemon squash, pink grapefruit and talc. This is rapier-like of intensity and bolshy of length. Will age very well. Screw cap. | 11.2% alc. | Drink 2022-2033 | $60 | NG

Ernest Hill Wines ★★★★

307 Wine Country Drive, Nulkaba, NSW 2325 **T** (02) 4991 4418 **www**.ernesthillwines.com.au
OPEN 7 days 10–5 **WINEMAKER** Mark Woods **EST.** 1999 **DOZENS** 6000 **VYDS** 12ha

This is part of a vineyard originally planted in the early '70s by Harry Tulloch for Seppelt
Wines; it was later renamed Pokolbin Creek Vineyard, and later still (in '99) the Wilson family
purchased the upper (hill) part of the vineyard, and renamed it Ernest Hill. (JH)

94 **Shareholders Shiraz 2019, Hunter Valley** A warm year, defined by exuberant sweet cherry fruit
and weight. Tamarind, pomegranate and candied orange zest, to boot. A bit sweet, I suppose, but
there is such inherent value, a nostalgic classicism and yet, a contemporary freshness about these
wines that is winning. It will age well. Screw cap. | 14% alc. | Drink 2021–2032 | $30 | NG

Gundog Estate ★★★★★

101 McDonalds Road, Pokolbin, NSW 2320 **T** (02) 4998 6873 **www**.gundogestate.com.au **OPEN** 7 days
10–5 **WINEMAKER** Matthew Burton **EST.** 2006 **DOZENS** 7000 **VYDS** 5ha

Matt Burton makes 4 different Hunter Semillons, and Shiraz from the Hunter Valley,
Murrumbateman and Hilltops. The Burton McMahon wines are a collaboration between
Matt Burton and Dylan McMahon of Seville Estate, and focus on the Yarra Valley. In '16,
Gundog opened a second cellar door at 42 Cork Street, Gundaroo. (JH)

97 **Burton McMahon D'Aloisio's Vineyard Chardonnay 2021, Yarra Valley** A clear, bright green gold.
A superb single-vineyard wine from the moment you put your nose in the glass, there's aromas of
mandarin, white stone fruits, fresh-cut camelias and a hint of white clover honey. Even better on
the palate, this is both powerful and restrained. Finishes saline and long. Screw cap. | 13% alc. |
Drink 2022–2027 | $40 | PR

96 **Burton McMahon Syme on Yarra Vineyard Pinot Noir 2021, Yarra Valley** A bright, medium crimson.
Poised with aromas of pomegranate, freshly picked strawberries and raspberries, as well as hints
of cardamon and sandalwood. Equally good on the palate, which is nuanced, even and beautifully
balanced. Subtle but with plenty of stuffing, this gorgeous and well-crafted wine finishes with fine,
gentle but firm tannins. Screw cap. | 13.6% alc. | Drink 2022–2027 | $40 | PR

Keith Tulloch Wine ★★★★★

989 Hermitage Road, Pokolbin, NSW 2320 **T** (02) 4998 7500 **www**.keithtullochwine.com.au
OPEN By appt Thurs–Sat 11–4, Sun 10–3 **WINEMAKER** Keith Tulloch, Brendan Kaczorowski,
Alisdair Tulloch **VITICULTURIST** Brent Hutton **EST.** 1997 **DOZENS** 10000 **VYDS** 12.7ha

Keith Tulloch is, of course, a member of the Tulloch family, which has played a leading role in
the Hunter Valley for over a century. Formerly a winemaker at Lindemans and Rothbury Estate,
he developed his own label in '97. There is the same almost obsessive attention to detail,
the same almost ascetic intellectual approach, the same refusal to accept anything but the
best as that of Jeffrey Grosset. In Apr '19 the winery became the first Hunter Valley winery to
become certified carbon neutral under the National Carbon Offset Standard (NCOS). (JH)

95 **Latara Vineyard Semillon 2021, Hunter Valley** Broader and waxier of feel, belying the tensile nature
of the cool year. Hewn of dark volcanic clays, imparting a warmth and amplitude. Rivets of talcy
acidity, phenolic chew and pungent mineral weld a streamlined wine of a beguiling generosity, focus
and force. Lemon squash, guava, jasmine, fennel and raw pistachio ricochet to a long finish. This will
age exceptionally well. Screw cap. | 10.5% alc. | Drink 2021–2034 | $35 | NG

Krinklewood Biodynamic Vineyard ★★★★☆

712 Wollombi Road, Broke, NSW 2330 **T** (02) 6579 1322 **www**.krinklewood.com **OPEN** Fri–Mon 10–5
WINEMAKER Valentina Moresco, PJ Charteris (Consultant) **EST.** 1981 **DOZENS** 7500 **VYDS** 20ha

Krinklewood is a family-owned certified biodynamic organic winery. Every aspect of the
property is managed in a holistic and sustainable way; Rod Windrim's extensive herb crops,
native grasses and farm animals all contribute to biodynamic preparations to maintain healthy
soil biology. The small winery is home to a Vaslin Bucher basket press and 2 Nomblot French
fermentation eggs, a natural approach to winemaking. (JH)

96 **Fortified Verdelho 2007, Hunter Valley** An impressive fortified. Impressive as much for its rancio
complexity, evoking varnish, roasted walnuts and blue cheese, as much as the impeccable poise
derived from the high-quality spirit in play and its integration. Excellent. Cork. | 17.5% alc. |
$65 | NG

Leogate Estate Wines ★★★★★

1693 Broke Road, Pokolbin, NSW 2320 **T** (02) 4998 7499 **www.**leogate.com.au **OPEN** 7 days 10–5
WINEMAKER Mark Woods **EST.** 2009 **DOZENS** 30000 **VYDS** 127.5ha

Since purchasing the substantial Brokenback Vineyard in 2009, Bill and Vicki Widin have wasted no time. Initially the Widins leased the Tempus Two winery but prior to the '13 vintage they completed the construction of their own winery and cellar door. They have had a string of wine show successes for their very impressive portfolio. Leogate has an impressive collection of back-vintage releases available on request. (JH)

| 97 | **Museum Release Reserve Semillon 2011, Hunter Valley** Exceptional semillon from a superlative vintage, at least in these parts. Tightly coiled, unleashing lemon balm, barley sugar, toasted hazelnut, quinine, buttered toast and lanolin accents from a spring of talcy, bright acidity. This is hitting middle age, rather than senescence. Give it another decade to unwind further, or enjoy the balletic pirouette of fruit, refinement, gentle aged complexity and tensile freshness now. Screw cap. | 11% alc. | Drink 2021–2026 | $70 | NG |

| 95 | **Museum Release Brokenback Vineyard Semillon 2017, Hunter Valley** This is a filigreed, lightweight, almost balletic expression, just pirouetting into adolescence. The sordid career into any mid-life crisis, eons away. And yet, I like the wine here. It will age, sure. But the lemon squash, tonic, citrus balm, Thai herbs and soapy lanolin feel, all attractive. The acidity, arguably better measured than its '11 sibling. A lovely wine now and in the making. Screw cap. | 11% alc. | Drink 2021–2029 | $30 | NG |

Margan Wines ★★★★★

1238 Milbrodale Road, Broke, NSW 2330 **T** (02) 6579 1317 **www.**margan.com.au **OPEN** 7 days 10–5
WINEMAKER Andrew Margan **VITICULTURIST** Andrew Margan **EST.** 1996 **DOZENS** 25 **VYDS** 100ha

Margan Vineyards was established by Andrew and Lisa Margan in '96. Today it incorporates 2 of the second generation, Alessa and Ollie, as viticulturist and winemaker respectively. Andrew continues to oversee the viticultural and winemaking side; Lisa, the tourism and hatted restaurant. The estate boasts 100ha of vines and the vineyards are largely on the lauded Fordwich Sill, a geological formation dating back 200 million years. (NG)

| 95 | **White Label Fordwich Hill Semillon 2021, Hunter Valley** If in doubt about the veracity of terroir, one only has to compare this to its edgier Ceres Hill sibling. Both lightweight, the textural similarities end there. This, more mellifluous. Greater flow, length of finish and ease of drinkability. Aromas of icy pole, lemongrass and tonic. This, too, will grow in stature with time. Screw cap. | 11.7% alc. | Drink 2023–2036 | $35 | NG |

McGuigan Wines ★★★★

447 McDonalds Road, Pokolbin, NSW 2320 **T** (02) 4998 4111 **www.**mcguiganwines.com.au **OPEN** 7 days 10–5 **WINEMAKER** Thomas Jung **EST.** 1992 **DOZENS** 4.3 million **VYDS** 2000ha

McGuigan Wines is an Australian wine brand operating under parent company Australian Vintage Ltd. McGuigan represents 4 generations of Australian winemaking and, while its roots are firmly planted in the Hunter Valley, its vine holdings extend across SA, from the Barossa Valley to the Adelaide Hills and the Eden and Clare valleys, into Vic and NSW. McGuigan Wines' processing facilities operate out of 3 core regions: the Hunter Valley, Murray Darling and the Barossa Valley. (JH)

| 91 | **Cellar Select Rosé 2021, Hunter Valley** 57%/43% shiraz/tempranillo. 10% barrel fermented. A pallid coral hue. Riffs on powdered musk, orange peel, strawberry and lavender. Fresh, delicate and refined. Easily drunk with a solid chill to mask the faintest lick of sweetness across the finish. Screw cap. | 12% alc. | Drink 2021–2022 | $22 | NG |

Meerea Park ★★★★★

Pavilion B, 2144 Broke Road, Pokolbin, NSW 2320 **T** (02) 4998 7474 **www.**meereapark.com.au
OPEN 7 days 10–5 **WINEMAKER** Rhys Eather **EST.** 1991 **DOZENS** 10000

This is the project of Rhys and Garth Eather, whose great-great-grandfather, Alexander Munro, established a famous vineyard in the 19th century, known as Bebeah. Meerea Park's cellar door is located at the striking Tempus Two winery, owned by the Roche family. It hardly need be said that the quality of the wines, especially with 5 years' cellaring, is outstanding. (JH)

BIG RIVERS
CENTRAL RANGES
HUNTER VALLEY
NORTHERN RIVERS
NORTHERN SLOPES
SOUTH COAST
SOUTHERN NSW
WESTERN PLAINS

95   **XYZ Semillon 2021, Hunter Valley** This wine is still in its infancy, but already has an abundance of juicy sweet citrus flavours, and a great future.   Screw cap. | 11% alc. | Drink 2021-2035 | $25 | JH

94   **Hell Hole Individual Vineyard Semillon 2021, Hunter Valley** Some wool and lanolin aromas are swept away the moment you first taste the lemon curd and zest on the palate, the DNA of all good young Hunter Valley semillons. Excellent cellaring prospect.   Screw cap. | 11% alc. | Drink 2026-2045 | $30 | JH

Mercer Wines

426 McDonalds Rd, Pokolbin, NSW 2320 **T** 1300 227 985 **WWW**.mercerwines.com.au **WINEMAKER** Aaron Mercer **EST.** 2020 **DOZENS** 2000

After several years at the bastion of organic Hunter Valley viticulture, Tamburlaine, Aaron Mercer has set out on his own under the eponymous banner, Mercer Wines. Aaron has been exposed to a litany of wine styles through his experience across the region, in addition to work in France, Germany and California. Yet it is the draw of the Hunter, where Mercer was born, that defines his current MO: crafting wines in small batches to showcase the Hunter's best turf, complemented at times with fruit from cooler reaches of inter-regional NSW. (NG)

91   **Preservative Free Rosé 2021, New South Wales** Shiraz. A pale coral colour. Juicier and slightly more plump and fruitier than its nebbiolo sibling, but no less fresh, frisky, light, evanescent and delicious. Exuberant riffs on musk stick, orange zest and red cherry, befitting its preservative-free idiom. Screw cap. | 12% alc. | Drink 2021-2022 | $22 | NG

90   **Rouge Preservative Free 2021, New South Wales** An intra-state blend of shiraz and montepulciano, made without any SO$_2$. A mid-weighted feel, pulpy and swiggable. I'd drink this chilled. Shiraz's reductive whiff of iodine melds with the garden herbal lift and ferrous nature of montepulciano. Gentle, mind you. Lithe tannins are soothed by gentle extraction and plenty of sass.   Screw cap. | 14% alc. | Drink 2021-2022 | $20 | NG

Molly Morgan Vineyard

496 Talga Road, Rothbury, NSW 2320 **T** (02) 4930 7695 **WWW**.mollymorgan.com **WINEMAKER** Usher Tinkler **VITICULTURIST** Jacob Wiseman **EST.** 1963 **DOZENS** 2000 **VYDS** 7.66ha

Established by the Roberts family in 1963, later acquired by a syndicate headed by Andrew Simon of Camperdown Cellars fame. The vineyard is named after an exceptionally resourceful woman who was twice convicted and sent to NSW, married 3 times (the last time when she was 60, her husband aged 31). Out of this improbable background she emerged as a significant benefactor of the sick, earning the soubriquet 'Queen of the Hunter'. (JH)

93   **MoMo Semillon 2018, Hunter Valley** An aged release, this semillon is true to form: lightweight yet strident; balletic yet intense of flavour. Lemon curd, sherbet, glazed quince and dried straw, with adolescence dawning and middle age at least several years down the track.   Screw cap. | 11.5% alc. | Drink 2021-2030 | $25 | NG

Mount Eyre Vineyards

173 Gillards Road, Pokolbin, NSW 2320 **T** 0438 683 973 **WWW**.mounteyre.com **OPEN** At Garden Cellars, Hunter Valley Gardens **WINEMAKER** Andrew Spinaze, Mark Richardson, Michael McManus **VITICULTURIST** Neil Grosser **EST.** 1970 **DOZENS** 3000 **VYDS** 25ha

This is the venture of 2 families whose involvement in wine extends back several centuries in an unbroken line: the Tsironis family in the Peleponnese, Greece; and the Iannuzzi family in Vallo della Lucania, Italy. Their largest vineyard is at Broke, with a smaller vineyard at Pokolbin. (JH)

92   **Three Ponds Verdelho 2021, Hunter Valley** While cases will shift from the cellar door because of fruity riffs on guava and citrus, patchouli and jasmine scents and the sheer exuberance, there is something more serious about it than most. Drier, too. There is a wild fennel note and a white pepper trail of freshness, not dissimilar to quality Soave.   Screw cap. | 13% alc. | Drink 2021-2026 | $23 | NG

Mount Pleasant

401 Marrowbone Road, Pokolbin, NSW 2320 **T** (02) 4998 7505 **WWW**.mountpleasantwines.com.au **OPEN** Thurs-Mon 10-4 **WINEMAKER** Adrian Sparks, Jaden Hall **VITICULTURIST** Steve Ferguson **EST.** 1921 **VYDS** 88.2ha

While the vaunted history of craftsmanship here is indisputable, the reds have ebbed from the reductive tension championed by former Chief Winemaker Jim Chatto, to a more relaxed expression under new maker Adrian Sparks. Sparks seems to have a predilection for mid-weighted, lower-alcohol styles of red. The whites, too, feel less austere. Their fealty to the regional pedigree of steely, long-lived semillon, however, is clear. Winery of the Year in the Halliday Wine Companion 2017. (NG)

---

96 **Lovedale Semillon 2014, Hunter Valley** Lovedale has a stellar track record as one of the Hunter's greatest semillon sites. Scents of key lime pie, lemongrass, tonic, buttered Wonder bread and citrus curd. Very fine. Pixelated. The mid palate, tightly furled but marked by a chiaroscuro of balletic lightness and ample extract. Plenty of velocity and a long trajectory across the palate. Still an adolescent. Much in store. Screw cap. | 12% alc. | Drink 2022-2030 | $70 | NG

Pepper Tree Wines ★★★★★

86 Halls Road, Pokolbin, NSW 2320 **T** (02) 4909 7100 **www**.peppertreewines.com.au **OPEN** Mon-Fri 9-5, w'ends 9.30-5 **WINEMAKER** Gwyn Olsen **EST.** 1991 **DOZENS** 50000 **VYDS** 172.1ha

Pepper Tree is owned by geologist Dr John Davis. It sources the majority of its Hunter Valley fruit from its Davis Family Vineyard at Mount View, but also has premium vineyards at Orange, Coonawarra and Wrattonbully. The highly credentialled Gwyn Olsen ('12 Dux, Advanced Wine Assessment Course, AWRI; '14 Young Winemaker of the Year, Gourmet Traveller WINE; and '15 Len Evans Tutorial Scholar) has been winemaker since '15. (JH)

---

97 **Tallawanta Single Vineyard Shiraz 2011, Hunter Valley** A fascinating comparison with the other aged re-release, the Coquun. This, more refined. The tannins, a finer composition of oak and gravelly detail. The sweet terracotta, hoisin and worn leather, only Hunter. The savoury, moreish and mid-weighted tone, just as nuptial. Sous-bois, Asian medicine, tea and smoked biltong. Screw cap. | 14% alc. | Drink 2021-2030 | $150 | NG

96 **Single Vineyard Alluvius Semillon 2021, Hunter Valley** A fine Hunter semillon that is as juicy and optimally ripe – despite its light weight and low alcohol – as it is pixelated, vibrant and intense because of it. Lanolin, lemon squash, tonic and galangal notes stream along chalky acid rails. The finish, pointed and immensely long. Destined for fine things with a decade of patience. Screw cap. | 10.5% alc. | Drink 2021-2034 | $35 | NG

Pump Shed Chardonnay 2020, Wrattonbully This may well be the best wine under the Pepper Tree banner, tucking in a skein of mineral match-struck pungency amid folds of stone fruits, nougatine, a waxy mandarin scent with a lick of quinine to cumquat bitterness to finish. Impressive palate-staining intensity. The oak, nicely nestled. A countenance of generosity melded with a contemporary verve. Screw cap. | 13.8% alc. | Drink 2021-2028 | $50 | NG

Pooles Rock ★★★★☆

576 De Beyers Road, Pokolbin, NSW 2320 **T** (02) 4993 3688 **www**.poolesrock.com.au **OPEN** 7 days 10-5 **WINEMAKER** Xanthe Hatcher **EST.** 1988 **VYDS** 14.6ha

Pooles Rock was founded, together with the Cockfighter's Ghost brand, in 1988 by the late David Clarke OAM, and acquired by the Agnew family in '11 (who also own the neighbouring Audrey Wilkinson). Pooles Rock sources fruit from a number of wine regions, although its essential operations are based in the lower Hunter. The style is one of optimal ripeness, plump palate weight and precise structural latticework. (NG)

---

96 **Single Vineyard Semillon 2011, Hunter Valley** Superb aromas of candied citrus, glazed quince, buttered toast and lemon curd. Long and febrile of feel, despite the bottle maturation. This sits at a strident middle age, with plenty more to come. The finish is immense. Intense, despite the balletic weight, this drives across the palate as much as it coats it in doing so. A bit tangy, but … it makes one salivate in preparation for the next glass. Screw cap. | 12% alc. | Drink 2022-2030 | $75 | NG

RidgeView Wines  ★★★★★

273 Sweetwater Road, Pokolbin, NSW 2320 **T** (02) 6574 7332 **www**.ridgeview.com.au **OPEN** Thurs-Sun 10-5 **WINEMAKER** Darren Scott, Gary MacLean, Mark Woods **VITICULTURIST** Darren Scott **EST.** 2000 **DOZENS** 3000 **VYDS** 15ha

Ridgeview is an insider's secret, brimming with a solid suite of wines and some exceptional aged releases and older cellar stock. The address also boasts the funkiest retro label in all of the Hunter. In 2020 Ridgeview purchased a neighbouring property, Eagle's Nest. In lieu of the expansion, a new winery is slated for completion in '23. This will complement the established restaurant and its holistic culture of wines, local produce and herbs, all grown at the estate. (NG)

BIG RIVERS

CENTRAL RANGES

HUNTER VALLEY

NORTHERN RIVERS

NORTHEN SLOPES

SOUTH COAST

SOUTHERN NSW

WESTERN PLAINS

97　**Impressions Semillon 2010, Hunter Valley** Among the very finest aged Hunter semillons tasted. A superlative wine. Aged characteristics and depth of fruit find confluence with an underbelly of waxy freshness. This runs on, despite its aged embellishments: truffle, lemon butter, brioche, peat and bees wax. A stunning drink, it would be a shame to miss it. A regional totem. Screw cap. | 11.5% alc. | Drink 2021-2026 | $50 | NG | ♥

96　**Impressions Effen Hill Vineyard Shiraz 2015, Hunter Valley** An aged release from a challenging year. But this has blossomed. A penumbra of cherry cola and tamarind, tucked behind a veneer of leather and the fecund earth of the Hunter. Lacking the concentration of its '17 sibling, but more than making up for it with a digestible, mid-weighted drinkability. Poised, sappy, long and absolutely delicious. Screw cap. | 13.5% alc. | Drink 2021-2025 | $45 | NG

Stomp Wine 　　★★★★

504 Wilderness Road, Lovedale, NSW 2330 **T** 0409 774 280 **WWW**.stompwines.com.au **OPEN** Thurs-Mon 10-5 **WINEMAKER** Michael McManus **EST.** 2004 **DOZENS** 1000

After a seeming lifetime in the food and beverage industry, Michael and Meredith McManus moved to full-time winemaking. They set up Stomp Winemaking, a contract winemaker designed to keep small and larger parcels of grapes separate through the fermentation and maturation process, thus meeting the needs of boutique wine producers in the Hunter Valley. The addition of their own Stomp label is a small but important part of their business. (JH)

94　**Limited Release Fiano 2021, Hunter Valley** A great grape done justice. Excellent aromas: lemon pith, fennel and white pepper. As much textural intrigue as there is freshness. Skinsy and moreish. Resolute length and energy. Bravo! I'll like to taste this again in a few years. Riveting potential. Screw cap. | 12.5% alc. | Drink 2021-2026 | $28 | NG

Sweetwater Wines　　★★★★★

117 Sweetwater Road, Belford, NSW 2335 **T** (02) 4998 7666 **WWW**.sweetwaterwines.com.au **WINEMAKER** Bryan Currie **EST.** 1998 **VYDS** 16ha

Sweetwater Wines is a single-vineyard winery making semillon, shiraz and cabernet sauvignon, the wines made by Andrew Thomas from 2003 to '16 and all stored in a temperature-controlled underground wine cellar. The reason for the seemingly unusual focus on cabernet sauvignon is the famed red volcanic soil over limestone. (JH)

95　**Single Estate Semillon 2021, Hunter Valley** Fidelitous to the lanolin, grapefruit and lemon balm-doused nervy Hunter archetype, this lightweight also expresses whiffs of white pepper, sugar snap pea and a verdant undercarriage, not dissimilar to white bordeaux or quality Austrian grüner veltliner. Tensile, nicely chewy and very long, this is a beauty. Screw cap. | 11% alc. | Drink 2021-2033 | $27 | NG

Thomas Wines 　　★★★★★

28 Mistletoe Lane, Pokolbin, NSW 2320 **T** (02) 4998 7134 **WWW**.thomaswines.com.au **OPEN** 7 days 10-5 **WINEMAKER** Andrew Thomas **VITICULTURIST** Andrew Thomas **EST.** 1997 **DOZENS** 10000 **VYDS** 6ha

Andrew Thomas moved to the Hunter Valley from McLaren Vale to join the winemaking team at Tyrrell's Wines. After 13 years, he left to undertake contract work and to continue the development of his own label. He makes single-vineyard wines, underlining the subtle differences between the various subregions of the Hunter. The acquisition of Braemore Vineyard in Dec '17 was significant, giving Thomas Wines a long-term supply of grapes from one of the Hunter Valley's most distinguished semillon sites. (JH)

96　**Braemore Individual Vineyard Semillon 2021, Hunter Valley** Pungent lemongrass and lemon aromas carry through in a high-fidelity replay on the long palate with its glittering acidity. Screw cap. | 11% alc. | Drink 2026-2036 | $35 | JH

Braemore Cellar Reserve Semillon 2016, Hunter Valley An exquisite wine that suggests the style here was finer boned and less overt of fruit, in the past. Barley water, lemon oil and a strong waft of peat, not dissimilar to great aged champagne or Laphroaig. Lightweight and skeletal, yet of immense thrust, intensity of extract, drive and length. A bit tangy, to be churlish. Screw cap. | 10.8% alc. | Drink 2021-2026 | $65 | NG

94　**Will's Hill Shiraz 2019, Hunter Valley** Mid weighted and juicy of feel. A shift away from the glossier, more reductive expressions of the past, to a wine that is immensely pure, effusive of energy and deliciousness. Wild strawberry, clove, a whiff of vanilla and a diaphanous spread of fine-boned tannins, gentle oak and dutiful acidity. Screw cap. | 13.6% alc. | Drink 2021-2026 | $30 | NG

Tinklers Vineyard ★★★★☆

Pokolbin Mountains Road, Pokolbin, NSW 2320 **T** (02) 4998 7435 **WWW**.tinklers.com.au **OPEN** 7 days 10-5 **WINEMAKER** Usher Tinkler **EST**. 1946 **DOZENS** 7000 **VYDS** 41ha

Three generations of the Tinkler family have been involved with the property since 1942. Originally a beef and dairy farm, vines have been both pulled out and replanted at various stages and part of the adjoining 80+yo Ben Ean Vineyard has been acquired. The majority of the grape production is sold to McWilliam's and Tyrrell's. Usher was chief winemaker at Pooles Rock and Cockfighter's Ghost for over 8 years, before taking on full-time responsibility at Tinklers. (JH)

94   **School Block Semillon 2021, Hunter Valley** This is a benchmark expression. A filigreed, cooler vintage. Very good! Gin-and-tonic aromas muddled with rosemary, thyme and lemongrass. The acidity, juicy. A rail of phenolic pucker, an augment of complexity. This is a sinuous balancing act of the right degree of ripeness, immaculate detail and impressive length. A thoroughbred at a bargain price. Screw cap. | 11% alc. | Drink 2021-2029 | $25 | NG

Tyrrell's Wines ★★★★★

1838 Broke Road, Pokolbin, NSW 2321 **T** (02) 4993 7000 **WWW**.tyrrells.com.au **OPEN** Mon-Sun 9-4 by appt **WINEMAKER** Andrew Spinaze, Mark Richardson, Chris Tyrrell **VITICULTURIST** Andrew Pengilly **EST**. 1858 **DOZENS** 220000 **VYDS** 364ha

One of the most successful family wineries, a humble operation for the first 110 years of its life that has grown out of all recognition over the past 40 years. Tyrrell's has an awesome portfolio of single-vineyard semillons released when 5-6 years old. Its estate plantings include over 100ha in the Hunter Valley and 26ha in Heathcote. There are 11 blocks of vines older than 100 years in the Hunter Valley and the Tyrrell family owns 7 of those blocks. A founding member of Australia's First Families of Wine. (JH)

97   **Single Vineyard Stevens Shiraz 2018, Hunter Valley** The regional magic allows the power of this great shiraz to come from 13.5% alc. and neutral oak. It's Hunter Valley to its bootlaces, with decades to come, a steal in these days of $300+ wines coming from everywhere. Screw cap. | 13.5% alc. | Drink 2023-2058 | $50 | JH

      Single Vineyard Belford Semillon 2017, Hunter Valley Strap in for a fidelitous ride across the ebbs and flows of Hunter regality, when I taste this suite of semillon. The top-drawer, with few peers. Belford, a little more reticent and stonier than its Stevens brethren. Talc, wet pebbles strewn across a stream, lemongrass and citrus balm. But the texture, the opus. Still in need of time. Taut, linear and of pixelated detail and precision. Wait with bated breath. Screw cap. | 11% alc. | Drink 2021-2030 | $45 | NG

      Vat 1 Semillon 2017, Hunter Valley While I enjoy the open-knit approaches to crafting semillon across the region, this remains the bulletproof benchmark. Even here, there have been endeavours towards greater accessibility, with some lees inflection. A meld of the finest dry-grown plots conferring a carapace of talc, sandy mineral and effusive acidity that is, to be frank, indomitable. Descriptives, ineffable. The length, justifiable. Bury this. Screw cap. | 11.5% alc. | Drink 2021-2035 | $105 | NG

96   **Single Vineyard HVD Semillon 2017, Hunter Valley** Lightweight. A skitter of lemon zest, tamarind and quince, bulwarked with a talcy mineral pungency and a juicy acid kit. Long, tactile and pummelling of intensity. This is a late-released Hunter semillon, barely nudging middle age. Screw cap. | 10.5% alc. | Drink 2021-2029 | $45 | NG

Whispering Brook ★★★★☆

Rodd Street, Broke, NSW 2330 **T** (02) 9818 4126 **WWW**.whispering-brook.com **OPEN** Thurs-Sun 10.30-5 and by appt **WINEMAKER** Susan Frazier, Adam Bell **VITICULTURIST** Adam Bell, Neil Grosser **EST**. 2000 **DOZENS** 1100 **VYDS** 3ha

It took some time for partners Susan Frazier and Adam Bell to find the property on which they established their vineyard over 20 years ago. It has a combination of terra rossa loam soils on which the reds are planted, and sandy flats for the white grapes. A trip to Portugal in '07 inspired the planting of Portuguese varieties. The partners have also established an olive grove and accommodation, offering vineyard and winery tours. (JH)

95   **Semillon 2021, Hunter Valley** I love this vintage for wines of both colours: cool, attenuated and herbal complexity, its tattoo. The best wines, way beyond mere citrus balm and acid. Lightweight, yet a fine thrust of nettle, lemon squash, white pepper grind, dill, Thai herb and icy pole. The acidity, fine boned and juicy. The finish, taut, yet with nothing brittle, hard, or out of place. Very long. A fine wine that will reward mid- to longer-term cellaring. Screw cap. | 10.5% alc. | Drink 2022-2034 | $35 | NG

BIG RIVERS

CENTRAL RANGES

HUNTER VALLEY

NORTHERN RIVERS

NORTHERN SLOPES

SOUTH COAST

SOUTHERN NSW

WESTERN PLAINS

South Coast

Southern Highlands

Centennial Vineyards ⓎⓂⒶ ★★★★★

'Woodside', 252 Centennial Road, Bowral, NSW 2576 **T** (02) 4861 8722 **www**.centennial.net.au
OPEN 7 days 10–5 **WINEMAKER** Tony Cosgriff **EST.** 2002 **DOZENS** 10000 **VYDS** 28.65ha

Centennial Vineyards, jointly owned by wine professional John Large and investor Mark Dowling, covers 133ha of beautiful grazing land. Centennial purchased the 8.2ha Bridge Creek Vineyard in Orange to meet the challenge of the Southern Highlands' capricious weather. (JH)

91 **Bong Bong Quattro Bianco 2021, Southern Highlands Tumbarumba** A slinky, spunky blend of a delicious knockabout, the quality akin to the good, savoury, everyday whites of Europe. The apposite blend, perfect material for these cool-climate growing zones; 65% gris, with chardonnay, albariño and gewürz. Pistachio, lemon balm, grape spice and a pithy stone-fruit element. Unbeatable for a white at this price, at least in this expensive land. Chill, slug and smile. You have won the lottery!
Screw cap. | 12.5% alc. | Drink 2021-2023 | $20 | NG

Cherry Tree Hill ⓎⓂ ★★★★

12324 Hume Highway, Sutton Forest, NSW 2577 **T** (02) 8217 1409 **www**.cherrytreehill.com.au **OPEN** 7 days 10–5 **WINEMAKER** Anton Balog, Mark Balog **VITICULTURIST** Ian Evans **EST.** 2000 **DOZENS** 3500 **VYDS** 13.5ha

Gabi Lorentz began the establishment of the Cherry Tree Hill vineyard in '00 with the planting of cabernet sauvignon and riesling, soon followed by merlot, sauvignon blanc and chardonnay. Since then, 5.5ha of the merlot and cabernet have been re-grafted to pinot noir, destined for both still and sparkling wine. Gabi's inspiration was childhood trips on a horse and cart through his grandfather's vineyard in Hungary. Gabi's son David is now the owner and manager of the business. (JH)

92 **Chardonnay 2019, Yarra Valley** A well-crafted, medium-bodied, loosely knit expression, in the best sense. Plying a mineral pungency with a striving for real flavour, there is plenty on offer. Stone-fruit accents, honeydew melon, roasted almonds and praline. The oak, like a blowhole that stems the flow while liberating it when necessary, allowing the flavours to ebb and flow long. Lovely drinking.
Screw cap. | 13% alc. | Drink 2021-2025 | $25 | NG

Southern New South Wales

Canberra District

Clonakilla ⓎⓂ ★★★★★

3 Crisps Lane, Murrumbateman, NSW 2582 **T** (02) 6227 5877 **www**.clonakilla.com.au **OPEN** Mon-Fri 11–4, w'ends 10–5 **WINEMAKER** Tim Kirk, Chris Bruno **VITICULTURIST** Greg Mader **EST.** 1971 **DOZENS** 20000 **VYDS** 16ha

The indefatigable Tim Kirk, with an inexhaustible thirst for knowledge, is the winemaker and manager of this family winery founded by his father, scientist Dr John Kirk. It is not at all surprising that the quality of the wines is exceptional, especially the Shiraz Viognier, which has paved the way for numerous others but remains the icon. Demand for the wines outstrips supply, even with the '98 acquisition of an adjoining 20ha property by Tim and wife Lara Kirk. In '07 the Kirk family purchased another adjoining property. (JH)

96 **Riesling 2021, Canberra District** As pure as a spring day and smelling of a citrus orchard in bloom. A heady mix of lime and lemon sprinkled with ginger powder are just teasers, as this is complex and beguiling. The palate is long and defined by acidity as much as the power of the fruit. It has texture, succulence and a slickness rendering it assured and impressive. Screw cap. | 12% alc. | Drink 2021-2035 | $35 | JF

Collector Wines ⑨Ⓜ ★★★★★

7 Murray Street, Collector, NSW 2581 **T** (02) 6116 8722 **WWW**.collectorwines.com.au **OPEN** Thurs-Mon 10-4 **WINEMAKER** Alex McKay **EST.** 2007 **DOZENS** 6000 **VYDS** 6ha

Owner and winemaker Alex McKay makes exquisitely detailed wines, bending to the dictates of inclement weather on his doorstep, heading elsewhere if need be. He is known to not speak much, and when he does, his voice is very quiet. So you have to remain alert to appreciate his unparalleled sense of humour. No such attention is needed for his wines, which are consistently excellent, their elegance appropriate for their maker. A new cellar door will open in October 2022. (JH)

96   **Tiger Tiger Chardonnay 2019, Tumbarumba** One of the finest Tumbarumba chardonnays around. A perfect balance of stone fruit, grapefruit, mouth-watering smoky flinty sulphides with just the right amount of palate-buffering creamy lees to offset the electrifying acidity. Superb drink. Screw cap. | 12.9% alc. | Drink 2022-2029 | $38 | JF

95   **Lantern 2019, Hilltops** Spanish amigos, as in 54/41% tempranillo/touriga, with a splash of grenache to great effect. This has a core of excellent bright red-berried fruit and black cherries, but is savoury through and through. Lots of warm spices, freshly rolled tobacco with grainy savoury tannins working across the medium-bodied palate, with plenty of fresh acidity to close. Screw cap. | 13.2% alc. | Drink 2022-2028 | $30 | JF

94   **Marked Tree Red Shiraz 2019, Canberra District** An excellent dark red befitting a structured wine, but this is not weighty. Full of dark cherries, licorice, fennel plus cedary oak, yet it sits right in the savoury camp, with ripe tannins and a flourish across the medium-bodied palate to a lightly dry finish. Screw cap. | 13% alc. | Drink 2022-2030 | $30 | JF

Helm ⑨ ★★★★★

19 Butts Road, Murrumbateman, NSW 2582 **T** (02) 6227 5953 **WWW**.helmwines.com.au **OPEN** Fri-Mon 10-4 **WINEMAKER** Ken Helm **VITICULTURIST** Ben Osbourne **EST.** 1973 **DOZENS** 5000 **VYDS** 11ha

Ken Helm celebrated his 44th vintage in '20. Riesling has been an all-consuming interest, ultimately rewarded with rieslings of consistently high quality. He has also given much to the broader wine community, extending from the narrow focus of the Canberra District to the broad canvas of the international world of riesling. In '17 Helm completed construction of a separate 40000L insulated winery with a double-refrigeration system dedicated to the production of riesling, the old winery now producing cabernet sauvignon. (JH)

96   **Premium Riesling 2021, Canberra District** Such a composed and classy wine. Yes, it has lemon blossom, ginger spice and citrus flavours – and tantalisingly so – but there's a depth that rightly puts this into premium territory. Best of all, texture is its hallmark, with talc-like acidity and a sheen across the palate as it glides towards a long finish. Screw cap. | 11.5% alc. | Drink 2021-2035 | $60 | JF

Lark Hill ⑨Ⓜ ★★★★★

31 Joe Rocks Road, Bungendore, NSW 2621 **T** (02) 6238 1393 **WWW**.larkhill.wine **OPEN** Thurs-Mon 11-4 **WINEMAKER** Dr David Carpenter, Sue Carpenter and Chris Carpenter **EST.** 1978 **DOZENS** 6000 **VYDS** 12ha

The Lark Hill vineyard is situated at an altitude of 860m, offering splendid views of the Lake George escarpment. The Carpenters have made wines of real quality, style and elegance from the start, but have defied all the odds (and conventional thinking) with the quality of their pinot noirs in favourable vintages. Significant changes came in the wake of son Christopher gaining 3 degrees – including a double in wine science and viticulture through CSU – and the organic/biodynamic certification of the vineyard and wines in 2003. (JH)

95   **Dark Horse Vineyard Marsanne 2019, Canberra District** A racy style full of lively acidity yet flavourful with lemon, stone fruit, a touch of burnt butter and a beeswax character that's appealing. The palate is tight, with a balance of savouriness to the fruit flavours. Terrific wine and will continue to garner complexity in time. Screw cap. | 12.5% alc. | Drink 2021-2028 | $30 | JF

Mount Majura Vineyard ⑨🖛 ★★★★★

88 Lime Kiln Road, Majura, ACT 2609 **T** (02) 6262 3070 **WWW**.mountmajura.com.au **OPEN** 7 days 10-5 **WINEMAKER** Dr Frank van de Loo **VITICULTURIST** Leo Quirk **EST.** 1988 **DOZENS** 5000 **VYDS** 9.3ha

Vines were first planted in 1988 by Dinny Killen on a site on her family property that had been especially recommended by Dr Edgar Riek; its attractions were red soil of volcanic origin over limestone, with reasonably steep east and northeast slopes providing an element of frost

BIG RIVERS

CENTRAL RANGES

HUNTER VALLEY

NORTHERN RIVERS

NORTHEN SLOPES

SOUTH COAST

SOUTHERN NSW

WESTERN PLAINS

protection. The tiny vineyard has been significantly expanded since it was purchased in '99. The Mount Majura flagship remains the Canberra District Tempranillo, with volume and quality cementing its place. (JH)

95 **Riesling 2021, Canberra District** The 8.5g/L RS is perceptible, but so is the (undisclosed) acidity, for they balance each other sufficiently to make this an ideal wine for a sunny day. Minerality is the last piece of the jigsaw. Screw cap. | 12% alc. | Drink 2021-2030 | $30 | JH

Mondeuse 2021, Canberra District Mondeuse is a French variety that I find so appealing, as I do this wine. Firstly, it's refreshing and lively with a core of tangy, juicy, tart raspberries and black cherries with a sprinkle of pepper, fresh herbs and violets. Yet it has a strong savoury element of iodine, prosciutto and meaty reduction, finishing with fine tannins and raspberry-sorbet acidity. Screw cap. | 13% alc. | Drink 2023-2028 | $34 | JF

Nick O'Leary Wines ★★★★★

149 Brooklands Road, Wallaroo, NSW 2618 **T** (02) 6230 2745 **www**.nickolearywines.com.au **OPEN** By appt **WINEMAKER** Nick O'Leary **VITICULTURIST** Nick O'Leary **EST**. 2007 **DOZENS** 17000 **VYDS** 12ha

At the age of 28, Nick O'Leary had been involved in the wine industry for over a decade, working variously in retail, wholesale, viticulture and winemaking. Two years earlier he had laid the foundation for Nick O'Leary Wines. His wines have had extraordinarily consistent success in local wine shows and competitions since the first vintages, and are building on that early success in spectacular fashion. At the NSW Wine Awards '15, the '14 Shiraz was awarded the NSW Wine of the Year trophy, exactly as the '13 Shiraz was in the prior year – the first time any winery had won the award in consecutive years. (JH)

96 **Heywood Tempranillo 2021, Canberra District** A new wine and a very welcome one in the classy Nick O'Leary stable. There's more structure to this compared with its sibling, Seven Gates, and more savoury. Pastilles, raspberries and cherries, earthy with baking spices, freshly rolled tobacco and potpourri. Fuller bodied with stealth-like tannins driving long across the palate. Top stuff. Screw cap. | 13.5% alc. | Drink 2022-2028 | $34 | JF

White Rocks Riesling 2021, Canberra District O'Leary's 3 rieslings are basically made the same, it's where the fruit is sourced that makes the big difference. This from the Westering vineyard, one of the oldest riesling sites in the Canberra District, nudging 50 years. The wine's a babe in terms of youth and its charm. Grapefruit and lime, zest and pith, minerally and tight, with ultra-refreshing acidity and a finish that lingers long after the sip has gone. Screw cap. | 12% alc. | Drink 2022-2035 | $38 | JF | ♥

95 **Riesling 2021, Canberra District** Always reliable and a very good go-to drink, because it's juicy and refreshing without any brittleness to the acidity. It's also full of freshly squeezed Indian limes and wet pebbles with a touch of lemon curd. The finish is impressively long. Screw cap. | 12% alc. | Drink 2021-2029 | $25 | JF

Seven Gates Tempranillo 2021, Canberra District More depth than a joven style, yet this retains such a purity of fruit. Red currants and cherries come infused with sarsaparilla, woodsy spices and turmeric. The medium-bodied palate delights with bright acidity with some tension throughout and spot-on decisive tempranillo tannins. Screw cap. | 13.5% alc. | Drink 2022-2028 | $32 | JF

Heywood Red Blend 2021, Canberra District A blend of 40/40/20% tempranillo/shiraz/sangiovese. This is a ripper. While it charms with upfront fruit flavours and lots of spice, it's a savoury wine with drinkability writ large. Lighter framed, juicy, tangy acidity and fine, almost silky, tannins. I'd enjoy this in cool or warm weather. Screw cap. | 13.5% alc. | Drink 2022-2026 | $34 | JF

Heywood Riesling 2021, Canberra District Comes out punching with apple and lemon flavours, a waft of blossom and a daikon radish savouriness. It's racy with bright acidity in the mix and finishes with terrific length. Screw cap. | 12% alc. | Drink 2021-2031 | $34 | JF

Ravensworth ★★★★★

312 Patemans Lane, Murrumbateman, ACT 2582 **T** (02) 6226 8368 **www**.ravensworthwines.com.au **OPEN** By appt in Sept **WINEMAKER** Bryan Martin **VITICULTURIST** Bryan Martin **EST**. 2000 **DOZENS** 8000 **VYDS** 3.4ha

Ravensworth is led by innovative winemaker Bryan Martin, his wife Jocelyn, plus his brother David. Bryan takes an organic approach, eschewing chemicals, preventing soil compaction and allowing the vines to thrive in what he describes as 'natural forestry principles'. He also sources fruit for Ravensworth's other labels including the Regional. In '20, a winery and cellar were completed, the latter made with straw bales and filled with large-format oak, Italian amphorae, ceramic eggs and concrete vessels: all expressing Bryan's desire to experiment and craft minimum-intervention wines with texture. (JF)

Murrumbateman Riesling 2021, Canberra District Such a yin-and-yang wine, as it has texture and depth yet is spritely and vibrant. There's so much flavour and delight, with its infusion of lemonade (without the sweetness), ginger beer and daikon, as this dips into savoury territory; a citrusy tang then a fine line of acidity pulling it altogether to form a complete wine. Refreshing, complex and utterly delicious. Screw cap. | 11.5% alc. | Drink 2021-2028 | $30 | JF

Pinot Gris 2021, Canberra District If you want pinot gris that's dilute of colour and without tannin, leave now. If you like it full of flavour, texture and complexity, then come join the party. This is fab and yes, it is an amber wine. It's a pale orangey pink and tastes of negroamaro, with lots of pink grapefruit, ginger-poached pears, Sichuan pepper (without the numbing effect) and a dusting of baking spices. The palate is alive with fine phenolics and acidity. It's a vim-and-vigour drink. Screw cap. | 12.5% alc. | Drink 2021-2025 | $30 | JF

The Long Way Around Tinto 2021, Swan Valley Hilltops Blend of 90yo grenache from the Swan Valley (65%), with tempranillo/graciano from Hilltops and a little monastrell from Ricca Terra Farm in the Riverland. Yep, long way around. A very good Iberian outcome. It's super-savoury, even if it has a core of dark red fruit plus pomegranate juice. Earthy, with lots of Middle Eastern spices from sumac to a more complex ras el hanout, with grainy and lightly if pleasantly drying tannins. It gets better and better in the glass; moreish with every sip. Screw cap. | 14% alc. | Drink 2022-2026 | $32 | JF

REGION

Gundagai

Tumblong Hills

1149 Old Hume Highway, Gundagai, NSW 2722 **T** 0401 622 808 **www**.tumblonghills.com **OPEN** Thurs–Sun 11–4 **WINEMAKER** Simon Robertson **VITICULTURIST** Simon Robertson **EST** 2009 **DOZENS** 10000 **VYDS** 200ha

This large vineyard was established by Southcorp Wines in the '90s, as part of 'Project Max', an initiative to honour Max Schubert of Penfolds Grange fame. It was acquired in '09 by business partners Danny Gilbert, Peter Leonard and Peter Waters. They were able to secure the services of viticulturist and general manager Simon Robertson, who knew the vineyard like the back of his hand, his experience stretching across the wine regions of Southern New South Wales. In '11, investors Wang Junfeng and Handel Lee came onboard. (JH)

Table of Plenty Fiano 2021, Gundagai Honeysuckle, stone fruit and Mediterranean herbs offer varietal context. The palate soft and giving with texture in the mix and lemon sherbet acidity keeping it fresh and lively. Screw cap. | 12.5% alc. | Drink 2022-2023 | $19 | JF

Table of Plenty Nebbiolo Rosé 2021, Gundagai A light copper blush sets the scene. Strawberries, blood orange and raspberry-like acidity with a slip of texture add to the appeal. Screw cap. | 13.5% alc. | Drink 2022-2023 | $19 | JF

REGION

Hilltops

Grove Estate Wines

4100 Murringo Road, Young, NSW 2594 **T** (02) 6382 6999 **www**.groveestate.com.au **OPEN** 7 days 9.00-4.30 **WINEMAKER** Brian Mullany, Tim Kirk, Bryan Martin **EST** 1989 **DOZENS** 4000 **VYDS** 100ha

Grove Estate Vineyard was re-established in 1989 by Brian and Suellen Mullany on the site where grapes were first planted in Lambing Flat (Young) in 1861 by Croatian settlers who brought vine cuttings with them from Dalmatia. Further plantings in '98 were made on their Bit O' Heaven Vineyard, the 2 sites with vastly different soils. The wines are made at Clonakilla by Tim Kirk and Bryan Martin. (JH)

Shiraz 2020, Hilltops An outrageous vibrant purple hue, so it starts off right. A solid mix of plums, squishy currants, lots of woodsy spices and extract but overall, it's juicy and appealing. There's fruit-oak sweetness across the full-bodied palate yet halted by vice-like tannins and a bitter finish. It is also somewhat raw, perhaps indicative of its youth. Time should help out. Good wine and great value too. Screw cap. | 14.5% alc. | Drink 2022-2029 | $22 | JF

BIG RIVERS

CENTRAL RANGES

HUNTER VALLEY

NORTHERN RIVERS

NORTHERN SLOPES

SOUTH COAST

SOUTHERN NSW

WESTERN PLAINS

Self-dubbed 'The Wine State', South Australia has seven zones including the Adelaide Super Zone, which is an odd assembly of three of the seven, not to mention chunks of otherwise nameless land.

When international wine and lifestyle tourists finally return, the region that will be foremost in their minds is the **Barossa Valley**, an easy drive northeast of Adelaide. For many, it is the home of Australia's best shiraz wines, with Penfolds Grange the splendidly opulent ultimate icon. Cabernet sauvignon is often united with shiraz in Australia's definitive blend. À la mode grenache is fresher and more vibrant in its familiar partnership with shiraz and mourvèdre, and flying solo more frequently and confidently than ever.

The cooler temperatures of **Eden Valley** and **High Eden** grow elegant shiraz and bring riesling into the limelight, with flavours of lime and Meyer lemon fruit. This variety is grist for the mill in the **Clare Valley**; here, slate rock, limestone and red earth give riesling its gravitas, likewise shiraz, the second-most widely planted, well in advance of cabernet sauvignon. **Adelaide Hills** is the final region on the Mount Lofty Ranges zone. Pinot noir has the lion's share of red plantings, three times greater than shiraz, but thumped by the region's hero of sauvignon blanc, along with chardonnay and pinot gris.

The grouping of the five regions in the Fleurieu zone is logical, all enjoying a Mediterranean/maritime climate: an even accumulation of warmth (seasonal and diurnal) with a dry summer and cool nights. **McLaren Vale** spans the expanse between the cool of the Adelaide Hills and the moderating influence of St Vincent Gulf; dark-chocolate-riddled shiraz, satisfyingly generous yet varietally accurate cabernet and the thrill of modern grenache are its mainstays. **Langhorne Creek** is the other important player, and the most underrated region in Australia, producing red wines with rivers of plush shiraz and cabernet sauvignon comprising the majority of the total crush. **Currency Creek** is a scaled-down mirror image of Langhorne Creek.

The Limestone Coast zone of six regions has three big names. **Coonawarra** hung its hat on shiraz until 1955 (1955 Wynns Michael Hermitage a still-superb great Australian shiraz), thereafter on cabernet sauvignon (1963 Mildara 'Peppermint Pattie' likewise famous).

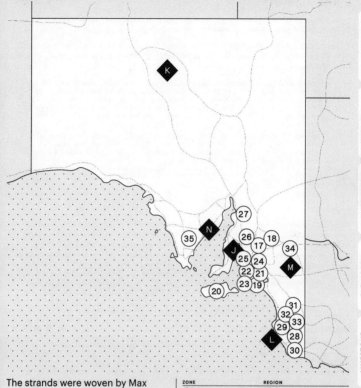

BAROSSA

FLEURIEU

MOUNT LOFTY
RANGES

FAR NORTH

LIMESTONE
COAST

LOWER MURRAY

THE PENINSULAS

The strands were woven by Max Schubert with the 1962 Bin 60A Coonawarra Cabernet Kalimna Shiraz, the all-time greatest red wine. **Padthaway** produces wines of consistent quality and yield across shiraz, chardonnay, cabernet sauvignon and pinot gris/grigio (in order of size), plus seven other varieties. **Wrattonbully** is a slimmed down version of Padthaway, with the dubious distinction of growing more pinot gris/grigio than chardonnay, but neither can challenge the red-wine duo of cabernet sauvignon (full of blackcurrant and plum) and generous, fleshy shiraz.

ZONE	REGION	
J* Barossa	17	Barossa Valley
	18	Eden Valley
Fleurieu	19	Currency Creek
	20	Kangaroo Island
	21	Langhorne Creek
	22	McLaren Vale
	23	Southern Fleurieu
Mount Lofty Ranges	24	Adelaide Hills
	25	Adelaide Plains
	26	Clare Valley
K Far North	27	Southern Flinders Ranges
L Limestone Coast	28	Coonawarra
	29	Mount Benson
	30	Mount Gambier
	31	Padthaway
	32	Robe
	33	Wrattonbully
M Lower Murray	34	Riverland
N The Peninsulas	35	Southern Eyre Peninsula
* Adelaide Super Zone		

Byrne Vineyards  ★★★★★

PO Box 15, Kent Town BC, SA 5071 **T** (08) 8132 0022 **www**.byrnevineyards.com.au **WINEMAKER** Mark Robinson, Phil Reedman **MW EST.** 1963 **DOZENS** 120000 **VYDS** 200ha

The Byrne family has been involved in the SA wine industry for 3 generations, with vineyards in the Clare Valley and Riverland. Wine styles include vine-dried, field blends, vegan-friendly wines and regional wines. (JH)

95   **Calcannia Grenache 2021, Clare Valley** Jubey, spicy and mineral on the nose, with layers of raspberry humbug, red licorice, anise and even a hint of ginger. In the mouth, the exactitude of the '21 vintage comes to the fore. This is precise and restrained, almost lean, with rivulets of flavour that flow across the tongue. Really sensational. The oak is largely imperceptible, save for a spicy, supporting role, which gives the fruit ample room to shine with its own light. Marvellous.
Screw cap. | 15% alc. | Drink 2022-2030 | $28 | EL

     Calcannia Sangiovese 2021, Clare Valley Concentrated, black and brooding, with dense, silky tannins and poignant purple fruit. There is buoyancy in the fruit, despite the river of texture that flows through the mouth. The back palate is really moreish. A lot going on and it's all good.
Screw cap. | 15% alc. | Drink 2022-2029 | $28 | EL

Chain of Ponds ★★★★

8 The Parade West, Kent Town, SA 5067 (postal) **T** (08) 7324 3031 **www**.chainofponds.com.au
WINEMAKER Greg Clack **EST.** 1985 **DOZENS** 20000

It is years since the Chain of Ponds brand was separated from its then 200ha of estate vineyards, which were among the largest in the Adelaide Hills. It does, however, have long-term contracts with major growers. Prior to the '15 vintage, Greg Clack came onboard as full-time chief winemaker. In May '16 Chain of Ponds closed its cellar door and moved to Project Wine's small-batch processing facility at Langhorne Creek. (JH)

94   **Grave's Gate Shiraz 2020, Adelaide Hills** It hits well above its pricepoint – outstanding value here – to deliver a joyous Hills shiraz experience in deep spicy aromas and fruits with black cherry, plum, violet and an earthy nuance. A fine line of supple tannins brings length and balance. Screw cap. | 14.5% alc. | Drink 2021-2026 | $20 | JP

Dandelion Vineyards ★★★★★

PO Box 138, McLaren Vale, SA 5171 **T** (08) 8323 8979 **www**.dandelionvineyards.com.au
WINEMAKER Elena Brooks **EST.** 2007 **VYDS** 124.2ha

Elena Brooks crafts full-bodied wines across South Australia's premium regions: Adelaide Hills, Eden Valley, Langhorne Creek, McLaren Vale, Barossa Valley and Fleurieu Peninsula. She endeavours to draw upon vineyards untempered by over-management, as much as she strives for a softer impact in the winery. As a result, Dandelion wines are increasingly bright, transparent and stamped by a more sensitive oak regime than in the past. (NG)

94   **Pride of the Cabernet Sauvignon 2020, Fleurieu** A medium- to full-bodied exercise with cabernet, the tannins neatly controlled, but still able to proclaim its patrician upbringing, blackcurrant and bramble fruits to the fore. Screw cap. | 14.5% alc. | Drink 2025-2035 | $30 | JH

Hesketh Wine Company ★★★★

28 The Parade, Norwood, SA 5067 **T** (08) 8362 8622 **www**.heskethwinecompany.com.au **OPEN** Mon-Thurs 10-4, Fri-Sat 10-10, Sun 10-6 **WINEMAKER** James Lienert, Keeda Zilm, Andrew Hardy **EST.** 2006 **DOZENS** 40000

Headed by Jonathon Hesketh, this is part of WD Wines Pty Ltd, which also owns Parker Coonawarra Estate (see separate entry), St John's Road and Vickery Wines. Jonathon spent 7 years as the global sales and marketing manager of Wirra Wirra, and 2.5 years as general manager of Distinguished Vineyards in NZ. He is also the son of Robert Hesketh, one of the key players in the development of many facets of the SA wine industry. A new cellar door opened in 2022. (JH)

92   **Regional Selections Riesling 2021, Eden Valley** Classic aromas of freshly squeezed lime juice and grapefruit with hints of Bickford's lime cordial, Christmas lily, almond paste, kaffir lime and crushed stone. Tight and focused throughout its length, driving along with limey precision, just a touch of textural interest and a sapid, saline to its porcelain-like framework of acidity. Great value from a wonderful Eden Valley vintage. Screw cap. | 11% alc. | Drink 2021-2031 | $24 | DB

Project Wine ★★★☆

83 Pioneer Road, Angas Plains, SA 5255 **T** (08) 8537 0600 **www**.projectwine.com.au **WINEMAKER** Peter Pollard **EST.** 2001 **DOZENS** 155000

Originally designed as a contract winemaking facility, Project Wine has developed a sales and distribution arm that has rapidly developed markets both domestic and overseas. Located in Langhorne Creek, it sources fruit from most key SA wine regions, including McLaren Vale, Barossa Valley and Adelaide Hills. (JH)

93 **Drop Zone Riesling 2021, Clare Valley** The '21 vintage is a beautiful prism. Through this looking glass, we see the effects of a restrained and cool year – effortless acidity, voluminous fruit and presence in the mouth, offered with tension and very fine phenolics. Green apple skins, lime flesh and a hint of kiwi. Gorgeous stuff here. Screw cap. | 13% alc. | Drink 2022-2029 | $27 | EL

Quarisa Wines ★★★☆

743 Slopes Road, Tharbogang, NSW 2680 (postal) **T** (02) 6963 6222 **www**.quarisa.com.au **WINEMAKER** John Quarisa **EST.** 2005

John Quarisa has had a distinguished career as a winemaker spanning over 20 years, working for some of Australia's largest wineries including McWilliam's, Casella and Nugan Estate. He was also chiefly responsible in 2004 for winning the Jimmy Watson Trophy (Melbourne) and the Stodart Trophy (Adelaide). Production has risen in leaps and bounds, doubtless sustained by the exceptional value for money provided by the wines. (JH)

89 **Mrs Q Sangiovese 2021, Adelaide Hills** This sangiovese is living life large. There's no denying the generosity on hand; the deep, inky colour, the powerful flavour base ripe in black fruits and plums with a persistent spicy thread of aniseed, clove and cacao. That said, it's nicely controlled by a fine but firm tannin presence. Screw cap. | 14.8% alc. | Drink 2022-2026 | $19 | JP

88 **Q Malbec 2021, Riverina** There is an impressive flow of blueberry, mulberry and iodine here, lit by blazing florals. This is packed with flavour while offering the sort of oomph that the shopper in this zone is all over. Screw cap. | 14% alc. | Drink 2021-2026 | $17 | NG

Johnny Q Petite Sirah 2020, Riverina A monster truck! Inky, opaque and foreboding of density. Purple fruits, lavender and lilac. Huge, palate-staining tannins. Some mocha-bourbon oak, augmenting the impact. Far from finessed, complex or discreet, yet if big flavour at a price is the MO, look no further. Screw cap. | 14.5% alc. | Drink 2021-2028 | $17 | NG

Sister's Run ★★★★

PO Box 148, McLaren Vale, SA 5171 **T** (08) 8323 8979 **www**.sistersrun.com.au **WINEMAKER** Elena Brooks **EST.** 2001

Sister's Run is now part of the Brooks family empire, the highly experienced Elena Brooks making the wines. The Stiletto and Boot on the label are those of Elena, and the motto 'The truth is in the vineyard, but the proof is in the glass' is, I (James) would guess, the work of marketer extraordinaire husband Zar Brooks. (JH)

92 **Bethlehem Block Gomersal Cabernet Sauvignon 2019, Barossa Valley** Unctuous blackberry fruit leads the charge here with hints of blackcurrant jelly, blackstrap licorice, dark chocolate, cedar, oak spice and a blast of choc-mint on the back end. There's oodles of black-fruited entertainment here; it's supple and ripe, the tannins are superfine, sinking way back into the fruit and it flows nicely across the tongue. Good-value drinking. Screw cap. | 14% alc. | Drink 2021-2028 | $23 | DB

91 **Calvary Hill Lyndoch Shiraz 2019, Barossa Valley** Ginger-spiced, ripe red and dark plum fruits wash over a backdrop of Asian spice, milk chocolate, jasmine and earth, for a most enticing first sniff. The fruit attack on the palate fans out nicely and shows plummy exuberance, packed with exotic spice, earth, softly spoken oak and pressed flowers. The wine tightens on the exit and the acidity kicks in brightly as the tail lights fade. Screw cap. | 14.5% alc. | Drink 2021-2028 | $23 | DB

The Pawn Wine Co. ★★★★

10 Banksia Road, Macclesfield, SA 5153 **T** 0438 373 247 **www**.thepawn.com.au **WINEMAKER** Tom Keelan **VITICULTURIST** Tom Keelan **EST.** 2004 **DOZENS** 10000 **VYDS** 35ha

The Pawn Wine Co. began as a partnership between Tom Keelan and Rebecca Willson (Bremerton Wines) and David and Vanessa Blows. Tom was for some time manager of Longview Vineyards at Macclesfield in the Adelaide Hills, and consulted to the neighbouring vineyard, owned by David and Vanessa. In '17 Tom and Rebecca purchased David and

Vanessa's share. David still supplies grapes to the Pawn Wine Co., and Tom works very closely with David and his 3 sons to produce food-friendly wines that reflect their origins. (JH)

94 **Fiano 2021, Langhorne Creek** Fiano is a difficult customer at the best of times, but here it roars defiantly, its depth and power driving the palate through the finish and lingering aftertaste.
Screw cap. | 12% alc. | Drink 2021-2031 | $26 | JH

Thistledown Wines

★★★★★

c/- Revenir, Peacock Road North, Lenswood, SA 5240 **T** 0424 472 831 **www.**thistledownwines.com
WINEMAKER Giles Cooke MW **EST.** 2010 **DOZENS** 10000

Thistledown is a conflation of wisdom, foresight and strident confidence; an assemblage of talent, superb old-vine sites and remarkable wines that have, with a few others, established a firmament at the top of the grenache totem in this country. Giles Cooke and Fergal Tynan – each a Master of Wine, historian and lover of the world's finest grenache – became tired of international stereotypes of Australian wine. With vast experience respectively making and selling wines from Spain, they began to carve out a niche defined by filigreed precision, thirst-slaking tannins and crunchy red fruit elements under the local guidance of maker Peter Leske. (NG)

97 **Our Fathers Just Like Heaven Roussanne 2021, McLaren Vale** A not-for-profit label with all proceeds going towards mental health charities. Exceptional wine, here! Riffs on Asian pear, rooibos, quince, preserved lemon, hazelnut and dried herb, whisk me to Avignon and environs. Like an unctuous Meursault, with a Mediterranean sheen. Viscous and detailed of phenolics, yet paradoxically taut, with a slippery mineral underbelly propelling it to scintillating length. We should be proud of wines like this coming from these shores. Screw cap. | 14% alc. | Drink 2021-2028 | $30 | NG

Sands of Time Single Vineyard Blewitt Springs Grenache 2021, McLaren Vale Raspberry, lilac and rosehip behind. The tannins, a saline scape of bridling force that stretch from the attack to the long, chalky finish. Delicious. Concrete ferment, layered bunches and destemmed material to promote perfume and a mescal whiff of the best parts beyond a border of control. Saliva-sapping energy.
Screw cap. | 14.5% alc. | Drink 2022-2031 | $90 | NG

96 **She's Electric Old Vine Single Vineyard Grenache 2021, McLaren Vale** The Vagabond is superlative, but this is extraordinary! The tannins, taut, febrile and wound across a spool of sage, thyme and blood orange zest. The drive of red cherry, rhubarb and Mediterranean herb is palate staining, without ever reneging on its sandy, vibrant and effortless tout. Incredibly complex. Scintillating length. Kerpow! Screw cap. | 14.5% alc. | Drink 2022-2028 | $65 | NG

The Quickening Shiraz 2020, Barossa A striking wine, as juicy as quicksilver on the first whiff and taste, before the spicy, savoury whole-bunch nuances come into play. Has the X-factor.
Screw cap. | 14.5% alc. | Drink 2022-2040 | $50 | JH

Our Fathers Shiraz 2018, Barossa Made to the exactitude that one expects from this address, with all profits imparted to mental-health causes. While the region cannot deliver the finesse, mid-weighted balletic energy and complexity, perhaps, of the northern Rhône, it can deliver vinous fortitude and a latent power that, in the right hands, has its own stamp of elegance without straying into the galumphing, sweet, clumsily oaked grind of so many. Here, a prime example. Violet, crushed black rock, mace, pepper grind, salumi, clove, lilac and five spice. A textural thread, of detailed complexity woven very long. Superlative! Screw cap. | 14% alc. | Drink 2021-2028 | $50 | NG

ZONE

Barossa

REGION

Barossa Valley

1837 Barossa

★★★★

119-131 Yaldara Drive, Lyndoch, SA 5351 **T** (08) 7200 1070 **www.**1837barossa.com.au/ **OPEN** Mon-Sun 11-5 **WINEMAKER** Guido Auchli, Peter Gajewski, Ben Cooke **VITICULTURIST** Michael Heinrich **EST.** 1999 **VYDS** 25ha

The ambition of the Swiss tech entrepreneurial Auchli family, 1837 Barossa commemorates the date on which Colonel William Light named the Barossa. Red wines hail exclusively from the estate near Lyndoch, while whites are sourced from Eden Valley growers. Viticulture is overseen by fifth-generation grower Michael Heinrich, with a philosophy of minimal chemical input. (TS)

90 **Summer Breeze Pinot Rosé 2021, Eden Valley** A pale, pale pink rosé produced from pinot noir and pinot grigio, showing characters of redcurrant, raspberry and ruby red grapefruit along with hints of stone, jasmine, almond paste and green apple. A little phenolic swirl adds texture and mouthfeel and the wine finishes crisp, clean and dry with a red-fruited flourish. Screw cap. | 12% alc. | Drink 2022-2025 | $20 | DB

Brave Souls Wine ★★★★

12 Clevedon Street, Botany, NSW, 2019 (postal) **T** 0420 968 473 **www**.bravesoulswine.com.au
WINEMAKER Corey Ryan, Simon Cowham, David Fesq **VITICULTURIST** Simon Cowham **EST.** 2017 **DOZENS** 3500

The story of Brave Souls and its co-founder Julia Weirich has a strong Australian can-do air about it, albeit with German beginnings. Julia obtained her degree in industrial engineering and decided to travel to Australia, where in '13 she became marketing coordinator at Fesq & Co. She later took off for winemaking experience at Bass Phillip, NZ, Burgundy, southern and central Italy and South Africa, eventually returning to Australia to Fesq to take the new role of European Wine Manager, and to Sons of Eden making Brave Souls Wine. In 2020, Julia returned overseas and the winemaking is now undertaken by Corey Ryan and Simon Cowham of Sons of Eden, alongside David Fesq.

95 **The Able Seaman 2020, Barossa Valley** A blend of 59/27/14% grenache/shiraz/mourvèdre. Plump and juicy aromatics bound forth – plum jam along with red cherry and mulberry lift. Packed firmly with spice and earthen notes, a little purple floral note flitting around above. Great density, flow and plush fruit presence. Lovely drinking. Screw cap. | 14.5% alc. | Drink 2021-2029 | $29 | DB

Brothers at War ★★★★★

58 Murray Street, Tanunda, SA 5252 **T** 0405 631 889 **www**.brothersatwar.com.au **OPEN** 7 days 11-5
WINEMAKER Angus Wardlaw **VITICULTURIST** Chris Alderton **EST.** 2013 **DOZENS** 5000 **VYDS** 15ha

Brothers Angus and Sam Wardlaw are the men behind this exciting addition to the contemporary Barossa wine scene and, as the name suggests, they could have possibly had the odd rumble as they were growing up under the watch of their father, Barossa winemaker, David Wardlaw. Established in 2013 with a small intake of shiraz, the brothers gathered pace over the ensuing years, adding vigneron Chris Alderton to the mix and today the formidable trio craft a superb range of pure-fruited, vibrant wines from across the Barossa and Eden Valleys. They riff on the classic grape Barossa varieties in a modern, elegant style that speaks clearly of their regional roots. Brothers at War is a young winery with a very bright future indeed. (DB)

97 **Peace Keeper Grenache 2021, Barossa Valley** A red-purple hue, with great clarity and detail, the pure plummy fruits underscored with floral flourishes along with ginger spice and a calm, airy sense of space on the palate. The Peace Keeper is a wonderfully composed and balanced wine with nary a hair out of place. Superb drinking and astonishing value for money. Screw cap. | 13.5% alc. | Drink 2021-2031 | $38 | DB | ♥

David Franz ★★★★☆

94 Stelzer Road, Stone Well, SA 5352 **T** 0417 454 556 **www**.david-franz.com **OPEN** 7 days 11-5
WINEMAKER David Franz Lehmann **VITICULTURIST** David Franz Lehmann **EST.** 1998 **DOZENS** 6600 **VYDS** 33.92ha

David Franz (Lehmann) is one of Margaret and Peter Lehmann's sons. He took a very circuitous path around the world before establishing his eponymous winery. His wife Nicki accompanied him on his odyssey and, together with their 3 children, 2 dogs, a mess of chickens and a surly shed cat, all live happily together in their house and winery. (JH)

94 **Gewürztraminer 2021, Eden Valley** A head-spinningly perfumed gewürtztraminer. Aromas of citrus fruits infused with characters of Turkish delight, rosewater, lychees, bath salts, white flowers and crushed stone. The aromas transpose neatly over to the palate, yet it is bone dry, savoury and sapid; nary a note of the variety's sometimes gloopy lack of detail. This is a wonderful rendition of the grape. Screw cap. | 12.6% alc. | Drink 2022-2032 | $27 | DB

Plane Turning Right 2017, Barossa Valley 43/40/14/3% merlot/petit verdot/malbec/cabernet sauvignon. Aged in seasoned oak hogsheads for 24 months on full lees. A complex and captivating blend with juicy plummy fruits underscored by complex notes of black and red currants, exotic spice, sage, spearmint, olive tapenade, washed-rind cheese and dried citrus rind. Sleek and savoury with a meaty edge. Screw cap. | 13.5% alc. | Drink 2022-2028 | $27 | DB

Dorrien Estate ★★★★★

Cnr Barossa Valley Way/Siegersdorf Road, Tanunda, SA 5352 **T** (08) 8561 2235 **www**.dorrienestate.
com.au **WINEMAKER** Nick Badrice **EST.** 1982 **DOZENS** 1 million **VYDS** 109.6ha

Dorrien Estate is the physical base of the vast Cellarmasters network – the largest direct
sales outlet in Australia. It also makes wine for many producers across Australia at its modern
winery, which has a capacity of 14.5 million litres in tank and barrel; however, a typical make of
each wine will be little more than 1000 dozen. (JH)

95 **Mockingbird Hill Dr J.W.D. Bain Riesling 2021, Clare Valley** Like walking through an apple orchard:
blossoms, apples and the occasional grassy interlude. This typifies the capacity for the beauty
that '21 is so frequently leaving in its wake. Chalky, talcy, minerally and fine, with a plume of flavour
through the finish. A big yes. Screw cap. | 12% alc. | Drink 2022-2032 | $30 | EL

Eperosa ★★★★★

Lot 552 Krondorf Road, Tanunda, SA 5352 **T** 0428 111 121 **www**.eperosa.com.au **OPEN** Fri-Sat 11-5
WINEMAKER Brett Grocke **EST.** 2005 **DOZENS** 1000 **VYDS** 8.75ha

Eperosa owner and Wine Companion 2021 Winemaker of the Year Brett Grocke qualified as a
viticulturist in '01. He is ideally placed to secure small parcels of organically managed grapes,
hand-picked, whole-bunch fermented and foot-stomped, and neither filtered nor fined. The
wines are of impeccable quality – the use of high-quality, perfectly inserted, corks will allow
the wines to reach their full maturity decades hence. (JH)

96 **L.R.C. Shiraz 2020, Barossa Valley** With 2% riesling to give it some added spark. Deep damson
plum and blackberry fruit, packed with exotic spice, roasting meats, violets and savoury nuance.
Gorgeous texture and flow in the mouth. Meaty-edged plummy fruits and abundant spice, gravelly
tannin and a bright, savoury flick to its tail. Cork. | 13.9% alc. | Drink 2021-2035 | $60 | DB

First Drop Wines ★★★★

38 Barossa Valley Way, Nuriootpa, SA 5355 **T** 0488 299 233 **www**.firstdropwines.com **OPEN** Wed-Sat
10-4, Sun 11-4 **WINEMAKER** John Retsas, Kurt Northam **EST.** 2004 **DOZENS** 30000

First Drop Wines HQ is in the striking 'Home of the Brave' building on the southern edge of
Nuriootpa in the Provenance Barossa precinct. John Retsas is the man behind the dynamic
brand, with its striking wine labels and delicious wines sourced from vineyards across the
Barossa, Adelaide Hills and McLaren Vale. There is a heavy emphasis on the 'alternative'
(appropriate) varieties with Italian and Portuguese grape varieties making their savoury and
delicious presence felt. (DB)

94 **Mother's Milk Barossa Shiraz 2020, Barossa Valley** A wonderful, plushly-fruited Barossa shiraz
packed full of vibrant satsuma plum and juicy blueberry characters, underscored by hints of
maraschino cherry, Asian spice, violets, turned earth, roasting meats and a nuance of softly spoken
oak. There's depth of fruit and intensity here, but also a sense of sapid juiciness with ripe, fine, sandy
chocolatey tannins adding ample support. The wine fans out with a plume of spiced plum fruits on
the finish. Wonderful value. Screw cap. | 14.5% alc. | Drink 2021-2030 | $28 | DB

Gomersal Wines ★★★★

203 Lyndoch Road, Gomersal, SA 5352 **T** (08) 8563 3611 **www**.gomersalwines.com.au **OPEN** Thurs-Sun
10-4 **WINEMAKER** Barry White **VITICULTURIST** Barry White **EST.** 1887 **DOZENS** 10200 **VYDS** 20.2ha

The 1887 establishment date has a degree of poetic licence. In 1887 Friedrich W Fromm
planted the Wonganella Vineyards, following that with a winery on the edge of the Gomersal
Creek in '91; it remained in operation for 90 years, finally closing in 1983. In 2000 a group
of friends 'with strong credentials in both the making and consumption ends of the wine
industry' bought the winery and re-established the vineyard. (JH)

91 **GSM 2019, Barossa Valley** Mid red-purple hues with aromas of red plum, red cherry and cranberry
along with gingery spice, violets, red licorice, earth and mocha. At the lighter end of medium
bodied, with fine tannin, bright acidity and a spicy fan of red and dark fruits on the finish. Excellent
value here. Screw cap. | 14.8% alc. | Drink 2022-2028 | $20 | DB

91 **Riesling 2021, Clare Valley** Clare Valley riesling is loved for a reason; it is lush, generous and laden
with citrus, while the acidity is like a coiled spring within. There's an aspect of tartness to this –
like green apple skin, but is counterbalanced by fine pithy acid. This is all that, and through the
lens of the cool, restrained and even '21 vintage, it is all the better. Screw cap. | 12.5% alc. |
Drink 2022-2029 | $20 | EL

Greenock Creek Wines ★★★★★

450 Seppeltsfield Road, Marananga SA 5355 **T** (08) 8563 2898 **www**.greenockcreekwines.com.au **OPEN** 7 days 11–5 **WINEMAKER** Alex Peel, Peter Atyeo **VITICULTURIST** Peter Atyeo **EST.** 1984 **DOZENS** 4000 **VYDS** 22ha

Founders Michael and Annabelle Waugh deliberately accumulated a series of old dryland, low-yielding Barossa vineyards back in the '70s, aiming to produce wines of unusual depth of flavour and character. The Waughs retired in '18 and the business was purchased by a group headed by Sydney-based Jimmy Chen. Peter Atyeo stayed on as assistant winemaker and manager, with Alex Peel (formerly Ross Estate and Yaldara) stepping in as winemaker. (JH)

97   **Fifteen Claims Shiraz 2019, Barossa Valley** Intense and concentrated blackberry, black plum and black cherry fruit notes with plenty of cedary oak nuance and hint of deep, dark spice, formic acid, salted black licorice, Old Jamaica chocolate, fig jam and earth. Weighty, full bodied and super-concentrated, with ripe, sandy tannins retreating back into the fruit and intense blackberry jam and a cedary plume on the long finish. Cork. | 15% alc. | Drink 2022-2042 | $150 | DB

Groom ★★★★★

28 Langmeil Road, Tanunda, SA 5352 (postal) **T** (08) 8563 1101 **www**.groomwines.com **WINEMAKER** Daryl Groom, Lisa Groom, Jeanette Marschall **EST.** 1997 **DOZENS** 2000 **VYDS** 27.8ha

The full name of the business is Marschall Groom Cellars, a venture established by David and Jeanette Marschall and their 6 children, and Daryl and Lisa Groom and their 4 children. Daryl was a highly regarded winemaker at Penfolds before he moved to Geyser Peak in California. Years of discussion between the families resulted in the purchase of a 35ha block of bare land adjacent to Penfolds' 130yo Kalimna Vineyard. The next acquisition was an 8ha vineyard at Lenswood in the Adelaide Hills. (JH)

96   **Shiraz 2020, Barossa Valley** Deeply coloured with aromas of satsuma plum and blueberry compote. Lovely fruit weight and spice-laden mid palate, with pitch-perfect flow and balance, fine pillowy tannins for support and an extended spicy finish. Great drinking now but will cellar well, too. Cork. | 14.7% alc. | Drink 2021-2038 | $50 | DB

95   **Bush Block Zinfandel 2020, Barossa Valley** Impressively pure blackberry and black cherry-fruit characters, dredged deeply with fruitcake spice with hints of mince pies, Old Jamaica chocolate, earth and well-judged vanillin oak. Great flow, balance and pure, savoury-edged appeal. Go zinfandel! Cork. | 14.9% alc. | Drink 2028-2035 | $30 | DB

Hayes Family Wines ★★★★★

102 Mattiske Road, Stone Well, SA 5352 **T** 0499 096 812 **www**.hayesfamilywines.com **OPEN** Sat 11–4.30 or by appt **WINEMAKER** Andrew Seppelt **EST.** 2014 **DOZENS** 1000 **VYDS** 5ha

Hayes Family Wines is a small family-owned wine producer nestled among organically farmed vineyards in Stone Well on the western ridge of the Barossa Valley. The Hayes family has decades of agriculture and business experience. (JH)

97   **Redman Vineyard Shiraz 2019, Coonawarra** From an outstanding vintage that has produced wines with a superb texture and structure to the medium to full-bodied palate. While the tannins are plentiful, they are ripe and bend to the array of blackberry and blueberry flavours. Screw cap. | 13.6% alc. | Drink 2029-2059 | $60 | JH

Head Wines ★★★★★

PO Box 58, Tanunda, SA 5352 **T** 0413 114 233 **www**.headwines.com.au **OPEN** By appt Feb-Apr **WINEMAKER** Alex Head **EST.** 2006 **DOZENS** 6000

Head Wines is the venture of Alex Head. In 1997, he finished a degree in biochemistry from Sydney University. Experience in fine wine stores, importers and an auction house was followed by vintage work at wineries he admired. The names of the wines reflect his fascination with Côte-Rôtie in the Northern Rhône Valley. The 2 aspects in Côte-Rôtie are known as Côte Blonde and Côte Brune. In each case, open fermentation (with whole bunches) and basket pressing precedes maturation in French oak. (JH)

97   **Wilton Hill Barossa Ranges Shiraz 2019, Eden Valley** The colour is a saturated red purple, giving a hint of the intensity to come. Dark and black fruit of impressive density abound, cut deeply with spice and earth. It's a wonderfully expressive wine, both of latent fruit power and of site. The balance is pitch perfect, with ample tannin and mineral-like acid support. Very impressive. Diam. | 14.8% alc. | Drink 2021-2041 | $149 | DB

96   **The Contrarian Shiraz 2020, Barossa** An expressive, fragrant bouquet 100% in tune with red cherry fruits, freshness and vitality foremost from start to finish. The urge to have a second glass will be omnipresent.   Screw cap. | 13.5% alc. | Drink 2022-2035 | $39 | JH

95   **Rosé 2021, Barossa** 50/45/5% grenache/mataro/viognier. A heady bouquet and ultra-complex palate has made the investment of time and money worthwhile.   Screw cap. | 13.5% alc. | Drink 2021-2025 | $27 | JH

       Head Red GSM 2020, Barossa The rich bouquet, hinting at luscious fruits, doesn't deceive. A vibrant, supple trifecta of cherry, plum and raspberry.   Screw cap. | 14.5% alc. | Drink 2021-2031 | $27 | JH

94   **Heart & Home Dry Red 2020, Barossa** 79/21% cabernet sauvignon and shiraz. This is all about cabernet sauvignon kicking up its heels in the Barossa Valley and making no apologies for doing so. There is an edge of authority to its expression provided by the firm tannins, shiraz ending any suggestion of excess force. Bargain on a grand scale.   Screw cap. | 14.5% alc. | Drink 2021-2031 | $23 | JH

       Head Red Shiraz 2020, Barossa A medium-bodied blend of cherry, plum and blackberry fruits, complexed by ripe though savoury tannins. Excellent balance. Screw cap 14.5% alc. | Drink 2022-2041 | $27 | JH

Hentley Farm Wines

Cnr Jenke Road/Gerald Roberts Road, Seppeltsfield, SA 5355 **T** (08) 8562 8427 **www.**hentleyfarm.com.au **OPEN** 7 days 10-4 **WINEMAKER** Andrew Quin **EST.** 1997 **DOZENS** 20000 **VYDS** 44.7ha

Keith and Alison Hentschke purchased Hentley Farm in 1997, as a mixed farming property with an old vineyard. Keith studied agricultural science at Roseworthy, later adding an MBA. During the '90s he had a senior production role with Orlando, before moving on to manage Fabal, one of Australia's largest vineyard management companies. Establishing a great vineyard like Hentley Farm required all of his knowledge. Situated on the banks of Greenock Creek, the vineyard has red clay loam soils overlaying shattered limestone, lightly rocked slopes and little topsoil. (JH)

95   **Riesling 2021, Eden Valley** Bright straw-green; a vibrant bouquet and palate puts lime and a wisp of passionfruit in a setting of dry, minerally acidity. Crisp and crunchy, but ultimately fruit-driven. Screw cap. | 11% alc. | Drink 2021-2031 | $25 | JH

       MC Riesling 2021, Barossa Valley There's a wonderful aromatic profile here; a steely, almost Germanic peachiness among the crisp, focused lime and citrus fruits cut with frangipani and almond blossom. Great velocity and texture with pitch-perfect tension between fruit and acidity and a vivid, crisp, refreshing line. Screw cap. | 11% alc. | Drink 2021-2035 | $35 | DB

       OD Riesling 2021, Barossa Valley Pale straw with beautifully composed, freshly squeezed lime, grapefruit and juicy white peach, along with hints of orange blossom, almond paste and stone. Pure and just lovely to drink, the wine sits at 21g/L RS but the bright acidity tends to rein that sugar in. The wine finishes off-dry, clean and absolutely delicious. Screw cap. | 9% alc. | Drink 2021-2035 | $35 | DB

       The Stray Grenache Shiraz 2020, Barossa Valley The final blend completed with the addition of zinfandel. A bright, breezy and juicy red wine demanding to be enjoyed without delay, ablaze with red fruits, but calm in extract and alcohol. Minimal oak all the better. Screw cap. | 14.5% alc. | Drink 2021-2029 | $32 | JH

Hewitson

66 Seppeltsfield Road, Nuriootpa, SA 5355 **T** (08) 8212 6233 **www.**hewitson.com.au **OPEN** Mon, Tues, Thurs-Sat 11-4.30 **WINEMAKER** Dean Hewitson **VITICULTURIST** Dean Hewitson **EST.** 1996 **DOZENS** 25000 **VYDS** 12ha

Dean Hewitson was a winemaker at Petaluma for 10 years, during which time he managed to do 3 vintages in France and one in Oregon, as well as undertaking his master's at the University of California, Davis. It is hardly surprising that the wines are immaculately made from a technical viewpoint. (JH)

94   **Belle Ville Rosé 2021, Barossa Valley** A blend of mourvèdre and cinsault. At once complex and juicy, sweetness engendered by the fruit, not RS. High quality. Screw cap. | 12.5% alc. | Drink 2021-2022 | $26 | JH

       Gun Metal Riesling 2021, Eden Valley This wastes no time in imparting its message of Rose's lime juice and a squeeze of Meyer lemon and of grapefruit. The acidity is there of course, but it's essentially gentle. All of which makes this ready now (and later, if you wish). Screw cap. | 12.5% alc. | Drink 2021-2029 | $28 | JH

Kaesler Wines

★★★★☆

Barossa Valley Way, Nuriootpa, SA 5355 **T** (08) 8562 4488 **www**.kaesler.com.au **OPEN** 7 days 11–5 by appt **WINEMAKER** Reid Bosward, Stephen Dew **EST.** 1990 **DOZENS** 20000 **VYDS** 36ha

The first members of the Kaesler family settled in the Barossa Valley in 1845. The vineyards date back to 1893, but the Kaesler family ownership ended in 1968. Kaesler Wines was eventually acquired by a small group of investment bankers (who have since purchased Yarra Yering), in conjunction with former Flying Winemakers Reid and Bindy Bosward.

94 **Old Vine Semillon 2021, Barossa Valley** A tautly stretched and precise Barossa semillon with pristine fruit characters of lemon and crunchy green apple along with hints of almond meal, lanolin, soft spice, dried herbs and white flowers. There's a dot of clotted cream on the palate which is finely formed and possesses a wonderfully pure, stony, citrus-flecked finish. Drink gleefully or cellar. Screw cap. | 11.5% alc. | Drink 2021-2035 | $25 | DB

Kalleske

★★★★

6 Murray Street, Greenock, SA 5360 **T** (08) 8563 4000 **www**.kalleske.com **OPEN** 7 days 10–5 **WINEMAKER** Troy Kalleske **VITICULTURIST** Kym Kalleske **EST.** 1999 **DOZENS** 10000 **VYDS** 50ha

The Kalleske family has been growing and selling grapes on a mixed farming property at Greenock for over 140 years. Sixth-generation Troy Kalleske, with brother Tony, established the winery and created the Kalleske label in '99. The vines vary in age, with the oldest dating back to 1875. All are grown biodynamically. (JH)

92 **Rosina Rosé 2021, Barossa Valley** 92/8% grenache/shiraz. Such a pretty-smelling wine, with aromas of redcurrant, raspberry and strawberries, brushed with jasmine and soft spice. Fragrant in the mouth too, with a wash of bright red fruit, crushed stone and floral flourish. It finishes dry and savoury. Screw cap. | 12.5% alc. | Drink 2021-2023 | $22 | DB

Clarry's GSM 2021, Barossa Valley For me, Clarry's GSM has always been a wine that emphasises the fruit density that is on display from Moppa and Greenock. Fruit-pure with a sense of latent power, minimal interruption from oak and both impressive fruit density and enjoyment. Screw cap. | 14.5% alc. | Drink 2021-2028 | $23 | DB

JMK Shiraz VP 2021, Barossa Valley A luscious shiraz-based VP. Heady plum and blackberry jam characters along with hints of cassis, brandy snaps, figs, chocolate cake, baking spice and kirsch. Intense and heady with a sweetly unctuous palate, chewy tannin backbone and rich, fruitcake finish. Screw cap. | 18.5% alc. | Drink 2021-2035 | $25 | DB

91 **Florentine Single Vineyard Chenin Blanc 2021, Barossa Valley** Pale strawy in the glass with aromas of crunchy pear, melon and yellow plum with hints of almond paste, white flowers and stone. Crunchy pear fruit again on the palate, with bright acidity, plentiful drive and a gentle phenolic tweak on the dry finish. Screw cap. | 12% alc. | Drink 2021-2024 | $22 | DB

Laughing Jack

★★★★★

194 Stonewell Road, Marananga, SA 5355 **T** (08) 8562 3878 **www**.laughingjackwines.com.au **OPEN** Fri-Sat 10–4 **WINEMAKER** Shawn Kalleske **EST.** 1999 **DOZENS** 5000 **VYDS** 38.88ha

The Kalleske family has many branches in the Barossa Valley. Laughing Jack is owned by Shawn, Nathan, Ian and Carol Kalleske, and Linda Schroeter. Vine age varies considerably, with old dry-grown shiraz the jewel in the crown. A small part of the grape production is taken for the Laughing Jack Shiraz. (JH)

96 **Moppa Hill Gold Seam Cabernet Sauvignon 2019, Barossa Valley** There is a solid wall of ripe blackberry, blackcurrant and black cherry at this wine's core. Hints of spice, licorice, dark chocolate and lighter wafts of briar, dried herbs, cedar, vanillin and earth. A wonderful example of top-drawer Barossa cabernet sauvignon with impeccable balance, precision and grace; pitch-perfect sinewy tannin support and a gorgeous swell of spicy, pure black fruits on the lengthy finish. Screw cap. | 14% alc. | Drink 2022-2042 | $40 | DB | ♥

MBK

★★★★

14 Meredyth Street, Millswood, SA 5034 **T** 0402 114 808 **WINEMAKER** Steve Baraglia **EST.** 2014 **DOZENS** 400

MBK (and parent company, Mabenki) is derived from the names of the three founders: Mario Barletta, Ben Barletta and Kim Falster. Brothers Ben and Mario came from a retail background (Walkerville Cellars, Adelaide), Kim Falster is their wine-loving friend. The company started

BAROSSA

FLEURIEU

MOUNT LOFTY RANGES

FAR NORTH

LIMESTONE COAST

LOWER MURRAY

THE PENINSULAS

in 2014, but its genesis was back in 1993, making 'house wine' to sell in the store. They have never missed a vintage, but wines were sold exclusively to a private customer base. (EL)

94   **Watervale Riesling 2021, Clare Valley** Scintillating, taut, and extreme knife-edge stuff here. Limes, apples and pears are lit up by pithy, saline acidity. Bright and gorgeous – Clare Valley routinely brings the lovely voluminous base of flavour, while still achieving that almost-austere acid. Awesome.   Screw cap. | 12% alc. | Drink 2022-2030 | $22 | EL

Orlando ★★★★★

Barossa Valley Way, Rowland Flat, SA 5352 **T** (08) 8521 3111 **www**.pernod-ricard-winemakers.com
WINEMAKER Ben Thoman **EST.** 1847 **DOZENS** 10000 **VYDS** 14ha

Orlando is the parent who has been separated from its child, Jacob's Creek (see separate entry). While Orlando is over 170 years old, Jacob's Creek is little more than 45 years old. For what are doubtless sound marketing reasons, Orlando aided and abetted the separation. (JH)

96   **Steingarten Riesling 2021, Eden Valley** No longer a single-vineyard wine, today, it is a blend of 2 separate blocks but retains the name of the famous walled vineyard. It's still a belter ... pristine citrus fruits, a crystalline acid line that crackles and pulses through the fruit with sapid zeal and focus and a tubular, powerful palate shape that is much admired. It's a ripper.   Screw cap. | 11% alc. | Drink 2021-2040 | $50 | DB

     Centenary Hill Shiraz 2017, Barossa Sporting a very glossy, classy aromatic profile of pristine plum and berry fruits, with a sheen of cedary oak, spice and dark chocolate. Wonderfully balanced with an elegant, detailed palate shape, fine, sandy tannin support and a sense of enduring drive and grace. Screw cap. | 14.5% alc. | Drink 2021-2036 | $75 | DB

Penfolds ⑨Ⓜ⒜ ★★★★★

30 Tanunda Road, Nuriootpa, SA 5355 P16 **T** (08) 8568 8408 **www**.penfolds.com **OPEN** 7 days 10-5
WINEMAKER Peter Gago **EST.** 1844

Penfolds is the star in the crown of Treasury Wine Estates (TWE) but its history predates the formation of TWE by close on 170 years. Its shape has changed in terms of its vineyards, its management, its passing parade of great winemakers and its wines. There is no other single winery brand in the New or the Old World with the depth and breadth of Penfolds. Retail prices range from less than $20 to $950 for Grange, which is the cornerstone, produced every year, albeit the volume determined by the quality of the vintage, not by cash flow. (JH)

98   **Reserve Bin A Chardonnay 2020, Adelaide Hills** There is a resolute conviction and assuredness to this wine that sets it apart among the greatest and longest-lived of all. A textbook exemplar of Kym Schroeter's wizardry of uniting profound gunflint reduction, high-tensile white fruits and lightening acidity with uber-classy oak that exerts nothing like the presence expected of 86% new barrels. Brilliant, powder-fine mineral texture wraps every detail in seamless unity. For all that there is to astonish about this release, it is its monumental line and sheer, undeviating length that really set it apart.   Screw cap. | 12.5% alc. | Drink 2030-2045 | $125 | TS

     Yattarna Bin 144 Chardonnay 2019, South Eastern Australia The tension, endurance and sheer molecular detail of Yattarna propels it to the pinnacle of Australia's pointy chardonnay pyramid, and '19 follows in the hallowed footsteps of the sublime '18. This is a vintage that demands a great deal of time to unfurl. Tight, compact, focused and immensely determined, it leads out in its virile youth with the finest struck flint and gunpowder. A pinpoint singularity of white-fruit precision focuses a laser line of pure white acidity that projects from its core through a finish of astounding line, length and promise. Powder-fine, crystalline minerality surges long and strong. Another epic Yattarna. Vintage on vintage, has Yattarna now ascended to become Penfolds' greatest wine of all? Screw cap. | 12.5% alc. | Drink 2034-2049 | $175 | TS | ♥

97   **St Henri Shiraz 2018, South Australia** The effortless, unassuming self-assuredness of St Henri holds a unique and beloved place in the assemblage of Penfolds heroes, and '18 marks a particularly special release. Accomplished, spicy, glossy black fruits of grand integrity unfold to magnificent effect in the glass, contrasting a fine-boned frame of rigid yet graceful, powder-fine tannins that carry a finish of long-lingering line and alluring appeal. I look forward to spectating from the sidelines as its fruit slowly unfurls over the decades to come. An adorable St Henri that exemplifies all that this label stands for.   Cork. | 14.5% alc. | Drink 2028-2058 | $135 | TS

96   **Bin 51 Riesling 2021, Eden Valley** This cascades from the glass in a torrent of lily blossom, talc, fresh lemon, lime and Granny Smith apple. Yet for all its exuberance, it is honed and streamlined like only a cool season can achieve. The palate follows a focused line of magnificent tension, powder-fine mineral structure and the scintillating acid drive of cool nights. The most precise and enthralling Bin 51 of the recent era, irresistible now, and with a grand future before it.   Screw cap. | 11% alc. | Drink 2021-2041 | $40 | TS

Peter Lehmann

★★★★★

Para Road, Tanunda, SA 5352 **T** (08) 8565 9555 **www**.peterlehmannwines.com **OPEN** By appt **WINEMAKER** Nigel Westblade, Tim Dolan, Brett Smith, Brooke Blair **VITICULTURIST** Jade Rogge **EST.** 1979 **DOZENS** 750000

The seemingly indestructible Peter Lehmann (the person) died in June 2013, laying the seeds for what became the last step in the sale of the minority Lehmann family ownership in the company. The Hess Group of California had acquired control in '03 (leaving part of the capital with the Lehmann family) but a decade later it became apparent that Hess wished to quit its holding. Various suitors put their case forward but Margaret Lehmann (Peter's widow) wanted ongoing family, not corporate, ownership. Casella thus was able to make the successful bid in Nov '14, followed by the acquisition of Brand's Laira in Dec '15. (JH)

94 **H&V Riesling 2021, Eden Valley** Pale straw in the glass with aromas of freshly squeezed limes, Granny Smith apple crunch, Bickford's lime cordial and hints of orange blossom, crushed quartz and lighter notes of almond paste and fennel. Expansive and concentrated on the palate with a core of limey fruit pulsing through the wine. The light tweak of phenolics adds texture and appeal and a crisp line of acidity provides propulsion across the tongue. Good stuff in a strong vintage. Screw cap. | 11.5% alc. | Drink 2021–2031 | $25 | DB

Pirathon

★★★★

979 Light Pass Road, Vine Vale, SA 5352 **T** www.pirathon.com **OPEN** By appt **WINEMAKER** Adam Clay **VITICULTURIST** Tony Marshall **EST.** 2005 **DOZENS** 9000 **VYDS** 22ha

Pirathon primarily focuses on full-bodied Barossa Valley shiraz from the north-western districts of Greenock (contract-grown) and Maranaga (estate-grown). A new 480t winery was completed in '21. (JH)

90 **Blue Shiraz 2020, Barossa Valley** Purple red in the glass with an exuberant nose of juicy satsuma plum, jasmine, Asian spice, cherry pie and licorice. There's a slurpy edge to this one, with heady ripe plum and black fruits, abundant spice, fine tannin and brisk line. Good juicy drinking and great value. Screw cap. | 14.5% alc. | Drink 2022–2026 | $18 | DB

Purple Hands Wines

★★★★★

24 Vine Vale Road, Tanunda, SA 5352 **T** 0401 988 185 **www**.purplehandswines.com.au **WINEMAKER** Craig Stansborough **VITICULTURIST** Craig Stansborough **EST.** 2006 **DOZENS** 3000 **VYDS** 14ha

The finely honed, contemporary Barossa wines of Purple Hands are borne out of a partnership between Mark Slade and winemaker Craig Stansborough. Their home estate, the Stansborough vineyard, lies in the far south of the Barossa Valley. Purple Hands captures the purity and elegance that is possible when the raw materials are in good hands. (DB)

96 **Grenache 2020, Barossa Valley** A springtime basket of red flowers and fruits fill the senses, with a bright, almost tangy, back-palate and finish. Purple Hands at its best – and happiest. Screw cap. | 14% alc. | Drink 2022–2032 | $30 | JH

Running With Bulls

★★★★

40 Eden Valley Road, Angaston SA 5353 **T** (08) 8561 3200 **www**.runningwithbulls.com.au **WINEMAKER** Sam Wigan **EST.** 2008 **DOZENS** 19000

Running With Bulls is the Hill-Smith Family's foray into value- and flavour-packed, Spanish-inspired wines under the helmsmanship of winemaker Sam Wigan. These 'alternative' (or 'appropriate' varieties) are well suited to the Barossa Valley. Running With Bulls have consistently released excellent wines every year – full of character and inherent drinkability while remaining strong to their Barossa roots. (DB)

92 **Garnacha 2021, Barossa Valley** A pinot-esque and wonderfully perfumed Barossa garnacha (grenache) with vibrant aromas of red and yellow plum, mulberry, watermelon, strawberry and raspberry, with hints of Asian spice, ginger cake, cola and violets. Fleshy and juicy, with a spacious mouthfeel, loads of crunchy red and blue fruits, abundant spice, bright line and gypsum-like tannins. Super-value juicy drinking. Screw cap. | 14.5% alc. | Drink 2021–2026 | $23 | DB

91 **Tempranillo 2021, Barossa Valley** Bright red purple in the glass, with oodles of spicy, plummy fruit immediately jumping out. Hints of brown spices, cola, licorice, blueberry danish, maraschino cherries and earth. Plenty of bright acid crunch, tight, gritty tannin grip and cola-infused back fruits on the medium-length finish. Screw cap. | 14% alc. | Drink 2022–2028 | $23 | DB

Saltram ★★★★☆

Murray Street, Angaston, SA 5353 **T** (08) 8561 0200 **www**.saltramwines.com.au **OPEN** Thurs-Mon 10-5 **WINEMAKER** Alex MacKenzie **EST.** 1859 **DOZENS** 150000

There is no doubt that Saltram has taken strides towards regaining the reputation it held 30 or so years ago. Grape sourcing has come back to the Barossa Valley for the flagship wines. The red wines, in particular, have enjoyed great show success over the past decade with No. 1 Shiraz and Mamre Brook leading the charge. (JH)

96   **Mr Pickwick's Limited Release Particular Tawny NV, Barossa Valley** Head-spinning complexity with detailed red fruits, mince pies, baking spice, roasting nuts, candied citrus rind and earth. Incredibly fresh and vivid with a finish that just keeps on going. Just lovely. Cork. | 19.5% alc. | $75 | DB

Seabrook Wines ★★★★

1122 Light Pass Road, Tanunda, SA 5352 **T** (08) 8563 0368 **www**.seabrookwines.com.au **OPEN** Thurs-Mon 11-5 **WINEMAKER** Hamish Seabrook **EST.** 2004 **DOZENS** 3000 **VYDS** 10.1ha

Hamish Seabrook is the youngest generation of a proud Melbourne wine family once involved in wholesale and retail distribution, and as leading show judges of their respective generations. Hamish too, is a wine show judge but was the first to venture into winemaking, working with Best's and Brown Brothers in Victoria before moving to SA with wife Joanne. In 2008 Hamish set up his own winery on the family property in Vine Vale, having previously made the wines at Dorrien Estate and elsewhere. (JH)

92   **Lineage Cabernet Malbec 2019, Barossa Valley** A deeply coloured wine with a slab of opulent blackberry and mulberry fruit with hints of deep spice, turned earth, licorice and cedar. It shows impressive balance and flow with rich fruit, gravelly tannin pull and is flush with juicy dark fruit on the finish. Screw cap. | 14% alc. | Drink 2021-2028 | $22 | DB

91   **Lineage Mataro Rosé 2021, Barossa Valley** Pale copper-tinged pink in the glass, with aromas of delicate redcurrant, raspberry and strawberry fruit with hints of soft spice, watermelon, almond blossom and stone. Flush with red fruits and a little slinky texture to boot, the wine finishes crisp with fresh acidity and a white blossom, strawberry flourish. Screw cap. | 12.5% alc. | Drink 2021-2023 | $22 | DB

Seppeltsfield ★★★★★

730 Seppeltsfield Road, Seppeltsfield, SA 5355 **T** (08) 8568 6200 **www**.seppeltsfield.com.au **OPEN** 7 days 10.30-5 **WINEMAKER** Fiona Donald, Charlie Seppelt, Matthew Pick, Henry Slattery **VITICULTURIST** Kingsley Fuller **EST.** 1851 **DOZENS** 50000 **VYDS** 648ha

The historic Seppeltsfield property and its bounty of old fortified wines was originally established by the Seppelt family in 1851. Warren Randall now owns in excess of 90% of its capital. Randall, former sparkling winemaker for Seppelt Great Western in the '80s, has led a revival of Seppeltsfield, gradually restoring the heritage-listed property. The estate's 1888 gravity cellar is back in full operation and a tourism village has been established. The 100 Year Old Paras have no parallel anywhere else in the world and the conjunction of 100 years of devoted stewardship (think former cellarmaster James Godfrey) and climate, terroir and varieties have had an outcome that can never, ever, be duplicated. (JH)

97   **Para 21 Year Old Tawny 2001, South Australia** Medium tawny in the glass with amber flashes and notes of roasting nuts, candied citrus rinds, burnt toffee, butterscotch, brandy snaps, rancio and Christmas cake, with layers and layers of spice below. Unctuous, with head-spinning complexity and length of finish, with a seam of freshness that drives the flavours across the tongue and off into the distance. Screw cap. | 20.4% alc. | $95 | DB

Small Victories Wine Co ★★★★

3-5 Tanunda Road, Nuriootpa, SA, 5355 **T** (08) 8568 7877 **www**.smallvictorieswine.com **OPEN** Fri-Mon 11-4 **WINEMAKER** Julie Ashmead **EST.** 2021

Sisters-in-law Jules and Bec Ashmead work at Elderton as winemaker (Jules) and production/ logistics (Bec). The decision to create Small Victories came about after the constant search for wines that were interesting and a little different. In the end, they made their own. Sales from the wines support 2 local charities, Variety and Trees For Life. The label has a strong focus on sustainability, including environmentally friendly packaging, lightweight bottles and recycled cardboard cartons. And the reason for the name? The 2 friends believe in celebrating our small victories each day. (JP)

---

93 **Shiraz 2021, Eden Valley** Vibrant and vivid characters of super-ripe plums with high tones of raspberry and blueberry, hints of exotic spice, musk, jasmine and licorice. Boisterous and exuberant with super-pure fruit and chalky tannins. Put simply, it's about plummy joyful consumption without pretence. Screw cap. | 14.5% alc. | Drink 2022-2026 | $27 | DB

Vermentino 2021, Riverland Pretty gorgeous, really. Nashi pears, crunchy summer apples, juniper and little pockets of cassis and white currant. The mid palate loops and curls around the mouth, leaving swathes of refreshing, saline acid and vibrant fruit through the finish. Delicious. Screw cap. | 12.5% alc. | Drink 2021-2024 | $27 | EL

Sons of Eden ★★★★★

Penrice Road, Angaston, SA 5353 **T** (08) 8564 2363 **www**.sonsofeden.com **OPEN** 7 days 11–6
WINEMAKER Corey Ryan **VITICULTURIST** Simon Cowham **EST.** 2000 **DOZENS** 9000 **VYDS** 60ha

Corey Ryan and Simon Cowham both learnt and refined their skills in the vineyards and cellars of Eden Valley. Corey is a trained oenologist with over 20 vintages under his belt, having cut his teeth as a winemaker at Henschke. Thereafter he worked for Rouge Homme and Penfolds in Coonawarra, backed up by winemaking stints in the Rhône Valley. In '07 he won the Institute of Masters of Wine scholarship. Simon has had a similarly international career covering such diverse organisations as Oddbins, UK, and the Winemakers' Federation of Australia. He worked for Yalumba as technical manager of the Heggies and Pewsey Vale vineyards. (JH)

97 **Zephyrus Shiraz 2019, Barossa** Deeply coloured; a finely structured wine of great class as befits the vintage, the whole bunches lifting the red-fruit aromatics on the predominantly blackberry/black cherry foundations. Screw cap. | 14.5% alc. | Drink 2025-2039 | $45 | JH

96 **Notus Grenache 2021, Barossa Valley** Bright ruby with purple flashes in the glass and aromas of finely poised red cherry, red plum and macerated raspberry fruits, cut with gingery spice, floral high tones and all the vibrancy and verve you'd expect from a top-flight grenache. Medium bodied, pure fruit edged with exotic spice, powdery tannin support and a bright line equals a sense of effortless drinkability. Screw cap. | 14.5% alc. | Drink 2022-2032 | $54 | DB

95 **Marschall Shiraz 2020, Barossa Valley** You get a generous bang for your buck with this elegant, medium-bodied shiraz, supple and fresh, with finely strung tannins and oak. Screw cap. | 14.5% alc. | Drink 2023-2040 | $29 | JH

94 **Freya Riesling 2021, Eden Valley** A mouth-watering and lip-smacking riesling that reflects the punctilious vinification in its freshness and finesse, citrusy acidity drawing out the long finish. Screw cap. | 12.5% alc. | Drink 2021-2030 | $25 | JH

Kennedy GSM 2020, Barossa Valley Ripe plummy goodness from the first sip, with light floral facets flitting around above the fruit, which sits on a base of exotic spice, earth, kirsch and roasting meats. Superfine sandy tannins lend support. It has a lively line, great balance and presents both super drinking and great value. Screw cap. | 14.5% alc. | Drink 2022-2032 | $30 | DB

Spinifex ★★★★★

PO Box 511, Nuriootpa, SA 5355 **T** (08) 8564 2059 **www**.spinifexwines.com.au **OPEN** At Vino Lokal, Tanunda **WINEMAKER** Peter Schell **VITICULTURIST** Peter Schell **EST.** 2001 **DOZENS** 6000 **VYDS** 12ha

Peter Schell and Magali Gely are a husband-and-wife team from NZ who came to Australia in the early '90s to study oenology and marketing at Roseworthy College. They have spent 4 vintages making wine in France, mainly in the south where Magali's family were vignerons for generations near Montpellier. The wines are made in open fermenters, basket pressed, with partial wild (indigenous) fermentation and relatively long post-ferment maceration. (JH)

97 **Single Vineyard Moppa Shiraz 2019, Barossa Valley** From the deep colour and vivid crimson edge through to the finish, this wine sings a song of purity and intensity. The black fruits, the background of earth, oak and lifted spice simply serve to throw you back to shiraz of great quality, thanks to the skill of winemaker Peter Schell. Screw cap. | 14.5% alc. | Drink 2025-2050 | $60 | JH

96 **Single Vineyard Moppa Grenache 2020, Barossa Valley** It's all red plum and cherry fruit with a splash of raspberry coulis, along with hints of spice, ginger cake, earth and stone. It's concentrated but 40% whole bunches in the ferment opens the wine up beautifully, highlighting the crunchy, pure fruit, fine sandy tannin and savoury palate shape. Wonderful drinking. Screw cap. | 14.7% alc. | Drink 2021-2031 | $45 | DB

Bête Noir 2019, Barossa Valley It's elegant yet powerful, with ripe blackberry, licorice and a touch of plum. However long you wait, it will be there waiting for you. Bargain. Screw cap. | 14.5% alc. | Drink 2024-2049 | $39 | JH

Dominion Shiraz 2019, Barossa Valley As with all of Pete's wines, the leitmotif is fruit purity writ large. Here it's juicy damson plum and black cherries sheathed in purple floral flecks that I often see in wines from the foot of the eastern range. Deep spice, a touch of polished leather, fine long-chain tannins that cascade through the wine and a simmering sense of latent power. It's a wine of great depth but there is a sense of grace present also, which is a wonderful thing. Screw cap. | 14.5% alc. | Drink 2021–2038 | $60 | DB

94 **Syrah 2021, Barossa** Deep purple red in the glass, it's a rollicking, crunchy, bright and sapid ride with a gorgeous plume of plummy fruit, cut with spice and floral nuance, whole-bunch amaro notes and a sense of space, clarity and detail that brings a smile to the face. Such a wonderful drink and great value. Screw cap. | 14% alc. | Drink 2022–2029 | $30 | DB

St Hallett ★★★★★

St Hallett Road, Tanunda, SA 5352 **T** (08) 8563 7070 **www**.sthallett.com.au **OPEN** 7 days ,10–5 by appt **WINEMAKER** Helen McCarthy **EST.** 1944 **DOZENS** 210000

St Hallett sources all grapes from within the Barossa GI and is synonymous with the region's icon variety – shiraz. The winemaking team continues to explore the geographical, geological and climatic diversity of the Barossa, manifested through individual processing of all vineyards and single-vineyard releases. In '17, St Hallett was acquired by Accolade. (JH)

96 **Blackwell Shiraz 2019, Barossa** Bright-rimmed crimson purple. A perfectly balanced and poised medium-bodied shiraz, with a lustrous, succulent palate and a texture akin to Thai silk, tannins sufficient for the job and no more. Screw cap. | 14.5% alc. | Drink 2025–2042 | $55 | JH

St Hugo ★★★★★

2141 Barossa Valley Way, Rowland Flat, SA 5352 **T** (08) 8115 9200 **www**.sthugo.com **OPEN** Fri–Mon 10.30–4.30 **WINEMAKER** Peter Munro **EST.** 1983 **DOZENS** 50000 **VYDS** 57ha

This is a stand-alone business within Pernod Ricard, focused on the premium and ultra-premium end of the market. There is a restaurant with kitchen garden, and self-catering accommodation is available in a 19th-century stone cottage. (JH)

96 **Barossa Grenache Shiraz Mataro 2021, Barossa Valley** Vivid red purple in the glass, super-ripe plum and blueberry notes are lead by wafts of frangipani over a base of exotic spice, amaro herbs, licorice, earth and cherry danish. A very modern, juicy take on the classic blend, with pure, juicy fruit, tight ripe tannin and a finish that lingers beautifully. It's just great, spicy drinking. Screw cap. | 14.5% alc. | Drink 2022–2032 | $50 | DB

Cabernet Sauvignon 2019, Coonawarra This is massive, the oak a central part of the experience right now. However, at the time of tasting, this wine still has a year and a bit to go before release. The time will be crucial for the ample black and red fruit to soak up that oak, step up on its shoulders and ride the chariot with muscle and power. Concentrated and focused; this will be great in time. The Feb '23 release date: well judged. Screw cap. | 14% alc. | Drink 2023–2043 | $50 | EL

Thorn-Clarke Wines ★★★★★

266 Gawler Park Road, Angaston, SA 5353 **T** (08) 8564 3036 **www**.thornclarkewines.com.au **OPEN** Fri–Sun 10–5 by appt **WINEMAKER** Peter Kelly **VITICULTURIST** Steve Fiebiger **EST.** 1987 **DOZENS** 90000 **VYDS** 222ha

Established by David and Cheryl Clarke (née Thorn), and son Sam, Thorn-Clarke is one of the largest family-owned estate-based businesses in the Barossa. Their winery is close to the border between the Barossa and Eden valleys and 3 of their 4 vineyards are in the Eden Valley. The fourth vineyard is at St Kitts, at the northern end of the Barossa Ranges. The quality of grapes retained for the Thorn-Clarke label has resulted in a succession of trophy and gold medal–winning wines at very competitive prices. (JH)

95 **Sandpiper Riesling 2021, Eden Valley** The floral bouquet is shy, the palate anything but. It explores the world of citrus fruits and adds some tropicals. An interplay between piercing acidity and fruit sweetness draws out the length of the palate and adds to the overall enjoyment, acidity having the last word. Screw cap. | 11.5% alc. | Drink 2021–2031 | $25 | JH

Tim Smith Wines

★★★★

996 Light Pass Road, Vine Vale, SA 5352 **T** 0416 396 730 **www** timsmithwines.com.au **OPEN** By appt **WINEMAKER** Tim Smith **EST.** 2001 **DOZENS** 6000 **VYDS** 1ha

After many years working at Barossa producers such as Yalumba, St Hallett, Charles Melton and Château Tanunda, today Tim Smith plies his vinous craft from his shed in Vine Vale at the foot of the eastern range of the Barossa Valley. Making wines under his own label since 2002, it was perhaps Tim's time working harvest for Chapoutier, Gabriel Meffre and Domaine du Mandeville in France's Rhône valley, that have most strongly shaped where Tim's wines are today. (DB)

94   **Riesling 2021, Eden Valley** A wonderfully fragrant Eden Valley riesling from the strong '21 vintage. Classic regional aromas of freshly squeezed lime juice and Bickfords lime cordial with hints of Christmas lily, frangipani, almond paste and wet stone. These aromas transpose pitch-perfect on to the crisp, dry palate. It displays wonderful fruit purity, drive and tension, finishing with a stony, fresh lime blast and a cleansing, moreish appeal. Such great value.   Screw cap. | 11.5% alc. | Drink 2021-2031 | $28 | DB

Torbreck Vintners

★★★★★

348 Roennfeldt Road, Marananga, SA 5352 **T** (08) 8562 4155 **www** torbreck.com **OPEN** 7 days 10-5 by appt **WINEMAKER** Ian Hongell, Scott McDonald **VITICULTURIST** Nigel Blieschke **EST.** 1994 **DOZENS** 70 000 **VYDS** 112ha

Torbreck Vintners was already one of Australia's best-known producers of high-quality red wine when, in Sept 2013, wealthy Californian entrepreneur and vintner Peter Kight (of Quivira Vineyards) acquired 100% ownership of the business. Talented winemaker Ian Hongell joined the team in '16. Shiraz (and other Rhône varieties) is the focus. Wines are unfined and unfiltered. (JH)

95   **Hillside Vineyard Shiraz Roussanne 2020, Barossa Valley** Co-fermentation dialling the colour saturation up to Spinal Tap levels here. Intense and pure black cherry, plum and blackberry fruits are cut with deep spice, licorice and earth. Weighty and concentrated with a toothsome, muscular frame, deep resonant black fruits, assertive fine tannin and simmering latent power on the finish. There's a lot of fruit heft and bang for your buck here.   Cork. | 15% alc. | Drink 2021-2031 | $33 | DB

Turkey Flat

★★★★★

67 Bethany Road, Tanunda, SA 5352 **T** (08) 8563 2851 **www** turkeyflat.com.au **OPEN** 7 days 11-5 **WINEMAKER** Mark Bulman **EST.** 1990 **DOZENS** 20 000 **VYDS** 47.83ha

The establishment date of Turkey Flat is given as 1990 but it might equally have been 1870 (or thereabouts), when the Schulz family purchased the Turkey Flat Vineyard; or 1847, when the vineyard was first planted – to the very old shiraz that still grows there today and the 8ha of equally old grenache. The business is run by sole proprietor Christie Schulz. (JH)

94   **Butchers Block Shiraz 2020, Barossa Valley** Fragrant and lifted ripe plum and dark berry fruits with hints of exotic spice, violets, chocolate and underlying wafts of roasting meats, pressed flowers and light amaro herbs. The addition of a small amount of whole bunches to the ferment seems to open the wine up and let a little more light in, along with spice and textural elements. Pure of fruit with long, sandy tannins and a juicy finish, the Butchers Block provides excellent value and delicious drinking. Screw cap. | 14.1% alc. | Drink 2021-2026 | $25 | DB

Utopos

★★★★★

PO Box 764, Tanunda, SA 5352 **T** 0409 351 166 **www** utopos.com.au **WINEMAKER** Kym Teusner **EST.** 2015 **DOZENS** 1500 **VYDS** 20ha

The fates were kind when Neil Panuja, a friend of Kym Teusner's from 'the big smoke', said he had the wish to get into fine-wine production and asked that Kym keep an eye out for something special. Shortly thereafter, a vineyard that Kym had coveted from his beginnings in the Barossa Valley came onto the market. The 20ha vineyard was duly acquired, Kym investing in a small share. The depleted stony soils consistently produce low yields of high-quality grapes that loudly proclaim their Barossan origin. The name they have given the business is the root word of Utopia. Everything is just so right: great vineyard, great winemaker, great story, great packaging. (JH)

96   **Grenache 2021, Barossa Valley** Bright red purple in the glass with aromas of juicy plum, red cherry fruits, exotic spice, gingerbread, violets, earth and red licorice. The fruit weight is spot on, pure yet with a distinct sense of space. The aromas transpose over onto the palate, which shows a chalky tannin texture and shimmering acid line. It's a cracker. Screw cap. | 14.5% alc. | Drink 2022-2032 | $70 | DB

  Shiraz 2019, Barossa Valley Deep red purple in the glass, with a perfumed cascade of satsuma plum and macerated blackberry characters, underscored by hints of baking spice, licorice, dark chocolate, vanilla and cedar. The balance is impeccable, with great fruit purity and detail throughout its length; the classy, cedary cut of French oak perhaps a little more noticeable on the palate. Deep, resonant and long, with über-ripe tannins and a sense of brightness to its form. Cork. | 14.5% alc. | Drink 2021-2038 | $70 | DB

Vanguardist Wines ★★★★★

121A Radford Road, Seppeltsfield, SA 5355 **T** 0487 193 053 **www**.vanguardistwines.com **OPEN** By appt **WINEMAKER** Michael John Corbett **VITICULTURIST** Michael John Corbett **EST.** 2014 **DOZENS** 2000 **VYDS** 7.5ha

Vanguardist Wines maker, Michael John Corbett, draws on established sources across South Australia to craft a delicious swag of Mediterranean-inspired wines of textural intrigue. A card of neutral wood, ambient ferments and plenty of whole-bunch is dealt with a deft hand. The results, often compelling. Corbett's opus is grenache, specifically Blewitt Springs grenache, hewn of the region's low-yielding elevated old vineyards. His ripeness barometer challenges notions of what is optimal, flirting with marginal levels of alcohol on the lower side. (NG)

96   **Grenache 2020, McLaren Vale** I have always appreciated the style here: a pinosity of red fruits with a firm yet svelte etching of nebbiolo-esque bristly tannins. Sometimes, though, the ripeness was on the south side of ideal. Not this year! This sits pretty on a dial between elegance and sappier fruit, still defined by signature fine-boned tannic latticework and saline freshness. Darker cherry, anise, mint, thyme, rosemary and sandalwood. A whiff of orange zest, too. This address is now at the top of the stylistic totem pole and one of the few true regional benchmarks. Diam. | 14.1% alc. | Drink 2021-2027 | $56 | NG

Z Wine ★★★★★

Shop 3, 109-111 Murray Street, Tanunda, SA 5352 **T** (08) 8563 3637 **www**.zwine.com.au **OPEN** Sun-Thurs 10-8, Fri-Sat 10-late **WINEMAKER** Janelle Zerk **EST.** 1999 **DOZENS** 10000

Z Wine is the partnership of sisters Janelle and Kristen Zerk, whose heritage dates back 5 generations at the Zerk Vineyard in Lyndoch. Vineyard resources include growers that supply old-vine shiraz, old bush-vine grenache and High Eden riesling. Both women have completed degrees at the University of Adelaide (Janelle winemaking and Kristen wine marketing). Janelle also has vintage experience in Puligny-Montrachet, Tuscany and Sonoma Valley. (JH)

96   **Roman Old Vine GSM 2021, Barossa Valley** The colour is fresh and full, the perfumed aromas and flavours of all manner of cinnamon spice, through licorice, dark chocolate, and velvety blackberry on the palate and into the lingering, bright finish. Screw cap. | 14.5% alc. | Drink 2022-2041 | $40 | JH

95   **August Old Vine Grenache 2021, Barossa Valley** Old vines, modern grenache style, picked while all the perfume and exotic spices of grenache are in high relief throughout the long palate. Best of all is the absence of heat on the juicy finish. Screw cap. | 14.5% alc. | Drink 2023-2031 | $35 | JH

  Saul Riesling 2021, Eden Valley Scents of citrus, apple, white peach and powder puff float in the glass, giving way to the more direct mix of lime and lemon on the long travel through to the finish and aftertaste of the palate. High-quality wine. Screw cap. | 11.5% alc. | Drink 2023-2036 | $35 | JH

REGION
Eden Valley

Flaxman Wines ★★★★★

662 Flaxmans Valley Road, Flaxmans Valley, SA 5253 **T** 0411 668 949 **www**.flaxmanwines.com.au **OPEN** Thurs-Fri, Sun 11-4, Sat 11-5 **WINEMAKER** Colin Sheppard **EST.** 2005 **DOZENS** 1200 **VYDS** 2ha

After visiting the Barossa Valley for over a decade, Melbourne residents Colin and Fi Sheppard decided on a tree change and in '04 found a small, old vineyard overlooking Flaxmans Valley, consisting of 90yo riesling, 90yo shiraz and 70yo semillon. Colin has worked at various Barossa wineries and his attention to detail (and understanding of the process) is reflected in the consistent high quality of the wines. (JH)

94 **Riesling 2021, Eden Valley** A beautiful perfumed nose with fragrant Christmas lily and citrus blossom notes coming to the fore, along with fresh lime juice and stone. The wine displays excellent fruit purity and texture on the palate, the crystalline acidity reining everything in nicely and driving it forward to a pure Bickford's Lime crescendo. Screw cap. | 12.5% alc. | Drink 2021-2030 | $30 | DB

Gatt Wines ★★★★

417 Boehms Springs Road, Flaxman Valley, SA 5235 **T** (08) 8564 1166 **www**.gattwines.com
WINEMAKER David Norman **VITICULTURIST** Gil Rogers **EST**. 1972 **DOZENS** 8000 **VYDS** 56.24ha

When you read the hyperbole that sometimes accompanies the acquisition of an existing wine business, about transforming it into a world-class operation, it is easy to sigh and move on. When Ray Gatt acquired Eden Springs, he proceeded to translate words into deeds. As well as the 19.15ha Eden Springs Vineyard, he also acquired the historic Siegersdorf Vineyard (now 21.79ha) on the Barossa floor and the neighbouring Graue Vineyard (15.3ha). (JH)

90 **Riesling 2020, High Eden** Pale straw with notes of Bickford's lime cordial, grapefruit, tangerine, almond paste, orange blossom and stone. Pure and endearing, there's an almost stone-fruit richness to the palate shape, along with a nervy acidity that drives the wine forward. Screw cap. | 12.5% alc. | Drink 2022-2028 | $20 | DB

Heggies Vineyard ⓘ ★★★★☆

Heggies Range Road, Eden Valley, SA 5235 **T** (08) 8561 3200 **www**.heggiesvineyard.com **OPEN** By appt
WINEMAKER Marc van Halderen **EST**. 1972 **DOZENS** 15000 **VYDS** 62ha

Heggies was the second of the high-altitude (570m) vineyards established by the Hill-Smith family. Plantings on the 120ha former grazing property began in 1973; the principal varieties are riesling, chardonnay, viognier and merlot. There are also 2 special plantings: a 1.1ha reserve chardonnay block and 27ha of various clonal trials. (JH)

95 **Botrytis Riesling 2021, Eden Valley** The tightrope walk and tension between fruit sweetness and acidity is delicious and fascinating in equal measure here, with characters of lime-edged apricot drops, lemon barley, dried honey, gingerbread and a dusting of soft spice and jasmine. Floral and head-spinningly pure on the palate, with nary a hint of cloying. A clean, precise bolt of pure botrytis fruit and spice on the finish lingers beautifully. Screw cap. | 10.5% alc. | Drink 2021-2028 | $28 | DB | ♥

94 **Estate Riesling 2021, Eden Valley** A cracking lime-pure '21 riesling, with it's gorgeous blossomy perfume, quartz-like minerality and swift, sherbety cadence across the tongue. It's a great Heggies release. Screw cap. | 11.5% alc. | Drink 2021-2031 | $26 | DB

Henschke ⓘ ★★★★★

1428 Keyneton Road, Keyneton, SA 5353 **T** (08) 8564 8223 **www**.henschke.com.au **OPEN** Mon-Sat 9-4.30 & public hols 10-3 **WINEMAKER** Stephen Henschke **VITICULTURIST** Prue Henschke **EST**. 1868 **DOZENS** 30000 **VYDS** 100ha

Henschke is the foremost medium-sized wine producer in Australia. Stephen and Prue Henschke have taken a crown jewel and polished it to an even greater brilliance. The wines hail from the Eden Valley (the majority), the Barossa Valley or the Adelaide Hills. There's a compelling logic and focus – no excursions to McLaren Vale, Coonawarra, etc. Recognition as Winery of the Year in the '21 Companion is arguably long overdue. (JH)

98 **Julius Riesling 2021, Eden Valley** One of two joint winners for Halliday Wine Companion Riesling of the Year 2023. Citrus and passionfruit blossom soar as you swirl the glass, and the palate achieves the seemingly impossible with the volume of turbo-charged fruit. It reaches every receptor in the mouth and there's no hint of added acidity, the balance and length faultless. Screw cap. | 11.5% alc. | Drink 2021-2034 | $47 | JH | ♥

97 **Peggy's Hill Riesling 2021, Eden Valley** The blossom-filled bouquet surges instantly from the glass, citrus leading, apple tucked in close behind, the palate every bit as expressive. The crisp acidity provides the framework to carry the long finish and aftertaste; world class for a song. Screw cap. | 12% alc. | Drink 2021-2031 | $25 | JH

Hutton Vale Farm ⓘⓜ ★★★★☆

65 Stone Jar Road, Angaston, SA 5353 **T** (08) 8564 8270 **www**.huttonvale.com **OPEN** By appt
WINEMAKER Kym Teusner **EST**. 1960 **DOZENS** 1500 **VYDS** 27.1ha

John Howard Angas arrived in SA in 1843 and inter alia gave his name to Angaston, purchasing and developing significant farming property close to the still embryonic town. He named

FLEURIEU

MOUNT LOFTY RANGES

FAR NORTH

LIMESTONE COAST

LOWER MURRAY

THE PENINSULAS

part of this Hutton Vale and it is this property that is now owned and occupied by his great-great-grandson John and wife Jan Angas. Since 2012, the Angases grow the grapes and Kym Teusner is responsible for the winemaking, sales and marketing of Hutton Vale wines. The vineyards were badly affected by a grass fire in Aug '14. While much of the vineyard has regenerated, some of the oldest grenache vines were completely destroyed. (JH)

96   **Shiraz 2018, Eden Valley** A special vineyard that routinely expresses blueberries laced with graphite, sheets of hung deli meat, raspberry, ground white pepper, fresh nutmeg and littered with crushed pink peppercorns. No matter how it is made, or by whom, the fruit shines in a way that evokes memories of the nearby landscape ... towering gum trees, exposed granite boulders in places, and fresh, open air. This is spicy, layered and nuanced. It's really good.   Screw cap. | 14.4% alc. | Drink 2022-2039 | $75 | EL

Leo Buring

Sturt Highway, Nuriootpa, SA 5355 **T** 1300 651 650 **WINEMAKER** Tom Shanahan **EST.** 1934

Between 1965 and 2000, Leo Buring was Australia's foremost producer of rieslings, with a rich legacy left by former winemaker John Vickery. After veering away from its core business into other varietal wines, it has now refocused on riesling. Top of the range are the Leopold Derwent Valley and the Leonay Eden Valley rieslings.(JH)

97   **Leonay DWY17 Riesling 2021, Eden Valley** All the Leonay hallmarks are here: precision, detail, clarity and drive. What I really love about these wines is their tubular palate shape of achingly pure, limey fruit, topped with notes of Christmas lily and stone. The concentration on the palate is impressive, all compressed lime juice and floral top-notes, the wine coiling at first before accelerating off across the tongue with a cracking pace, leaving a finish that lingers beautifully. It's a classic.   Screw cap. | 11% alc. | Drink 2021-2038 | $40 | DB | ♥

94   **Dry Riesling 2021, Eden Valley** Thoroughly impressive, given the challenging vintage. This has been extracted with considerable aplomb, from fruit relatively unscathed. The finish, slightly bitter, but not unattractive. Otherwise, redcurrant, spearmint, lilac, chilli and a brush of thyme across an effortless finish. Mid weighted, characterful and altogether, a remarkable effort. The price, a steal. Screw cap. | 13.5% alc. | Drink 2021-2035 | $20 | DB

Millon Wines

48 George Street, Williamstown, SA 5351 **T** (08) 8524 6691 **WWW**.millonwines.com.au **WINEMAKER** Angus Wardlaw **EST.** 2013 **DOZENS** 20000

Millon Wines has 3 vineyards: one in the Eden Valley, the second in the Barossa Valley and the third in the Clare Valley. Winemaker Angus Wardlaw, with a degree in wine science from CSU and experience in the Clare Valley as winemaker at Kirrihill Wines, 'believes the Eden Valley is the future of the Barossa'. He makes the Millon wines with a minimalist approach. (JH)

91   **The Impressionist Riesling 2021, Eden Valley** Pale straw with green flashes in the glass. Aromas of freshly squeezed lime and grapefruit, with some green apple cut and hints of orange and almond blossom and crushed stone. Sapid and brisk, with a lovely crystalline profile and plenty of drive and clarity.   Screw cap. | 12% alc. | Drink 2021-2031 | $18 | DB

Mountadam Vineyards Ⓥ

High Eden Road, Eden Valley, SA 5235 **T** 0427 089 836 **WWW**.mountadam.com.au **OPEN** By appt **WINEMAKER** Caitlin Brown **VITICULTURIST** Caitlin Brown **EST.** 1972 **DOZENS** 30000 **VYDS** 148ha

Founded by the late David Wynn for the benefit of winemaker son Adam, Mountadam was purchased by Möet Hennessy Wine Estates in 2000. In '05, Mountadam returned to family ownership when it was purchased by David and Jenni Brown from Adelaide. David and Jenni have worked to bring the original Mountadam property back together with the purchase of Mountadam Farm in '07 and the High Eden Vineyard from TWE in '15. (JH)

91   **Five-Fifty Pinot Noir Rosé 2021, Eden Valley** Pale, pale pink in the glass with aromas of raspberry, red cherry and pomegranate with hints of white flowers, crushed stone, marzipan and watermelon. Bright, savoury, clean and crisp with excellent tension and a finish that echos with morello cherry and almond paste. Lovely.   Screw cap. | 14.5% alc. | Drink 2020-2025 | $20 | DB

90   **Five-Fifty Cabernet Sauvignon 2019, Barossa** Awash with red and blackcurrants, dark spice, maraschino cherries, cedar, dark chocolate and dried herbs. Varietal and true with rich black fruits on the palate and a slight meaty edge that adds interest. Compact and pure.   Screw cap. | 14.5% alc. | Drink 2020-2028 | $20 | DB

Pewsey Vale Vineyard ⓘ ★★★★★

Eden Valley Road, Eden Valley, SA 5353 **T** (08) 8561 3200 **WWW**.pewseyvale.com **OPEN** By appt
WINEMAKER Louisa Rose **EST.** 1847 **DOZENS** 20000 **VYDS** 65ha

Pewsey Vale was a famous vineyard established in 1847 by Joseph Gilbert. It was appropriate that when the Hill-Smith family began the renaissance of the Eden Valley plantings in 1961, it should do so by purchasing Pewsey Vale and establishing 50ha of riesling. In '77 the Riesling also finally benefited from being the first wine to be bottled with a Stelvin screw cap. While public reaction forced the abandonment of the initiative for almost 20 years, Pewsey Vale never lost faith in the technical advantages of the closure. (JH)

95 **Prima 25GR Riesling 2021, Eden Valley** I've always enjoyed the Prima. Those fresh lime and crunchy apple notes are there, sluiced with soft spice and heady blossom notes, but I love the dance between sweetness and acid, the tension and the tempering effect of the acidity on the perception of sweetness. It's about balance and the Prima gets it right, especially in the impressive 2021 vintage. Screw cap. | 9% alc. | Drink 2021-2031 | $30 | DB

1961 Block Single Vineyard Estate Riesling 2020, Eden Valley Aromas of freshly squeezed lime juice with notes of lemon myrtle, almond blossom, crushed stone and perhaps a vague honeysuckle note further in the distance. It's a purely focused wine; quartzy and sapid with wonderful clarity, detail and drive. Screw cap. | 12.5% alc. | Drink 2021-2035 | $35 | DB

Yalumba ⓘⓐ ★★★★★

40 Eden Valley Road, Angaston, SA 5353 **T** (08) 8561 3200 **WWW**.yalumba.com **OPEN** 7 days 11–4
WINEMAKER Louisa Rose (chief), Kevin Glastonbury, Sam Wigan, Heather Fraser, Will John **EST.** 1849
DOZENS 930000 **VYDS** 180ha

Owned and run by the Hill-Smith family, Yalumba has a long commitment to quality and great vision in its selection of vineyard sites, new varieties and brands. It has always been a serious player at the top end of full-bodied Australian reds and was a pioneer in the use of screw caps. It has a proud history of lateral thinking and rapid decision-making by a small group led by Robert Hill-Smith. (JH)

97 **The Virgilius Viognier 2019, Eden Valley** Yalumba has firmly positioned itself at the pointy end of the Australian viognier hierarchy with its Virgilius. It's a style more in line with the wines of the northern Rhône than the usual overtly apricotty numbers we often see from the Antipodes. Steely and textural with savoury-shaped stone fruits and a light dusting of apricot and citrus fruits, along with notes of marzipan, dried honey and light ginger spice. It boasts a savoury, stony palate shape and a light tweak of phenolics on the finish, which is fruit-pure and enduring. Screw cap. | 13% alc. | Drink 2021-2027 | $50 | DB | ♥

The Menzies Cabernet Sauvignon 2017, Coonawarra An icon in Australian wine, Yalumba's Coonawarra-born Menzies Cabernet Sauvignon has long stood at the pointy end of our country's fine-wine pyramid, and I'm sure many will fondly remember occasions when a well-cellared example of the Menzies has knocked their socks off. Nothing's changed, perhaps the oak has been dialled back a little, but that classic, herbal-flecked blackberry and blackcurrant fruit at its core is all elegance and latent power. Fine spice and graphite-like tannins lay down layers on the palate. The finish is long and with impeccable balance, trailing off with a vapour trail of blackcurrant, cedar and olive tapenade. It's a classic. Cork. | 14.5% alc. | Drink 2021-2041 | $60 | DB | ♥

96 **Vine Vale Grenache 2020, Barossa Valley** A wonderful, bunchy grenache that ticks all the boxes. Red fruited and fragrant with a deep seam of souk-like spice and gingerbread, notes of macerated raspberry and strawberry, a splash of soy, dried herbs, pressed flowers and lighter meaty tones. Medium bodied with a pure, savoury fruit flow that makes the wine seem very comfortable in its own skin. Balanced tannins and on-point acidity provide structure and cadence. Effortless drinking. Screw cap. | 14% alc. | Drink 2021-2031 | $40 | DB

The Signature Cabernet Sauvignon Shiraz 2018, Barossa There is a resonance and depth to this release that I really like. Wonderfully pure and concentrated blackberry and plum fruits, layered with spice, dark chocolate, earth, cedar and oak nuance. Succulent and sinewy in the mouth, it flexes considerable muscle, yet remains purely fruited and approachable even at this stage of its evolution. Rich and balanced with fine, ripe tannin and plenty of energy for such depth of fruit. Lovely. Cork. | 14.5% alc. | Drink 2021-2050 | $65 | DB

REGION

Currency Creek

Shaw Family Vintners ★★★☆

369 Myrtle Grove Road, Currency Creek, SA 5214 **T** (08) 8555 4215 **www**.shawfamilyvintners.com **OPEN** Mon–Fri 9–5 **WINEMAKER** Brie Overcash, Brooke Blair **EST**. 2001 **DOZENS** 60000 **VYDS** 414ha

Shaw Family Vintners was established in the early '70s by Richard and Marie Shaw and sons Philip, Nathan and Mark when they planted shiraz at McLaren Flat. Extensive vineyards were acquired and developed in McLaren Vale (64ha) and Currency Creek (350ha), and a winery at Currency Creek. In Apr '17 the winery, vineyards, stock and brands were purchased by Casella Family brands and are now managed by the next generation of Casella and Shaw families. (JH)

90   **Stonemason Shiraz 2019, Currency Creek** Wow. Finding wines at this price and quality – we are in unicorn land. Luscious notes of black cherry and dark chocolate have balanced, ripe tannins to provide texture and structure.   Screw cap. | 14.5% alc. | Drink 2022–2025 | $15 | JH

REGION

Kangaroo Island

Bay of Shoals Wines ★★★★☆

49 Cordes Road, Kingscote, Kangaroo Island, SA 5223 **T** (08) 8553 0289 **www**.bayofshoalswines.com.au **OPEN** 7 days 11–5 **WINEMAKER** Kelvin Budarick **EST**. 1994 **DOZENS** 5000 **VYDS** 15ha

John Willoughby's vineyard overlooks the Bay of Shoals, which is the northern boundary of Kingscote, Kangaroo Island's main town. Planting of the vineyard began in 1994. In addition, 460 olive trees have been planted to produce table olives. (JH)

95   **Albariño 2021, Kangaroo Island** Don't bother searching for perfumes first up on the bouquet, for they aren't there. The palate is another matter, packed with intense flavours ranging through Granny Smith apple, blood orange and grapefruit, causing a traffic jam as each elbows their siblings, which only serves to sharpen their defences. Will stand up to every type of Asian dish. The '21 vintage magic is not to be gainsaid.   Screw cap. | 12% alc. | Drink 2021–2028 | $30 | JH

False Cape Wines ★★★★

1054 Willson River Road, Dudley East, SA 5222 **T** 0447 808 838 **www**.falsecapewines.com.au **OPEN** 7 days 11–5 **WINEMAKER** Greg Follett, Nick Walker **VITICULTURIST** Jamie Helyar **EST**. 1999 **DOZENS** 6000 **VYDS** 30ha

Julie and Jamie Helyar's False Cape Vineyards links third-generation Kangaroo Island farming with third-generation Langhorne Creek grape growers. It is the largest vineyard on Kangaroo Island with 30ha of vines. Wines are made by Julie's brother, Greg Follett, of Lake Breeze in Langhorne Creek; Nick Walker of O'Leary Walker makes the Riesling. False Cape is entirely off-grid, completely relying on solar power; the red grape varieties are dry-grown, free-range turkeys providing pest control management and sheep are used for weed management during winter. (JH)

94   **Willson River Riesling 2021, Kangaroo Island** Lovely riesling, with an even flow from the first sip to the finish. Lime, Meyer lemon and grapefruit float on crisp, natural acidity.   Screw cap. | 12% alc. | Drink 2022–2032 | $22 | JH

       Unknown Sailor Cabernet Merlot 2019, Kangaroo Island The colour is excellent, crimson through to the rim. The mouthfeel of this medium-bodied blend is compelling, fruit, tannins and oak coalesce, blackcurrant at its centre.   Screw cap. | 14% alc. | Drink 2023–2030 | $27 | JH

Springs Road Wines ★★★★

761 Playford Highway, Cygnet River, Kangaroo Island, SA 5233 **T** 0499 918 448 **www**.springsroad. com.au **OPEN** 7 days 12–5 Oct–Apr, Wed–Mon 12–4 May–Sept **WINEMAKER** Joch Bosworth **VITICULTURIST** Joch Bosworth **EST**. 1994 **DOZENS** 4000 **VYDS** 11ha

The Springs Road vineyards were established in 1994 on a small sheep property and are now owned and operated by Joch Bosworth and Louise Hemsley-Smith from Battle of Bosworth in McLaren Vale. The vineyards have been managed organically since Louise and Joch took over in 2016, and are awaiting certification. The wine label is adapted from Louis de Freycinet's 1808 map of Southern Australia, 'Terre Napoléon'. (JH)

94   **Little Island Red 2021, Kangaroo Island** A powerful, yet inherently full-bodied wine, with blackberry to the fore. Needs time, but has balance and will repay extended cellaring. Screw cap. | 14.5% alc. | Drink 2025-2040 | $25 | JH

The Islander Estate Vineyards ★★★★★

78 Gum Creek Road, Cygnet River, SA 5223 **T** (08) 8553 9008 **WWW**.iev.com.au **OPEN** Thurs-Tues 12-5 **WINEMAKER** Jacques Lurton, Yale Norris **VITICULTURIST** Jacques Lurton, Yale Norris **EST**. 2000 **DOZENS** 8000 **VYDS** 10ha

Jacques Lurton established a close-planted vineyard. The wines are made and bottled at the onsite winery. The property was ravaged by the terrible Jan '20 bushfire which consumed the entire vineyard, its infrastructure, the house, the laboratory and the office, which became the sacrificial lamb slowing the fire sufficiently to allow the protection of the winery and its stock of bottled wine. Business partner Yale Norris cut back every vine down to 20cm hoping that shoots would appear. If the regeneration ceases, the entire vineyard will be pulled out and replanted. (JH)

96   **Boundary Track Shiraz 2018, Kangaroo Island** Still holding a crimson edge to the hue, it is a beautifully made wine with silky tannins and fruit freshness, the oak playing a nigh on unseen hand. One glass insists on another. Screw cap. | 13.5% alc. | Drink 2028-2048 | $75 | JH

94   **The Red Shiraz 2021, Kangaroo Island** The crimson magenta hue is striking. Positively juicy, with black cherry and plum fruit; tannin extract minimal. Altogether unusual wine, and it would be interesting to buy 6 or so bottles and track its development over the next 5 years or more. Screw cap. | 14% alc. | Drink 2023-2048 | $25 | JH

Pinot Gris 2021, South Australia While the back label shows South Australia, the winery says Adelaide Hills is the region, and the wine in the mouth is emphatically cool grown. Its exceptional power and texture is derived from wild ferment of the pressings in used French oak, the balance cool-fermented in stainless steel. Screw cap. | 12.5% alc. | Drink 2022-2027 | $30 | JH

Sauvignon Blanc 2021, Kangaroo Island Pale quartz green. Classic sauvignon blanc flavours, ranging from snow pea to wild herbs to gooseberry. No compromises needed – nor used. Revels in the exceptional vintage, flawless mouthfeel and balance. Screw cap. | 13% alc. | Drink 2022-2023 | $30 | JH

REGION

Langhorne Creek

Angas & Bremer ★★★★

8 The Parade West, Kent Town, SA 5067 **T** (08) 8537 0600 **WWW**.angasandbremer.com.au **WINEMAKER** Peter Pollard **EST**. 2017 **DOZENS** 7500

Langhorne Creek's climate is profoundly driven by the Southern Ocean and its average altitude of 20m, lower than that of any other region on the mainland. You might expect ample rainfall, but its growing season total of just 161mm makes irrigation essential. The net outcome is a climate that proffers generous yields with a lower-than-average need for sprays, reducing soil compaction by tractors and the overall cost per tonne of grapes. Thus most growers have organic accreditation, Angas & Bremer included. (JH)

91   **Touriga Nacional 2020, Langhorne Creek** By some distance the best of these releases, the bright crimson-purple colour setting the pace. It's only just into medium-bodied territory, the flavours of red and blue fruits cosseted by gentle spicy, earthy tannins. Ready now, but will hold for a few years. Value plus. Screw cap. | 14% alc. | Drink 2021-2025 | $20 | JH

90   **The Creek 2019, Langhorne Creek** A 44/28/21/5/2% blend of grenache, touriga, malbec, graciano and shiraz; a master blend, though it's the first 3 parts that run the show. The wine will please almost all who know the price, and others who don't even know that. It's got some jujube/glacé cherry fruit flavours, and isn't necessarily dry, but it will stand up for all those home-delivered pizzas and such like. Screw cap. | 14.5% alc. | Drink 2022-2023 | $20 | JH

Angas Plains Estate ★★★★

317 Angas Plains Road, Langhorne Creek, SA 5255 **T** (08) 8537 3159 **www**.angasplainswines.com.au
OPEN Mon–Fri 11–5, Sat 12–4 **WINEMAKER** Peter Douglas, Phillip Cross **VITICULTURIST** Phillip Cross
EST. 1994 **DOZENS** 3000 **VYDS** 15.2ha

In '94 Phillip and Judy Cross began the Angas Plains Estate plantings. The location on ancient Angas River flood plains, together with cooling evening breezes from the local Lake Alexandrina, proved ideally suited to the red varieties. Skilled contract winemaking has resulted in some excellent wines from the estate-grown shiraz and cabernet sauvignon. (JH)

94   **PJs Cabernet Sauvignon 2019, Langhorne Creek** Bright crimson-purple hue. Here the oak is more obvious than that of its shiraz sibling, but the depth of the blackcurrant and black-olive fruit handles the competition with panache. Value plus.   Screw cap. | 14.5% alc. | Drink 2022-2027 | $25 | JH

Ben Potts Wines ★★★★★

The Winehouse, 1509 Langhorne Creek Road, Langhorne Creek, SA 5255 **T** (08) 8537 3029
www.benpottswines.com.au **OPEN** 7 days 10–5 **WINEMAKER** Ben Potts **EST.** 2002

Ben Potts is the 6th generation to be involved in grapegrowing and winemaking in Langhorne Creek, the first being Frank Potts, founder of Bleasdale Vineyards. Ben completed the oenology degree at CSU, and ventured into winemaking on a commercial scale in 2002 (aged 25). (JH)

96   **Fiddle's Block Shiraz 2019, Langhorne Creek** Delicious shiraz showing the sense of place to perfection; small red and black berry fruits on a medium-bodied framework of spicy, savoury fruit and oak tannins; lip-smacking finish and aftertaste. Trophy Best Shiraz at Langhorne Creek Wine Show '21.   Screw cap. | 14.8% alc. | Drink 2022-2042 | $40 | JH

Bleasdale Vineyards ★★★★★

1640 Langhorne Creek Road, Langhorne Creek, SA 5255 **T** (08) 8537 4000 **www**.bleasdale.com.au
OPEN 7 days 10–5 **WINEMAKER** Paul Hotker, Matt Laube **VITICULTURIST** Sarah Keough **EST.** 1850 **VYDS** 45ha

One of the most historic wineries in Australia; in '20 it celebrated 170 years of continuous winemaking by the direct descendants of the founding Potts family. Not so long before the start of the 21st century, its vineyards were flooded every winter by diversion of the Bremer River, which provided moisture throughout the dry, cool, growing season. In the new millennium, every drop of water is counted. (JH)

98   **The Iron Duke Cabernet Sauvignon 2020, Langhorne Creek** Halliday Wine Companion Cabernet Sauvignon of the Year 2023. A best-of-the-best barrel selection. The bright colour is as it should be, the bouquet rimmed with the violets that are often talked about (not by me, until, that is, you come across a wine such as this). Notes of cedar and cassis are not far behind in their appeal. Then the glory of this magnificent wine's palate takes total control of all the senses, the sheer intensity of the fruit making the finely tempered tannins and French oak applaud from the wings of the stage. Screw cap. | 14% alc. | Drink 2025-2050 | $79 | JH | ♥

96   **Generations Malbec 2020, Langhorne Creek** Typical intense malbec colour. Winemaker Paul Hotker has this wine on a string, dancing to his every command. This has the gravitas of a great red wine that just happens to be made from malbec; its mouth-watering intensity of forest blackberries, cloves and black olive drawn out on the finish by ripe tannins. Trophy and top gold Royal Adelaide Wine Show '21, gold Perth Royal Wine Awards '21. Screw cap. | 14% alc. | Drink 2022-2035 | $35 | JH | ♥

95   **Chardonnay 2021, Adelaide Hills** Wild ferment and mlf in French puncheons (25% new), matured for 9 months. White peach and grapefruit flavours jostle for primacy, neither achieving it. Nor does the mlf or oak – this is a wine of and for all. Screw cap. | 12.5% alc. | Drink 2022-2032 | $30 | JH

    Second Innings Malbec 2020, Langhorne Creek Bright colour. A highly aromatic bouquet with the particular spice – half pepper, half clove – of Bleasdale Vineyards. The palate is a broad church of plum, blackberry and red cherry – and a hint of clove on the finish. Outstanding value. Screw cap. | 14% alc. | Drink 2022-2032 | $22 | JH

    Wellington Road Shiraz Cabernet 2020, Langhorne Creek A 50/50% blend, the cabernet crushed, the shiraz destemmed; open fermented and 8–12 days on skins. Pressed to French puncheons (25% new) for 12 months' maturation. Clever winemaking has optimised the high-quality grapes in a full-bodied framework that will underwrite long-term cellaring. Screw cap. | 14% alc. | Drink 2025-2035 | $32 | JH

    Frank Potts 2020, Langhorne Creek A 76/15/7/2% blend of cabernet sauvignon, malbec, petit verdot and merlot. Bright, near vivid, crimson; an elegant cabernet-driven wine, with notes of cedar, cigar box and cassis on the bouquet and palate alike. It's medium bodied and lithe, an English gentleman's claret. Screw cap. | 14% alc. | Drink 2023-2030 | $35 | JH

Generations Shiraz 2020, Langhorne Creek Opens with a bright crimson-red hue. It has the inherent pliable mouthfeel of Langhorne Creek that offers the widest window of opportunity to drink half and cellar half. It has varietal plum, blackberry, licorice and spice flavours held within a silken web of fine tannins. Drink any place at any time. Screw cap. | 14% alc. | Drink 2025-2035 | $35 | JH

94   **Pinot Gris 2021, Adelaide Hills** This will come as a surprise for those expecting another ho-hum white wine. There is both flavour and texture complexity, largely nashi pear and citrus, plus tropical and spice slants. Screw cap. | 12.5% alc. | Drink 2021-2025 | $22 | JH

Riesling 2021, Adelaide Hills Cool fermented with some solids to build texture. Neatly balances 8.4g/L TA and 5.5g/L RS. The perfumed apple- and citrus-blossom bouquet introduces a dangerously enjoyable wine, with freshness its calling card. Screw cap. | 11% alc. | Drink 2022-2031 | $30 | JH

Bremerton Wines ★★★★★

15 Kent Town Road, Langhorne Creek, SA 5255 **T** (08) 8537 3093 **www**.bremerton.com.au **OPEN** 7 days 10-5 **WINEMAKER** Rebecca Willson **EST.** 1988 **DOZENS** 30000 **VYDS** 120ha

Bremerton has been producing wines since 1988. Rebecca Willson (chief winemaker) and Lucy Willson (marketing manager) were the first sisters in Australia to manage and run a winery. They have 120ha of premium vineyards (80% of which goes into their own labels). (JH)

97   **B.O.V. 2018, Langhorne Creek** A 'best of vintage' barrel blend of 76/24% shiraz/cabernet sauvignon. Vivid crimson-purple colour. This transcends the normal face of Langhorne Creek thanks to the pure intensity of a remarkable wine that has the ability to cruise through 30+ years. Blackberry and blackcurrant wrap around each other on a juicy, supple palate. Diam. | 14.5% alc. | Drink 2025-2055 | $85 | JH

96   **Old Adam Shiraz 2019, Langhorne Creek** One of Bremerton's 3 red wine flagbearers, its style is as consistent as possible, courtesy of 20 months' maturation in French and American oak, and long-standing estate blocks in a region that imparts its special softness. It delivers a superbly balanced wine, with luscious dark berry fruits at its core, marrying this with quality oak that partners just-so tannins. A wine that will add yet more to its elegance over the decades to come. Diam. | 14.5% alc. | Drink 2024-2044 | $56 | JH

95   **Special Release Fiano 2021, Langhorne Creek** This has a striking bouquet, ranging from honeysuckle through to the fresh-squeezed lemon that carries it into the multidimensional, mouth-watering crystalline acidity. This is such a great variety, requiring nothing from the winemaker other than making the right decision on the harvest date. Screw cap. | 12% alc. | Drink 2022-2027 | $24 | JH

94   **Special Release Grenache 2021, Langhorne Creek** Bright clear colour. Adventurous vinification also used by some highly regarded pinot noir makers. One-third whole-bunch carbonic maceration within some ferments, then crushed and destemmed for completion of fermentation and 8 months in stainless steel and aged barriques. A mix of wild strawberry, and a film of spicy, earthy tannins on the mouth-watering finish. Screw cap. | 14.5% alc. | Drink 2022-2025 | $24 | JH

Gipsie Jack Wine Co ★★★★☆

The Winehouse, 1509 Langhorne Creek Road, Langhorne Creek, SA 5255 **T** (08) 8537 3029 **www**.gipsiejack.com.au **OPEN** 7 days 10-5 **WINEMAKER** John Glaetzer, Ben Potts **EST.** 2004

The partners of Gipsie Jack are John Glaetzer and Ben Potts, named after John Glaetzer's Jack Russell dog Gipsie. Glaetzer and Potts say, 'We want to make this label fun, like in the 'old days'. No pretentiousness, no arrogance, not even a back label. A great wine at a great price, with no discounting.' (JH)

95   **Dolcetto 2019, Langhorne Creek** Light ruby-red hue; the aromas, flavours and light- to medium-bodied palate are all encapsulated by the colour. It's red-fruit dominant, the mouthfeel beguiling, with silky tannins and a fresh finish. Truly delicious, great value. Trophy and gold medal Best Alternative Variety (White or Red) Langhorne Creek Wine Show '21. Screw cap. | 14.5% alc. | Drink 2022-2029 | $22 | JH

94   **Malbec 2019, Langhorne Creek** Good crimson-purple colour, the bouquet and palate reaffirming the unique symbiotic bond between Langhorne Creek and malbec, with exotic spiced plum and earth flavours, and a moderately firm, mouth-watering finish. Screw cap. | 14.8% alc. | Drink 2022-2032 | $22 | JH

Killibinbin ★★★☆

PO Box 10, Langhorne Creek, SA 5255 **T** (08) 85373382 **www**.killibinbin.com.au **WINEMAKER** Jim Urlwin **VITICULTURIST** Guy Adams **EST.** 1997 **DOZENS** 12000 **VYDS** 20ha

In late 2010 Guy and Liz Adams (of Metala Vineyards fame) acquired the Killibinbin brand. Production has grown significantly since that time, but the wines continue to be sourced solely from the Metala Vineyards (20ha are dedicated to Killibinbin). (JH)

BAROSSA

FLEURIEU

MOUNT LOFTY RANGES

FAR NORTH

LIMESTONE COAST

LOWER MURRAY

THE PENINSULAS

93   **Secrets 2019, Langhorne Creek** A 62/32/6% estate blend of cabernet sauvignon/shiraz/petit verdot. It's supple and smooth, the blackberry and blackcurrant fruit fresh, in best Langhorne Creek style and weight. Extraordinary value.   Screw cap. | 14.5% alc. | Drink 2022-2032 | $15 | JH

Kimbolton Wines ★★★★★

29 Burleigh Street, Langhorne Creek, SA 5255 **T** (08) 8537 3002 **www**.kimboltonwines.com.au
OPEN 7 days 11-4 **WINEMAKER** Contract **EST.** 1998 **DOZENS** 2500 **VYDS** 55ha

The Kimbolton property originally formed part of the Potts Bleasdale estate. In 1946 it was acquired by Henry and Thelma Case, grandparents of current owners brother and sister Nicole Clark and Brad Case. The grapes from the vineyard plantings are sold to leading wineries, with small amounts retained for the Kimbolton label. The name comes from a medieval town in Bedfordshire, UK, from which some of the family's ancestors emigrated. (JH)

94   **Cabernet Sauvignon 2019, Langhorne Creek** The youthful colour is a good start. Punches well above its price weight. The fragrant bouquet offers a seamless fusion of fruit and oak, the palate following with alacrity. Blackcurrant/cassis, gently cedary oak, and perfectly balanced and integrated tannins make this a high-quality, all-purpose wine.   Screw cap. | 14% alc. | Drink 2022-2032 | $25 | JH

Lake Breeze Wines ★★★★★

Step Road, Langhorne Creek, SA 5255 **T** (08) 8537 3017 **www**.lakebreeze.com.au **OPEN** 7 days 10-5
WINEMAKER Greg Follett **EST.** 1987 **DOZENS** 20000 **VYDS** 90ha

The Folletts have been farmers at Langhorne Creek since 1880, and grapegrowers since the 1930s. Part of the grape production is sold, but the quality of the Lake Breeze wines is exemplary, with the red wines particularly appealing. Best Value Winery in the 2022 Companion. (JH)

98   **The Drake Cabernet Sauvignon Shiraz 2016, Langhorne Creek** When the wine first enters the mouth you begin to question whether there can be too much of a good thing, until the wine soars on the finish with a satin and velvet stream of incredible purity and length. To be released Sep '22.   Screw cap. | 14.6% alc. | Drink 2026-2046 | $80 | JH | ♥

97   **Section 54 Shiraz 2020, Langhorne Creek** This is a wonderfully elegant wine with a profusion of red and black berry fruits sustained by its silky mouthfeel, fine tannins a constant thrumming on the finish and aftertaste.   Screw cap. | 14.5% alc. | Drink 2023-2040 | $26 | JH

   Arthur's Reserve Cabernet Sauvignon Malbec 2019, Langhorne Creek This is an utterly beautiful wine, intensely focused yet silky and elegant. Trophies in '21 may continue to be awarded until May '22 when the wine is released.   Screw cap. | 14% alc. | Drink 2022-2041 | $48 | JH | ♥

96   **Old Vine Grenache 2021, Langhorne Creek** The brilliantly clear crimson-purple hue announces a beautiful wine, bursting with juicy red fruits backed up by fine-spun tannins giving a savoury farewell.   Screw cap. | 14.5% alc. | Drink 2022-2035 | $28 | JH

95   **Cabernet Sauvignon 2020, Langhorne Creek** The crust of tannins and oak that surrounds the polished blackcurrant fruit will soften until its release and continue thereafter for many years.   Screw cap. | 14% alc. | Drink 2023-2040 | $28 | JH

   Malbec 2020, Langhorne Creek Deep, vibrant purple crimson. Layer upon layer of fruit, satsuma plum, tendrils of licorice and a sprinkle of dark chocolate fruit. Langhorne Creek and malbec walk together.   Screw cap. | 14.5% alc. | Drink 2022-2040 | $30 | JH

Watkins ★★★★

59 Grants Gully Road, Chandlers Hill, SA, 5159 **T** 0422 418 845 **www**.watkins.wine **OPEN** Fri-Sat
11-6, Sun 11-5 **WINEMAKER** Sam Watkins **EST.** 2019 **DOZENS** 6500 **VYDS** 150ha

Sibling trio Ben, Sam and Jo Watkins, under the guidance of parents David and Ros Watkins, have established Watkins as a new label based at their Chandlers Hill winery and cellar door. They are tapping into their well-established estate vineyards there and in Langhorne Creek: both regions' vines are maritime influenced, with afternoon sea breezes tempering summer ripening temperatures. Winemaker Sam Watkins has worked in Napa Valley, USA, and Porto, Portugal, as well as Orange, NSW, Coonawarra, Barossa and McLaren Vale, SA. Brother Ben is commercial director, and sister Jo is brand director and cellar door manager. (TL)

90   **Limited Bright Red Grenache Sangiovese 2021, Langhorne Creek** An interesting cross between a rosé and a light dry red. It's not sweet, yet is all about red berry and pomegranate seeds that have a biting freshness. The colour alone will drive sales at high speed.   Screw cap. | 13.5% alc. | Drink 2022-2022 | $20 | JH

Shiraz 2020, Langhorne Creek There's plenty to chew on in this supple, rich, warmly-accented wine which will repay cellaring as it slims down with age in bottle. Screw cap. | 14% alc. | Drink 2024-2034 | $20 | JH

McLaren Vale

Angove Family Winemakers ★★★★★

Bookmark Avenue, Renmark, SA 5341 **T** (08) 8580 3100 **www**.angove.com.au **OPEN** Mon-Fri 10-5, Sat 10-4, Sun & public hols 10-3 **WINEMAKER** Tony Ingle, Paul Kernich, Ben Horley, Amelia Anspach **VITICULTURIST** Nick Bakkum **EST.** 1886 **DOZENS** 500 **VYDS** 300ha

Founded in 1886, Angove Family Winemakers is one of Australia's most successful wine businesses – a fifth-generation family company with a tradition of excellence and an eye for the future. In early '19 Angove acquired the celebrated 12.7ha Angel Gully Vineyard in Clarendon from Primo Estate, and renamed the vineyard Angels Rise. Angove is committed to remaining privately owned and believes remaining in family hands enables the company to be master of its own destiny. (JH)

98 **Warboys Vineyard Grenache 2019, McLaren Vale** The perfumed, flowery bouquet of red berries and spices heralds a vibrant, glistening palate, the texture and structure are tannin-free zones (yet neither fined nor filtered). Screw cap. | 14.5% alc. | Drink 2022-2029 | $75 | JH

95 **Family Crest Shiraz 2019, McLaren Vale** You'd never guess Angove is a recent arrival in McLaren Vale. This is a near-perfect illustration of varietal character with eiderdown tannins underlying a Magimix blend of dark chocolate and blood plum fruit. Generosity is its calling card, and it won't die any time soon. A multipurpose player with food. Screw cap. | 14.5% alc. | Drink 2023-2039 | $25 | JH

Aphelion Wine ★★★★★

18 St Andrews Terrace, Willunga, SA 5172 **T** 0404 390 840 **www**.aphelionwine.com.au **OPEN** By appt **WINEMAKER** Rob Mack **EST.** 2014 **DOZENS** 2500

When you consider the credentials of winemaker Rob Mack and co-founder Louise Rhodes Mack, great oaks come to mind. Rob has accumulated 2 degrees in accounting and management in '07, and wine science from CSU in '16. He scaled the heights of direct marketing as wine buyer and planner for Laithwaites Wine People, and spent the next 18 months as production manager for Direct Wines in McLaren Vale. He has worked with 5 wineries, 4 in McLaren Vale. Rob was voted Young Gun of Wine '18 and Aphelion won Best Small Producer at the McLaren Vale Wine Show in '19. (JH)

96 **Brini Single Vineyard Grenache 2021, McLaren Vale** An exploration of Blewitt Springs, likely the finest subregion for the finest grape in the country – grenache. A single site in the northeast corner on sandy loams. Very pinot-like. Sandalwood, bergamot, camphor, sapid sour cherry, lapsang and Asian spiced-plum notes drive across a patina of herb-flecked tannins, all skeletal and fibrous. This is very fine. The plumpest of these single-site expressions, yet the most complete. Screw cap. | 14.5% alc. | Drink 2022-2028 | $70 | NG

Aramis Vineyards ★★★★

411 Henley Beach Road, Brooklyn Park, SA 5032 **T** (08) 8352 2900 **www**.aramisvineyards.com **WINEMAKER** Renae Hirsch (red), Peter Leske (white) **VITICULTURIST** Daniel Lavrencic **EST.** 1998 **DOZENS** 12 000 **VYDS** 26ha

Aramis Vineyards was founded in '98 by Lee Flourentzou. Located barely 2km from the Gulf of St Vincent, it is one of the coolest sites in McLaren Vale, planted to shiraz (18ha) and cabernet sauvignon (8ha), the 2 varieties best suited to the site. This philosophy leads Aramis to source grapes from other regions that best represent each variety, including sauvignon blanc and chardonnay from Adelaide Hills and riesling from Eden Valley. (JH)

92 **White Label Sauvignon Blanc 2021, Adelaide Hills** Boasting the kind of exuberant Hills' sauvignon grapefruit, citrus, green apple intensity we have come to love. It bounces with energy in the glass! Tight in zippy acidity, there is a flourish of snow pea and spice which gets the mouth-watering and, suddenly, you're thinking of Asian dishes for dinner. Screw cap. | 11.5% alc. | Drink 2021-2025 | $22 | JP

BAROSSA

FLEURIEU

MOUNT LOFTY RANGES

FAR NORTH

LIMESTONE COAST

LOWER MURRAY

THE PENINSULAS

Battle of Bosworth ★★★★

92 Gaffney Road, Willunga, SA 5172 **T** (08) 8556 2441 **www**.battleofbosworth.com.au **OPEN** 7 days 11–5 **WINEMAKER** Joch Bosworth **EST.** 1996 **DOZENS** 15000 **VYDS** 80ha

Owned and run by Joch Bosworth (viticulture and winemaking) and partner Louise Hemsley-Smith (sales and marketing), this winery takes its name from the battle that ended the War of the Roses, fought on Bosworth Field in 1485. The vineyards were established in the early '70s in the foothills of the Mount Lofty Ranges. The vines are fully certified A-grade organic. The Spring Seed Wine Co wines are made from estate vineyards. (JH)

93   **Puritan Shiraz 2021, McLaren Vale** While these sort of pulpy, whole-berry, gently extracted wines are now ubiquitous here, this address was one of the first to craft them well. Violet. Iodine parlayed as dried nori. Blueberry. Pepper and clove and star anise. The finish long, while crackling across the palate with a contagious energy. Juicy and beautifully articulated. This vintage, this stellar effort, is the prototype for zero-preservative shiraz. Screw cap. | 14.5% alc. | Drink 2021-2023 | $22 | NG

92   **Chardonnay 2021, McLaren Vale** Good drinking. Plays a flinty mineral chord, offsetting the Vale's inclination towards riper fruit, from canned peach to dried mango. The oak, nestled nicely. Mid weighted and juicy across the mid palate. The finish boasts tension and flare, as much as an ease of approachability. A foil for those who seek ample flavour, as much a vehicle for those pinning for freshness and linearity. Well done. Screw cap. | 13% alc. | Drink 2021-2026 | $25 | NG

Bekkers ⊙ ★★★★★

212–220 Seaview Road, McLaren Vale, SA 5171 **T** 0408 807 568 **www**.bekkerswine.com **OPEN** Thurs-Sat 10–4 or by appt **WINEMAKER** Emmanuelle Bekkers **VITICULTURIST** Toby Bekkers **EST.** 2010 **DOZENS** 1500 **VYDS** 18ha

Bekkers brings together 2 high-performing, highly experienced and highly credentialled business and life partners. Toby Bekkers graduated with an honours degree in applied science in agriculture from the University of Adelaide, and over the ensuing years has had broad-ranging responsibilities as general manager of Paxton Wines in McLaren Vale, and as a leading exponent of organic and biodynamic viticulture. Emmanuelle was born in Bandol in the south of France, and obtained 2 university degrees, in biochemistry and oenology, before working for the Hardys in the south of France, which led her to Australia and a wide-ranging career, including Chalk Hill. (JH)

97   **Grenache 2020, McLaren Vale** If anybody believes that other varieties in this country can match the world-class persuasions of McLaren Vale grenache they are sorely mistaken. Here, thorough evidence. A rich wine, harnessing the riper tendencies of the vintage while promoting fragrance, a diaphanous levity to the tannic latticework and that uncanny pinosity that makes grenache like this so compelling. Svelte, dense and yet so fresh. Molten raspberry, crushed black rock, Berger spice and orange peel. A faint whiff of mescal and clove derived from the whole-bunch inclusion (20%) imbues additional savouriness. This is very fine. Screw cap. | 14.5% alc. | Drink 2022-2030 | $90 | NG

Bondar Wines ⊙ ★★★★★

148 McMurtrie Road, McLaren Vale, SA 5171 **T** 0460 898 158 **www**.bondarwines.com.au **OPEN** Fri-Sun 11–5 **WINEMAKER** Andre Bondar **VITICULTURIST** Ben Lacey **EST.** 2013 **DOZENS** 3000 **VYDS** 13.5ha

Husband and wife Andre Bondar and Selina Kelly began a deliberately unhurried journey in 2009, which culminated in the purchase of the celebrated Rayner Vineyard post-vintage '13. Andre had been a winemaker at Nepenthe wines for 7 years, and Selina had recently completed a law degree. They changed focus and began to look for a vineyard capable of producing great shiraz. The Rayner Vineyard had all the answers: a ridge bisecting the land, Blewitt Springs sand on the eastern side; and the Seaview, heavier clay loam soils over limestone on the western side. (JH)

97   **Violet Hour Shiraz 2020, McLaren Vale** A beautiful wine in every dimension – its crimson colour, haunting perfumed bouquet, caressing the mouth with its perfectly ripened fruit, superfine tannins, and subtle but relevant oak. One of the great bargains. Screw cap. | 14% alc. | Drink 2022-2035 | $30 | JH

    Midnight Hour Shiraz 2020, McLaren Vale 100% whole-bunch fermentation has produced an exotic array of foresty flowers, intense but finely balanced juicy, small berry fruits and sheer, silky tannins somewhere in the mix, oak ditto. Has the stamp of authority of a great wine. 60 dozen made. Screw cap. | 14% alc. | Drink 2026-2041 | $40 | JH

96   **Grenache Rosé 2021, McLaren Vale** Pale salmon pink; full-on perfume of rose petals and bath powder, but it's the intensity of the brilliantly juicy palate that makes this so special. Screw cap. | 13% alc. | Drink 2021-2025 | $27 | JH

  Rayner Vineyard Grenache 2021, McLaren Vale From the cool, attenuated '21 vintage, this is a showcase of persimmon, Seville orange and the pithiest pucker from a sour cherry I am yet to experience. Raspberry bon-bon shifts to the domineering flavour with air. The tannins, white pepper-clad and moreish. Sandy, saline and gritty. Very fine. A protean expression, shifting endlessly with air to a succulent vibrato. Entrenched in the pantheon of the Vale. Screw cap. | 13.8% alc. | Drink 2021-2027 | $40 | NG

  Junto GSM 2020, McLaren Vale 68/10/9/7/5/1% grenache/shiraz/mataro/carignan/cinsaut/counoise. Bright, clear crimson; a perfumed, red-fruited, spiced bouquet lights the way, the palate making off with this opening by adding high-quality tannins. Whether or not a shotgun marriage, it comes together in glistening unison. Drink 2021-2031 | $28 | JH

95   **Chardonnay 2020, Adelaide Hills** Early pickup of green-gold colour; no surprise that it should be fragrant, layered and complex, with roasted almond through to white-fleshed stone fruit and grapefruit. Screw cap. | 13% alc. | Drink 2022-2030 | $35 | JH

Brash Higgins ★★★★★

California Road, McLaren Vale, SA 5171 **T** (08) 8556 4237 **www**.brashhiggins.com **OPEN** By appt
WINEMAKER Brad Hickey **EST.** 2010 **DOZENS** 1000 **VYDS** 7ha

American Brad Hickey arrived in Australia to work vintage '07 in McLaren Vale, where he met his now partner Nicole Thorpe. Together they established Brash Higgins in 2010. Brad has a varied background, including 10 years as head sommelier at some of the best New York restaurants, then a further 10 years of baking, brewing and travelling to the best-known wine regions of the world. Both the estate vineyard and the winery are certified organic. (JH)

97   **R/SM Field Blend Riesling Semillon 2020, McLaren Vale** It took me a while to get my head around these bedfellows, planted – serendipitously as it turns out – alongside each other. I can only conclude that this wine is venerable. Stunning, even. Perhaps I was falling into the dull trap of seeking varietal personality when, in fact, this is all about place and a courageous textural interplay, from grainy truffled lees traits, to candied quince, rooibos and lemon-peel skinsy chutney, a staining degree of briny salinity and Blewitt Springs sandiness. The breadth of well-positioned oak, too. This drinks and feels like a top expression from the Loire, with an ersatz manzanilla-meets-maritime veil. Formidably long, moreish and extremely impressive. Wow! Screw cap. | 13.5% alc. | Drink 2022-2026 | $39 | NG | ♥

96   **NDV Amphora Project Nero d'Avola 2020, McLaren Vale** Dark, spiced cherry scents meld with bitters, bergamot, anise, clove, sassafras and cardamom. The tannins, a gristly bristle, corral the teeming fruit and confer a welcome savouriness. This is a serious nero d'Avola of impact, immaculate detail and a textural precision that unravels with each sip. Far from the pulpy, vapid expressions that too often define the domestic norm. Excellent wine here. The mandala of moreish tannins, its opus. Screw cap. | 14.5% alc. | Drink 2022-2030 | $45 | NG | ♥

Chalk Hill ★★★★★

56 Field Street, McLaren Vale **T** (08) 8323 6400 **www**.chalkhillwines.com.au **OPEN** 7 days 11-6
WINEMAKER Renae Hirsch **VITICULTURIST** Jock Harvey **EST.** 1973 **DOZENS** 20000 **VYDS** 89ha

The growth of Chalk Hill has accelerated after passing from parents John and Diana Harvey to grapegrowing sons Jock and Tom. Both are heavily involved in wine industry affairs. Further acquisitions have seen the vineyards now span each district of McLaren Vale. The Alpha Crucis series is especially praiseworthy. (JH)

98   **Alpha Crucis Old Vine Grenache 2020, McLaren Vale** Halliday Wine Companion Grenache of the Year 2023. The bouquet is expressive and enticing, as is the gorgeous, juicy and mouth-watering medium-bodied palate. Moving the wine back and forth in the mouth unlocks rivulets of earthy spices, running through the pomegranate and red forest fruits. Precision and purity. Screw cap. | 14% alc. | Drink 2022-2030 | $55 | JH | ♥

96   **Alpha Crucis Clarendon Syrah 2020, McLaren Vale** The best of the 3 subregional expressions. An effortless flow from the attack to the finish, as echoes of the northern Rhône mesh with a warmer Australian idiom: red and blue fruits, bergamot, nori, sassafras, clove, turmeric, sandalwood and souk spice. This is really exceptional as far as syrah/shiraz goes in these parts. Mid-weighted feel. So easy to drink. A long, intricate glide. Gorgeous grape tannins. The oak, a mere addendum. Exceptional drinking. Screw cap. | 14% alc. | Drink 2021-2030 | $55 | NG | ♥

Chapel Hill ★★★★★

1 Chapel Hill Road, McLaren Vale, SA 5171 **T** (08) 8323 8429 **www**.chapelhillwine.com.au
OPEN 7 days 11–5 **WINEMAKER** Michael Fragos, Bryn Richards **VITICULTURIST** Rachel Steer **EST**. 1971
DOZENS 70000 **VYDS** 44ha

A leading medium-sized winery in McLaren Vale. In late 2019 the business was purchased from the Swiss Thomas Schmidheiny group – which owns the respected Cuvaison winery in California and vineyards in Switzerland and Argentina – by Endeavour Drinks (part of the Woolworths group). Wine quality is unfailingly excellent. The red wines are not filtered or fined, and there are no tannin or enzyme additions, just SO_2 – natural red wines. (JH)

96 **1948 Vines Grenache 2020, McLaren Vale** This is an incredibly exciting wine. Known for reliable wines, this address has suddenly come to play ball with the artisans! There is nothing heavy or clumsy about this, as with so much grenache from bigger companies. Just old-vine sap cleaved by finely tuned extraction, sound choice of oak and some bunches in the mix. A sandy, gently gritty tannic frame contains kirsch, Asian plum, sandalwood and bergamot notes. The effect is svelte, fresh and lively. Pinosity a-go-go. The weight and intensity, effortless of feel. Thoroughly impressive, boding so well for the future of this great variety. Screw cap. | 14.5% alc. | Drink 2021-2028 | $65 | NG

Gorge Block Cabernet Sauvignon 2016, McLaren Vale One of 3 bottle-aged releases from this venerated site to commemorate 50 years of existence. The finest, I suppose, as much as I cherish the '12. Finer because of its detail, the refined weave of its tannins, unwinding across notes of cassis, bouquet garni, green olive, sage and licorice. Finer, because of the suave intensity, the build across the palate, the thrust of fruit and parry of structure. Finer, because I keep going back. Screw cap. | 14.5% alc. | Drink 2022-2038 | $75 | NG

Cooter & Cooter ★★★★

82 Almond Grove Road, Whites Valley, SA 5172 **T** 0438 766 178 **www**.cooter.com.au **WINEMAKER** James Cooter, Kimberly Cooter **EST**. 2012 **DOZENS** 800 **VYDS** 23ha

The cursive script on the Cooter & Cooter wine labels was that of various Cooter family businesses operating in SA since 1847. James comes from a family with more than 20 years in the wine industry. Kimberley is also a hands-on winemaker; her father is Walter Clappis, a veteran McLaren Vale winemaker. (JH)

91 **Watervale Riesling 2021, Clare Valley** An exceptional, cool and attenuated vintage in the Clare. Dry grown, hand picked, fermented cool with plenty of solids to impart a bit more breadth and generosity than the steely archetype. Lime blossom, tangerine and lemon zest are catapulted across a dry and austere mid-weighted palate by a battery of talcy acidity. Screw cap. | 12% alc. | Drink 2021-2029 | $23 | NG

Coriole ★★★★★

Chaffeys Road, McLaren Vale, SA 5171 **T** (08) 8323 8305 **www**.coriole.com **OPEN** 7 days 11–5 **WINEMAKER** Duncan Lloyd **EST**. 1967 **DOZENS** 30000 **VYDS** 48.5ha

While Coriole was established in 1967, the cellar door and gardens date back to 1860, when the original farm houses that now constitute the cellar door were built. The oldest shiraz forming part of the estate plantings was planted in 1917, and since '85, Coriole has been an Australian pioneer of sangiovese and the Italian white variety fiano. Coriole celebrated its 50th anniversary in '19, presumably counting from the year of its first commercial wine release. (JH)

94 **Fiano 2021, McLaren Vale** Long a pioneer of this outstanding variety, recent critical acclaim and gradual acceptance by the punter is iterated as greater confidence in the vineyard and winery. More concentration, detail and a certain fealty to the better example of Campania, fiano's spiritual home, the result. Glazed quince, bitter almond, pistachio, apricot and wild fennel. A sluice of welcome phenolics defies the long finish as much as the saline acidity. Very good. Great vintage, to boot. Screw cap. | 13% alc. | Drink 2021-2025 | $28 | NG

Sangiovese 2020, McLaren Vale Has all the attributes expected of sangiovese, most obviously the play between all the cherries of the rainbow; from fresh, to sour, to poached, backed by superfine tannins. It's a wine I would drink now or over time. Screw cap. | 14.1% alc. | Drink 2021-2029 | $28 | JH

Dune Wine ★★★★★

PO Box 9, McLaren Vale, SA 5171 **T** 0403 584 845 **www**.dunewine.com **WINEMAKER** Duncan and Peter Lloyd **EST.** 2017 **DOZENS** 1700 **VYDS** 8ha

This is the project of Duncan and Peter Lloyd (of Coriole fame) using fruit sourced from a single vineyard in Blewitt Springs. The brothers grew up immersed in a world of wine, olive oil, illegal goat's cheese and great food. Both worked in kitchens from the age of 13 and continued to develop a love of good food and wine. Duncan studied winemaking before leaving McLaren Vale to work in Tasmania and Margaret River, and then in Chianti and the Rhône Valley. Peter also left the area after university, with eclectic occupations in France and England. (JH)

95   **The Empty Quarter 2020, McLaren Vale** A co-fermented blend of shiraz, grenache and mourvèdre, plus a little negroamaro. Notes of plum and glacé cherry on the bouquet are outgunned by the black and red fruits and firm tannins of the medium- to full-bodied palate, with an unexpected juicy finish. Intriguing wine. Screw cap. | 14.3% alc. | Drink 2022-2027 | $28 | JH

        Desert Sands Shiraz 2019, McLaren Vale The lowest-yielding cuvée, such is the density, savouriness and pliancy of the tannins, al dente as they stream across the gums to ensure the fruit, no matter how ripe, maintains a sense of decorum. Chiselled. Blue-fruit aspersions, creamy-ish oak (10% new) and loads of star anise, cocoa powder and tapenade. Serious texture, without being too cerebral. Screw cap. | 14.4% alc. | Drink 2021-2029 | $32 | JH

94   **Blewitt Springs Shiraz 2020, McLaren Vale** A harmonious array of red and black cherries whipped together with hints of nutmeg and cinnamon, all of which linger on the finish and aftertaste. Screw cap. | 14.2% alc. | Drink 2021-2035 | $28 | JH

Gemtree Wines ★★★★★

167 Elliot Road, McLaren Flat, SA 5171 **T** (08) 8323 0802 **www**.gemtreewines.com **OPEN** 7 days 11-5 **WINEMAKER** Mike Brown, Joshua Waechter **VITICULTURIST** Melissa Brown **EST.** 1998 **DOZENS** 90000 **VYDS** 123ha

Gemtree Wines is owned and operated by husband-and-wife team Melissa and Mike Brown. Mike (winemaker) and Melissa (viticulturist) firmly believe it is their responsibility to improve the land for future generations, and the vineyards are farmed organically and biodynamically. (JH)

95   **Cinnabar GSM 2021, McLaren Vale** A fine nose reminiscent of Asian plum, pumice, kirsch, thyme and rosemary of the Southern Rhône. Nothing is heavy, desiccated, too sweet or out of sorts. A swathe of chalky, pungent tannins corral, direct, impart tension and make me salivate for the next glass. Exceptional GSM. Screw cap. | 14% alc. | Drink 2022-2028 | $26 | NG

Grounded Cru ★★★★★

49 Ingoldby Road, McLaren Flat, SA 5052 **T** 0438 897 738 **www**.groundedcru.com.au **OPEN** By appt **WINEMAKER** Geoff Thompson, Matt Jackman **VITICULTURIST** Geoff Thompson, Matt Jackman **EST.** 2015 **DOZENS** 18000

Established as a brand in 2015 with an inaugural release of wines in '17, Grounded Cru draws fruit from high-quality vineyards in McLaren Vale, Langhorne Creek and the Adelaide Hills. Thompson was formerly chief winemaker at McPherson Wines in Nagambie. Conversely, his approach at Grounded Cru is one that seeks textural intrigue over obvious fruit, with European styling melded to Australian generosity. The Mediterranean varieties on offer are superlative, boasting poise and savoury tannins laden with briar. (NG)

95   **Cru GSM 2020, McLaren Vale** 66/28/6% grenache/shiraz/mourvèdre. A fine nose of cardamom, white pepper and clove. Refined, as much as it is jubilant. Raspberry bon-bon, licorice strap, salumi and violet. Best, though, the chiffon screen of tannins that direct the wine long. Lovely drinking. Screw cap. | 14.5% alc. | Drink 2021-2026 | $30 | NG

Hardys ★★★★★

202 Main Road, McLaren Vale, SA 5171 **T** (08) 8329 4124 **www**.hardyswines.com **OPEN** Sun-Fri 11-4, Sat 10-4 **WINEMAKER** Nic Bowen **VITICULTURIST** Adam Steer **EST.** 1853

The Thomas Hardy and the Berri Renmano group merged in 1992 and prospered over the next 10 years. This led to another merger in '03, with Constellation Wines of the US and BRL Hardy, creating the largest wine group in the world (the Australian arm was known as Constellation Wines Australia or CWA); but it is now part of the Accolade Wines group. The various Hardys wine brands are Eileen Hardy and Thomas Hardy wines. (JH)

BAROSSA

FLEURIEU

MOUNT LOFTY RANGES

FAR NORTH

LIMESTONE COAST

LOWER MURRAY

THE PENINSULAS

95   **HRB Riesling 2021, Tasmania Clare Valley Eden Valley** A highly sophisticated riesling with a dry Germanic twang, more pronounced than the typical Australian. By this I mean the meld of bath-salt freshness and phenolics; lime cordial, quince, lemon balm, fennel and stone-fruit inflections; juicy acidity, rather than the brittle norm. A glimpse of yonder, while still firmly entrenched in the culture of home. Lightweight and energetic. Intense of flavour and beautifully tactile. This evinces class and authority. Very good.   Screw cap. | 12.4% alc. | Drink 2021-2031 | $35 | NG

Hedonist Wines

Rifle Range Road, McLaren Vale, SA 5171 **T** (08) 8323 8818 **www**.hedonistwines.com.au
WINEMAKER Walter Clappis, Kimberly Cooter, James Cooter **EST.** 1982 **DOZENS** 18000 **VYDS** 35ha

Walter Clappis has been making wine in McLaren Vale for 40 years, and over that time has won innumerable trophies and gold medals, including the prestigious George Mackey Memorial Trophy with his '09 The Hedonist Shiraz. Daughter Kimberly and son-in-law James Cooter (both with impressive CVs) support him on the winery floor. The NASAA-certified organic and biodynamic estate plantings of shiraz, cabernet sauvignon, tempranillo and grenache are the cornerstones of the business. (JH)

93   **The Hedonist Shiraz 2020, McLaren Vale** Nicely done. Richly flavoured, suave of feel and long limbed of tannins. A bit of heat, but easily ignored amid a cornucopia of palate-staining dark fruits, pepper grind, charcuterie and an exotic spice kitchen that alludes to the northern Rhône rather than traditional sweetness of the Vale. A steal, glimpsing a great deal more sophistication than the price tag suggests.   Screw cap. | 14% alc. | Drink 2022-2030 | $25 | NG

Inkwell

PO Box 33, Sellicks Beach, SA 5174 **T** 0430 050 115 **www**.inkwellwines.com **OPEN** By appt
WINEMAKER Dudley Brown **EST.** 2003 **DOZENS** 800 **VYDS** 12ha

Inkwell was born in 2003 when Dudley Brown returned to Australia from California and bought a rundown vineyard on the serendipitously named California Road. He inherited 5ha of neglected shiraz, and planted an additional 7ha to viognier (2.5ha), zinfandel (2.5ha) and heritage shiraz clones (2ha). The 5-year restoration of the old vines and establishment of the new reads like the ultimate handbook for aspiring vignerons, particularly those who are prepared to work non-stop. The reward has been rich.

96   **Black and Blue Late Harvest Fortified Zinfandel 2018, McLaren Vale** A very fine expression, far more about elegance, detail and composure, than sheer heft. Roasted chestnut, sassafras, maraschino cherry and amaro-like herbal lift. Long and gorgeous. A plume of freshness, belying the spiritous core.   Cork. | 16.4% alc. | $40 | NG

     Black and Blue Late Harvest Fortified Zinfandel 2017, McLaren Vale Sticky date, turmeric, cardamom, sandalwood, cinnamon, candied orange zest and an ineffable spice trail that draws me to journeys in Morocco and visits to many a souk. Real pile-driving walnut rancio complexity. Sanguine, wood smoky and very fine.   Cork. | 16.8% alc. | $40 | NG

94   **Infidels Primitivo 2019, McLaren Vale** This is delicious. Always idiosyncratic, the wines here are woven with plentiful stories to tell. And surely, that is the point of good wine. Organically farmed. No adds aside from a psychologically reassuring dollop of SO$_2$. Well-appointed French and sweeter American oak, lubricating a spool of tamarind, sangria and blood plum, all spreading across an interface of dusty, pliant tannins and saline freshness.   Cork. | 14.1% alc. | Drink 2021-2026 | $30 | NG

Kangarilla Road

44 Hamilton Road, McLaren Flat, SA 5171 **T** (08) 8383 0533 **www**.kangarillaroad.com.au **OPEN** Mon-Fri 9-4.30, w'ends 11-4 **WINEMAKER** Kevin O'Brien **VITICULTURIST** Kevin O'Brien **EST.** 1997 **DOZENS** 30000 **VYDS** 5ha

In January 2013, Kangarilla Road founders Kevin and Helen O'Brien succeeded in breaking the mould for a winery sale, crafting a remarkable win-win outcome. They sold their winery and surrounding vineyard to Gemtree Wines, which has had its wine made at Kangarilla Road since '01 under the watchful eye of Kevin. The O'Briens have retained their adjacent JOBS vineyard and the Kangarilla Road wines continue to be made by Kevin at the winery. Luck of the Irish, perhaps. (JH)

95   **The Veil 2018, McLaren Vale** Seeded with flor and left in older oak for 3 years. Delicious. Chamomile, saltbush, preserved Moroccan lemon and some lees-derived almond biscuit. The finish, nicely firm and bitter. Wonderfully savoury. Prodigiously versatile. Drink this with hard cheese, Thai salads ... or, as my imagination goes into over-drive, just be creative.   Screw cap. | 13.5% alc. | Drink 2021-2027 | $35 | NG

Kay Brothers ★★★★★

57 Kays Road, McLaren Vale, SA 5171 **T** (08) 8323 8211 **WWW**.kaybrothers.com.au **OPEN** 7 days 11–4 **WINEMAKER** Duncan Kennedy **VITICULTURIST** Duncan Kennedy **EST**. 1890 **DOZENS** 10 500 **VYDS** 22ha

A traditional winery with a rich history and just over 20ha of priceless old vines. The red and fortified wines can be very good. Of particular interest is Block 6 Shiraz, made from 125yo vines. Both vines and wines are going from strength to strength. Celebrated its 130th anniversary in '20. (JH)

95 **Basket Pressed Mataro 2020, McLaren Vale** This address has turned a corner over the last few years. For the better. Fidelity to this great variety is embedded in leather, tapenade, pastrami, licorice strap and hung-game riffs. Plenty of blue and black fruits, too, expanding nicely across the persistent finish. Savouriness, the tattoo. Screw cap. | 14.5% alc. | Drink 2022-2030 | $29 | NG

Koomilya ★★★★★

Amery Road, McLaren Vale SA 5171 **T** (08) 8323 8000 **WWW**.koomilya.com.au **OPEN** 7 days 11–4 **WINEMAKER** Stephen Pannell **EST**. 2015 **DOZENS** 2000 **VYDS** 13ha

The Koomilya vineyard is wedged between the original Upper Tintara vineyard planted in 1862, and the Hope Farm or Seaview vineyard established in the early 1850s. In '12, Stephen and his wife Fiona embarked on rejuvenating it with organic farming, weeding the native bush and removing olive trees to create biochar to return as charcoal to the soil. Plantings of new varieties have followed, with a small set of wines created to specifically reflect the location, accent and circumstances of the seasons throughout each particular vintage. (TL)

97 **Cabernet Touriga 2018, McLaren Vale** Halliday Wine Companion Other Red of the Year 2023. This is exceptional, although not for the faint of heart. A mid-weighted and immensely savoury wine that is compact, portentous and so tightly bound to a ferrous orb of tannins that it makes one revel in the anticipation of the next sip. Italian of feel. Steely of resolve. Earthenware, herb, violet, biltong and a dusty swathe of dried plum and tobacco. The tannins are reminiscent of certain Wendouree cuvées or better, great Tarasi. They are a forcefield of enticement, confidence and saliva-sucking moreishness. I want to drink this whole bottle solo, so good is it. A stellar wine hailing from a spellbinding site. Screw cap. | 13% alc. | Drink 2022-2033 | $70 | NG | ♥

Lino Ramble ★★★★

11 Gawler Street, Port Noarlunga, SA 5167 **T** 0409 553 448 **WWW**.linoramble.com.au **OPEN** By appt **WINEMAKER** Andy Coppard **EST**. 2012 **DOZENS** 3500

After 20 years of working for other wine companies, big and small, interstate and international, Andy Coppard and Angela Townsend say, 'We've climbed on top of the dog kennel, tied a cape around our necks, held our breaths, and jumped'. And if you are curious about the name, the story has overtones of James Joyce's stream of consciousness mental rambles. (JH)

93 **Solitaire Grillo 2020, McLaren Vale** I like this. Broader and more textural than other whites in the suite. Almond meal, freshly lain tatami straw, lemon drop, quince paste and the saline wisp of the maritime zone that is the Vale. Long, chewy, pithy and persuasive. Screw cap. | 12.8% alc. | Drink 2022-2024 | $25 | NG

92 **Yoyo Pinot Gris 2021, Adelaide Hills** A slinky gris, with a spurt of unresolved CO_2 to provide perk and aromatic lift. Nashi pear, baked apple and a sluice of peppery freshness. Gently mid weighted, yet real thrust of fruit and parry of freshness. Lovely drink. Screw cap. | 12.4% alc. | Drink 2022-2024 | $25 | NG

mazi wines ★★★★☆

5 Wilbala Road, Longwood, SA 5153 **T** 0406 615 553 **WWW**.maziwines.com.au **WINEMAKER** Alex Katsaros, Toby Porter **EST**. 2016 **DOZENS** 1500

Lifelong friends Toby Porter and Alex Katsaros always talked about making wine together as an adjunct to their day jobs in wine. Toby has been a winemaker at d'Arenberg for 15+ years and Alex had 10 years' experience working with alternative varieties here and abroad. They decided to only make rosé, and more power to them in doing so. The aim is to produce fresh wines with vibrant fruit, normally by crushing and pressing the grapes for a cool ferment in stainless steel, but maturation in old French oak can (and has) been used to build palate complexity without sacrificing fruit. (JH)

BAROSSA

FLEURIEU

MOUNT LOFTY RANGES

FAR NORTH

LIMESTONE COAST

LOWER MURRAY

THE PENINSULAS

95 **Mataro Cinsault Grenache Rosé 2021, McLaren Vale** Arguably one of the finest rosés in the country. The caveat: the lighter hued, herb-doused and gently grippy Provençal style is light years away from most Aussie gear. I prefer it this way. One can push the style to the point of flavourless vapidity, but mercifully, these guys aren't going that way. This is an ode to classicism, the triumvirate of varieties synergistic with the greatest from the south of France, albeit, with some oomph from the Vale. A superlative vintage to boot, exuding scented fruit that is neither too muscular, nor anaemic. Poised. Classy. A musk stick hue. Riffs on glazed red cherry, poached strawberry, Seville orange zest, lavender and thyme. The finish, as reliant on a taper of gentle acidity, as it is on a skein of impeccably tuned phenolics. Long, crunchy and sappy. Superlative rosé here. Screw cap. | 12.5% alc. | Drink 2021-2022 | $24 | NG

Ministry of Clouds

765 Chapel Hill Road, McLaren Vale, SA 5171 **T** 0417 864 615 www.ministryofclouds.com.au
OPEN By appt **WINEMAKER** Julian Forwood, Bernice Ong **VITICULTURIST** Richard Leask **EST.** 2012 **DOZENS** 5000
VYDS 9.6ha

These wines have always been good, but today the best expressions are defined by McLaren Vale, rather than too much external dabbling. Tim Geddes long made the wines, yet today the team is a triumvirate, with former Wedgetail Estate maker Chris Parsons joining the fray at the new winery. Julian and Bernice craft this and shape that, while Chris is the technical raft. (NG)

97 **Kintsugi 2018, McLaren Vale** 85/10/5% grenache, mataro and shiraz. A deliciously spicy and lively bouquet, and a medium-bodied palate travelling along the same pathway to a long and juicy finish. To be gulped, not sipped, thanks to its modest alcohol. Screw cap. | 14.2% alc. | Drink 2022-2032 | $85 | JH

96 **Shiraz 2020, McLaren Vale** A wine that is at once complex and fresh, with blackberry, red and black cherry and licorice, aided and abetted by shapely tannins and integrated oak. Screw cap. | 14.5% alc. | Drink 2025-2035 | $32 | JH

Grenache 2020, McLaren Vale Superb colour, vivid and clear; the scented, spicy, flowery bouquet leads a red berry/cherry/piquant palate, savoury elements increasing overall complexity. Screw cap. | 14.3% alc. | Drink 2022-2032 | $40 | JH

95 **Riesling 2021, Clare Valley** Pure. Intense. Focused. Long. Lime. Citrus. Apple. All in capital letters. Screw cap. | 12.4% alc. | Drink 2021-2031 | $32 | JH

Grenache Carignan 2021, McLaren Vale Exceptional. Prosaic, I suppose, but the natural buttress of carignan's astringency, wildness and natural acidity obviate Aussie grenache's inherent sweetness. So good! I am having difficult spitting this, such is the first base of saliva-inducing structure. The kirsch, tapenade, white pepper and lavender, a distant second. My favourite wine of the stable. Screw cap. | 14.3% alc. | Drink 2021-2026 | $32 | NG

Mr Riggs Wine Company

169 Douglas Gully Road, McLaren Flat, SA 5171 **T** 1300 946 326 www.mrriggs.com.au **WINEMAKER** Ben
Riggs **EST.** 2001 **DOZENS** 28000 **VYDS** 12ha

With over a quarter of a century of winemaking experience, Ben Riggs is well established under his own banner. Ben sources the best fruit from individual vineyards in McLaren Vale, Clare Valley, Adelaide Hills, Langhorne Creek, Coonawarra and from his own Piebald Gully Vineyard (shiraz and viognier). Each wine expresses the essence of not only the vineyard but also the region's terroir. The vision of the Mr Riggs brand is unpretentious and personal: 'To make the wines I love to drink'. He drinks very well. (JH)

96 **JFR Shiraz 2019, McLaren Vale** A massive wine (and bottle), opaque in colour, and equally densely packed into the mouth, with blackberry, dark chocolate and licorice; oak and ripe tannins filling any chance omission with yet more flavour. Strictly for those who love full-bodied wines. Diam. | 14.5% alc. | Drink 2024-2039 | $50 | JH

94 **Montepulciano d'Adelaide 2020, Adelaide Hills** Anyone wondering about the potential of the montepulciano grape in this country need wonder no more. It's in good hands. Ben Riggs combines some Aus-Italian sensibility here, promoting the grape's noteworthy tannin:acid profile with some stellar fruit intensity. Red plums, cherry and dried herbs aplenty, with warm and earthy savoury notes to complete the picture. Goes down very easily. Screw cap. | 14.5% alc. | Drink 2021-2028 | $30 | JP

Mitolo Wines

141 McMurtrie Road, McLaren Vale, SA 5171 **T** (08) 8323 9304 www.mitolowines.com.au
OPEN Thurs-Mon 10-5 **WINEMAKER** Ben Glaetzer **EST.** 1999 **DOZENS** 40000

Mitolo had a meteoric rise once Frank Mitolo decided to turn a winemaking hobby into a business. In 2000 he took the plunge into the commercial end of the business, inviting Ben Glaetzer to make the wines. Split between the Jester range and single-vineyard wines, Mitolo began life as a red wine–dominant brand but now produces a range of varietals. (JH)

92   **Jester Shiraz 2020, McLaren Vale** A solid house wine with plenty of flavour, good value, nicely managed tannins and a whiff of tradition within a more contemporary-styled package. Dark cherry, plum, lilac, iodine, a smear of olive and a trail of peppery freshness. Thoroughly impressive at the price. Screw cap. | 14.5% alc. | Drink 2022-2030 | $25 | NG

Morgan Simpson ★★★★

PO Box 39, Kensington Park, SA 5068 **T** 0417 843 118 **www**.morgansimpson.com.au **WINEMAKER** Richard Simpson **EST**. 1998 **DOZENS** 1200 **VYDS** 17.1ha

Morgan Simpson was founded by SA businessman George Morgan (since retired) and winemaker Richard Simpson, a CSU graduate. The grapes are sourced from the Clos Robert Vineyard, planted to shiraz (9ha), cabernet sauvignon (3.5ha), mourvèdre (2.5ha) and chardonnay (2.1ha), established by Robert Allen Simpson in 1972. Most of the grapes are sold, the remainder used to provide the reasonably priced, drinkable wines for which Morgan Simpson has become well known: they are available through their website. (JH)

90   **Two Clowns Chardonnay 2019, McLaren Vale** A little lacking across the mid palate, but a minor gripe. A little tired, perhaps. But plump and savoury in all. A meld of phenolics and acidity drives this. Far better than what I anticipated. Reminiscent of an easy-goer from the Mâconnais. Best drunk soon. Screw cap. | 12% alc. | Drink 2021-2025 | $20 | NG

Nick Haselgrove Wines ★★★★☆

13 Blewitt Springs Road, McLaren Flat, SA 5171 **T** (08) 8383 0886 **www**.nhwines.com.au **OPEN** Mon-Sun 10-3 by appt **WINEMAKER** Nick Haselgrove **EST**. 1981 **DOZENS** 12000 **VYDS** 12ha

After various sales, amalgamations and disposals of particular brands, Nick Haselgrove now owns The Old Faithful (the flagship), Blackbilly, Clarence Hill, James Haselgrove and The Wishing Tree brands. (JH)

96   **James Haselgrove Futures Shiraz 2019, McLaren Vale** A burly wine, but the sheath of ground pepper, clove, cardamom, salumi, blue and black fruits, Asian five-spice, anise and root beer is toned by well-applied oak and 28 months' maturation. Therein, serving it well. Each glass reveals more and despite the challenges of the torrid growing season, this is fresh and savoury and meandering on a bouillon, umami and saline sense. Reminiscent of something from the Rhône, a personal love affair. Very good. Bravo! Screw cap. | 14% alc. | Drink 2021-2035 | $75 | NG

Oliver's Taranga Vineyards ★★★★★

246 Seaview Road, McLaren Vale, SA 5171 **T** (08) 8323 8498 **www**.oliverstaranga.com **OPEN** 7 days 10-4 **WINEMAKER** Corrina Wright **VITICULTURIST** Don Oliver **EST**. 1839 **DOZENS** 10000 **VYDS** 90ha

William and Elizabeth Oliver arrived from Scotland in 1839 to settle in McLaren Vale. Six generations later, members of the family are still living on the Whitehill and Taranga farms. Corrina Wright (the Oliver family's first winemaker) makes the wines. In '21 the family celebrated 180 years of grapegrowing. (JH)

96   **The Banished Fortified Grenache NV, McLaren Vale** Spiritous aromas of date, cardamom, ginger, mahogany, old stained timber, tobacco and the spices of a Moroccan souk. A blend with an average age of 20 years, meaning that some of the wines are considerably older still. Fine depth and spread across the palate. Turmeric and cardamom linger. Multitudinous and immensely rewarding, albeit, in small doses. Screw cap. | 19% alc. | $50 | NG

Ruthless Ruth Muscat NV, McLaren Vale Olive edges skirting a mahogany hue. Scents of molasses, roasted almonds, hazelnuts and walnut, with rancio-driven closet and old cheese. Brilliant gear! This straddles the edges of overt, fresh and pointed restraint. Intense, layered and profoundly long. Screw cap. | 19% alc. | $60 | NG

Orbis Wines ★★★★

307 Hunt Road, McLaren Vale, SA 5171 **T** 0466 986 318 **www**.orbiswines.com.au **OPEN** By appt **WINEMAKER** Lauren Langfield, Nick Dugmore, Samuel Smith **VITICULTURIST** Richard Leask **EST**. 1960 **VYDS** 26ha

BAROSSA
FLEURIEU
MOUNT LOFTY RANGES
FAR NORTH
LIMESTONE COAST
LOWER MURRAY
THE PENINSULAS

Orbis Wines hail from a site of 32ha at an elevation of 150m, planted in the 1960–70s. The old-vine shiraz was recently complemented with tempranillo, while grenache, albariño, montepulciano, nero d'Avola and fiano will soon be coming on steam. Owners Brad Moyes and Kendall Grey's fervent belief that these varieties will define McLaren Vale's future underlies a holistic culture in the truest sense: regenerative farming, recycled timber, solar power, polyculture in the vineyard, the abolishment of heavy machinery and the negation of tin-foil seals and screw caps, are some of their efforts in the name of bona fide sustainability, carbon neutrality and the promotion of biodiversity. These ethics are appropriated to minimally invasive harvest and wine-making practises in the hands of Samuel J Smith and Nick Dugmore, from hand picking, a reliance on indigenous yeasts and zero sulphur additions. (NG)

94   **Tempranillo Rosé 2021, McLaren Vale** A very fine rosé, resplendent with a lustrous tangerine hue and rails of salty tannins, pliant enough to wind their way around a densely packed core of musk, bergamot, persimmon and pomegranate. This drinks like a lighter red such is its versatility, mid weight, freshness and the whiff of seriousness to its structural latticework. Excellent drinking, far from the ersatz Provençal blueprint. I love this. Bravo!   Screw cap. | 12.5% alc. | Drink 2022-2024 | $30 | NG

Paralian Wines   ★★★★★

21 Eden Terrace, Port Willunga, SA 5171 **T** 0413 308 730 **www**.paralian.com.au **OPEN** By appt
WINEMAKER Skye Salter, Charlie Seppelt **EST.** 2018 **DOZENS** 450

Charlie Seppelt and Skye Salter met in '08 working the vintage at Hardys Tintara in McLaren Vale. Charlie's first exposure to McLaren Vale was as a vintage casual at d'Arenberg and it was vinous love at first sight. They headed off overseas, a high point undertaking vintage in Burgundy. He headed back to Australia, she went on to the Languedoc, seemingly ideal, but found it as depressing as Burgundy had been inspirational. They agreed McLaren Vale, and in particular Blewitt Springs, was the place they wanted to make grenache and shiraz with high fragrance and brightness. (JH)

96   **Springs Hill Vineyard Shiraz 2021, McLaren Vale** An exceptional nose of crushed pepper, dill, clove and a 'je ne sais quoi' peaty wildness reminiscent of Cornas. Long and taut, shimmering with licorice, blue fruits, dried nori accents and the spice elements as they reverberate across the dense, tightly packed palate. Plenty floral, too. This is an exceptional Blewitt Springs wine. The finish is chewy, pixelated, saline, pithy and so beautifully shaped. This is a very rare occasion when shiraz trumps grenache.   Screw cap. | 14% alc. | Drink 2022-2032 | $42 | NG

Paxton   ★★★★☆

68 Wheaton Road, McLaren Vale, SA 5171 **T** (08) 8323 9131 **www**.paxtonwines.com **OPEN** 7 days 10-5
WINEMAKER Dwayne Cunningham, Kate Goodman (Consultant) **EST.** 1979 **DOZENS** 32000 **VYDS** 82.5ha

David Paxton is of one Australia's most successful and respected viticulturists, with a career spanning over 40 years. He started his successful premium grower business in 1979 and has been involved with planting and managing some of the most prestigious vineyards in McLaren Vale, Barossa Valley, Yarra Valley, Margaret River and Adelaide Hills for top global wineries. There are 6 vineyards in the family holdings in McLaren Vale. All are certified organic and biodynamic, making Paxton one of the largest biodynamic producers in Australia. (JH)

95   **Quandong Farm Single Vineyard Shiraz 2020, McLaren Vale** A powerful gush of fruit, and even more so tannins, the saving grace being that they are ripe. Bramble, blackberry and dark chocolate are all in the passing parade.   Screw cap. | 13.5% alc. | Drink 2023-2035 | $30 | JH

94   **NOW Shiraz 2021, McLaren Vale** Deep, bright crimson. No preservative also means no oak, and managing the ferment is not drop-dead easy. This has a run stream of cherry (red and black), plum and blackberry with a smooth gloss of tannins. Well done, indeed.   Screw cap. | 14% alc. | Drink 2022-2024 | $25 | JH

Primo Estate   ★★★★★

McMurtrie Road, McLaren Vale, SA 5171 **T** (08) 8323 6800 **www**.primoestate.com.au **OPEN** 7 days 11-4
WINEMAKER Joseph Grilli, Daniel Grilli, Tom Garrett **EST.** 1979 **DOZENS** 30000 **VYDS** 34ha

Joe Grilli has always produced innovative and excellent wines. The biennial release of the Joseph Sparkling Red (in its tall Italian glass bottle) is eagerly awaited, the wine immediately selling out. Also highly regarded are the vintage-dated extra virgin olive oils. (JH)

96 **Pecorino 2021, Adelaide Hills** The highly floral bouquet is left on the wayside by the richness and succulence (not sweetness) of the palate. It strikes a further blow with its titanium backbone of acidity. Screw cap. | 12.5% alc. | Drink 2021-2025 | $28 | JH

Joseph The Fronti NV, McLaren Vale Superlative, managing to capture the decadent richness of the style as much as an uncanny detail, freshness and drinkability. Muscat, the grape. Frontignan, a town in the Languedoc. Scents of the Moroccan souk: incense, cardamom, orange peel, cinnamon and grape spice. Mahogany. Decay. Turkish delight. Liquid promise. It's all here. Take a whiff and recline. Screw cap. | 17% alc. | $50 | NG

Samson Tall ★★★★☆

219 Strout Road, McLaren Vale, SA 5171 **T** 0488 214 680 **www**.samsontall.com.au **OPEN** 7 days 11-5 **WINEMAKER** Paul Wilson **EST**. 2016 **DOZENS** 500

Paul Wilson and Heather Budich purchase grapes from local growers, making the wine in a small winery on their property. The cellar door is a small church built in 1854, the winery and church (with a small historic cemetery) surrounded by gardens and a vineyard. Paul has learned his craft as a winemaker; all of the wines are well made and the grapes well chosen. (JH)

95 **Mataro Cinsault Rosé 2021, McLaren Vale** Very good. Less flirtatious than its grenache sibling. More earthenware, savoury, herbal, ferrous and firm of tannic twine. Fresh as. To use the clichéd term 'food wine' undersells this. This is a mid-weighted rosé of chew over mere zip, punching with the country's finest. Screw cap. | 12% alc. | Drink 2021-2022 | $25 | NG | ♥

94 **Grenache 2020, McLaren Vale** A very modest price for a meld of fruit of this pedigree: Hatwell, Slate Creek and Marmont sites, 78, 110 and 80 years of age, respectively. A warm year, to be sure. But the twine of 30% whole bunches and properly extracted tannins, manages to corral most of the excess. Fine tannins! Blood plum, fecund strawberry, white pepper. A tad sweet. A bit lactic. Big oak (1500L foudre for 12 months) not only the righteous way but – in a region where too many handle grenache in used barriques – the courageous choice. Fine drive and sinuous length from a producer nudging the pantheon, if not already in it. Screw cap. | 14.5% alc. | Drink 2021-2027 | $30 | NG

SC Pannell ★★★★★

60 Olivers Road, McLaren Vale, SA 5171 **T** (08) 8323 8000 **www**.pannell.com.au **OPEN** 7 days 11-4 **WINEMAKER** Stephen Pannell **EST**. 2004 **DOZENS** 15000 **VYDS** 9ha

The only surprising piece of background is that it took Steve Pannell and wife Fiona so long to cut the painter from Constellation/Hardys and establish their own winemaking and consulting business. Steve radiates intensity and his extended experience has resulted in wines of the highest quality. The Pannells have 2 vineyards in McLaren Vale, the first planted in 1891 with a precious 3.6ha of shiraz. (JH)

96 **Aglianico 2020, McLaren Vale** A warmer year like this seems to have proven beneficial to this sturdy, ferruginous and late-ripening variety. Make no mistake, it is as emblematic of our vinous future as grenache, despite being a relative arriviste. If you like savoury wines laden with dried tobacco, graphite, black cherry and licorice, harnessed by tannins of mettle and stridency like few others, here's your ticket to ride! Screw cap. | 14% alc. | Drink 2021-2030 | $42 | NG

Scarpantoni Estate ★★★★

Scarpantoni Drive, McLaren Flat, SA 5171 **T** (08) 8383 0186 **www**.scarpantoniwines.com **OPEN** Mon-Fri 9-5, w'ends & public hols 11.30-4.30 **WINEMAKER** Michael and Filippo Scarpantoni, David Fleming **EST**. 1979 **DOZENS** 37000 **VYDS** 40ha

Scarpantoni has come a long way since Domenico Scarpantoni purchased his first vineyard in 1958. He worked for Thomas Hardy at its Tintara winery, then as vineyard manager for Seaview Wines and soon became one of the largest private grapegrowers in the region. The winery was built in '79 with help from sons Michael and Filippo, who continue to manage the company. (JH)

94 **Montepulciano 2021, McLaren Vale** By far the best wine in this suite, attesting to the promise of sturdy, late-ripening Italian varieties in the region, particularly when endowed with ferrous tannins – lithe and drawn gently – and saline freshness. This stands out like the proverbial promised land. Macerated cherry, clove, beef bouillon, lilac and licorice strap. But it is the mould of pulpy, impeccably extracted whole berries and the intuitive varietal DNA, structured and pointed in the right direction, that win me over. Screw cap. | 14% alc. | Drink 2021-2028 | $25 | NG

BAROSSA

FLEURIEU

MOUNT LOFTY RANGES

FAR NORTH

LIMESTONE COAST

LOWER MURRAY

THE PENINSULAS

Semprevino ★★★★

271 Kangarilla Road, McLaren Vale, SA 5171 **T** 0417 142 110 **www**.semprevino.com.au
WINEMAKER Russell Schroder **EST.** 2006 **DOZENS** 800

Semprevino is the venture of Russell Schroder and Simon Doak, who became close friends while at Monash University in the early 1990s. Russell is the prime mover, who, after working for CRA/Rio Tinto for 5 years, left on a 4-month trip to Western Europe and became captivated by the life of a vigneron. Returning to Australia, he enrolled at CSU, obtaining his wine science degree in 2005. Between '03 and '06 he worked vintages in Italy and Victoria, coming under the wing of Stephen Pannell at Tinlins. (JH)

93 **GSM 2020, McLaren Vale** This is good. Reminiscent of quality Côtes du Rhône, with a swirl of purple fruits and florals, sluiced with Mediterranean herb, iodine and some smoked-meat extract. The tannins, gently fibrous against the effortless flow of fruit. An acceptable whiff of reduction, imparts tension. Mid weighted, plump and extremely versatile. Screw cap. | 14.6% alc. | Drink 2021-2026 | $26 | NG

Serafino Wines ★★★★★

Kangarilla Road, McLaren Vale, SA 5171 **T** (08) 8323 0157 **www**.serafinowines.com.au **OPEN** Mon-Fri 10-4.30, w'ends & public hols 10-4.30 **WINEMAKER** Michelle Heagney **EST.** 2000 **DOZENS** 30000 **VYDS** 121ha

After the sale of Maglieri Wines to Beringer Blass in 1998, Maglieri founder Serafino (Steve) Maglieri acquired the McLarens on the Lake complex originally established by Andrew Garrett. Serafino Wines has won a number of major trophies in Australia and the UK, Steve Maglieri awarded a Member of the Order of Australia in Jan '18. (JH)

94 **Cabernet Sauvignon 2019, McLaren Vale** Bordeaux's maritime climate for cabernet sauvignon is replicated in McLaren Vale, albeit in a warmer mode, providing a generous style that doesn't lose the variety's signature of blackcurrant, nor the region's lick of dark chocolate. This is an inviting medium-to full-bodied wine, the contributions of tannins and French oak dextrously handled. Bargain. Screw cap. | 14.5% alc. | Drink 2024-2034 | $28 | JH

Sew & Sew Wines ★★★☆

97 Pennys Hill Road, The Range, SA 5172 **T** 0437 763 139 **www**.sewandsewwines.com.au **OPEN** By appt
WINEMAKER Jodie Armstrong **VITICULTURIST** Jodie Armstrong **EST.** 2015 **DOZENS** 3500

Winemaker and viticulturist Jodie Armstrong has worked in the wine industry for more than 20 years. She sources grapes from the vineyards that she manages, her in-depth knowledge of these vineyards allowing her to grow and select premium fruit. She makes the wines in friends' wineries 'where collaboration is a source of inspiration'. (JH)

92 **Sashiko Series Nero 2020, McLaren Vale** A play on the usual GSM with mataro (aka mourvèdre) joined by nero d'Avola playing the role of shiraz and aglianico assuming a savoury, tannic third party. It is an enticing blend in black cherry, spiced plum and red licorice, spiced up through the middle palate and finishing fresh and juicy. Screw cap. | 14% alc. | Drink 2021-2028 | $25 | JP

Shingleback ★★★★☆

3 Stump Hill Road, McLaren Vale, SA 5171 **T** (08) 8323 7388 **www**.shingleback.com.au **OPEN** 7 days 10-5 **WINEMAKER** John Davey, Dan Hills **VITICULTURIST** Paul Mathews, John Davey **EST.** 1995 **DOZENS** 150000 **VYDS** 120ha

Brothers Kym and John Davey planted and nurture their family-owned and sustainably managed vineyard on land purchased by their grandfather in the '50s. Shingleback has been a success story since its establishment. Its 120ha of estate vineyards are one of the keys to that success, which includes winning the Jimmy Watson Trophy in 2006 for the '05 D Block Cabernet Sauvignon. (JH)

95 **Davey Estate Single Vineyard Shiraz 2019, McLaren Vale** A compellingly endowed shiraz which has managed to emerge from its oak womb with a supple, seductive medium-bodied palate that has an energetic savoury finish, which is the high point of the wine. Three trophies McLaren Vale Wine Show '20. Screw cap. | 14% alc. | Drink 2024-2034 | $25 | JH

Three Dark Horses

★★★★

307 Schuller Road, Blewitt Springs, SA 5171 **T** 0405 294 500 **WWW.**3dh.com.au **WINEMAKER** Matt Broomhead **VITICULTURIST** Matt Broomhead **EST.** 2009 **DOZENS** 5000 **VYDS** 8.9ha

Three Dark Horses is the project of former Coriole winemaker Matt Broomhead. After vintages in southern Italy (2007) and the Rhône Valley, he returned to McLaren Vale in late 2009 and, with his father Alan, buys quality grapes, thanks to the many years of experience they both have in the region. The third dark horse is Matt's grandfather, a vintage regular. Part of the vineyard is sand soil–based interspersed with ironstone, a highly desirable mix for shiraz and cabernet sauvignon. (JH)

93   **Grenache Touriga 2020, McLaren Vale** At this price, the wine is very good – not merely in a domestic sense, but in an international one. Jubey. Ripe. Savoury. Round. Floral. Fresh. The reductive hand, a little out of the holster. Touriga, floral and peppery. The grenache, warm and soothing and finer boned. Delicious drinking. The tannins and acidity, a finessed patina. Screw cap. | 14.5% alc. | Drink 2021-2026 | $25 | NG

92   **Shiraz 2020, McLaren Vale** A torrid year, but harnessed beautifully. At this pricing tier, impregnable. Oodles of blue fruits, iodine, clove, salumi, tapenade and white-pepper-laced freshness hit the varietal high points. A bit reductive/neoprene, but this has become the Australian means of mitigating low acidity while imparting a sense of tension. Impressive within the constructs. Screw cap. | 14.5% alc. | Drink 2021-2027 | $25 | NG

91   **Preservative Free Shiraz 2021, McLaren Vale** This address provides stellar value. The wines, inevitably delicious. Archetypal gently extracted shiraz, sans SO_2. Wild fermented. Playing the sassy florals of partial carbonic influence with aplomb. Pithy blue fruits, a waft of spice and a frame of the right sort of gently applied oak, this goes down with very little effort after a brisk chill. Best enjoyed in its fruity primacy. Screw cap. | 14.5% alc. | Drink 2022-2024 | $22 | NG

Varney Wines

★★★★★

62 Victor Harbor Road, Old Noarlunga, SA 5168 **T** 0450 414 570 **WWW.**varneywines.com.au **OPEN** Thurs-Mon 11-5 **WINEMAKER** Alan Varney **EST.** 2017 **DOZENS** 1500

Alan Varney's Australian career grew out of a vintage stint with d'Arenberg into an 11-year employment, much of it as senior winemaker. He is a brilliant winemaker, saying, 'I am not afraid to step out of the box and go with my intuition ... I only use old seasoned oak with no fining or filtration.' He has built an environmentally sensitive winery alongside wife Kathrin's restaurant, Victor's Place, overlooking the Onkaparinga Gorge. Varney Wines were the Wine Companion 2021 Best New Winery. (JH)

96   **GSM 2019, McLaren Vale** Best GSM in the land? Very possibly. Suave, taut, streamlined, savoury. Wonderfully pliant and spicy, with a seasoning (15%) of whole bunches. Mourvèdre's hung game, to kick off. Clove, anise, pepper, blue and black fruits, cardamom and violet, otherwise. Measured, compact and dense. Perfectly extracted. Each tannin a finely wrought rivet, serving to weld a superb wine of precision and latent force. Screw cap. | 14% alc. | Drink 2021-2027 | $32 | NG

95   **GSM 2020, McLaren Vale** As Rhône-like as it gets. Grenache (55%), the kirsch, sandalwood and white pepper. Shiraz (25%), the florals and salumi. But there is far more to this: old vines, propitious siting and the confidence to extract with an MO of savoury complexity and strident tannins that ready one for the fifth glass rather than one sip ... before lights out. Screw cap. | 14.2% alc. | Drink 2021-2028 | $32 | NG

     Fiano 2019, Langhorne Creek Alan Varney certainly knows what he's doing. The scented, slightly peppery bouquet is a logical forerunner to the skilfully engineered, grapefruit-accented palate. A wine to stand tall with any food style. Screw cap. | 12.4% alc. | Drink 2021-2024 | $28 | JH

Vigena Wines

★★★★★

210 Main Road, Willunga, SA 5172 **T** 0433 966 011 **OPEN** .By appt **WINEMAKER** Ben Heide **EST.** 2010 **DOZENS** 20000 **VYDS** 15.8ha

Vigena Wines is principally an export business. In recent years the vineyard has been revitalised, with one significant change: chardonnay has been grafted to shiraz, giving the business a 100% red wine focus. (JH)

96   **Cabernet Sauvignon 2020, McLaren Vale** This is by far the best wine of the suite, at least in its current equilibrium of force and intensity of cassis and black olive flavours, supported by a verdant chassis and cylinders of vanilla-pod oak and saline freshness. Perfectly varietal. Undeniably classy. The structural mettle, no matter how strong, feels suited to the quality of fruit and scattered herbal notes. While I have said that some wines will come around at this address, this is already delicious. No doubt it will become even more so after a decade. Cork. | 14.5% alc. | Drink 2022-2035 | $65 | NG

Vigna Bottin ★★★★☆

192 Main Road, Willunga SA 5172 **T** 0414 562 956 **WWW**.vignabottin.com.au **OPEN** Fri 11–4, Sat–Sun 11–5 **WINEMAKER** Paolo Bottin **EST**.2006 **DOZENS** 1500 **VYDS** 15.22ha

The Bottin family migrated to Australia in 1954 from Treviso in northern Italy where they were grapegrowers. The family began growing grapes in McLaren Vale in '70, focusing on mainstream varieties for sale to wineries in the region. When son Paolo and wife Maria made a trip back to Italy in '98, they were inspired to do more, and, says Paolo, 'my love for barbera and sangiovese was sealed during a vintage in Pavia. I came straight home to plant both varieties in our family plot. My father was finally happy!' (JH)

95 **Fiano 2021, McLaren Vale** I enjoy tasting this family's wines. Each year, an incremental ascendancy of quality and integrity: hand picked, partially wild fermented on skins for 10 days to impart flavour and textural moxie, a bit of barrel, blending and time on lees with some stirring. This brims with pear, wild fennel, raw almond and citrus verbena. The finish, salty and firm, the phenolics directing the intense wave of flavour. As prescient as it is fine drinking. Screw cap. | 12.8% alc. | Drink 2021–2025 | \$27 | NG

WayWood Wines ★★★★☆

67 Kays Road, McLaren Vale, SA 5171 **T** (08) 8323 8468 **WWW**.waywoodwines.com **OPEN** By appt **WINEMAKER** Andrew Wood **VITICULTURIST** Andrew Wood **EST**. 2005 **DOZENS** 1500 **VYDS** 3ha

This is the culmination of Andrew Wood and Lisa Robertson's wayward odyssey. Andrew left his career as a sommelier in London and retrained as a winemaker, working in Portugal, the UK, Italy and the Granite Belt, settling in McLaren Vale in early '04. Working with Kangarilla Road winery for the next 6 years, while making small quantities of shiraz, cabernets and tempranillo from purchased grapes, led them to nebbiolo, montepulciano and shiraz. (JH)

97 **LBVP Shiraz 2017, McLaren Vale** The late-bottled (LB) evolution of '17 VP, decanted to 100L barrels in '19 for a further 2 years' maturation. Very smart. The spirit impeccably embedded into the fray of dark cherry, camphor, raspberry bon-bon and molten black rock. A tautly arched bow of gritty, seamlessly melded tannins, corrals any excess. The finish, endless. Excellent domestic fortified. Screw cap. | 19% alc. | \$40 | NG

Wirra Wirra Vineyards ★★★★★

255 Strout Road, McLaren Vale, SA 5171 **T** (08) 8323 8414 **WWW**.wirrawirra.com **OPEN** Mon–Sat 10–5, Sun & public hols 11–5 **WINEMAKER** Paul Smith, Tom Ravech, Kelly Wellington, Grace Wang **VITICULTURIST** Anton Groffen **EST**. 1894 **DOZENS** 140000 **VYDS** 21.5ha

Wirra Wirra has established a formidable reputation. The wines are of exemplary character, quality and style. Managing director Andrew Kay and the winemaking team of Paul Smith, Tom Ravech and Kelly Wellington forge along the path of excellence first trod by the late (and much loved) Greg Trott, the pioneering founder of modern-day Wirra Wirra. Its acquisition of Ashton Hills in '15 added a major string to its top-quality bow. (JH)

94 **Church Block Cabernet Sauvignon Shiraz Merlot 2019, McLaren Vale** This satisfies all the criteria for a blend such as this: bright colour and fresh black and red fruits, undaunted by the extended time in barrel, and satisfying ripe tannins. And a gold-plated bargain. Screw cap. | 14.5% alc. | Drink 2022–2039 | \$22 | JH

Woodstock ★★★★

215 Douglas Gully Road, McLaren Flat, SA 5171 **T** (08) 8383 0156 **WWW**.woodstockwine.com.au **OPEN** 7 days 11–4 **WINEMAKER** Ben Glaetzer **EST**. 1905 **DOZENS** 22000 **VYDS** 18.44ha

The Collett family is among the best known in McLaren Vale, the late Doug Collett AM was known for his World War II exploits flying Spitfires and Hurricanes with the RAF and RAAF, returning to study oenology at Roseworthy Agricultural College and rapidly promoted to take charge of SA's largest winery, Berri Co-operative. In 1973 he purchased the Woodstock estate, built a winery and in '74 he crushed its first vintage. Son Scott Collett became winemaker in '82 and has won numerous accolades; equally importantly, he purchased an adjoining shiraz vineyard planted circa 1900 and a bush-vine grenache vineyard planted in '30. In '99 he joined forces with Ben Glaetzer, passing responsibility for winemaking to Ben, but retaining responsibility for the estate vineyards. (JH)

93 **Audacity Rosé 2021, McLaren Vale Langhorne Creek** A 65/25/7/3% blend of vermentino/grenache/ mataro/shiraz. Some bloom and red berry scents on the bouquet are followed by a palate that is not only fresh, but adds flavours of pomegranate and forest strawberries. Screw cap. | 11.5% alc. | Drink 2021-2023 | $24 | JH

90 **Sauvignon Blanc 2021, Adelaide Hills** My, it certainly packs a lot of cool-climate sauvignon pleasure into the pricepoint. Fabulous value for money here. Ripe tropical fruits mingle with grapefruit, lime, apple and lantana. The palate is the key to this wine, it brings both depth of flavour, texture and a fruit-tingle sweet spot, all the while gracefully rolling along via juicy acidity to the finish. Screw cap. | 13% alc. | Drink 2021-2025 | $19 | JP

Yangarra Estate Vineyard ★★★★★

809 McLaren Flat Road, Kangarilla SA 5171 **T** (08) 8383 7459 **WWW**.yangarra.com.au **OPEN** Mon-Sat 11-5 **WINEMAKER** Peter Fraser **VITICULTURIST** Michael Lane **EST**. 2000 **DOZENS** 15000 **VYDS** 100ha

This is the Australian operation of Jackson Family Wines, one of the leading premium wine producers in California, which in 2000 acquired the 172ha Eringa Park Vineyard from Normans Wines (the oldest vines dated back to 1923). The renamed Yangarra Estate Vineyard is the estate base for the operation and has moved to certified biodynamic status with its vineyards. Peter Fraser has taken Yangarra Estate to another level altogether with his innovative winemaking and desire to explore all the possibilities of the Rhône Valley red and white styles. Peter was named Winemaker of the Year in the Wine Companion 2016. (JH)

97 **Roux Beaute Roussanne 2020, McLaren Vale** Arguably the finest white wine in the Vale. A few contenders. A lustrous deep yellow. Saline, as is so much in these parts. Then a decompression of rooibos, the ripest lemon that sits as a figment of the imagination, raw pistachio and green olive- brine martini. Thick, intense, powerful and yet, tiptoeing across a drawbridge of phenolics, almost the daintiest powerhouse that I've pirouetted with. Screw cap. | 13.5% alc. | Drink 2022-2037 | $65 | NG

Ovitelli Grenache 2020, McLaren Vale Always an exciting proposition. A transparent grenache of pixelated precision. As reminiscent of its nebbiolo brethren as it is of pinot. A shimmering red- fruited veil. Gritty, attenuated tannins derived from old vines (1946) and a long, gentle agitation in ceramic eggs. Like biting into the juiciest raspberry that bridles the perfect edge of ripeness, before sucking on sandstone. Long is an understatement. This is among Australia's greatest wines from the country's finest cultivar. Screw cap. | 14.5% alc. | Drink 2022-2032 | $75 | NG | ♥

96 **Ovitelli Blanc 2020, McLaren Vale** 50/25/12/9/4% grenache blanc/roussanne/clairette/piquepoul/ bourboulenc, all of the southern Rhône and well at home here. Taut, salty and nascent of feel. Then, an explosion with air. Loads in store. Lanolin, sea salt, skinsy quince notes, nashi pear, baked apple and preserved Moroccan lemon. Yet it is the texture that compels, from the first rail of chew, to the last lattice of saliva-sucking bite and pithy mealiness. Stay tuned. This is only the beginning of the ascension. Screw cap. | 13% alc. | Drink 2022-2035 | $65 | NG

Zonte's Footstep ★★★★☆

The General Wine Bar, 55a Main Road, McLaren Flat, SA 5171 **T** (08) 7286 3083 **WWW**. zontesfootstep.com.au **OPEN** Mon-Sat by appt **WINEMAKER** Brad Rey **VITICULTURIST** Brad Rey **EST**. 2003 **DOZENS** 20000 **VYDS** 214.72ha

Brad Rey is the kingpin of a small group of winemakers and wine marketers who in 2003 decided it was time to do their own thing in McLaren Vale. Scott Collett's family are multi- generation grape growers and makers; Anna Fisher provides business management skills; and the Heath family own the 215ha organically run vineyards in the Finniss River district whence the grape requirements of Zonte's organic wines are supplied.

95 **Violet Beauregard Malbec 2021, Langhorne Creek** Standard no-frills vinification, but this is a wine that is anything but standard. Its depth and breadth of dark berry fruits, licorice, spice and plum coat the palate with flavours that draw you back up repeatedly. Wonderful stuff; hail the vintage! Screw cap. | 14% alc. | Drink 2022-2032 | $30 | JH

BAROSSA

FLEURIEU

MOUNT LOFTY RANGES

FAR NORTH

LIMESTONE COAST

LOWER MURRAY

THE PENINSULAS

Mount Lofty Ranges

Michael Hall Wines ★★★★★

103 Langmeil Road, Tanunda, SA 5352 **T** 0448 911 835 **WWW**.michaelhallwines.com **OPEN** Fri-Sat 11-5 or by appt **WINEMAKER** Michael Hall **EST**. 2008 **DOZENS** 2500

Michael Hall came to Australia in 2001 to pursue winemaking – a lifelong interest – and undertook the wine science degree at CSU, graduating as dux in '05. His vintage work in Australia and France is a veritable who's who of producers: in Australia with Cullen, Giaconda, Henschke, Shaw + Smith, Coldstream Hills and Veritas; in France with Domaine Leflaive, Meo-Camuzet, Vieux Telegraphe and Trevallon. He is now involved full-time with his eponymous brand and the wines are as impressive as his experience suggests they should be. (JH)

96   **Pinot Noir 2020, Piccadilly Valley Lenswood** Low rainfall throughout led to a very small crop and a wine of highly concentrated flavour, astonishingly so. Intense aromas of red cherry, redcurrant, fine spices, a hint of red licorice and musk. Draws power as it builds in the mouth. A supple and smooth palate with composed open-weave tannins. Power and grace. Screw cap. | 13.5% alc. | Drink 2021-2032 | $60 | JP

Adelaide Hills

Catlin Wines ★★★★☆

39B Sydney Road, Nairne, SA 5252 **T** 0411 326 384 **WWW**.catlinwines.com.au **WINEMAKER** Darryl Catlin **EST**. 2013 **DOZENS** 2000

Darryl Catlin grew up in the Barossa Valley with vineyards as his playground, picking bush-vine grenache for pocket money as a youngster. Stints with Saltram, the Australian Bottling Company and Vintner Imports followed in his 20s, before he moved on to gain retail experience at Adelaide's Royal Oak Cellar, London's Oddbins and McKay's Macquarie Cellars. Next, he studied for a winemaking degree while working at Adelaide's East End Cellars. Then followed a number of years at Shaw + Smith, rising from cellar hand to winemaker, finishing in '12 and establishing his own business the following year. (JH)

95   **Nitschke Riesling 2021, Adelaide Hills** The winemaker typically makes Clare riesling but here takes a stab at Adelaide Hills riesling. The result shows the potential of the grape in the region. Riesling brightness is turned down, the spice and charm factor turned up and the result is rather special. Spring wildflowers, lavender, apple, lime and spice scents are transformed on to the palate with depth and concentration. Not to mention, generous mouthfeel and persistence. A stunning wine. Screw cap. | 11.5% alc. | Drink 2021-2025 | $32 | JP

94   **GB's Montepulciano Rosé 2021, Adelaide Hills** Now, this is different. Montepulciano as a rosé brings its plums, cherries and Italian herbals to the party and it's quite a tasty, lightly savoury treat. Confection-pink hues translate into a lifted aromatic fragrance but it is the bright flavours and textural mouthfeel that will suddenly arrest the tastebuds. A perfect versatile food-match rosé right here. Screw cap. | 12.5% alc. | Drink 2021-2025 | $22 | JP

Charlotte Dalton Wines ♀♛ ★★★★★

Factory 9, 89-91 Hill Street, Port Elliot, SA 5212 **T** 0466 541 361 **WWW**.charlottedaltonwines. com.au **OPEN** Fri-Mon 11-3 (7 days 26 Dec-26 Jan) **WINEMAKER** Charlotte Hardy **EST**. 2015 **DOZENS** 1200

Charlotte Hardy has been making wines for 20 years, with a star-studded career at Craggy Range (NZ), Château Giscours (Bordeaux) and David Abreu (California), but has called SA home since 2007. Her winery is part of her Basket Range house, which has been through many incarnations since starting life as a pig farm in 1858. (JH)

94   **Love You Love Me Semillon 2019, Adelaide Hills** You don't see a lot of Hills semillon, but maybe this smart, intelligently made wine heralds a change. A very confident, expressive semillon with 3 years under its belt and showing jasmine, apple blossom and white flower aromas, spiced apple, lemongrass, spice. Rich in flavour, creamy in texture but delivered with a tangy juiciness that makes you have to have another sip. Screw cap. | 12% alc. | Drink 2022-2025 | $30 | JP

BAROSSA
FLEURIEU
MOUNT LOFTY RANGES
FAR NORTH
LIMESTONE COAST
LOWER MURRAY
THE PENINSULAS

Coates Wines ⓘ ★★★★★

185 Tynan Road, Kuitpo, SA 5172 **T** 0417 882 557 **WWW**.coates-wines.com **OPEN** W'ends & public hols 11–5 **WINEMAKER** Duane Coates **EST**. 2003 **DOZENS** 2500

Duane Coates has a bachelor of science, a master of business administration and a master of oenology from the University of Adelaide; for good measure he completed the theory component of the MW program in 2005. His original intention was to simply make a single barrel of wine employing various philosophies and practices outside the mainstream; there was no plan to move to commercial production. The key is organically grown grapes. (JH)

96   **The Riesling 2021, Adelaide Hills** Among the finest rieslings in the land, by virtue of the intelligence behind its craftsmanship, as much as the deliciousness of the results: kaffir lime, talc and blossom. Few surprises there. Yet the fleck of oak and further latticework derived from natural yeast, lees and grape skins, spiels an intriguing narrative more Germanic of feel and texturally compelling than the domestic norm. Very impressive.   Screw cap. | 12% alc. | Drink 2022–2030 | $35 | NG | ♥

     The Reserve Chardonnay 2020, Adelaide Hills Very high-quality chardonnay here. A warm year, not without its challenges. But in these hands, stone-fruit accents stream long, corralled by classy vanilla-pod oak and crunchy acidity. Plenty of dried porcini, toasted hazelnut and nougatine at its core. A wine that feels latent; reticent even, despite its power, persistence and length. This will age well.   Screw cap. | 13% alc. | Drink 2022–2030 | $35 | NG | ♥

95   **The Semillon Sauvignon Blanc 2021, Adelaide Hills** Oak is the orb around which this classic bordeaux blend should gravitate. Without it, the meld is zesty, fruity and too often, ordinary. With it, the stars align. Here, optimally ripe parcels mesh with fresher portions. All fermented spontaneously in used French wood. The result, giddy. Guava, hedgerow and sugar snap peas find effortless confluence with tatami hay, spearmint and lemon balm. This will age beautifully over the short–medium term.   Screw cap. | 13% alc. | Drink 2021–2026 | $30 | NG

     The Chardonnay 2021, Adelaide Hills A fine, long-focused lens on classy domestic chardonnay. The meld of nougat lees, vanillin oak and pithy glazed stone fruits, finely tuned. Praline, quinine, orange verbena and toasted cashew, too. The finish, precise, measured and extremely long. This stands to go the distance.   Screw cap. | 13% alc. | Drink 2022–2030 | $35 | NG

     The Mourvèdre 2021, McLaren Vale Fermented wild. Unfined and unfiltered. The sort of wine, unfettered and pure of intent, that could be considerably more expensive. Blueberry and florals. A twine of ferrous tannic persuasion, dried tobacco and a verdant smattering of herb. The finish, long and persuasive.   Screw cap. | 14% alc. | Drink 2022–2031 | $35 | NG

CRFT Wines ⓘ ★★★★★

45 Rangeview Drive, Carey Gully, SA 5144 **T** 0413 475 485 **WWW**.crftwines.com.au **OPEN** Fri–Sun 12–5 **WINEMAKER** Candice Helbig, Frewin Ries **VITICULTURIST** Candice Helbig, Frewin Ries **EST**. 2012 **DOZENS** 1000 **VYDS** 1.9ha

Life and business partners NZ-born Frewin Ries and Barossa-born Candice Helbig crammed multiple wine lives into a relatively short period, before giving up secure jobs and establishing CRFT in '13. Frewin's CV includes Cloudy Bay and the iconic Sonoma pinot noir producer Williams Selyem, among others. Candice trained as a laboratory technician before moving to winemaking at Hardys, gaining her degree in oenology and viticulture from CSU and on to Boar's Rock and Mollydooker. The Arranmore vineyard was purchased in '16, gaining NASAA organic certification in '19, and wines are made with a minimal-intervention approach. (JH)

95   **Arranmore Vineyard Grüner Veltliner 2021, Piccadilly Valley** Vegan friendly. Of the 3 grüners produced at CRFT, Arranmore is the floral and spiced beauty, fine-boned and linear. Lifted aromas of apple blossom, white peach, lemon thyme and citrus. A wave of summer fruits, citrus and spice envelops the tastebuds nicely, tempered by a firm line of crisp, bright acidity.   Screw cap. | 13.5% alc. | Drink 2021–2025 | $31 | JP

Deviation Road ⓘ ★★★★★

207 Scott Creek Road, Longwood, SA 5153 **T** (08) 8339 2633 **WWW**.deviationroad.com **OPEN** 7 days 10–5 **WINEMAKER** Kate Laurie **EST**. 1999 **DOZENS** 8000 **VYDS** 11.05ha

Continuing a 5-generation family winemaking tradition, Hamish and Kate Laurie created their first wine from the 30yo Laurie family-owned vineyard on Deviation Road in '02. In '04 Hamish and Kate purchased their property at Longwood, which is the current home to 4ha of shiraz and pinot noir, the winery and tasting room. Disgorging equipment from Kate's family's Manjimup winery, originally imported from Champagne, was shipped to the Adelaide Hills in '08 enabling the first Deviation Road traditional method sparkling wine release. (JH)

96   **Altair Brut Rosé NV, Adelaide Hills** 55/45% pinot noir/chardonnay. Base vintage '18; 40 months on lees. Disgorged Oct '21. 8g/L dosage. A finely beaded, salmon-pink sparkling that rates among Australia's best. Confidently presented with complexity and poise, Altair wears a delicate sheen of savoury autolysis with almonds, baked pastry, poached pear, bright red berries aromas. Layer upon layer of delicate flavour, texture and depth. Runs fine, long and so impressive. All class. Cork. | 12.5% alc. | $38 | JP | ♥

95   **Sauvignon Blanc 2021, Adelaide Hills** Typically pure and super-expressive for a Hills sauvignon, dressed in Tahitian lime, green mango, gooseberry and citrus. Feel the depth of fruit and intensity of flavour on the palate: so, so impressive. Clean, tangy and supple, with a snow-pea-shoot green finish. Screw cap. | 12.5% alc. | Drink 2021-2025 | $30 | JP

Geoff Weaver

2 Gilpin Lane, Mitcham, SA 5062 (postal) **T** (08) 8272 2105 **www**.geoffweaver.com.au **WINEMAKER** Geoff Weaver **EST.** 1982 **DOZENS** 3000 **VYDS** 12.3ha

This is the business of one-time Hardys chief winemaker Geoff Weaver. The Lenswood vineyard was established between 1982 and '88, and invariably produces immaculate riesling and sauvignon blanc and long-lived chardonnays. The beauty of the labels ranks supreme. (JH)

95   **Single Vineyard Sauvignon Blanc 2021, Adelaide Hills** This is an excellent example of a sauvignon that is super-tasty now, but with so much potential still to explore. So versatile. Well composed, crisp and balanced in lime, citrus, apple, green mango and spice. It softens through to the finish, maintaining a chalky clean texture. Screw cap. | 13.5% alc. | Drink 2021-2026 | $30 | JP

Hahndorf Hill Winery

38 Pain Road, Hahndorf, SA 5245 **T** (08) 8388 7512 **www**.hahndorfhillwinery.com.au **OPEN** Mon-Sat 10.30-4 **WINEMAKER** Larry Jacobs **EST.** 2002 **DOZENS** 6000 **VYDS** 6.5ha

Larry Jacobs and Marc Dobson purchased Hahndorf Hill Winery in 2002. Larry and Marc established the near-iconic Mulderbosch Wines in '88. It was purchased at the end of '96 and the pair eventually found their way to Australia and Hahndorf Hill. Now a specialist in Austrian varieties, they have imported 6 clones of grüner veltliner and 2 clones of St Laurent into Australia and also produce blaufränkisch and zweigelt. In '16 the winery was awarded Best Producer Under 100t at the Adelaide Hills Wine Show, and their wines too have had trophy and medal success. (JH)

96   **GRU Grüner Veltliner 2021, Adelaide Hills** Has more weight and gravitas than its siblings, but the same balance and length: it's a crying shame that I don't methodically lay down the Hahndorf Hill grüners for a decade or so to watch their development, giving the same reward as fine rieslings. Screw cap. | 13% alc. | Drink 2021-2030 | $30 | JH

Heirloom Vineyards

PO Box 39, McLaren Vale, SA 5171 **T** (08) 8323 8979 **www**.heirloomvineyards.com.au **WINEMAKER** Elena Brooks **EST.** 2004

Another venture for winemaker Elena Brooks and her husband Zar. They met during the 2000 vintage and one thing led to another. Dandelion Vineyards and Zonte's Footstep came along first, and continue, but other partners are involved in those ventures. The lofty aims of Heirloom are 'to preserve the best of tradition, the unique old vineyards of SA, and to champion the best clones of each variety, embracing organic and biodynamic farming'. (JH)

96   **Shiraz 2020, McLaren Vale** The deep – verging on opaque – colour rings a bell warning of the arrival of an exotic full-bodied shiraz, arguing the toss on varietal expression (unctuous blackberry and licorice) and sense of place (dark chocolate) with ripe, gently chewy tannins and a benison of oak. Screw cap. | 14.5% alc. | Drink 2022-2040 | $40 | JH

Howard Vineyard

53 Bald Hills Road, Nairne, SA 5252 **T** (08) 8188 0203 **www**.howardvineyard.com **OPEN** 7 days by appt **WINEMAKER** Tom Northcott **VITICULTURIST** Tom Northcott **EST.** 1998 **DOZENS** 6000 **VYDS** 70ha

Howard Vineyard is a family-owned Adelaide Hills winery set among towering gum trees, and terraced lawns. All the wines are estate-grown. Winemaker Tom Northcott has a bachelor degree in viticulture and oenology from Adelaide University, and has worked vintages in the South of France, Barossa Valley, Western Australia and Tasmania. (JH)

90 **Rosé 2021, Adelaide Hills** Cabernet Sauvignon/merlot/cabernet franc. A tasty, pale rosé for the price, brimming with cherries, strawberries and a dusting of light spice. Works the mouth with juicy acidity and a pleasurable amount of texture. Screw cap. | 12.5% alc. | Drink 2021-2023 | $20 | JP

La Linea ★★★★★

36 Shipsters Road, Kensington Park, SA 5068 (postal) **T** (08) 8431 3556 **www**.lalinea.com.au
WINEMAKER Peter Leske **VITICULTURIST** Peter Leske **EST.** 2007 **DOZENS** 4000 **VYDS** 6.64ha

La Linea is a partnership between experienced wine industry professionals Peter Leske (ex-Nepenthe) and David LeMire MW. Peter was among the first to recognise the potential of tempranillo in Australia and his knowledge of it is reflected in the 3 wine styles made from the variety. The pair pioneered mencia – the red variety from northwest Spain – in the Hills. They also produce the off-dry riesling 25GR (25g/L RS) under the Vertigo label. (JH)

95 **Tempranillo Rosé 2021, Adelaide Hills** This has everything you need or want in a good rosé, from bountiful red berries, mid-palate textural goodness and a long-running spiciness across the palate to versatility at the table. Quite an accomplishment. And all of that at a reasonable price. Screw cap. | 12.5% alc. | Drink 2021-2025 | $24 | JP

Mencia 2020, Adelaide Hills Mencia is making itself home in the Hills and McLaren Vale. The Mediterranean variety loves a Mediterranean climate. It fully opens with some air and then wait for the deep spice, dark-berry, cherry and herbal lift. A touch of undergrowth adds a savoury note. Sweeping tannins play across an expansive palate through to a dry finish. Screw cap. | 13.5% alc. | Drink 2021-2026 | $29 | JP

La Prova ★★★★★

102 Main Street, Hahndorf, SA 5245 **T** (08) 8388 7330 **www**.laprova.com.au **OPEN** first w'end of the month 11–5 or by appt **WINEMAKER** Sam Scott **EST.** 2009 **DOZENS** 5000

Sam Scott's great-grandfather worked in the cellar for Max Schubert and passed his knowledge down to Sam's grandfather. Sam enrolled in business at university, continuing the casual retailing with Booze Brothers – which he'd started while at school – picking up the trail with Baily & Baily. Next came wine wholesale experience with David Ridge, selling iconic Australian and Italian wines to the trade. This led to a job with Michael Fragos at Tatachilla in 2000 and since then he has been the 'I've been everywhere man', working all over Australia and in California. He moved to Bird in Hand winery at the end of '06, and from there he took the plunge on his own account. (JH)

95 **Nebbiolo Rosato 2021, Adelaide Hills** The producer understands nebbiolo oh, so well. Here, he brings lift and energy, delicacy and strength to a pretty complex rosato. Red cherry, dried strawberry, almond biscuit and a dash of pepper are the basis for the exploration. But just look at the tannin and acid management here: so bright, clean and enduring. Screw cap. | 12.8% alc. | Drink 2021-2025 | $26 | JP | ♥

Pinot Grigio 2021, Adelaide Hills Energy to burn here with an impressive purity of fruit. Citrus-blossom aromatics fill the glass alongside crab apple, lemon curd and grapefruit. The line and length, catapulted by the freshest acidity, is mighty energising. Screw cap. | 12.5% alc. | Drink 2021-2024 | $26 | JP

Fiano 2021, Adelaide Hills A tour de force of winemaking, the bouquet raising questions despatched to the 4 corners of the field by the palate, with its racy intensity of lemon and Meyer lemon in the lead; honey, nuts and salt flapping on the side. Screw cap. | 13.3% alc. | Drink 2021-2027 | $28 | JH

94 **Aglianico Rosato 2021, Adelaide Hills** Aglianico is a southern Italian variety, here picked early just as the red fruits start to show, and given minimal skin contact. It has an ethereal bouquet with savoury red crabapple aromas, and a deliberately bone dry palate. Will go anywhere. Screw cap. | 12.5% alc. | Drink 2021-2027 | $26 | JH

Sangiovese 2020, Adelaide Hills A fine-edged sangiovese, very smart, with a tickle of the kind of savouriness that winemaker Sam Scott usually seeks. Dark, soused cherries, plum, spice, earth, briar are delivered clean and composed with a light, caper-like lift to finish. Delish. Screw cap. | 13.9% alc. | Drink 2021-2026 | $26 | JP

Living Roots Best New Winery ★★★★★

159 Tynan Rd, Kuitpo SA 5201 **T www**.livingrootswine.com **OPEN** By appt **WINEMAKER** Sebastian Hardy, Anthony Neilson **EST.** 2016 **DOZENS** 400

Summed up perfectly in their own words: 'Living Roots is an urban winery in the Finger Lakes region of New York and a not-so-urban winery in the Adelaide Hills region of South Australia. It was founded by husband-and-wife team Sebastian (an Adelaide native and 6th generation

BAROSSA
FLEURIEU
MOUNT LOFTY RANGES
FAR NORTH
LIMESTONE COAST
LOWER MURRAY
THE PENINSULAS

winemaker) and Colleen Hardy (a New York native and marketer). The intercontinental label pays homage to family heritage while also branching out to new vineyards, styles and techniques. Best New Winery in the Halliday Wine Companion 2023. (JH)

96   **Grenache 2020, McLaren Vale** High-quality wine from start to finish; good depth to the colour, fragrant berries, flowers and spices on a bouquet that tells you there is a perfectly proportioned and composed palate, the tannins caressing the red and purple fruits. Diam. | 13.8% alc. | Drink 2022-2030 | $34 | JH

95   **Montepulciano 2020, Limestone Coast** Intense deep purple core; the bouquet stands aside to leave the exultant power of the sultry black fruits to tell the tale. A 'no, beg your pardon' full-bodied red wine. Diam. | 12.6% alc. | Drink 2025-2040 | $34 | JH

    Pepperberry Shiraz 2018, Adelaide Hills The bouquet exudes licorice, black cherries and berries, pepper and a waft of cinnamon stick. The freshness of the long finish is a highlight. Diam. | 13.4% alc. | Drink 2023-2038 | $34 | JH

Lobethal Road Wines ★★★★

2254 Onkaparinga Valley Road, Mount Torrens, SA 5244 **T** (08) 8389 4595 **www**.lobethalroad.com **OPEN** Thurs-Mon 11-5 **WINEMAKER** Michael Sykes **VITICULTURIST** David Neyle **EST**. 1998 **DOZENS** 7500 **VYDS** 10.5ha

Dave Neyle and Inga Lidums bring diverse, but very relevant, experience to the Lobethal Road vineyard. Dave has been in vineyard development and management in SA and Tasmania since 1990. Inga has 25+ years' experience in marketing and graphic design in Australia and overseas, with a focus on the wine and food industries. The property is managed with minimal chemical input. (JH)

93   **Sauvignon Blanc 2021, Adelaide Hills** A star performer for the producer with its zippy, zesty exuberance for life. Aromas of green apple, lantana, lemon, lime and grapefruit and snow pea. A burst of energy on the palate, so zesty and nicely concentrated in flavour. Super-juicy and ready to go. Screw cap. | 12.5% alc. | Drink 2021-2025 | $25 | JP

92   **Pinot Gris 2021, Adelaide Hills** The winemaker regards 2021 as a perfect growing season. It's produced a lovely gris, graceful and fine-featured. White flowers, apple blossom, nashi pear and spice. Boasts a smooth, rolling light texture across the tongue with some brisk, sherbety acidity. Coming together slowly and looking good. Screw cap. | 12.8% alc. | Drink 2021-2026 | $25 | JP

Longview Vineyard ★★★★★

154 Pound Road, Macclesfield, SA 5153 **T** (08) 8388 9694 **www**.longviewvineyard.com.au **OPEN** Wed-Sun 11-3 **WINEMAKER** Peter Saturno, Brian Walsh **VITICULTURIST** Chris Mein **EST**. 1995 **DOZENS** 22 000 **VYDS** 60ha

With a lifelong involvement in wine and hospitality, the Saturno family has been at the helm of Longview since 2007. A new cellar door and kitchen was unveiled in '17, adding to 16 accommodation suites, a popular function room and unique food and wine events in the vineyard. (JH)

95   **Whippet Sauvignon Blanc 2021, Adelaide Hills** A standout sauvignon blanc from a standout region that is noted for the grape variety. From the more complex end of the spectrum, with layers of tropical fruits and citrus nicely melded to light grassy elements, citrus peel and lime. Concise and complex. Screw cap. | 12% alc. | Drink 2021-2025 | $25 | JP

94   **Macclesfield Grüner Veltliner 2021, Adelaide Hills** Engaging aromatics lift from the glass – peach blossom, honeysuckle, melon, citrus and apple. A fine, delicate grüner builds upon a crisp structure, with a touch of light herbal savouriness to close. Grüner clearly loves its new home in the Hills. Screw cap. | 12.5% alc. | Drink 2021-2025 | $30 | JP

Mike Press Wines ★★★☆

PO Box 224, Lobethal, SA 5241 **T** (08) 8389 5546 **www**.mikepresswines.com.au **WINEMAKER** Mike Press **EST**. 1998 **DOZENS** 12 000 **VYDS** 22.7ha

Mike and Judy Press established their Kenton Valley Vineyards in 1998, when they purchased 34ha of land in the Adelaide Hills at an elevation of 500m. They planted mainstream cool-climate varieties intending to sell the grapes to other wine producers. Even an illustrious 43-year career in the wine industry did not prepare Mike for the downturn in grape prices that followed and that led to the development of the Mike Press wine label. (JH)

89   **Single Vineyard Pinot Noir Rosé 2021, Adelaide Hills** Confection pink hues on this well-priced, attractive young rosé. Boasts plenty of simple, red-fruited appeal: strawberries, cherries, raspberries. Gently creamy to taste. Screw cap. | 13% alc. | Drink 2021–2023 | $13 | JP

88   **Single Vineyard Chardonnay 2021, Adelaide Hills** A simple, light and ripe style of fruit-driven chardonnay, unoaked. Boasts pear, peach and melon flavours topped with crunchy acidity. All upfront and ready to drink now. Screw cap. | 13% alc. | Drink 2021–2023 | $13 | JP

     Single Vineyard Sauvignon Blanc 2021, Adelaide Hills Fresh, crisp and varietally true to form with plenty of grapefruit, lime and passionfruit aromas. Smooth and supple across the palate with green mango, melon notes. Soft, sweet finish. Screw cap. | 13% alc. | Drink 2021–2023 | $13 | JP

Mt Lofty Ranges Vineyard ⑨⑪⑭   ★★★★★

Harris Road, Lenswood, SA 5240 **T** (08) 8389 8339 **www**.mtloftyrangesvineyard.com.au **OPEN** Fri–Sun & public hols 11–5 **WINEMAKER** Peter Leske, Taras Ochota **EST**. 1992 **DOZENS** 3000 **VYDS** 4.6ha

Mt Lofty Ranges is owned and operated by Sharon Pearson and Garry Sweeney. Nestled high in the Lenswood subregion of the Adelaide Hills at an altitude of 500m, the very steep north-facing vineyard is pruned and picked by hand. The soil is sandy clay loam with a rock base of white quartz and ironstone, and irrigation is kept to a minimum to allow the wines to display vintage characteristics. (JH)

95   **Home Block Riesling 2021, Lenswood** Compared with the Aspire Riesling, here we see the opposite side of the riesling coin. A classic approach is taken and the fruit is up to the job, in dry lime, lemon, green apple and bright, clean, mineral notes. Taut and dry, with good line and length on show and impressive depth to boot – and it's still early days. Screw cap. | 12.5% alc. | Drink 2022–2026 | $30 | JP

Murdoch Hill ⑨   ★★★★★

260 Mappinga Road, Woodside, SA 5244 **T** (08) 7200 5018 **www**.murdochhill.com.au **OPEN** Thurs–Mon 11–4 **WINEMAKER** Michael Downer **EST**. 1998 **DOZENS** 5000 **VYDS** 17.3ha

A little over 20ha of vines have been established on the undulating, gum tree–studded countryside of Charlie and Julie Downer's 60yo Erika property, 4km east of Oakbank. Son Michael, with a bachelor of oenology degree from the University of Adelaide, is winemaker. (JH)

94   **Sauvignon Blanc 2021, Adelaide Hills** The white flowers of the bouquet move right towards jasmine, the palate veering left with flecks of grapefruit and snow pea, acidity brightening the finish. Screw cap. | 12% alc. | Drink 2022–2025 | $25 | JH

New Era Vineyards   ★★★★

PO Box 391, Woodside SA 5244 **T** 0413 544 246 **www**.neweravineyards.com.au **WINEMAKER** Robert Baxter, Iain Baxter **VITICULTURIST** Bob Baxter, Iain Baxter **EST**. 1988 **DOZENS** 1500 **VYDS** 15ha

The New Era vineyard is situated over a gold reef that was mined for 60 years until 1940, when all recoverable gold had been extracted. Much of the production is sold to other winemakers in the region. The small amount of wine made has been the subject of favourable reviews. (JH)

93   **Grüner Veltliner 2021, Adelaide Hills** Wild-fermented in both stainless steel and oak. Some winemaking thought has gone into the making of this grüner, delivering complex flavours in yellow apple, pear, ginger, lovage and white pepper. Entwined in a generous palate, textural and long offset by nicely by juicy acidity. Screw cap. | 13% alc. | Drink 2022–2025 | $27 | JP

Paracombe Wines ⑨⑪⑭   ★★★★

294b Paracombe Road, Paracombe, SA 5132 **T** (08) 8380 5058 **www**.paracombewines.com **OPEN** By appt **WINEMAKER** Paul Drogemuller **EST**. 1983 **DOZENS** 15000 **VYDS** 22.1ha

Paul and Kathy Drogemuller established Paracombe Wines in 1983 in the wake of the devastating Ash Wednesday bushfires. The winery is located high on a plateau at Paracombe, looking out over the Mount Lofty Ranges, and the vineyard is run with minimal irrigation and hand pruning to keep yields low. The wines are made onsite, with every part of the production process through to distribution handled from there. (JH)

93   **Pinot Blanc 2021, Adelaide Hills** One of those wines you keep returning to, each time discovering something new. It's the saline, oyster-shell and sea-spray quality that is central here: it's so clean and works the tastebuds in unison with honeysuckle, citrus blossom, preserved lemon and spiced apple.

BAROSSA

FLEURIEU

MOUNT LOFTY RANGES

FAR NORTH

LIMESTONE COAST

LOWER MURRAY

THE PENINSULAS

Conducts a purity of fruit flavour in tandem with a bright, crisp, lemon pithiness. One to watch. Screw cap. | 11% alc. | Drink 2021-2024 | $25 | JP

The Reuben 2017, Adelaide Hills 56/35/7/2% merlot/cabernet sauvignon/cabernet franc/malbec. The Reuben's lead grape can change from year to year, in '17 it's merlot's moment to take point. Immediately, there is a sense of elegance and fineness with plush plum, mulberry, brambly fruits and gentle spice, herbs. Medium in body, smooth in tannins with restrained, thoughtful oak, it's certainly one tidy wine package for the price. Screw cap. | 14.5% alc. | Drink 2021-2027 | $27 | JP

Patritti Wines ★★★★

13-23 Clacton Road, Dover Gardens, SA 5048 **T** (08) 8296 8261 **WWW**.patritti.com.au **OPEN** Mon-Sat 9-5 (7 days Dec) **WINEMAKER** James Mungall, Ben Heide **EST.** 1926 **DOZENS** 190000 **VYDS** 16ha

A family-owned and run business founded by Giovanni Patritti in 1926. Today it has 3 vineyard locations with a mix of old and new plantings. The most historic are patches are held by a long-term lease from the City of Marion, the oldest vines planted 1906. Today they are encircled by businesses of all kinds, residential housing and scattered remnants of vineyards which are actively protected by most residents and local planning boards. There are 6 ranges of wines. (JH)

96   **Marion Vineyard Grenache Shiraz 2020, Adelaide** Deeply coloured; rich aromas of spicy fruitcake and plum open the door to a beautifully cadenced spray of fresh red and purple fruits, with superfine tannins. Great value. Screw cap. | 13.5% alc. | Drink 2022-2033 | $40 | JH

Petaluma ★★★★★

254 Pfeiffer Road, Woodside, SA 5244 **T** (08) 8339 9390 **WWW**.petaluma.com.au **OPEN** 7 days 10-5 **WINEMAKER** Teresa Huezenroeder **VITICULTURIST** Mike Harms **EST.** 1976 **DOZENS** 130000 **VYDS** 240ha

The Petaluma range has been expanded beyond the core group of Croser sparkling, Clare Valley Riesling, Piccadilly Valley Chardonnay and Coonawarra Merlot. Newer arrivals of note include Adelaide Hills Viognier and Shiraz. The plantings in the Clare Valley, Coonawarra and Adelaide Hills provide a more than sufficient source of estate-grown grapes for the wines. A new winery and cellar door opened in 2015 on a greenfield site with views of Mount Lofty. In '17 Petaluma was acquired by Accolade. (JH)

96   **Croser Pinot Noir Chardonnay 2017, Piccadilly Valley** A traditional-method blend of 59/41% pinot noir/chardonnay. Abundant white peach and nectarine fruits, blanched almonds and a long, well-balanced finish. Looks as if it will handsomely repay a few more years on lees (preferably) or just with time in bottle. Diam. | 13% alc. | $42 | JH

Riposte ★★★★★

PO Box 256, Lobethal, SA 5241 **T** 0412 816 107 **WWW**.timknappstein.com.au **WINEMAKER** Tim Knappstein **EST.** 2006 **DOZENS** 14000

Tim Knappstein is a third-generation vigneron, his winemaking lineage dating back to 1893 in the Clare Valley. He made his first wines at the family's Stanley Wine Company and established his own wine company in the Clare Valley in 1976. After the sale of that company in '81, Tim relocated to Lenswood in the Adelaide Hills to make cool-climate wines. His quest has now been achieved with consistently excellent wines reflected in the winery's 5-star rating since the Wine Companion 2012. (JH)

95   **The Dagger Pinot Noir 2021, Adelaide Hills** The complete package here, immediately appealing and bright. Wrapped in perfectly ripe cherry fruits, bramble, plum, violet and dried herbs. Beautifully detailed, assisted by integrated oak, crunchy acid bite and leafy, savoury tannins. Impressive depth. Screw cap. | 13.5% alc. | Drink 2022-2028 | $24 | JP

The Foil Sauvignon Blanc 2021, Adelaide Hills Plenty of passionfruit, peach, lime, herbs, grass and cut apple here, combining the 2 halves – tropical and herbal – of the sauvignon personality beautifully. Acidity, smooth and bright, aids the delivery of these elements on the palate. Well sustained and with depth of flavour. Screw cap. | 12.5% alc. | Drink 2022-2024 | $24 | JP

The Scimitar Single Vineyard Riesling 2021, Clare Valley Raised in the Clare Valley, Tim Knappstein is a master riesling maker. His and his son's skills are in evidence here, with a masterclass in riesling celebrating depth of fruit and fantastic line and length. Lime juice, apple blossom, Golden Delicious apple and white peach are concentrated with flavours running deep. Linear and sleek in fine, chalky acidity and grapefruit pith. Stunning. Screw cap. | 11.5% alc. | Drink 2021-2031 | $24 | JP

The Stiletto Pinot Gris 2021, Adelaide Hills Embraces an almost Alsatian mentality in the delivery of this pinot gris with some deep-running layers of spice. Vibrant and enticing. Trademark apple, pear, lemon drop, dried fruit, bergamot and spice. Smooth and even with great persistence. Fine and elegant. Screw cap. | 12.5% alc. | Drink 2021-2024 | $24 | JP

The Katana Single Vineyard Chardonnay 2020, Adelaide Hills All class here, with the experienced hand of winemaker, Tim Knappstein, in evidence. Ripe, well-composed stone fruits, citrus, lime zest, nougat, jasmine with grilled-nut qualities of barrel fermentation, open and bright. Smooth, flavoursome and long through the finish. On point and delicious. Screw cap. | 13% alc. | Drink 2022-2026 | $29 | JP

BAROSSA
FLEURIEU
MOUNT LOFTY RANGES
FAR NORTH
LIMESTONE COAST
LOWER MURRAY
THE PENINSULAS

Shaw + Smith ⓠ

★★★★★

136 Jones Road, Balhannah, SA 5242 **T** (08) 8398 0500 **www.**shawandsmith.com **OPEN** 7 days 11-5
WINEMAKER Adam Wadewitz, Martin Shaw **VITICULTURIST** Murray Leake **EST.** 1989 **VYDS** 62ha

Cousins Martin Shaw and Michael Hill Smith MW already had unbeatable experience when they founded Shaw + Smith as a virtual winery in 1989. In '99 Martin and Michael purchased the 36ha Balhannah property, building the superbly designed winery in '00. It is here that visitors can taste the wines in appropriately beautiful surroundings. (JH)

96 **Sauvignon Blanc 2021, Adelaide Hills** A model of consistency over 32 vintages, Shaw + Smith Sauvignon Blanc continues to lead the way in '21 with a combination of fruit intensity and a seeming lightness of being. It's told in 2 parts; the first is exuberant tropicals, citrus and herbal interplay, but it quickly moves into a state of serious intensity, filigree acidity and mealy texture. That lasting impression saturates the tastebuds and stays with you. Screw cap. | 12% alc. | Drink 2021-2023 | $30 | JP | ♥

Riesling 2021, Adelaide Hills This is one of those sneaky wines that manage to hide their qualities until the finish and aftertaste, when all heaven breaks free. Its mix of lime, lemon, Granny Smith apple and white peach all demand a place. Screw cap. | 12% alc. | Drink 2023-2041 | $35 | JH

Sidewood Estate ⓠⓂⓐ

★★★★★

6 River Road Hahndorf, SA 5125 **T** (08) 8388 1673 **www.**sidewood.com.au **OPEN** Mon-Sun 11-5
WINEMAKER Darryl Catlin **VITICULTURIST** Mark Vella **EST.** 2004 **VYDS** 90ha

Sidewood Estate was established in 2004. It is owned by Owen and Cassandra Inglis who operate it as a winery and cidery. Situated in the Onkaparinga Valley, the vines weather the cool climate of the Adelaide Hills. Significant expenditure on regeneration of the vineyards was already well underway when Sidewood invested over $12 million in the expansion of the winery, increasing capacity from 500t to 2000t each vintage and implementing sustainable improvements. The expansion includes new bottling and canning facilities capable of handling 6 million bottles of wine and cider annually. A multimillion-dollar restaurant, cellar door and cidery was opened in 2020. (JH)

96 **Abel Pinot Noir 2019, Adelaide Hills** A light and open-weaved single-clone pinot. Bright brick red colour, a little shy to the nose, though thoroughly enticing, perhaps because of it. Shag-pile carpet softness on the palate offers a gentle feel, before you notice its fruit-driven acidity in a delicate wave of subtle and sophisticated pinot. As alluring as pinot can be. Screw cap. | 12.5% alc. | Drink 2020-2025 | $40 | TL

95 **Sauvignon Blanc 2021, Adelaide Hills** What do we ask of sauvignon blanc? We ask for this: a wine that combines tension and energy with simply joyous, live-for-the-moment fruit intensity. Kaffir lime, lemon zest, grapefruit, nettle and lemongrass moments dart in, out and around zippy acidity. Scintillating. Trophy Perth Royal Wine Awards 2021. Screw cap. | 12% alc. | Drink 2021-2024 | $22 | JP

94 **Mappinga Chardonnay 2020, Adelaide Hills** Makes an immediate creamy, buttery, complex impression with summery stone-fruit intensity, biscuit spice, nougat and citrus. The oak is well integrated, providing a background hum and vanillin creaminess. Plenty of flavour right here, and the price makes it a steal. Screw cap. | 12.5% alc. | Drink 2021-2026 | $25 | JP

Silver Lining

★★★★

60 Gleneagles Road, Mount Osmond, SA 5064 **T** 0438 736 052 **www.**silverliningwine.com.au
WINEMAKER Leigh Ratzmer, Marty Edwards **VITICULTURIST** Vitiworks, Simon Tolley **EST.** 2020 **DOZENS** 1200

The name alone says a lot about the positive and life-affirming attitude of this venture by Marty Edwards, whose love of the Adelaide Hills was nurtured by his family's pioneering involvement with The Lane Vineyard in Hahndorf. They have all left that business now but after being diagnosed with Parkinson's Disease in 2012, Marty decided he still had a lot more to give. He focused on his health and young family, but couldn't give up his passion for Hills vineyards and wines. Silver Lining Wines was the result, with proceeds going to Parkinson's Disease research. (TL)

92 **Sauvignon Blanc 2021, Adelaide Hills** Bristles with Adelaide Hills sauvignon blanc zesty swagger: kaffir lime leaf, grapefruit, nectarine and white peach with a splash of passionfruit. Energy to burn on the palate, with super bright limey acidity and citrus zestiness. Hits the sauvignon spot. Screw cap. | 12.5% alc. | Drink 2021-2025 | $25 | JP

Tapanappa

15 Spring Gully Road, Piccadilly, SA 5151 **T** (08) 7324 5301 **www**.tapanappa.com.au **OPEN** 7 days & public hols 11-4 **WINEMAKER** Brian Croser **EST**. 2002 **DOZENS** 2500 **VYDS** 16.7ha

Tapanappa was founded by Brian Croser in 2002. The word Tapanappa is probably derived from the local Aboriginal language and likely translates to 'stick to the path'. Through Tapanappa, Brian is continuing a career-long mission of matching the climate, soil and geology of distinguished sites to the right varieties, and then developing and managing the vineyards to optimise quality. Tapanappa is dedicated to producing unique 'wines of terroir' from its 3 distinguished sites in SA with its winery located in the heart of the Piccadilly Valley. (JH)

95 **Single Vineyard Riesling 2021, Eden Valley** Typically fragrant Eden Valley riesling aromas – they really are quite distinctive – in apple blossom, musk and white flowers, with lemon and lime zest. A delicate youngster, filigree fine acidity offsets a citrus-dominated, lively palate. Effortless in its beauty. Screw cap. | 13% alc. | Drink 2022-2031 | $35 | JP

Terre à Terre

15 Spring Gully Rd, Piccadilly SA 5151 **T** 0400 700 447 **www**.terreaterre.com.au **OPEN** At Tapanappa Wed-Sun 11-4 **WINEMAKER** Xavier Bizot **VITICULTURIST** Xavier Bizot **EST**. 2008 **DOZENS** 4000 **VYDS** 20ha

It would be hard to imagine 2 better-credentialled owners than Xavier Bizot (son of the late Christian Bizot of Bollinger fame) and wife Lucy Croser (daughter of Brian and Ann Croser). 'Terre à terre' is a French expression meaning down to earth. The vineyard area has increased, leading to increased production. In '15, Terre à Terre secured the fruit from one of the oldest vineyards in the Adelaide Hills, the Summertown Vineyard, which will see greater quantities of Daosa and a Piccadilly Valley pinot noir. (JH)

97 **Crayeres Vineyard Sauvignon Blanc 2021, Wrattonbully** This is a marvel. It has all of the sophistication and line of the Down to Earth Sauvignon Blanc, but it works within a startlingly streamlined framework of phenolics. This is slippery and supple in texture, with rivulets of flavour that ripple and course through the mouth, long after the wine has left. We are lucky to have the quality of sauvignon blanc that we do here in Australia and this is one of the very best. An amazing display of class. Screw cap. | 12.8% alc. | Drink 2022-2032 | $50 | EL | ♥

95 **Down to Earth Sauvignon Blanc 2021, Wrattonbully** Totally sophisticated; the fruit here is completely at one with the oak, which, save for the textural impact of soft, round shape, is largely invisible. This has persistent flow of flavour across the palate, trailing into a long and languid finish. Juniper, cassis, green apple skins, snow pea florals, brine, jasmine tea and blackberry bramble. Really smart. Restrained and seamless. Screw cap. | 12.8% alc. | Drink 2022-2028 | $32 | EL

The Lane Vineyard

5 Ravenswood Lane, Balhannah, SA 5244 **T** (08) 8388 1250 **www**.thelane.com.au **OPEN** 7 days 10-5 **WINEMAKER** Turon White **VITICULTURIST** Jared Stringer **EST**. 1993 **DOZENS** 25000 **VYDS** 75ha

The Lane Vineyard is one of the Adelaide Hills' elite wine tourism attractions, with a cellar door and restaurant that offers focused tastings by region and style, with endless views. Established by the Edwards family in '93, it was acquired by the UK's Vestey Group in '12, following their establishment of Coombe Farm in the Yarra Valley. Four distinct tiers of single-vineyard wines are produced at The Lane. (JH)

95 **Shiraz 2020, Adelaide Hills** Sometimes back labels can be useful for vinification information, and once in a blue moon are as accurate as this 'Aromas of forest fruits and clove followed by flavours of plum, black pepper and charcuterie with a silky texture and fine tannins.' Precisely. Screw cap. | 13.8% alc. | Drink 2022-2035 | $30 | JH

Tomich Wines

87 King William Road, Unley, SA 5061 **T** (08) 8299 7500 **www**.tomich.com.au **OPEN** Mon-Fri 9-5 **WINEMAKER** Randal Tomich **VITICULTURIST** Randal Tomich **EST**. 2002 **DOZENS** 40000 **VYDS** 85ha

Patriarch John Tomich was born on a vineyard near Mildura, where he learnt firsthand the skills and knowledge required for premium grape growing. He completed postgraduate studies in winemaking at the University of Adelaide in 2002 and embarked on the master of wine revision course from the Institute of Masters of Wine. His son Randal invented new equipment and techniques for tending the family's vineyard in the Adelaide Hills, resulting in a 60% saving in time and fuel costs. (JH)

94   **Woodside Vineyard Pinot Grigio 2021, Adelaide Hills** Adelaide Hills grigio is getting a reputation for a charming fineness and a lightness of touch with the grigio grape. It's explored here with an enticing, delicate perfume of spring blossom, honeysuckle, pear skin and freshly baked biscuits. Superfine acidity brings the palate alive. Beautiful brightness and balance. Delightful.   Screw cap. | 12.5% alc. | Drink 2021-2025 | $25 | JP

Wicks Estate Wines ★★★★★

21 Franklin Street, Adelaide, SA 5000 (postal) **T** (08) 8212 0004 **WWW**.wicksestate.com.au **WINEMAKER** Adam Carnaby **EST**. 2000 **DOZENS** 25000 **VYDS** 53.96ha

Tim and Simon Wicks had a long-term involvement with orchard and nursery operations at Highbury in the Adelaide Hills prior to purchasing their property at Woodside in '99. They planted fractionally less than 54ha of sauvignon blanc, shiraz, chardonnay, pinot noir, cabernet sauvignon, tempranillo and riesling. Wicks Estate has won more than its fair share of wine show medals over the years, the wines priced well below their full worth. (JH)

95   **Chardonnay 2021, Adelaide Hills** With ex-Seppelt winemaker Adam Carnaby at the helm, expectations are high. They are met in full with this terrific, fully-energised young chardonnay. Polished and focused in citrus and stone fruits, it shows additional complex ferment-derived characters as it works its way across the palate briskly. One more-ish chardonnay!   Screw cap. | 12.5% alc. | Drink 2022-2028 | $25 | JP

94   **Sauvignon Blanc 2021, Adelaide Hills** There's a lot of flavour here for such a small price. Has a foot in both sauvignon worlds, with an array of dusty herbals, gooseberry, Tahitian lime, green-skinned passionfruit and mango skin. Crisp acid crunch to close. Plenty to enjoy here. Does proud by the grape and the region.   Screw cap. | 12.5% alc. | Drink 2021-2025 | $20 | JP

Wine Architect ★★★★

38a Murray Street, Tanunda, SA 5352 **T** 0439 823 251 **WWW**.winearchitect.com.au **OPEN** Wed–Thurs 2-6, Fri 2-late, or by appt **WINEMAKER** Natasha Mooney **VITICULTURIST** Natasha Mooney, Caj Amadio **EST**. 2006 **DOZENS** 3000

This is a reasonably significant busman's holiday for Natasha Mooney, a well-known and highly talented winemaker whose 'day job' (her term) is to provide winemaking consultancy services for some of SA's larger wineries. This allows her to find small, unique parcels of grapes that might otherwise be blended into large-volume brands. She aims for mouthfeel and drinkability without high alcohol, and for that she should be loudly applauded. (JH)

94   **La Bise Rosé Grenache 2021, Adelaide Hills** Grenache blended with 15% pinot gris. A good rosé is a work of art. La Bise is a serious practitioner and it shows, in a wine of grace and charm, not to mention subtle flavour depth. Striking ruddy pink in colour. Gently scented dusty cherry, macerated strawberry, musk and dried herbs. Doesn't rush things on the palate, offering a dry, textural style with a crunchy red-fruit core. Of serious intent.   Screw cap. | 12.5% alc. | Drink 2021-2024 | $22 | JP

XO Wine Co ★★★★

13 Wicks Road, Kuitpo, SA 5172 **T** 0402 120 680 **WWW**.xowineco.com.au **WINEMAKER** Greg Clack, Kate Horstmann **EST**. 2015 **DOZENS** 1800

Greg Clack spent 11 years in McLaren Vale with Haselgrove Wines. In 2014 he took himself to the Adelaide Hills as chief winemaker at Chain of Ponds – this remains his day job, nights and days here and there devoted to XO. Kate has a degree in viticulture and oenology and a masters in wine business. XO's raison d'être revolves around small-batch, single-vineyard wines. The winemaking minimises wine movements, protecting freshness. (JH)

92   **Cherry Pie Light Red 2021, Adelaide Hills** 35/22/21/18/4% pinot noir/barbera/tempranillo/dolcetto/ grenache. The use of 100% carbonic maceration on pinot noir and dolcetto is made for this style of light dry red. It brings an extra level of liveliness and plummy sweet fruits to the fore. Ripe in black cherry, plum, spice and pepper with a touch of tasty amaro and firm tannins to close. Fab drinking early.   Screw cap. | 13% alc. | Drink 2021-2024 | $24 | JP

REGION

Adelaide Plains

Pure Vision Organic Wines ★★★

PO Box 258, Virginia, SA 5120 **T** 0412 800 875 **WWW**.purevisionwines.com.au **WINEMAKER** Joanne Irvine, Ken Carypidis **EST.** 2001 **DOZENS** 18000 **VYDS** 55ha

The Carypidis family runs 2 brands: Pure Vision and Nature's Step. The oldest vineyards were planted in 1975; organic conversion began in 2009. Growing grapes under a certified organic regime is much easier if the region is warm to hot and dry, conditions unsuitable for botrytis and downy mildew. The Adelaide Plains, where Pure Vision's vineyard is situated, is such a region. Ken Carypidis has been clever enough to secure the services of Joanne Irvine as co-winemaker. (JH)

88 **Nature's Step Organic Wild Ferment Pinot Grigio 2021, Adelaide Plains** A golden-blush colour introduces a soft and approachable young grigio nicely aromatic in honeysuckle, Golden Delicious apple, pear and white peach. Mild in flavour, nicely refreshing in soft acidity, it's a drink-now proposition. Screw cap. | 12.5% alc. | Drink 2022-2023 | $15 | JP

Cabernet Sauvignon 2020, Adelaide Plains Oak enjoys a background presence with black spiced fruits holding centre stage. For the price, there is a lot on offer from the fragrant violets, black fruits, anise and leafy appeal of the bouquet, to the nicely integrated palate. Firm, drying tannins to close. Screw cap. | 14.5% alc. | Drink 2022-2024 | $17 | JP

REGION

Clare Valley

Claymore Wines ⑨Ⓜ⑩ ★★★★☆

7145 Horrocks Way, Leasingham, SA 5452 **T** (08) 8843 0200 **WWW**.claymorewines.com.au **OPEN** Mon-Sat 11-5, Sun & public hols 11-4 **WINEMAKER** Rebekah Richardson **EST.** 1998 **DOZENS** 35000 **VYDS** 50ha

Claymore Wines is the venture of Anura Nitchingham, a medical professional who imagined this would lead the way to early retirement (which, of course, it did not). In '96 a 16ha block at Penwortham was purchased and planted to shiraz, merlot and grenache. Since then their portfolio has expanded to approximately 57ha, including 5 additional sites dotted from Auburn to Watervale. The wine labels are inspired by music that moves them: U2, Pink Floyd, Prince and more. (JH)

95 **Joshua Tree Riesling 2021, Clare Valley** The 2021 vintage was a godsend for almost all regions in South Australia, and the rieslings from this vintage are typified by balance and restraint across the board. In many cases, the wines produced this year are among the finest in decades – no small feat. This wine is generous and plump in the mouth, littered with green apples, ripe limes, nashi pears and juniper berries, punctuated by pockets of juicy, salty acidity. The wine is glorious now, but it will age gracefully too. Screw cap. | 12% alc. | Drink 2021-2031 | $22 | EL

94 **Dark Side of the Moon Shiraz 2020, Clare Valley** Blood plum, red licorice, blackberries, mulberries, raspberries and spice. This is a satisfying, dense and a compelling drink, especially at the price. Few places on the planet can achieve concentration in shiraz like South Australia can. It's very impressive. Screw cap. | 14.8% alc. | Drink 2021-2031 | $25 | EL

Clos Clare ⑨ ★★★★☆

45 Old Road, Watervale, SA 5452 **T** (08) 8843 0161 **WWW**.closclare.com.au **OPEN** W'ends 11-5 **WINEMAKER** Sam and Tom Barry **EST.** 1993 **DOZENS** 1600 **VYDS** 2ha

Clos Clare was acquired by the Barry family in '07. Riesling continues to be made from the 2ha unirrigated section of the original Florita Vineyard (the major part of that vineyard was already in Barry ownership). Its red wines come from a vineyard beside the Armagh site. (JH)

95 **Watervale Riesling 2021, Clare Valley** This is very smart. It is mineral, tightly coiled, powerful and sleek, all at once. The fruit is embedded in the acid; the acid likewise is wrapped in a sheath of talcy phenolics. Very fine ... I love the spool of flavour through the finish. Pristine. Stonking value for money. Screw cap. | 12% alc. | Drink 2022-2031 | $32 | EL

94 **Cemetery Block Shiraz 2018, Clare Valley** There's loads of spicy blackberries, blood plum and deli meat in here, with a fine, whippy splay of tannins that create pliable shape in the mouth. Mid weight. Smart. Delicious. Classy. Screw cap. | 14% alc. | Drink 2022-2028 | $28 | EL

Grosset ⑨

King Street, Auburn, SA 5451 **T** 1800 088 223 **WWW**.grosset.com.au **OPEN** 10-5 Wed-Sun (Spring) **WINEMAKER** Jeffrey Grosset, Brent Treloar **VITICULTURIST** Matthew O'Rourke **EST**. 1981 **DOZENS** 11000 **VYDS** 21ha

Jeffrey Grosset wears the unchallenged mantle of Australia's foremost riesling maker. Grosset's pre-eminence is recognised both domestically and internationally; however, he merits equal recognition for the other wines in his portfolio: Semillon Sauvignon Blanc from Clare Valley and Adelaide Hills, Chardonnay and Pinot Noir from the Adelaide Hills and Gaia, a bordeaux blend from the Clare Valley. Four estate-owned vineyards in the Clare Valley are certified organic and biodynamic. Best Value Winery in the Wine Companion 2018. (JH)

98 **G110 Riesling 2021, Clare Valley** Streamlined, long, lingering rivulets of spicy, almost austere riesling. It has integrity, shape and line, punctuated by detailed nuance and poise. It is spicy – even tense in its disposition – layered with nutmeg, spring flowers, brine, green apple skins, crushed limestone, mineral slate, snow pea tendril and even lemongrass. It is a kaleidoscope of flavour and texture, the puzzle pieces so small that it's hard to put them all together – describing it is a challenge (which is a good sign for the wine). It is enigmatic, statuesque and epic in every way. But it's also quiet, so do not underestimate it – make sure you tune in to its frequency. Screw cap. | 12.8% alc. | Drink 2022-2042 | EL | ♥

97 **Polish Hill Riesling 2021, Clare Valley** Grosset Polish Hill is always a supremely elegant, powerful wine with a proven track record of graceful ageing in the cellar, and a release such as this is the foundation upon which that reputation is built. This is concentrated, structured and long, with jasmine tea, saffron, lemon pith, aniseed, fennel flower, green apple skins and white pepper – all of which colour in the background for the lime flesh and Clare volume of flavour. Brilliant. Drink it now or cellar it as you normally would – it is sensational. Screw cap. | 12.9% alc. | Drink 2021-2041 | $72 | EL

Gaia 2019, Clare Valley Cabernet sauvignon and cabernet franc. 5000 bottles made. Elegant. This has grunt and low-down power, but the engine is built into a chassis of fine fruit and supple tannins. The acidity acts as the titanium bolt that holds it together, creating a strengthening framework of life and finesse. Blackberries, cassis, licorice, mulberry and raw cocoa, with nori, pink peppercorns and pastrami, blood plum, kelp and brine. Marvellous. Screw cap. | 13.7% alc. | Drink 2022-2042 | $89 | EL | ♥

96 **Alea Riesling 2021, Clare Valley** Alea ... the pretty, sweet thing in the family. Behind the incredibly attractive facade lies a complex, layered and wonderful wine that consists of exotic spice, citrus fruits and saline acidity, all shaped by fine, chalky structure. This '21 iteration is a precise and restrained version of itself, showing length, elegance and, most importantly, supreme deliciousness. Screw cap. | 12.3% alc. | Drink 2021-2036 | $44 | EL

Springvale Riesling 2021, Clare Valley Where the Polish Hill is the powerful, muscular one of the family, the Springvale is the often underestimated little sibling. Similarly powerfully structured, but leaning towards the spicy end of the spectrum rather than plum in the middle of fleshy fruit power. This is structured and saline, with layers of cut lime, red apple skins, saffron, turmeric and citrus pith. All of it encased in briny acidity and stretched out over an interminably long finish. Generous and structured at once. Super-smart. Screw cap. | 12.9% alc. | Drink 2021-2041 | $50 | EL

Jaeschke's Hill River Clare Estate ⑨ⓜ

406 Quarry Road, Clare, SA 5453 **T** (08) 8843 4100 **WWW**.hillriverclareestate.com.au **OPEN** 7 days 10-4 **WINEMAKER** Angela Meaney, Steve Braglia **VITICULTURIST** James Meyer **EST**. 1980 **DOZENS** 1750 **VYDS** 180ha

The Jaeschke family has been broadacre farming in the Hill River district for over 50 years. In May 2010 they purchased the neighbouring 180ha vineyard established by Penfolds in '80. It is planted to 17 varieties, including 21.2ha of riesling, the success of which has led to a stream of trophies and gold medals since '13, the first entry in wine shows. The venture began as the idea of daughter Michelle. That success, together with a cellar-door grant from PIRSA, led to the introduction of a cellar door, deck and lawn area for picnics, with barbeque facilities provided too. (JH)

91 **Single Vineyard Rosé 2021, Clare Valley** We live in a world where the pursuit of achieving the 'right' Provençal colour often comes at the cost of flavour. And might I remind everyone now: we do not drink colour. This rosé has more colour than most, and brings with it plenty of fleshy flavour – raspberry, pomegranate, cherries, lashings of spice, sprinkling of rose petals and a gently sweet little lick of RS (less than 2g/L) through the finish. A lot of uncomplicated pleasure here. Screw cap. | 12.6% alc. | Drink 2021-2023 | $20 | EL

Jeanneret Wines

★★★★☆

22 Jeanneret Road, Sevenhill, SA 5453 T (08) 8843 4308 WWW. jeanneretwines.com OPEN Mon-Sat 10-5 & public hols, Sun 12-5 WINEMAKER Ben Jeanneret, Harry Dickinson EST. 1992 DOZENS 18000 VYDS 36.5ha

Ben Jeanneret has progressively built the range and quantity of wines he makes at the onsite winery. In addition to the estate vineyards, Jeanneret has grape purchase contracts with owners of an additional 20ha of hand-pruned, hand-picked, dry-grown vines spread throughout the Clare Valley. The Rieslings are very good indeed. (JH)

| 94 | **Big Fine Girl Riesling 2020, Clare Valley** Cheesecloth, pie crust, lemon zest, apples and brine. This is plump and delicious - the textural palate really enhances the broadcast of fruit flavours, the juicy acid drags the wine across the palate and through into the long finish. This is a cool wine ... interesting, engaging, delicious, different. Like it. Screw cap. | 12.5% alc. | Drink 2021-2031 | $27 | EL |

Jim Barry Wines

★★★★★

33 Craig Hill Road, Clare, SA 5453 T (08) 8842 2261 WWW.jimbarry.com OPEN Mon-Sat 10-4 WINEMAKER Tom Barry, Ben Marx, Topsi Wallace VITICULTURIST Derrick Quinton EST. 1959 DOZENS 80000 VYDS 380ha

Jim Barry's wine business is led by Peter Barry; the third generation represented by Peter and Sue Barry's children, Tom, Sam and Olivia. Tom's wife is also called Olivia, and she (Olivia Hoffmann) has set a whirlwind pace, graduating with a bachelor of commerce from the University of Adelaide, then a master of wine business. Peter purchased the famed Florita Vineyard with his brothers in '86 (one of the oldest vineyards in the Clare Valley, planted in 1962). The second generation also purchased Clos Clare in '08. Jim Barry Wines is able to draw upon 345ha of mature Clare Valley vineyards, plus 35ha in Coonawarra. In Nov '16, Jim Barry Wines released the first commercial assyrtiko grown and made in Australia. A founding member of Australia's First Families of Wine. (JH)

| 97 | **The Florita Riesling 2021, Clare Valley** Tasted alongside the Florita Cellar Release ('15) and the Wolta Wolta ('19), and never was there a more achingly beautiful trio of wines. This ranks slightly higher than the Cellar Release due to its startling clarity, and scintillating, persuasive power. It will live forever and a day, and I bet at Cellar Release time in '27, when we see this wine again, you will be thanking your lucky stars you stocked up now, in '22. Astounding. Screw cap. | 12% alc. | Drink 2022-2042 | $55 | EL |

Loosen Barry Wolta Wolta Dry Riesling 2019, Clare Valley This is full on - intensely concentrated, penetrating flavour and acidity that is so seamlessly countersunk into all aspects of the experience that you barely notice any one aspect of it. And yet, as time slows in a moment of emergency, so too does this - it veritably suspends time. The flavour lives on interminably. I'm quivering in anticipation for the '21 release ... in the meantime, drinking this experiential wine. Screw cap. | 12.3% alc. | Drink 2022-2042 | $120 | EL

| 96 | **The McRae Wood Shiraz 2019, Clare Valley** Savoury, spicy and intense shiraz here, with emphasis on the savoury. This has layers of shaved hung deli meat, amaro herbs, a hint of bacon fat, mulberries, blood plums, salted licorice and tapenade, too. The tannins are firm, promising a long life in front of it, although everything is already so nicely integrated, you could drink it tonight. You could, but you shouldn't - it'll evolve so nicely over the years to come. Screw cap. | 14% alc. | Drink 2022-2039 | $60 | EL |

Cellar Release The Florita Riesling 2015, Clare Valley Released after 6 years in bottle, and when you drink it you'll agree this was a wise move. This is gloriously toasty: yellow flowers (there's a buttercup vibe through the finish), hinoki, Golden Delicious apples, preserved lemons, yellow peach, pulverised quartz, saline acidity and a creamy undercurrent of crushed nuts. This is verging on sublime. Or perhaps it just is. Screw cap. | 12.3% alc. | Drink 2022-2035 | $65 | EL

| 94 | **Crimson Gold Shiraz 2018, Clare Valley** Good thing that Jim Barry was into wine as well as horses, because this wine is more streamlined, sleek and impressive here than it sounds like its namesake ever was on the track. Gorgeous. Plenty of exotic spice, blood, hung deli meat, leather strap, raw cocoa and purple berries to capture and hold interest. Brilliant value. Screw cap. | 14% alc. | Drink 2022-2029 | $30 | EL |

Knappstein

★★★★★

2 Pioneer Avenue, Clare, SA 5453 T (08) 8841 2100 WWW.knappstein.com.au OPEN 7 days 10-4 WINEMAKER Michael Kane, Mike Farmilo (Consultant) EST. 1969 DOZENS 75000 VYDS 114ha

Knappstein's full name is Knappstein Enterprise Winery, reflecting its history before being acquired by Petaluma, then part of Lion Nathan, followed by Accolade. After a period of corporate ownership, Knappstein has now come full circle and is back in private ownership, purchased in '19 by Yinmore Wines. The wines are produced from the substantial mature estate Enterprise, Ackland, Yertabulti and The Mayor's vineyards. (JH)

95 **Ackland Single Vineyard Watervale Riesling 2021, Clare Valley** This is an acid-driven, lean and minerally riesling, with tight lemon, lime and grapefruit. If you thought the Enterprise was taut and terrific, it ain't got nothin' on this. With long sinewy muscles and a tense concoction of fruit on the palate, this is very good, if not a little austere in its youth, currently. Age it. Screw cap. | 12% alc. | Drink 2021-2036 | $30 | EL

Enterprise Vineyard Riesling 2021, Clare Valley The palate here is lean, restrained, minerally and fine, with crushed quartz, saline acidity, jasmine-tea tannins and layers upon layers of citrus pith, zest and flesh. Length of flavour shows the pedigree and ageability of the wine. Very smart indeed. Screw cap. | 12% alc. | Drink 2021-2036 | $30 | EL

Liz Heidenreich Wines ★★★★

PO Box 783, Clare, SA 5453 **T** 0407 710 244 **www**.lizheidenreichwines.com **WINEMAKER** Liz Heidenreich **EST.** 2018 **DOZENS** 2000 **VYDS** 6ha

In 1866, Liz Heidenreich's great-great-grandfather Georg Adam Heidenreich, a Lutheran minister, was sent from Hamburg to the Barossa Valley to provide religious care. In 1936, Liz Heidenreich's grandfather planted vines at Vine Vale; those vines still in production, still owned and managed by the Heidenreich family. Liz decided to follow her family heritage and enrolled in a post-graduate winemaking degree course at the University of Adelaide. She says her spiritual wine homes are the Barossa and Clare valleys. (JH)

94 **Watervale Riesling 2021, Clare Valley** Cut lime, lemon sherbet, white pepper and jasmine tea. Plenty going on here. There's an austerity to the acid, which is a refreshing counterpoint to the voluminous fruit. A beautiful wine. Screw cap. | 12.5% alc. | Drink 2022-2032 | $25 | EL

Mr Mick ★★★★

7 Dominic Street, Clare, SA 5453 **T** (08) 8842 2555 **www**.mrmick.com.au **OPEN** 7 days 10-5 **WINEMAKER** Tim Adams, Brett Schutz **EST.** 2011 **DOZENS** 30000 **VYDS** 195ha

This is the venture of Tim Adams and Pam Goldsack. The name was chosen to honour KH (Mick) Knappstein, a legend in the Clare Valley and the broader Australian wine community. Tim worked at Leasingham Wines with Mick between 1975 and '86, and knew him well. When Tim and Pam acquired the Leasingham winery in Jan 2011, together with its historic buildings, it brought the wheel full circle. (JH)

90 **Riesling 2021, Clare Valley** This delivers a classy and totally inline riesling for $17. That's not bad, considering the wines I used to drink for the same price back in the day. Lemon zest, lime flesh, green apples and a lick of chalk. Everything here, everything good. Screw cap. | 12.2% alc. | Drink 2021-2028 | $17 | EL

Rosé 2021, Clare Valley So it's a little bit sweet, it's got plenty of flavour (think along the lines of raspberry, pomegranate, watermelon and strawberry), it's vibrant and it's uncomplicated. The acid is pert enough to prop it all up, making for some seriously unfettered and delicious summer drinking. Value for money is hard to beat, here. Screw cap. | 11.5% alc. | Drink 2022-2023 | $17 | EL

Shiraz 2018, Clare Valley Surprisingly, 24 months in predominantly American oak has not yielded an oak bomb. Instead, the fruit has enough heft and weight to rise above the oak that encases it, and drives the wine across the mouth – powered by blackberries, cocoa, cassis, jubes and gentle spice. Compelling drinking for the money. Big bang for buck, if big flavour is your proclivity. Screw cap. | 14.7% alc. | Drink 2021-2027 | $17 | EL

Mitchell ★★★★

246 Hughes Park Road, Sevenhill via Clare, SA 5453 **T** (08) 8843 4258 **www**.mitchellwines.com **OPEN** 7 days 11-5 **WINEMAKER** Andrew Mitchell, Simon Pringle **VITICULTURIST** Angus Mitchell **EST.** 1975 **DOZENS** 15000 **VYDS** 70ha

One of the stalwarts of the Clare Valley, established by Jane and Andrew Mitchell, producing long-lived rieslings and cabernet sauvignons in classic regional style. A lovely old stone apple shed is the cellar door and upper section of the upgraded winery. Children Angus and Edwina are now working in the business, heralding generational changes. Over the years, the Mitchells have established or acquired 70ha of vineyards on 4 excellent sites, some vines over 60 years old; all are managed organically, with biodynamic composts used for over a decade. (JH)

BAROSSA

FLEURIEU

MOUNT LOFTY RANGES

FAR NORTH

LIMESTONE COAST

LOWER MURRAY

THE PENINSULAS

92   **Pinot Gris 2021, Clare Valley** A barrel ferment component is evident both aromatically and in the mouth, however it's subtle enough to work in concert with the fruit. Nashi pears, salted lychee and layers of white plum, crushed limestone and even snow pea tendrils. Lots to like, and framed by soft talcy phenolics. Very fresh.   Screw cap. | 13% alc. | Drink 2022-2025 | $25 | EL

Mount Horrocks ★★★★★

The Old Railway Station, Curling Street, Auburn, SA 5451 **T** (08) 8849 2243 **www**.mounthorrocks. com **OPEN** W'ends & public hols 10-5 **WINEMAKER** Stephanie Toole **EST**. 1982 **DOZENS** 3500 **VYDS** 9.4ha

Owner and winemaker Stephanie Toole has never deviated from the pursuit of excellence in the vineyard and winery. She has 3 vineyard sites in the Clare Valley, each managed using natural farming and organic practices. The attention to detail and refusal to cut corners is obvious in all her wines. The cellar door is in the renovated old Auburn railway station. (JH)

97   **Watervale Riesling 2021, Clare Valley** The scented white flower and lime blossom aromas promise much to come on the palate, and don't deceive. It is utterly delicious, with swathes of lime and pink grapefruit which are fruit-sweet (not RS). Absolutely out of the box.   Screw cap. | 12.6% alc. | Drink 2021-2036 | $37 | JH

96   **Cabernet Sauvignon 2020, Clare Valley** This is beautiful. A medium bodied, super-elegant, superfine cabernet. It remains true to its Clare roots with dark chocolate and cocoa scattered throughout the veritable forest of black and purple berries. The acidity is fresh and juicy and countersunk into all aspects of the fruit. In fact, the wine is so seamlessly dovetailed at all junctures (oak, fruit, acid, tannins), that is moves into the supple, slinky, willowy space. This is a truly beautiful wine.   Screw cap. | 14.3% alc. | Drink 2022-2038 | $60 | EL

      Cabernet Sauvignon 2019, Clare Valley Perfect colour. A polished and elegant wine that is in the heart of the best Clare Valley cabernets, with blackcurrant and cedar marking the bouquet and perfectly balanced medium to full-bodied palate. Its finish and aftertaste are special, too, as is the modest alcohol.   Screw cap. | 14% alc. | Drink 2025-2039 | $60 | JH

O'Leary Walker Wines ★★★★★

7093 Horrocks Highway, Leasingham, SA 5452 **T** 1300 342 569 **www**.olearywalkerwines.com **OPEN** Mon-Sat 10-4, Sun & public hols 11-4 **WINEMAKER** David O'Leary, Nick Walker, Jack Walker, Luke Broadbent **EST**. 2001 **DOZENS** 20000 **VYDS** 45ha

When David O'Leary and Nick Walker took the plunge in 2001 to establish their own winery and brand, they had more than 30 years' experience as winemakers for some of Australia's biggest wine groups. Initially the principal focus was on the Clare Valley with 10ha of riesling, shiraz and cabernet sauvignon as the main plantings. Thereafter attention swung to the Adelaide Hills where they now have 35ha of chardonnay, cabernet sauvignon, pinot noir, shiraz, sauvignon blanc and merlot. The vineyards were certified organic in '13. (JH)

98   **The Sleeper Reserve Shiraz 2018, Barossa Valley** A flying start ex high-quality fruit, and extended time on skins has worked exactly as intended; in the old wine-show terminology, full bodied, soft finish. A delicious shiraz now or 30 years hence.   Diam. | 14.5% alc. | Drink 2025-2050 | $70 | JH

94   **Pinotage 2021, Clare Valley** Plush black and red cherries adorn the front of the wine, while salted pomegranate, red apples and a wild, earthy element bring up the rear. The tannins are a highlight, being chewy, malleable and fun. All in all, this is a bit of a burster. I like it, as will others.   Screw cap. | 13% alc. | Drink 2022-2029 | $30 | EL

Penna Lane Wines ★★★★☆

Lot 51 Penna Lane, Penwortham via Clare, SA 5453 **T** 0403 462 431 **www**.pennalanewines.com.au **OPEN** Fri-Sun 11-5 **WINEMAKER** Peter Treloar, Steve Baraglia **EST**. 1998 **DOZENS** 4500 **VYDS** 4.37ha

Penna Lane is located in the beautiful Skilly Valley, 10km south of Clare. The estate vineyard includes shiraz, cabernet sauvignon and semillon and is planted at an elevation of 450m, which allows a long, slow ripening period, usually resulting in wines with intense varietal fruit flavours. (JH)

95   **Watervale Riesling 2021, Clare Valley** Fleshy, plump, pretty riesling with layers of sherbety fresh acid and fruit. Gorgeous. Delicious. Yum. 2021 rocks.   Screw cap. | 12.5% alc. | Drink 2021-2031 | $28 | EL

Rieslingfreak ★★★★★

103 Langmeil Road, Tanunda, SA 5352 **T** 0439 336 250 **www**.rieslingfreak.com **OPEN** Sat 11-4 or by appt **WINEMAKER** John Hughes, Belinda Hughes **VITICULTURIST** Richard Hughes **EST**. 2009 **DOZENS** 7500 **VYDS** 40ha

The name of John Hughes' winery leaves no doubt about his long-term ambition: to explore every avenue of riesling, whether bone-dry or sweet, coming from regions across the wine world, albeit with a strong focus on Australia. (JH)

96   **No. 2 Riesling 2021, Clare Valley** Crushed rock minerals are peppered into the fine, saline fruit. This is elegant and restrained, with layers of subtle flavour that reveal themselves over the course of drinking. What a wonderful wine – minerally and taut, with chalky phenolic structure that binds the fruit in place. While this is not the most complex wine in the line-up, it has so many different facets of flavour that it is impossible to underestimate. Just wait for the length of flavour to recede: you'll be waiting a while.   Screw cap. | 10.5% alc. | Drink 2021-2041 | $37 | EL

95   **No. 4 Riesling 2021, Eden Valley** Citrus pith and lime flesh dominate the very fine aromatics. On the palate, I am carried away on a sea of flavour, only just resurfacing through the finish to appreciate what has just occurred. Generous fruit ebbs and flows across the tongue, the acidity is threaded in and out in a fine, saliva-inducing web. On closer inspection there is white pepper, aniseed and fennel flower too. Another masterful release, at once voluminous and restrained, certainly enduringly long. The price is mind-blowing. This is the fine, delicate, spicy wine in the line-up. Screw cap. | 11% alc. | Drink 2021-2036 | $27 | EL

94   **No. 3 Riesling 2021, Clare Valley** Saffron and turmeric lace the aromatics, straying into the pink peppercorn and aniseed space. On the palate the wine is rich and intense, a very different shape to its peers, and all the better for it – its identity is clear and pronounced. Salted lemon, lime, crunchy green apple and white peach, too. Super-pleasurable and multidimensional. Astounding price. Screw cap. | 11% alc. | Drink 2021-2036 | $27 | EL

Sevenhill Cellars ★★★★☆

111c College Road, Sevenhill, SA 5453 **T** (08) 8843 5900 **www.**sevenhill.com.au **OPEN** 7 days 10-5 **WINEMAKER** Will Shields **EST.** 1851 **DOZENS** 25000 **VYDS** 96ha

One of the historical treasures of Australia; the oft-photographed stone wine cellars are the oldest in the Clare Valley and winemaking has been an enterprise within this Jesuit province since 1851. All the wines reflect the estate-grown grapes from old vines. In recent years, Sevenhill Cellars has increased its vineyard holdings from 74ha to 96ha and, naturally, production has risen. (JH)

94   **Inigo Cabernet Sauvignon 2019, Clare Valley** Cassis, red apples, blackberry pie and pomegranates. This is laden with aromas and spice: pink peppercorn, licorice and dark cocoa. The palate is concentrated and lithe, the wine lingering long after it is gone. The tannins are interesting: very fine, quite grippy, and they ride in tandem with the fruit, steering it through the long finish. Screw cap. | 14% alc. | Drink 2022-2036 | $28 | EL

Skillogalee ★★★★☆

Trevarrick Road, Sevenhill via Clare, SA 5453 **T** (08) 8843 4311 **www.**skillogalee.com.au **OPEN** 7 days 9.30-5 **WINEMAKER** Kerri Thompson **VITICULTURIST** Brendan Pudney **EST.** 1989 **DOZENS** 15000 **VYDS** 51ha

David and Diana Palmer established Skillogalee in 1989. In 2002 the Palmers purchased next-door neighbour Waninga Vineyard with 30ha of 30-year-old vines. David and Diana retired in July 2021, selling Skillogalee to the Clausen family. Talented winemaker Kerri Thompson (Wines by KT), who has long consulted to the Palmer family while making her own wines at Skillogalee, took over in the cellar from the 2022 vintage.

96   **Trevarrick Single Contour Riesling 2021, Clare Valley** '21 was a pristine vintage, producing wines just like this: so perfumed, lemon sherbet and citrus pith frill the edges of lime flesh, juniper berry and elderflowers. In the mouth the wine touches high notes of pure and crystalline fruit. It is spicy, fine and tense with layers of saline acidity. Worth the wait. Screw cap. | 12% alc. | Drink 2021-2036 | $53 | EL

Steve Wiblin's Erin Eyes ★★★★☆

58 Old Road, Leasingham, SA 5452 **T** 0418 845 120 **www.**erineyes.com.au **WINEMAKER** Steve Wiblin **EST.** 2009 **DOZENS** 2500

Steve Wiblin became a winemaker accidentally when he was encouraged by his mentor at Tooheys Brewery. He watched the acquisition of Wynns and Seaview by Penfolds and then Seppelt, before moving to Orlando. He moved from the world of big wineries to small when he co-founded Neagles Rock in 1997. In 2009 he left Neagles Rock and established Erin Eyes explaining, 'In 1842 my English convict forebear John Wiblin gazed into a pair of Erin eyes. That gaze changed our family make-up and history forever. In the Irish-influenced Clare Valley, what else would I call my wines but Erin Eyes?' (JH)

BAROSSA
FLEURIEU
MOUNT LOFTY RANGES
FAR NORTH
LIMESTONE COAST
LOWER MURRAY
THE PENINSULAS

95 **Pride of Erin Single Vineyard Reserve Riesling 2021, Clare Valley** Finer and more restrained than the Emerald Isle Riesling – the spices and layers are dovetailed into the acidity and phenolic texture more seamlessly here. Very long, refined and saline. Quite beautiful. Screw cap. | 11.5% alc. | Drink 2021-2036 | $35 | EL

Taylors

89A Winery Road, Auburn, SA 5451 **T** (08) 8849 1111 **www**.taylorswines.com.au **OPEN** Mon-Fri 9-5, w'ends 10-4 **WINEMAKER** Mitchell Taylor, Adam Eggins, Phillip Reschke, Chad Bowman, Thomas Darmody **VITICULTURIST** Peter Rogge **EST**. 1969 **DOZENS** 250000 **VYDS** 400ha

The family-founded and owned Taylors continues to flourish and expand – its vineyards are now by far the largest holding in the Clare Valley. Over the years there have been changes in terms of the winemaking team and the wine style and quality. Recent entries in international wine shows have resulted in a rich haul of trophies and gold medals for wines at all pricepoints. A founding member of Australia's First Families of Wine, the family celebrated 50 years in '19. (JH)

96 **St Andrews Riesling 2021, Clare Valley** Wow – what a beautiful wine. This is restrained and delicate, with layers upon layers of citrus blossom, nashi pears, Granny Smith apples, lime flesh and juniper berries, all of it coalescing and swirling on the palate as the tide eddies the shore. It is plump, after all of that – it has shape and generosity and volume. The acidity is salty and bright, urging the fruit through the long finish and encouraging it even further into the memory. What a wine. Screw cap. | 12% alc. | Drink 2021-2036 | $43 | EL

Tim Adams

156 Warenda Road, Clare, SA 5453 **T** (08) 8842 2429 **www**.timadamswines.com.au **OPEN** 7 days 10-4.30 **WINEMAKER** Tim Adams, Brett Schutz **VITICULTURIST** Mick Plumridge **EST**. 1986 **DOZENS** 60000 **VYDS** 195ha

Tim Adams and partner Pam Goldsack preside over a highly successful business. Having expanded the range of estate plantings with tempranillo, pinot gris and viognier, the business took a giant step forward in '09 with the acquisition of the 80ha Leasingham Rogers Vineyard from CWA, followed in '11 by the purchase of the Leasingham winery and winemaking equipment. The winery is now a major contract winemaking facility for the region. (JH)

95 **Skilly Ridge Riesling 2021, Clare Valley** This is an interesting wine: it has a preserved citrus austerity initially, but the wine quickly morphs into a toasty, rounded, opulent space which is littered with cheesecloth, baked pie crust, Golden Delicious apples and nashi pear. The length of flavour endures long after the wine is gone, making for a rather sumptuous drinking experience. I keep expecting the toastiness to lose its form through the finish, but it doesn't. It's very impressive. Screw cap. | 11.5% alc. | Drink 2021-2031 | $30 | EL

ZONE

Limestone Coast

REGION

Coonawarra

Bailey Wine Co ★★★★

PO Box 368, Penola, SA 5277 **T** 0417 818 539 **www**.baileywineco.com **WINEMAKER** Tim Bailey **EST**. 2015 **DOZENS** 750

After 2 decades living and working in Coonawarra, Tim Bailey decided to take a busman's holiday by establishing his own small wine business. Tim worked at Leconfield for 21 years, and has also worked in the Sonoma Valley of California, travelling through the Napa Valley as well as France. Tim has a simple philosophy: 'Find great growers in the regions and let the vineyard shine through in the bottle.' (JH)

95 **Hyde Park Vineyard Shiraz 2019, Grampians** Hyde Park Vineyard is 5km southwest of Great Western and shares the subregion's lively shiraz spice. It's very much evident in this wine, with its winding layers of cassia bark, bush mint and aniseed. Brings a natural buoyancy and energy to the grape against a background of blueberry, black fruits, savoury oak and fine, velvety tannins. The best of both worlds with good drinking now or later. Screw cap. | 14% alc. | Drink 2021-2033 | $30 | JP

Bellwether ★★★★★

14183 Riddoch Highway, Coonawarra, SA 5263 **T** 0417 080 945 **WWW**.bellwetherwines.com.au **OPEN** 7 days 12–4 **WINEMAKER** Sue Bell **VITICULTURIST** Mike Wetherall, Peter Bird, Nick and Heather Laycock, Ashley Ratcliff, Rob Bennett, the Chalmers family, Brett Proud **EST.** 2008 **DOZENS** 2500

Underpinning Sue Bell's winemaking philosophy is the impact of climate change and the need for future classic varieties to be grown in the right regions. In '08, Sue and business partner, Andrew Rennie, bought the historic Glen Roy shearing shed, built around 1868 and sitting on 6h of classic Aussie bush. It is now a winery and cellar door with space to host food, wine and music events. There's an extensive produce garden, a camping area and glamping, too. It's all part of her thoughtful plan to reconnect with the land sustainably and with purpose. (JF)

96 **Chardonnay 2017, Tasmania** A sun-kissed hue entices, as do the florals and stone-fruit aromatics, with a waft of ginger spice. This is complex, detailed and impressive. The palate is key with its tight acid line cutting through the richness of flavours resulting in a moreish and savoury wine. Screw cap. | 12.6% alc. | Drink 2021-2027 | $70 | JF

Cabernet Sauvignon 2016, Coonawarra The flagship red in the range is released with bottle age and always reveals an elegance. A neat fusion of cassis and potpourri, curry leaf, ironstone and earth with a sprinkling of woodsy spices. Medium bodied as it unfurls with fine, powdery tannins and great persistence. A contemplative wine in a way, yet equally lovely to drink. Screw cap. | 14% alc. | Drink 2021-2031 | $70 | JF

95 **Ant Series Malbec 2019, Wrattonbully** This savoury, juicy wine impresses and entices from the very start with its noir-red hue, followed by bold aromas and flavours. It's earthy, gravelly and ferrous, yet the full-bodied palate is smooth as velvet thanks to those plush tannins. This is a sophisticated malbec. Bravo. Screw cap. | 13.3% alc. | Drink 2022-2032 | $35 | JF

DiGiorgio Family Wines ★★★★

14918 Riddoch Highway, Coonawarra, SA 5263 **T** (08) 8736 3222 **WWW**.digiorgio.com.au **OPEN** 7 days 10–5 **WINEMAKER** Peter Douglas, Bryan Tonkin **EST.** 1998 **DOZENS** 25000 **VYDS** 353.53ha

Stefano DiGiorgio emigrated from Abruzzo, Italy, in 1952. Over the years, he and his family gradually expanded their holdings at Lucindale to 126ha. In '02 the family purchased the historic Rouge Homme winery and its surrounding 13.5ha of vines from Southcorp. The plantings have since been increased to over 350ha, the lion's share to cabernet sauvignon. The enterprise offers full winemaking services to vignerons on the Limestone Coast. (JH)

90 **Kongorong Riesling 2021, Mount Gambier** Spring florals and lime zest on the nose. In the mouth it gathers momentum, with green apples and pithy acidity, talcy texture the stars. Smart, mineral and very fine. The '21 vintage is a sensational lens through which to view this wine. Screw cap. | 11.9% alc. | Drink 2022-2028 | $20 | EL

Lucindale Shiraz 2020, Limestone Coast Really good intensity here, with savoury tannins shaping black forest fruits, and all of it wrapped in a slick, sweet oak box. Nicely done. Great value for money. Screw cap. | 14% alc. | Drink 2022-2027 | $20 | EL

Katnook ★★★★★

Riddoch Highway, Coonawarra, SA 5263 **T** (08) 8737 0300 **WWW**.katnookestate.com.au **OPEN** Mon–Fri 10–5, w'ends 12–5 **WINEMAKER** Dan McNicol **EST.** 1979 **DOZENS** 90000 **VYDS** 198ha

Katnook has taken significant strides since acquisition by Freixenet, the Spanish cava producer. The historic stone woolshed in which the second vintage in Coonawarra (1896) was made, and which has served Katnook since 1980, has been restored. Likewise, the former office of John Riddoch has been restored and is now the cellar door. In Mar '18 Freixenet announced that Henkell, the Oetker Group's sparkling wine branch, had acquired 50.67% of Freixenet's shares, creating the world's leading sparkling wine group. The brand was sold to Accolade in Aug '20. (JH)

97 **Prodigy Shiraz 2019, Coonawarra** Did someone say bacon fat? This is supremely aromatic and hedonistic – there is fresh maple, forest-fruit compote, salted licorice, raw cocoa, blood plum and mulberries. In the mouth the wine follows suit, the trump card – nay, the bower – is the web of savoury tannin that extends to all reaches of the mouth. This is chewy and good. A beautiful wine. Screw cap. | 14.2% alc. | Drink 2022-2042 | $129 | EL

BAROSSA

FLEURIEU

MOUNT LOFTY RANGES

FAR NORTH

LIMESTONE COAST

LOWER MURRAY

THE PENINSULAS

Leconfield ★★★★★

15454 Riddoch Highway, Coonawarra, SA 5263 **T** (08) 8323 8830 **WWW**.leconfieldwines.com
OPEN By appt **WINEMAKER** Paul Gordon, Greg Foster **VITICULTURIST** Bendt Rasmussen **EST.** 1974 **DOZENS** 25000
VYDS 43.7ha

Sydney Hamilton purchased the unplanted property that was to become Leconfield
in 1974, having worked in the family wine business for over 30 years until his retirement in
the mid '50s. When he acquired the property, and set about planting it, he was 76 and
reluctantly bowed to family pressure to sell Leconfield to nephew Richard in '81. Richard has
progressively increased the vineyards to their present level. (JH)

95   **Old Vines Riesling 2020, Coonawarra** Marmalade on buttered toast, spiced apples, salted citrus
and a weighty, almost voluminous countenance about it. It doesn't billow, like a Clare Valley riesling
does, or race like a riesling from the Great Southern. Rather it has a stately, concentrated and
measured presence of flavour in the mouth that lingers long after the wine has gone. Rich, engaging
and sinewy through the finish. Very smart.   Screw cap. | 13% alc. | Drink 2022-2037 | $28 | EL

Lindeman's (Coonawarra) ★★★★★

Level 8, 161 Collins Street, Melbourne, Vic 3000 (postal) **T** 1300 651 650 **WWW**.lindemans.com
WINEMAKER Brett Sharpe **EST.** 1965

Lindeman's Coonawarra vineyards have assumed a greater importance than ever thanks to
the move towards single-region wines. The Coonawarra Trio of Limestone Ridge Vineyard
Shiraz Cabernet, St George Vineyard Cabernet Sauvignon and Pyrus Cabernet Sauvignon
Merlot Malbec are all of exemplary quality. (JH)

96   **Coonawarra Trio St George Vineyard Cabernet Sauvignon 2019, Coonawarra** Wow – what a wine.
Classical, concentrated and almost sturdy, yet it shows a cascade of rippling flavour that flows over
the tongue. Interminable and muscly, this is a seriously sophisticated wine that proves the futility of
reinventing the wheel.   Screw cap. | 14% alc. | Drink 2021-2041 | $70 | EL

Parker Coonawarra Estate ★★★★★

15688 Riddoch Highway, Penola, SA 5263 **T** (08) 8737 3525 **WWW**.parkercoonawarraestate.com.au
OPEN 7 days 10-4 **WINEMAKER** James Lienert, Andrew Hardy, Keeda Zilm **EST.** 1985 **DOZENS** 30000
VYDS 20ha

Parker Coonawarra Estate is at the southern end of Coonawarra, on rich terra rossa soil over
limestone. It is now part of WD Wines, which also owns Hesketh Wine Company, St John's
Road, Vickery Wines and Ox Hardy. Production has risen substantially since the change of
ownership. (JH)

97   **First Growth 2018, Coonawarra** As true to Coonawarra for its structure, density and weight, as it is to
cabernet for its cassis, blackberries and spice. This is voluminous, expansive, and eminently classy,
with a pedigree of fruit that veritably floods the palate with flavour. It endures long into the finish,
telling us what we need to know about its capacity for ageing. The tannins too are expertly crafted,
countersunk into the fruit, and at no point intrusive to the experience.   Screw cap. | 14.5% alc. |
Drink 2022-2042 | $110 | EL | ♥

Penley Estate ★★★★★

McLeans Road, Coonawarra, SA 5263 **T** (08) 7078 1853 **WWW**.penley.com.au **OPEN** 7 days 10-4
WINEMAKER Kate Goodman, Lauren Hansen **EST.** 1988 **DOZENS** 48000 **VYDS** 111ha

In 1988, Kym, Ang and Bec Tolley joined forces to buy a block of land in Coonawarra – Penley
Estate was underway, the amalgamation of a fifth generation wine family Penfold and Tolley.
In 2015 Ang and Bec took full ownership of the company. They made a number of changes,
welcoming general manager Michael Armstrong and, even more importantly, appointing Kate
Goodman as winemaker. Behind the scenes Ang's husband David Paxton, one of Australia's
foremost viticulturists, has been working as a consultant, with improvements in vineyard
performance already evident. (JH)

97   **Helios Cabernet Sauvignon 2020, Coonawarra** Blackberry pie on the nose, this is concentrated and
pure in its expression of both Coonawarra (black fruit, eucalyptus and ferrous) and exotic spice.
On the palate the tannins are pronounced, and they certainly impact the fruit, but it is clear from
the sheer volume of flavour that swells in the mouth that they will be no match in time. They will
recede into the tidal wave of flavour and serve only to carry and guide the fruit through the finish, as
Helios' chariot drove him across the sky. Inchoate as this is, it will emerge a superstar.   Screw cap. |
14% alc. | Drink 2022-2042 | $150 | EL

95 **Francis Cabernet Franc 2021, Coonawarra** Juicy, bouncy, stemmy, crunchy cabernet franc: delicious. Blackberries, eucalyptus, pink peppercorns, red licorice, brine, bitter dark chocolate and even red snakes. This puts me firmly in mind of a nouveau wine from Chinon – drink it tonight to experience the joy and X-factor this wine has to offer. For those who insist on drinking cabernet throughout summer, this could be the answer. I think it would handle a gentle chill with grace.
Screw cap. | 14.5% alc. | Drink 2021-2026 | $30 | EL

94 **Giliam Light Dry Red 2021, Coonawarra** Blend of cabernet sauvignon, merlot and cabernet franc. Vanilla pod, raspberries, strawberries, licorice, a touch of coconut, red apples, pink peppercorns and mulberries from the bush in summer. Lots going on, and more of a mouthful than the name suggests. Tannins are plump, finely knit and omnipresent; they create a shapely tail through the finish. Screw cap. | 14.5% alc. | Drink 2021-2028 | $30 | EL

Tolmer 2020, Coonawarra Supple, elegant, fine-framed cabernet – hard to see where the 14.5% alcohol is hiding. This is super-pretty, fragrant and lithe, littered with red berries, flowers, blood plums and bay leaves. The palate is a little more substantive and weighty than the Phoenix, but that's to be expected for the extra money. This has presence and poise. Gorgeous. Screw cap. | 14.5% alc. | Drink 2021-2031 | $30 | EL

Reschke Wines

★★★★☆

CW Wines, 7089 Riddoch Highway, Padthaway, SA 5271 **T** (08) 8239 0500 **WWW**.cwwines.com
WINEMAKER Ben Wurst (Contract) **EST.** 1998 **DOZENS** 25000 **VYDS** 155ha

The Reschke family has been a landowner in Coonawarra for 100 years, with a large holding that is part terra rossa, part woodland. Cabernet sauvignon (with 120ha) takes the lion's share of the plantings, with merlot, shiraz and petit verdot making up the balance. In 2020, Reschke was purchased by Coonawarra-based CW Wines. (JH)

95 **Vitulus Shiraz 2020, Coonawarra** Gorgeous. Oak is evident, but the fruit has so much exuberant concentration that it hardly matters. This is a deeply satisfying rendition of Coonawarra shiraz. The brightness of the fruit is almost addictive, and very attractive. Hedonistic, but classy. Screw cap. | 14.5% alc. | Drink 2021-2031 | $30 | EL

94 **Bull Trader Shiraz 2020, Coonawarra** This is a bright, super-pretty, sweetly-fruited and gently spicy wine that shows the modern side of Coonawarra. The vinification is by no means groundbreaking, but the jubilant expression of fruit in the glass is this. This is delicious, verging on uncomplicated, and just a total delight. What fun for $20! Screw cap. | 14.5% alc. | Drink 2021-2027 | EL

Vitulus 2019, Coonawarra Dark, salted cassis and blackberry. In the mouth the wine is laced with a fine mineral seam of graphite tannins and saline acidity. This is very elegant, while also managing to convey great concentration of fruit. All things in balance, a classy wine to the end. Screw cap. | 14.5% alc. | Drink 2022-2037 | $30 | EL

Wynns Coonawarra Estate

★★★★★

77 Memorial Drive, Coonawarra, SA 5263 **T** (08) 8736 2225 **WWW**.wynns.com.au **OPEN** 7 days 10-5
WINEMAKER Sue Hodder, Sarah Pidgeon **VITICULTURIST** Ben Harris **EST.** 1897

Privileged to own the longest-established vineyards in the region, first planted by visionary pioneer John Riddoch in 1891, Wynns Coonawarra Estate still resides in the fabled triple-gabled winery that he built on Memorial Drive. Investments in rejuvenating and replanting key blocks – and skilled winemaking – have resulted in wines of far greater finesse and elegance. (JH)

97 **Davis Single Vineyard Cabernet Sauvignon 2019, Coonawarra** The last bottling of wine from the Davis vineyard was in '08. The aromas here are impossibly bright and deep. Blackberry and raspberry, blood and ferrous, creamy blackberry pie – crust as well. The acidity is saline and fresh. This is astoundingly beautiful. Driven by fruit and powered by a thundering undercurrent of soft tannin, this will surely live into its third decade with ease, and likely still retain some of the vibrancy. Inchoate though it is, a star is on the rise. Screw cap. | 13.8% alc. | Drink 2022-2052 | $90 | EL

John Riddoch Limited Release Cabernet Sauvignon 2019, Coonawarra Like the '18 that preceded it, this is a wine of stature, precision and endurance. The tannins are fine and omnipresent, but then a cabernet without tannins would be like a person without purpose. This is direct, forthright and confident, with a core of pure, soft and unfettered berry fruits that cascade over the tongue and trail through the interminable finish. The piercing intensity of fruit on the middle palate echoes in the mouth. Truly, sublime. Screw cap. | 13.5% alc. | Drink 2022-2052 | $150 | EL

Michael Limited Release Shiraz 2019, Coonawarra If this doesn't set your heart aflutter, I don't know what will. Featherlight and concentrated at once, this has tissue paper-fine layers of black cherry, blueberry, graphite, licorice, chalk and ferrous notes. The acidity is flowing and ripe, weaving the layers of flavour together; the oak, invisible. Another beautiful release, with undulating length through the finish. I bet it'll live an elegant age. Screw cap. | 14% alc. | Drink 2022-2052 | $150 | EL

BAROSSA

FLEURIEU

MOUNT LOFTY RANGES

FAR NORTH

LIMESTONE COAST

LOWER MURRAY

THE PENINSULAS

Mount Benson

Cape Jaffa Wines ★★★★

459 Limestone Coast Road, Mount Benson via Robe, SA 5276 **T** (08) 8768 5053 **www**.capejaffawines.com.au **OPEN** 7 days 11–4 **WINEMAKER** Anna and Derek Hooper **EST.** 1993 **DOZENS** 10000 **VYDS** 22.86ha

Cape Jaffa was the first of the Mount Benson wineries. Cape Jaffa's fully certified biodynamic vineyard provides 50% of production, with additional fruit sourced from a certified biodynamic grower in Wrattonbully. Having received the Advantage SA Regional Award in '09, '10 and '11 for its sustainable initiatives in the Limestone Coast, Cape Jaffa is a Hall of Fame inductee. (JH)

91   **Sauvignon Blanc 2021, Mount Benson** Lemongrass, crushed shell, jalapeño and juniper, mingle with green apple, pear and white pepper. The acidity is erring towards tart, but otherwise this is nice – the spice component elevates the experience. Screw cap. | 12.4% alc. | Drink 2021-2023 | $20 | EL

Mount Gambier

Coola Road ★★★☆

Private Mail Bag 14, Mount Gambier, SA 5291 **T** 0487 700 422 **www**.coolaroad.com **WINEMAKER** John Innes **EST.** 2013 **DOZENS** 1000 **VYDS** 13.5ha

Thomas and Sally Ellis are the current generation of the Ellis family, who have owned the Coola grazing property on which the vineyard is now established for over 160 years. They began planting the vineyard in the late '90s with pinot noir, and have since extended the range to include sauvignon blanc, chardonnay, riesling and pinot gris. As the largest vineyard owner in the region, they decided they should have some of the grapes vinified to bring further recognition to the area. (JH)

90   **Single Vineyard Riesling 2021, Mount Gambier** Tight, bright and light, this is diaphanous and quite gorgeous. Its highlight, and main attribute, is its delicacy, showing a fine array of sea spray, green apple, kiwi skin, jasmine tea and citrus blossom. Very pretty. Screw cap. | 11% alc. | Drink 2022-2028 | $20 | EL

Padthaway

Stonehaven ★★★

7089 Riddoch Highway, Padthaway, SA 5271 **T** (08) 8765 6140 **www**.stonehavenwines.com.au **OPEN** 7 days 10–5 **WINEMAKER** Grant Semmens, Leisha Slattery, Sean Carney **EST.** 1998 **DOZENS** 500000 **VYDS** 400ha

Stonehaven was established by Constellation Brands in 1998. By 2011, the winery – built in '98 at a cost of more than $33 million – was in mothballs. The business changed hands a few times over the following decade and in '21, Stonehaven was purchased by Coonawarra-based CW Wines. The brand is expected to be relaunched and the facilities to form 'the cornerstone' of CW Wines' operations. (JH)

89   **Stepping Stone Shiraz 2020, Limestone Coast** Delicious. It's spicy, juicy and a little bit fruit-sweet with plenty of plump, plush fruit to keep things joyful. It's not complex, but there's a really satisfying backdrop of exotic spice and soft tannins to engage. At $13, you'd be pretty happy with this, I should imagine. Screw cap. | 14.5% alc. | Drink 2022-2024 | $13 | EL

Vintage Longbottom ★★★★☆

15 Spring Gully Road, Piccadilly, SA 5151 **T** (08) 8132 1048 **WWW**.vintagelongbottom.com
WINEMAKER Matt Wenk **EST.** 1998 **DOZENS** 48000 **VYDS** 94.9ha

Kim Longbottom has moved her wine business from Padthaway to the Adelaide Hills, where Tapanappa has taken on the responsibility of making 3 tiers of wines. At the top is Magnus Shiraz from Clarendon and Blewitt Springs; the middle is the H Range from the McLaren Vale floor districts; and there is a sparkling range from the Adelaide Hills. Her daughter Margo brings experience in fashion, digital marketing and business administration. (JH)

95   **H Sauvignon Blanc 2021, Adelaide Hills** The Longbottoms don't choose to employ the word fumé to describe this style of sauvignon, but it's certainly imbued with a light woody smokiness that is very attractive. It helps define the wine and its depth of flavour. White peach, lime, grapefruit and white florals edge into a soft mid-palate texture. Oak softens the grape's aggressive herbals while enhancing its length.   Screw cap. | 12.1% alc. | Drink 2021-2026 | $25 | JP

REGION
Wrattonbully

Smith & Hooper ★★★☆

Caves Edward Road, Naracoorte, SA 5271 **T** (08) 8561 3200 **WWW**.smithandhooper.com **OPEN** By appt
WINEMAKER Heather Fraser **EST.** 1994 **DOZENS** 15000 **VYDS** 62ha

Smith & Hooper can be viewed as simply one of many brands within the Hill-Smith family financial and corporate structures. However, it is estate-based, with cabernet sauvignon and merlot planted on the Hooper Vineyard in 1994; and cabernet sauvignon and merlot planted on the Smith Vineyard in '98. (JH)

90   **Merlot 2019, Wrattonbully** Layers of sweet fruit drive the palate, which is kept on track by very fine tannins and pert acidity. Compelling drinking for the price.   Screw cap. | 14.5% alc. | Drink 2021-2027 | $21 | EL

ZONE
Lower Murray

REGION
Riverland

Ricca Terra ★★★★

PO Box 305, Angaston, SA 5353 **T** 0411 370 057 **WWW**.riccaterra.com.au **WINEMAKER** Ashley Ratcliff
EST. 2017 **DOZENS** 10000 **VYDS** 80ha

Ricca Terra is the venture of Ashley and Holly Ratcliff. Ashley began his journey in wine in 1992 when he joined Orlando as a viticulturist, thereafter moving to Yalumba where he was winery manager for the vast Riverland winery and technical manager until '16. He was the recipient of 4 major state and federal industry awards, all focusing on viticulture in drought-prone regions. The wines are hand picked into 0.5t bins and chilled for 12 hours before transfer to the winery in the Barossa Valley. (JH)

91   **Bullets Before Cannonballs 2021, Riverland** Tempranillo, shiraz, lagrein and lambrusco. Juicy, black and brooding, this does a really good job of carrying oodles of black fruit within a medium-bodied frame. It's deceptively light, for all the flavour that is crammed in. Licorice, blackberries, star anise, black pepper, plums and resin. Lush and lively. Super-smart for the money.   Screw cap. | 14.5% alc. | Drink 2022-2027 | $23 | EL

90   **22 Degrees Halo Kaleidoscope of Mayhem Rosé 2021, Riverland** Grenache, mataro, nero d'Avola. Spicy, juicy and layered with medicinal strawberries, amaro/mountain herbs, some shaved deli meat, and ras el hanout … lots going on.   Screw cap. | 13.2% alc. | Drink 2022-2024 | $20 | EL

BAROSSA
FLEURIEU
MOUNT LOFTY RANGES
FAR NORTH
LIMESTONE COAST
LOWER MURRAY
THE PENINSULAS

Victoria

22151ha | 6 zones | 21 regions

If you look at a map of mainland Australia, you will see that viticulture in all states other than Victoria hugs the coastline, leaving vast areas of empty land devoid of vines. Victoria may only have six zones, but it has 21 contiguous regions evenly spread across the state.

Pride of place goes to the Port Phillip Zone, within one hour's drive from Melbourne. First up, the **Yarra Valley**, with fragrant red berry and spice pinot noir and intense, elegant chardonnay accounting for the lion's share of plantings, and smaller amounts of worthy shiraz and cabernet sauvignon attesting to the variations in altitude, aspect and soil. **Mornington Peninsula**'s maritime climate sees the majority of plantings given over to delicately framed pinot noir and chardonnay; pinot gris/grigio is the mouse that roared, with the cost per tonne inexplicably dwarfing Yarra Valley chardonnay and pinot noir. **Macedon Ranges** and **Sunbury** also fall in the pinot noir and chardonnay school, Macedon's cool climate propelling both varieties to ever greater heights. **Geelong** has several highly rated producers of cabernet sauvignon and powerful chardonnay and pinot noir, with shiraz in similar

vein. **Gippsland** is a zone with no regions – the only such example in this book. It does have a world-famous winery, though, Bass Phillip, which has made one of Australia's greatest pinot noirs since 1984.

To the Central Ranges. **Bendigo** is largely red wine country, led by faintly minty shiraz, next cabernet sauvignon, then merlot. The ubiquitous pinot gris/grigio is the top white variety. **Heathcote** has 15 red varieties planted, with shiraz in the lead, the wine with a beguiling warmth from the fruit (if not the alcohol). The white varieties are dominated largely by chardonnay: lay down your glasses. The wild and windswept **Strathbogie Ranges** plantings reflect its more than 600m altitude – pinot noir and chardonnay are the game here, followed by shiraz.

The North East Victoria zone has five regions, the hot **Rutherglen** the odd man out, producing gloriously rich fortified muscat and muscadelle (aka tokay, the name changed due to EU requirements). In terms of both quality and style, these have no equivalent elsewhere in the world. Historic **Beechworth** is a halfway house up the mountains, chardonnay made famous by Giaconda. The **King Valley** and

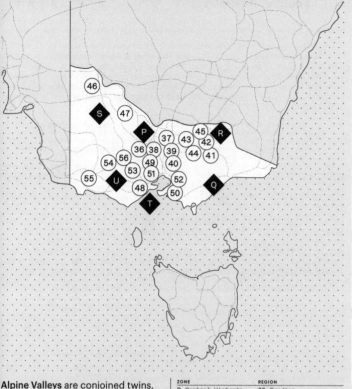

CENTRAL VICTORIA

GIPPSLAND

NORTH EAST VICTORIA

NORTH WEST VICTORIA

PORT PHILLIP

WESTERN VICTORIA

Alpine Valleys are conjoined twins, both with vineyards at very different altitudes, but the runaway success of prosecco, comprising almost half of total plantings.

The Western Victoria zone has three cool regions that dominate, led by the **Grampians**. Majestic, deeply coloured and infinitely complex shiraz makes up the bulk of plantings. **Henty** is the coldest region on the mainland; Seppelt Drumborg Vineyard and Crawford River are responsible for the vast majority of the glorious, long-lived riesling. **Pyrenees** hits the sweet spot with its shiraz (one-third of plantings) having the best of both climate worlds (cool and temperate), spice and licorice joining black fruits.

ZONE		REGION	
P	Central Victoria	36	Bendigo
		37	Goulburn Valley
		38	Heathcote
		39	Strathbogie Ranges
		40	Upper Goulburn
Q	Gippsland		
R	North East Victoria	41	Alpine Valleys
		42	Beechworth
		43	Glenrowan
		44	King Valley
		45	Rutherglen
S	North West Victoria	46	Murray Darling
		47	Swan Hill
T	Port Phillip	48	Geelong
		49	Macedon Ranges
		50	Mornington Peninsula
		51	Sunbury
		52	Yarra Valley
U	Western Victoria	53	Ballarat
		54	Grampians
		55	Henty
		56	Pyrenees

M. Chapoutier Australia ★★★★☆

141-143 High Street, Heathcote, Vic 3523 **T** (03) 5433 2411 **www**.mchapoutieraustralia.com
OPEN W'ends 10–5 or by appt **WINEMAKER** Michel Chapoutier **EST.** 1998 **DOZENS** 8000 **VYDS** 48ha

M. Chapoutier Australia is the eponymous offshoot of the famous Rhône Valley producer. The business focuses on vineyards in the Pyrenees, Heathcote and Beechworth with collaboration from Ron Laughton of Jasper Hill and Rick Kinzbrunner of Giaconda. After first establishing a vineyard in Heathcote adjacent to Jasper Hill, Chapoutier purchased the Malakoff Vineyard in the Pyrenees to create Domaine Terlato & Chapoutier. In '09 Michel Chapoutier purchased 2 neighbouring vineyards, Landsborough Valley and Shays Flat; all these are now fully owned by Tournon. (JH)

96 **...Ergo Sum Shiraz 2017, Beechworth** Vegan friendly. A wine that calls for more time in bottle and a decant before broaching. Starts dense and taut, but as it relaxes it loosens up, revealing a cool elegance. Baked plum, red and blue berries with licorice notes, florals and spice slowly transform on the palate into a lightly savoury style, all the while maintaining an even keel of fine tannin and balanced oak. Cork. | 14% alc. | Drink 2022–2031 | $68 | JP

Rouleur ★★★★☆

80 Laurens Street, North Melbourne, Vic 3051 **T** 0419 100 929 **www**.rouleurwine.com **OPEN** By appt
WINEMAKER Matthew East **EST.** 2015 **DOZENS** 2500

Owner Matt East's interest in wine began at an early age while he was growing up in the Yarra Valley and watching his father plant a vineyard in Coldstream. Between Feb '99 and Dec '15 his day job was in sales and marketing, culminating in his appointment in '11 as national sales manager for Wirra Wirra (which he had joined in '08). Following his retirement from that position, he set in motion the wheels of Rouleur. He lives in Melbourne, with the Yarra in easy striking distance for sourcing fruit and making wine (at Yering Farm in Coldstream). (JH)

95 **Chardonnay 2021, Yarra Valley** A wine with textural verve and phenolic persuasion. The oak, beautifully appointed. Candied quince, cherry plum, tangerine and chalk. Racy, yet chewy and saliva inducing. This is a delicious wine that retains freshness without sacrificing personality. Screw cap. | 12.9% alc. | Drink 2022–2030 | $34 | NG

Santa & D'Sas ★★★★

2 Pincott Street, Newtown, Vic 3220 **T** 0417 384272 **www**.santandsas.com.au **WINEMAKER** Andrew Santarossa, Matthew Di Sciascio **EST.** 2014 **DOZENS** 9000

Santa & D'Sas is a collaboration between the Santarossa and Di Sciascio families. Andrew Santarossa and Matthew Di Sciascio met while studying for a bachelor of applied science (wine science). Wines are released under the Valentino label (fiano, sangiovese and shiraz), are dedicated to Matthew's father; the remaining wines simply identify the region and variety. (JH)

94 **Prosecco NV, King Valley** A '21-based NV blend of prosecco from the Aussie home of the grape. So, so easy to love. This prosecco shines with the kind of purity of fruit that invites another sip. Making the most of their Italian heritage, the winemakers celebrate prosecco's inviting aperitif-style drinking in chalky lemon aromas and flavours, crunchy apple freshness and brisk acidity. Crown. | 11% alc. | $24 | JP

Shoofly | Frisk ★★★

PO Box 119, Mooroolbark, Vic 3138 **T** 0405 631 557 **www**.shooflywines.com **WINEMAKER** Ben Riggs, Garry Wall, Mark O'Callaghan **EST.** 2003 **DOZENS** 20000

This is a far-flung, export-oriented, business. It purchases a little over 620t of grapes each vintage. Ben Riggs makes Shoofly Shiraz and Chardonnay at Vintners McLaren Vale; Frisk Riesling and Prickly Riesling is made by Garry Wall at King Valley Wines. (JH)

88 **Shoofly Shiraz 2020, South Australia** Tanned hide, star anise, chocolate, red earth, hung deli meat and blackberries. This is a savoury, spicy wine with more secondary and tertiary characters than expected for its recent vintage. The finish rounds out a touch rugged, but plenty of varietal typicity for the money. Screw cap. | 14.5% alc. | Drink 2022–2024 | $17 | EL

The Flying Winemaker ★★★☆

801 Glenferrie Road, Hawthorn, Vic 3122 (postal) **T** 0413 960 102 **www**.eddiemcdougallwines.com.au **WINEMAKER** Eddie McDougall, Lilian Carter **VITICULTURIST** Eddie McDougall, Lilian Carter **EST.** 2007 **DOZENS** 1000

The Flying Winemaker is the brainchild of Eddie McDougall, award-winning winemaker, wine judge, columnist and TV personality. Eddie has made wines with the likes of Vietti (Barolo), Mas de Daumas Gassac (Languedoc), Deep Woods Estate (Margaret River), Giant Steps (Yarra Valley) and O'Leary Walker (Clare Valley). Eddie holds a bachelor of international business from Griffith University and a post-graduate diploma of wine technology and viticulture from the University of Melbourne. He spearheaded the acquisition of Wairarapa's Gladstone Vineyard in '18, where he took on the role of CEO and chief winemaker. (JH)

90 **Pinot Grigio 2021, King Valley** The winemaker catches the King Valley grigio style very well, pursuing a brisk, cool-climate line and length fleshed delicately in green apple, honeysuckle, hay and clean herbals. Provides both a soft mid-palate texture and brisk acidic finish. Screw cap. | 13% alc. | Drink 2022-2024 | $20 | JP

The Hairy Arm ⓘ ★★★★

18 Plant Street, Northcote, Vic 3070 **T** 0409 110 462 **www**.hairyarm.com **OPEN** By appt **WINEMAKER** Steven Worley **VITICULTURIST** Steven Worley **EST.** 2004 **DOZENS** 1000 **VYDS** 3ha

Steven Worley graduated as an exploration geologist, then added a master of geology degree, followed by a postgraduate diploma in oenology and viticulture. Until Dec '09 he was general manager of Galli Estate Winery. The Hairy Arm started as a university project in '04, and has grown from a labour of love to a commercial undertaking. (JH)

93 **Merrifolk Cote Nord Syrah 2020, Yarra Valley** A bright crimson cherry. Black plum and peppercorns along with some savoury, black olive and bay leaf. Full of flavour, there are some plum skins on the palate and the tannins are fine and chalky. An impressive, well-priced wine for early- to mid-term drinking. Screw cap. | 14% alc. | Drink 2022-2028 | $26 | PR

The Happy Winemaker ★★★★

16 Maddern Street, Black Hill, Vic 3350 **T** 0431 252 015 **www**.thehappywinemaker.com.au **WINEMAKER** Jean-Paul Trijsburg **EST.** 2015 **DOZENS** 700 **VYDS** 1ha

Jean-Paul Trijsburg graduated with an agronomy degree from the Wageningen University in the Netherlands and followed this with a joint MSc in viticulture and oenology in Montpellier, France and Geisenheim, Germany. In between degrees he headed to Burgundy in 2007. The experience left him with a love of all things French, but he went on to work in wineries in Pomerol, the Rheingau, Rioja, Chile and South Africa. Since '12, he has called Australia home, having worked for Hanging Rock Winery in the Macedon Ranges and Lethbridge Wines in Geelong. He and wife Jessica live in Ballarat and, following the arrival of their second son, Jean-Paul runs a nearby 1ha vineyard of pinot noir. Jean-Paul moved from his garage-cum-winery to Hanging Rock for the '19 vintage. (JH)

94 **Grenache Rosé by Jean-Paul 2021, Heathcote** Wild fermentation in 5-8yo French barriques. Lights up in vibrant red berries – cherry, raspberry and macerated strawberries – with spice and a hint of musk. The winemaker likes to build texture into his wines, but this has something else, a concentration of flavour that runs deep and fresh and bright and long. Delicious. Screw cap. | 12.5% alc. | Drink 2022-2024 | $25 | JP

Trifon Estate Wines ★★★☆

PO Box 258, Murchison, Vic 3610 **T** (03) 9432 9811 **www**.trifonestatewines.com.au **WINEMAKER** Glenn Eberbach, Amelie Mornex **VITICULTURIST** Sam Gallo, Ben Rose (consultant) **EST.** 1998 **DOZENS** 90000 **VYDS** 312ha

Trifon Estate has flown under the radar since it was established in 1998. Since that time 312ha of vines have been planted to 16 varieties, the lion's share to shiraz (83.26ha), cabernet sauvignon (47.93), merlot (42.74), chardonnay (38.79ha) and sauvignon blanc (23.76ha). (JH)

92 **Lagoon View Museum Release Semillon 2012, Central Victoria** A bottle-aged semillon is a rarity in these parts, but as it hits 10 years old, this semillon – with a touch of off-dry sweetness (7.5g/L) – sings. Lemon butter, toast, barley sugar, lime rind and lemon balm make an immediate impact aroma-wise. Light on its feet, it combines a warm texture with bright, lively acidity, all the while, bottle-aged characters maintain a complex hold on the palate. Screw cap. | 12.5% alc. | Drink 2022-2025 | $25 | JP

Central Victoria

REGION
Bendigo

Mandurang Valley Wines ⚲🍴🅰 ★★★★

77 Fadersons Lane, Mandurang, Vic 3551 **T** 0417 357 688 **www**.mandurangvalleywines.com.au **OPEN** Mon-Fri by appt. W'ends & public hols 11-5 **WINEMAKER** Wes Vine, Steve Vine **EST.** 1995 **DOZENS** 2500 **VYDS** 3ha

Wes and Pamela Vine planted their first vineyard at Mandurang in '76 and started making wine as a hobby. Commercial production began in '93, and an additional vineyard was established in '97. Wes became full-time winemaker in '99. Son Steve has progressively taken greater responsibility for the winemaking, while Wes is spending more time developing export markets. Pamela manages the cellar door cafe. (JH)

92 **Riesling 2021, Bendigo** Bright as a button. Gentle in grapefruit, lime, apple fruit and preserved-lemon aromas, but opens up on the palate showing some vivacious charm. Smooth, even and crisp with great length sustained by fine, chalky acidity. Screw cap. | 12.2% alc. | Drink 2021-2027 | $22 | JP

Sutton Grange Winery ⚲🍴🅰 ★★★★★

Carnochans Road, Sutton Grange, Vic 3448 **T** (03) 8672 1478 **www**.suttongrange.com.au **OPEN** W'ends 11-5 **WINEMAKER** Chris Smailes **EST.** 1998 **DOZENS** 6000 **VYDS** 12ha

Sutton Grange, a 400ha property, in the foothills of Leanganook near Harcourt, combines a horse training facility with grape growing and winemaking. The wine side of the business dates back to '98 and a chance lunch at the property with modern-day Bendigo wine pioneer, Stuart Anderson (founder Balgownie) and local winemaker, Alec Epis. Vines went in soon after, with Stuart Anderson's Burgundy-born son-in-law, Gilles Lapalus, installed as winemaker in '01. The experienced wine-making hand of Melanie Chester (ex Seppelt) from '15 took the Sutton Grange name to greater heights, regularly winning major trophies and accolades, most notably for her Syrah. In '22 Mel passed the baton to Chris Smailes, (ex Blue Pyrenees Estate). (JP)

95 **Fairbank Rosé 2021, Central Victoria** A blend of cabernet sauvignon, shiraz, sangiovese and viognier. Copper pink tea rose hues are easy on the eye, the perfumed strawberry, raspberry fruit, bracken and light musk aromas and flavours equally inviting. Screw cap. | 12.5% alc. | Drink 2022-2024 | $35 | JP | ♥

Fairbank Syrah 2020, Central Victoria. In keeping with the Fairbank Syrah style, we see an elegant expression of the grape, deep and engaging in black fruits, blueberry, pepper, spice and chocolate. Juicy fruit on the palate is nicely wrapped in fine tannins, driving the wine towards a smooth finish. Screw cap. | 13.5% alc. | Drink 2022-2032 | $35 | JP

Water Wheel ⚲ ★★★★

Bridgewater-Raywood Road, Bridgewater-on-Loddon, Vic 3516 **T** (03) 5437 3060 **www**.waterwheelwine.com **OPEN** Mon-Fri 9-5, w'ends 12-4 **WINEMAKER** Bill Trevaskis, Amy Cumming **EST.** 1972 **DOZENS** 35000 **VYDS** 136ha

Peter Cumming, with more than 2 decades of winemaking under his belt, has quietly built on the reputation of Water Wheel year by year. The winery is owned by the Cumming family, which has farmed in the Bendigo region for more than 50 years, with horticulture and viticulture special areas of interest. Water Wheel continues to make wines that over-deliver at their modest prices. (JH)

93 **Viognier 2020, Bendigo** Aromas of bright ginger, honeysuckle, apricot and yellow peach with orange peel, showing some pretty inviting complexity. Viscous with weight and a warm creaminess across the palate. Screw cap. | 14.4% alc. | Drink 2021-2026 | $24 | JP

Goulburn Valley

Arli Wine ★★★☆

2/540 Goulburn Valley Highway, Shepparton North, Vic 3531 **T** 0427 529 183 **www**.arliwine.com.au **WINEMAKER** John Kremor **EST.** 2021 **DOZENS** 300

Raised on his parents' vineyard in Merbein, John Kremor was destined for a life in wine. His first job was at BRL Hardy in Buronga, working his way up from the laboratory and cellar into the role of assistant winemaker. During his time there, he and his partner, Leanna, also redeveloped a local dried-fruit property with cabernet sauvignon and chardonnay, selling the fruit to a local winery. A work opportunity outside of wine took him to the Goulburn Valley in the late '90s. In '21 John returned to his first love, sourcing and making small parcels of wine from the Goulburn Valley region. (JP)

90 **Dookie Hills Riesling 2021, Central Victoria** A smart price for an attractive, citrus-focused riesling. Whereas the floral, citrus and apple aromas are quite delicate, the palate is altogether different: firm and dry with an emerging textural quality. Lemon pith, lime and grapefruit are carried well along a lively acid line. Screw cap. | 12.3% alc. | Drink 2021-2027 | $15 | JP

Box Grove Vineyard ⓘⓜⓐ ★★★★

955 Avenel-Nagambie Road, Tabilk, Vic 3607 **T** 0409 210 015 **www**.boxgrovevineyard.com.au **OPEN** By appt **WINEMAKER** Sarah Gough **EST.** 1995 **DOZENS** 2500 **VYDS** 28.25ha

This is the venture of the Gough family, with industry veteran (and daughter) Sarah Gough managing the vineyard, winemaking and marketing. Having started with 10ha each of shiraz and cabernet sauvignon under contract to Brown Brothers, Sarah decided to switch the focus of the business to what could loosely be called 'Mediterranean varieties'. Osteria (an Italian word meaning a place that serves wine and food) hosts tastings and meals prepared by visiting Melbourne chefs. (JH)

94 **Prosecco 2021, Nagambie Lakes** Brings a savoury layer to prosecco, striking a different chord, bringing preserved lemon, grapefruit pith, nashi pear and apple. Crunchy, enlivening acidity. A prosecco that fits both aperitif style and will match nicely with food. Screw cap. | 11.7% alc. | $25 | JP

Dalfarras ⓘⓜ ★★★★

PO Box 123, Nagambie, Vic 3608 **T** (03) 5794 2637 **www**.dalfarras.com.au **OPEN** Mon-Sat 9-5, Sun 11-5 **WINEMAKER** Alister Purbrick **EST.** 1991 **DOZENS** 8750 **VYDS** 20.97ha

The project of Alister Purbrick and artist wife Rosa (née Dalfarra), whose paintings adorn the labels of the wines. Alister is best known as winemaker at Tahbilk, the family winery and home, but this range of wines is intended to (in Alister's words) 'Allow me to expand my winemaking horizons and mould wines in styles different from Tahbilk'. (JH)

90 **Prosecco 2021, Victoria** An engaging young prosecco, with a touch of herbal interplay among the lemony citrus and apply varietal notes. Bright and tangy, it introduces a textural quality on the palate with some bready notes. Chalky dry on the finish. Cork. | 11% alc. | $20 | JP

Nero d'Avola 2019, Nagambie Lakes Voluptuous and soft, fragrant and juicy, there is a lot to be said for this little charmer, employing the new Italian kid on the block, nero d'Avola. Dried herb, dark cherry, leaf and cinnamon with woody oak nicely integrated. Bright as a button and ready to go. Screw cap. | 13% alc. | Drink 2021-2024 | $20 | JP

McPherson Wines ★★★★

199 O'Dwyer Road, Nagambie, Vic 3608 (postal) **T** (03) 9263 0200 **www**.mcphersonwines.com.au **WINEMAKER** Jo Nash **EST.** 1968 **DOZENS** 500000 **VYDS** 262ha

McPherson Wines is, by any standards, a substantial business. Made at various locations from estate vineyards and contract-grown grapes, they represent very good value across a range of labels. Winemaker Jo Nash has been at the helm for many years and co-owner Alistair Purbrick (Tahbilk) has a lifetime of experience in the industry. Quality is unfailingly good. (JH)

92   **Don't tell Gary 2020, Central Victoria** If you haven't already guessed, Gary is the McPherson accountant. A fun title for a wine that enjoys some pretty schmick and expensive oak which is slurped up easily by this super-generous, ripe shiraz. Over-delivers for the price in deep, dark, sweet berries and plums, earth, dark chocolate, toasted spice and nicely integrated oak that brings warmth and immediate drinkability.   Screw cap. | 15% alc. | Drink 2022-2028 | $24 | JH

90   **MWC Cabernet Sauvignon 2019, Victoria** This is one confident, finely tuned cabernet worth getting to know better. It strides into view, raising swirls of autumnal leafiness, black fruits, cinnamon, nutmeg and undergrowth. Tidy and balanced with concentration, it ties the fruit, tannin and oak together, and elegantly so.   Screw cap. | 13.9% alc. | Drink 2021-2027 | $19 | JP

Tahbilk ★★★★★

254 O'Neils Road, Tabilk, Vic 3608 **T** (03) 5794 2555 **WWW.**tahbilk.com.au **OPEN** Mon–Fri 9–5, Sat–Sun 10–5 **WINEMAKER** Alister Purbrick, Alan George, Brendan Freeman **VITICULTURIST** Richard Flatman **EST.** 1860 **DOZENS** 120000 **VYDS** 221.5ha

In 2020, Tahbilk celebrated its 160th birthday. For 5 generations, the Purbrick family have tended vines and protected the delicate watering holes and landscape of their property outside Nagambie. The family has moved fast in securing a more sustainable future, re-establishing natural wetlands, revegetating 160ha of land with indigenous trees and plants, achieving carboNZero certification in '16 and beginning the journey in '21 to convert its vineyards to accredited organic. In '22, Alister Purbrick stepped down as CEO but will continue to be involved in industry boards. Tahbilk is a founding member of Australia's First Families of Wine and was the Companion's Winery of the Year in '16. (JP)

96   **BDX Blend Old Block Vines 2019, Nagambie Lakes** It's also a statement wine; it says 'look at what cabernet sauvignon and friends can do in the Nagambie Lakes', a region more often associated with shiraz. Intriguing and complex, it immediately makes an impact with lifted aromas of blackberry, dark spices, an autumnal leafiness and dusty earth encased in violet aromatics. Fills the mouth with flavour and a fine, trimmed elegance.   Screw cap. | 14% alc. | Drink 2022-2034 | $67 | JP

    Eric Stevens Purbrick Cabernet Sauvignon 2018, Nagambie Lakes Some years it is the ESP Shiraz that shines the brightest, and some years it is the ESP Cabernet. The '18 vintage was such a year for cabernet, producing impressive depth of flavour, concentration and, above all, elegance. Leafy black fruit, clove, anise and sweet earth scents. Boasts depth, length and firm line as fine tannins guide the palate, embracing intense fruit, spice and a touch of cigar box complexity.   Screw cap. | 14.5% alc. | Drink 2022-2035 | $72 | JP

95   **Marsanne 2021, Nagambie Lakes** The Nagambie Lakes shared the great vintage for whites, and Tahbilk didn't miss out here, oozing with honeysuckle, lime and custard apple, the signature of acidity neatly tying the parcel up for now or in a decade or 2.   Screw cap. | 13% alc. | Drink 2025-2031 | $20 | JH

    Viognier 2021, Nagambie Lakes The perfection of the growing season has provided a luxurious wine, packed with flavours spanning ripe stone fruits through to shafts of fresh ginger, and a sprightly mouthfeel. Breaks all the rules of convention.   Screw cap. | 13.5% alc. | Drink 2021-2024 | $21 | JH

    Grenache Mourvèdre Rosé 2021, Nagambie Lakes Boasts concentrated flavour and a degree of complexity not generally seen at this price. Morello cherry, raspberry, rose and cardamom spice up this confection-pink rosé. Juicy energy in the mouth. Flavour is intense and runs deep, with a firm tannin grip as company. A rosé to savour.   Screw cap. | 13% alc. | Drink 2021-2026 | $22 | JP

    Cane Cut Marsanne 2019, Nagambie Lakes One of the many faces of marsanne, which once again reveals the delicate beauty and quiet strength of the grape. Light golden hues introduce a concentrated perfume of jasmine, citrus blossom, cumquat, stone fruit and mandarin rind. Runs long and smooth across the palate, luscious and so, so moreish. 500ml bottle.   Screw cap. | 11% alc. | Drink 2022-2025 | $26 | JP

    Museum Release Marsanne 2016, Nagambie Lakes A fabulous follow-up vintage to the excellent '15, encapsulating all the beauty of the Rhône grape that comes with bottle age. The characters we see in youth remain: the honeysuckle, jasmine florals and citrus force. Built around them are complexing additions through age, of hay, almond meal, pear skin and apricot nut. Acidity is firm but also soft. Stunning value, as always.   Screw cap. | 13% alc. | Drink 2022-2031 | $26 | JP

Tar & Roses ★★★★★

61 Vickers Lane, Nagambie, Vic 3608 **T** (03) 5794 1811 **WWW.**tarandroses.com.au **OPEN** first w'end each month 10–4 **WINEMAKER** Narelle King **EST.** 2006 **DOZENS** 40000

Tar & Roses produces wines inspired by the classic Mediterranean varietals and was named after the signature characteristics of nebbiolo. The name also ties back to the winemaking team behind the venture, the legendary Don Lewis and his winemaking partner Narelle King. Narelle is carrying on the Tar & Roses tradition after Don's passing in 2017. (JH)

95 **Lewis Riesling 2021, Central Victoria** So much budding complexity waiting to break through, with lifted floral aromatics, lemon, lime, citrus peel and a touch of exotic lemongrass. Concentrated on the palate, saturated in citrus intensity and length with a ribbon of apply spice with bright acidity that keeps on going. Screw cap. | 13% alc. | Drink 2021-2028 | $26 | JP

94 **Sangiovese 2021, Central Victoria** Thoughts immediately rush to pizza, it's that kind of sangiovese. Gets the tastebuds singing with the first rush of black cherry scents with redcurrant, thyme and pepper. Seriously smashable with its vibrancy, its mix of dark chocolate, cola, cherry, licorice and light savouriness running across the palate. Plenty of charm. Screw cap. | 13.5% alc. | Drink 2021-2028 | $27 | JP

Heathcote

Bull Lane Wine Company ★★★★

PO Box 77, Heathcote, Vic 3523 **T** 0427 970 041 **www**.bulllane.com.au **WINEMAKER** Simon Osicka **VITICULTURIST** Alison Phillips **EST**. 2013 **DOZENS** 500

After a successful career as a winemaker with what is now TWE, Simon Osicka, together with viticulturist partner Alison Phillips, returned to the eponymous family winery just within the eastern boundary of the Heathcote region in '10. Spurred on by a decade of drought impacting on the 60yo dry-grown vineyard, and a desire to create another style of shiraz, Simon and Alison spent considerable time visiting Heathcote vineyards with access to water in the lead-up to the '10 vintage. After the weather gods gave up their tricks of '11, Bull Lane was in business. (JH)

95 **Marsanne 2021, Heathcote** The maker captures the grape's warmth and complexity easily in a good year like '21. An array of ripe scents and flavours in citrus, peach, spiced apple, mandarin skin, apricot kernel, with honeysuckle and jasmine florals. Skin contact has contributed to the wine's gentle creaminess and almond-nougat light savouriness. Screw cap. | 13.5% alc. | Drink 2022-2027 | $30 | JP

Heathcote Estate ★★★★★

Drummonds Lane, Heathcote, Vic 3523 (postal) **T** (03) 5974 3729 **www**.yabbylake.com **OPEN** 7 days 10-4 **WINEMAKER** Tom Carson, Chris Forge, Luke Lomax **EST**. 1999 **DOZENS** 5000 **VYDS** 34ha

Heathcote Estate and Yabby Lake Vineyard are owned by the Kirby family of Village Roadshow Ltd. They purchased a prime piece of Heathcote red Cambrian soil in 1999. The wines are matured exclusively in French oak. The arrival of the hugely talented Tom Carson as group winemaker in 2008 has added lustre to the winery and its wines. (JH)

96 **Single Vineyard Shiraz 2020, Heathcote** Superlative wine showing great elegance. Concentrated ripe dark plum, blackberries, dried herbs, earthy sweetness, violet and more. The palate is laid out long in soft, ripe tannins, mouth-filling with an impressive regional and varietal declaration. Screw cap. | 13.5% alc. | Drink 2022-2030 | $50 | JP

Idavue Estate ★★★★

470 Northern Highway, Heathcote, Vic 3523 **T** 0429 617 287 **www**.idavueestate.com **OPEN** W'ends 10.30-5 **WINEMAKER** Andrew Whytcross, Sandra Whytcross **EST**. 2000 **DOZENS** 600 **VYDS** 5.7ha

Owners and winemakers Andrew and Sandra Whytcross produce award-winning wines; the vineyard managed by Andy, the winery run using normal small-batch winemaking techniques. The Barrelhouse cellar door is adorned with music paraphernalia and guitars, and regularly holds blues music events. (JH)

94 **Shiraz 2019, Heathcote** The alcohol reading might look on the high side but read the wine, it's surprisingly light on its feet, to the point of elegance. Plenty of toasty oak, spice and blackberry aromas with hints of dusty cacao. Smooth and svelte on the palate, with ripe black and plum flavours, fine tannins and a hint of eucalyptus. Screw cap. | 15% alc. | Drink 2021-2031 | $30 | JP

Jasper Hill ★★★★★

88 Drummonds Lane, Heathcote, Vic 3523 **T** (03) 5433 2528 **www**.jasperhill.com.au **OPEN** By appt **WINEMAKER** Ron Laughton, Emily McNally **EST**. 1979 **DOZENS** 2000 **VYDS** 26.5ha

CENTRAL VICTORIA

GIPPSLAND

NORTH EAST VICTORIA

NORTH WEST VICTORIA

PORT PHILLIP

WESTERN VICTORIA

The red wines of Jasper Hill, crafted by father-daughter team Ron Laughton and Emily McNally, are highly regarded and much sought after. The low-yielding dry-grown vineyards are managed organically and tended by hand. The family celebrated their 40th vintage in '21. (JH)

95   **Lo Stesso Fiano 2021, Heathcote** Another stunning interpretation of the Italian grape by Emily McNally, delving deep into its repertoire of forthright pear and apple and finds additional layers of dried fruits, guava, mango skin, nougat and spice. Rolled in texture and topped by delicious acidity. Screw cap. | 12.5% alc. | Drink 2022-2026 | $30 | JP

Kennedy ★★★★☆

Maple Park, 224 Wallenjoe Road, Corop, Vic 3559 (postal) **T** (03) 5484 8293 **www.**kennedyvintners. com.au **WINEMAKER** Glen Hayley, Gerard Kennedy **VITICULTURIST** Barney Touhey **EST.** 2002 **DOZENS** 3000 **VYDS** 29.2ha

Having been farmers in the Colbinabbin area of Heathcote for 27 years, John and Patricia Kennedy were on the spot when a prime piece of red Cambrian soil on the east-facing slope of Mount Camel Range became available for purchase. The Shiraz is made in small open fermenters, using indigenous yeasts and gentle pigeage before being taken to French oak for maturation. John and Patricia's geologist son Gerard returned to the family business in '15 and oversees the winemaking and activities in the vineyard. (JH)

93   **Pink Hills Rosé 2021, Heathcote** Summer-smart in light copper and orange peel hues, with the scent of red berries, spice and a fleck of pepper. Bone dry, which brings the delicacy of fruit to the forefront, finishing with a nice little sherbety surprise. Screw cap. | 13% alc. | Drink 2021-2025 | $25 | JP

      Henrietta Tempranillo 2021, Heathcote A punchy, deep purple-hearted youngster with a lot of go, Henrietta makes quite an entrance. Lively licorice and bush herbs join with ripe, sweet blackberry fruits, pomegranate and savoury woody spice. Flows evenly and long through a full-bodied palate with a lilting peppery thread. Screw cap. | 14% alc. | Drink 2022-2028 | $24 | JP

Paul Osicka ★★★★★

Majors Creek Vineyard at Graytown, Vic 3608 **T** (03) 5794 9235 **www.**paulosickawines.com.au **OPEN** By appt **WINEMAKER** Simon Osicka **EST.** 1955 **VYDS** 13ha

The Osicka family arrived from Czechoslovakia in the early '50s. Vignerons in their own country, their vineyard in Australia was the first new venture in central and southern Victoria for over half a century. Simon Osicka held senior winemaking positions at Houghton, Leasingham, and as group red winemaker for Constellation Wines Australia, interleaved with vintages in Italy, Canada, Germany and France. The fermentation of the red wines has changed from static to open fermenters and French oak has replaced American. Extensive retrellising of the 65yo estate plantings is now complete. Paul Osicka, Simon's father, passed away in 2019 after 50 vintages and over 60 years of involvement in the vineyards. (JH)

97   **Shiraz 2019, Heathcote** The lively bouquet offers fluttering wafts of spices crossing into dabs of French oak, but gives little advance notice of the depth and intensity of the black fruits wrapped in a fine skein of ripe tannins. A Grampians-like twist is all the better for that in the hands of Simon Osicka. Screw cap. | 14.5% alc. | Drink 2022-2040 | $38 | JH

Sanguine Estate ★★★★★

77 Shurans Lane, Heathcote, Vic 3523 **T** (03) 5433 3111 **www.**sanguinewines.com.au **OPEN** W'ends & public hols 10-5 **WINEMAKER** Mark Hunter **VITICULTURIST** Mark Hunter **EST.** 1997 **DOZENS** 15000 **VYDS** 28ha

The Hunter family – parents Linda and Tony, their children Mark and Jodi and their respective partners Melissa and Brett – have 21.5ha of shiraz and a 'fruit salad block'. Low-yielding vines and the magic of the Heathcote region have produced Shiraz of exceptional intensity, which has received rave reviews in the US. With the ever-expanding vineyard, Mark has become full-time vigneron and winemaker, and Jodi has taken over from her father as CEO and general manager. (JH)

96   **Inception Shiraz 2019, Heathcote** It's a beauty. Impressive depth of colour (as usual), opens to reveal fragrant musky, violet, spice and black fruits. Fruit power is well managed by the vibrant spice and oak integration and fine tannins. Screw cap. | 14.8% alc. | Drink 2021-2033 | $40 | JP

95   **Progeny Shiraz 2020, Heathcote** Progeny retains its well-known vibrancy and immediate drinking appeal. Deep, dense purple hues introduce lifted aromas of blackberry, briar, earth and violet. The winemaker believes that although there is less than 2% viognier, it makes its presence felt. I believe him. There is an aromatic appeal to this wine where the fruit is allowed free rein, with just a nod to French oak (20% new).The result is a wine of flavour and depth. Screw cap. | 14.8% alc. | Drink 2021-2030 | $25 | JP

Tellurian ★★★★★

408 Tranter Road, Toolleen, Vic 3551 **T** 0431 004 766 **www**.tellurianwines.com.au **OPEN** W'ends 11-4.30 or by appt **WINEMAKER** Tobias Ansted **EST**. 2002 **DOZENS** 7000 **VYDS** 32ha

The vineyard is situated on the western side of Mount Camel at Toolleen, on the red Cambrian soil that has made Heathcote one of the foremost regions in Australia for the production of shiraz (Tellurian means 'of the earth'). Viticultural consultant Tim Brown not only supervises the certified organic Tellurian estate plantings, but also works closely with the growers of grapes purchased under contract for Tellurian. (JH)

95 **Marsanne 2021, Heathcote** Marsanne, like its sibling Rhône grapes (both white and red), is naturally attuned to the Heathcote landscape. It gets to showcase its richness and textural qualities here, its honeysuckle lifted florals, leatherwood honey and spice with exotic Asian pear, quince paste, baked apple and peach. A warm, waxy mouthfeel is freshened by crisp, clean acidity. Screw cap. | 13.5% alc. | Drink 2022-2027 | $30 | JP

REGION
Strathbogie Ranges

Baddaginnie Run ★★★☆

PO Box 579, North Melbourne, Vic 3051 **T** (03) 9348 9310 **www**.baddaginnierun.net.au **WINEMAKER** Sam Plunkett **EST**. 1996 **DOZENS** 2500 **VYDS** 24ha

Winsome McCaughey and Professor Snow Barlow (Professor of Horticulture and Viticulture at the University of Melbourne) spend part of their week in the Strathbogie Ranges, and part in Melbourne. The business name, Seven Sisters Vineyard, reflects the seven generations of the McCaughey family associated with the land since 1870; Baddaginnie is the nearby township. (JH)

92 **Shiraz 2019, Strathbogie Ranges** Brilliant black cherry red-purple hue, very attractive. What a sparky introduction, all Damson plum, cherry, black berries, aniseed and spice. The sweet, plummy theme is ongoing throughout this wine, which is more a drink-now than drink-later style. Fresh, clean and generously fruity, it highlights the mineral-edged Bogies style beautifully. Screw cap. | 14.9% alc. | Drink 2021-2024 | $21 | JP

Fowles Wine ★★★★★

1175 Lambing Gully Road, Avenel, VIC 3664 **T** (03) 5796 2150 **www**.fowleswine.com **OPEN** 7 days, 9-5 **WINEMAKER** Lindsay Brown, Sam Atherton **VITICULTURIST** Glenn Chisholm **EST**. 1968 **DOZENS** 80000 **VYDS** 145ha

This family-owned winery is led by Matt Fowles, with chief winemaker Lindsay Brown heading the winemaking team. Marketing is energetic, with the well-known Ladies who Shoot their Lunch label also available, presented in a 6-bottle gun case. (JH)

95 **Ladies who Shoot their Lunch Wild Ferment Shiraz 2019, Strathbogie Ranges** On the more generous side, this vintage, but still there is tremendous vitality and complexity to the wine. Fragrant red fruits, plum, anise, spice and violet aromas. Fresh and even to taste, with firm tannins the launch pad for dark cherry, plum, red licorice, dried herbs and a long, pepper-dusted finish. Screw cap. | 14.9% alc. | Drink 2021-2030 | $35 | JP

REGION
Upper Goulburn

Delatite ★★★★☆

390 Pollards Road, Mansfield, Vic 3722 **T** (03) 5775 2922 **www**.delatitewinery.com.au **OPEN** 7 days 10-5 **WINEMAKER** Andy Browning **VITICULTURIST** David Ritchie **EST**. 1982 **DOZENS** 16000 **VYDS** 28ha

With its sweeping views across to the snow-clad alps, this is uncompromising cool-climate viticulture. Increasing vine age (the earlier plantings were between 1968-82, others between '84-2011) and the adoption of organic (and partial biodynamic) viticulture, have also played a role in providing the red wines with more depth and texture. The white wines are all wild-yeast fermented and are as good as ever. (JH)

95 **Pinot Gris 2021, Upper Goulburn** An ultra-cool-climate vineyard meets its match in this young, complex, texturally exciting pinot gris. They were made for each other. A light blush colour indicates some skin contact, a good sign, before aromas burst in lively aromatics: citrus blossom, honeysuckle, green apple and spice. Glides across the tongue in spiced apple, pear and nougat with just a hint of sweetness. Screw cap. | 13% alc. | Drink 2022-2028 | $30 | JP

Ros Ritchie Wines ★★★★☆

Magnolia House, 190 Mount Buller Road, Mansfield, 3722 **T** 0448 900 541 **www**.rosritchiewines.com **OPEN** Fri 5-8, w'ends & public hols 11-4 **WINEMAKER** Ros Ritchie **EST.** 2008 **DOZENS** 2000 **VYDS** 7ha

Ros Ritchie was winemaker at the Ritchie family's Delatite winery from 1981 to 2006, but moved on to establish her own winery with husband John in '08 on a vineyard near Mansfield. They became shareholders in Barwite Vineyards in '12 and in '14 established their new winery there. All vineyards are managed with minimal spray regimes. The cellar door is located at the historic Magnolia House at Mansfield, open on select weekends, hosting seasonal wine dinners and special events. (JH)

95 **Barwite Vineyard Riesling 2021, Upper Goulburn** Ros Ritchie established her early reputation on the almost fragile beauty of her rieslings. Super-cool-climate riesling remains one of her great strengths. Longevity is assured with the '21 with its filigree-fine lemony acidity a firm basis for floral citrus blossom, lime and lemon aromas and a palate that is crisp, dry and imbedded with a gentle spice which lifts the whole wine. Screw cap. | 11.9% alc. | Drink 2022-2031 | $27 | JP

ZONE

Gippsland

Lightfoot Wines ★★★★☆

717 Calulu Road, Bairnsdale, Vic 3875 **T** (03) 5156 9205 **www**.lightfootwines.com **OPEN** Fri-Sun 11-5 **WINEMAKER** Alastair Butt, Tom Lightfoot **VITICULTURIST** Tom Lightfoot **EST.** 1995 **DOZENS** 10000 **VYDS** 29.3ha

Formerly Lightfoot & Sons. Brian and Helen Lightfoot first established a vineyard of predominantly pinot noir and shiraz, with some cabernet sauvignon and merlot, on their Myrtle Point farm in the late '90s. The soils were found to be similar to that of Coonawarra, with terra rossa over limestone. In the early days, most of the grapes were sold to other Victorian winemakers, but with the arrival of Alistair Butt (formerly of Brokenwood and Seville Estate) and sons Tom and Rob taking over the business around '08 (Tom in the vineyard and cellar, Rob overseeing sales and marketing), the focus has shifted to producing estate wines. Cabernet and merlot have since been replaced with more chardonnay, some gamay and pinot grigio, but pinot noir retains the top spot. (TS)

95 **Myrtle Point Vineyard Chardonnay 2021, Gippsland** Such an enjoyable, easy to drink wine but with plenty of definition and complexity. Lemony freshness infuses white nectarine and a touch of cedary spice from the oak – 10 months in a mix of barrel sizes (15% new) and perfectly integrated. It feels light and breezy across the palate, then some creamy lees kicks in to bolster it out and lively acidity ensuring the finish lingers. Screw cap. | 12.5% alc. | Drink 2021-2029 | $30 | JF

Tambo Estate ★★★★

96 Pages Road, Tambo Upper, Vic 3885 **T** 0418 100 953 **www**.tambowine.com.au **OPEN** Thurs-Sun 11-5 **WINEMAKER** Alastair Butt **VITICULTURIST** Bill Williams **EST.** 1994 **DOZENS** 1940 **VYDS** 5.11ha

Bill and Pam Williams returned to Australia in the early '90s after 7 years overseas, and began the search for a property which met the specific requirements for high-quality table wines established by Dr John Gladstones in his masterwork Viticulture and Environment. They chose a property in the foothills of the Victorian Alps on the inland side of the Gippsland Lakes, with predominantly sheltered, north-facing slopes. They planted a little over 5ha: 3.4ha to chardonnay, as well as a little cabernet sauvignon, pinot noir and sauvignon blanc. They are mightily pleased to have secured the services of Alastair Butt (one-time winemaker at Seville Estate). (JH)

---

94   **Lakes Cabernet Sauvignon 2019, Gippsland** What's pleasing about this is the subtlety and gentleness throughout. It's lovely to drink, with its delicate flavours of currants, blueberries and blackberries, pastille and licorice with a smattering of woodsy spices and tapenade. Medium bodied, with fine tannins and nothing else to consider except to pour it. Screw cap. | 13.8% alc. | Drink 2021–2029 | $28 | JF

North East Victoria

Acres Wilde ★★★

1185 Glenrowan-Boweya Road, Taminick, Vic 3675 **T** 0427 701 017 **www**.acreswilde.com.au
WINEMAKER Chris Beach **EST.** 2011 **DOZENS** 260

Chris Beach made his way into the wine industry after working in various farming pursuits; beef, dairy, orchards and tractor driving. Along the way there was also overseas travel and stints at snow resorts and in the building industry. However, the past 15 years have been spent in the vineyards and wineries of North East Victoria. He is currently working as a cellar hand at a Glenrowan winery, making his own wine under his own label in his down time. Grapes are bought in and all winemaking processes are performed by him. At first, his 'winery' was a brick garage, but he is now happy to report that he has moved up in the world and is utilising a large tin shed. Grapes are fermented in half-tonne picking bins, hand plunged, basket pressed, and he says he prefers to follow a minimal approach as much as possible. (JP)

---

89   **Classic Muscat NV, Rutherglen** It may not be the most complex Classic Muscat, but it certainly boasts strong luscious and delicious factors – very important! – in dried fruits, nougat, fig and fruitcake. Clean and fresh. 500ml. Screw cap. | 17.3% alc. | Drink 2022–2022 | $15 | JP

88   **Ruby #1 NV, North East Victoria** A blend of 3 vintages and regions – 2013 Glenrowan, 2014 King Valley, 2015 Rutherglen. Attractive floral aromatics mix with dark berries, anise, licorice and spice. Nicely matched spirit at play here, elevating the fruit. Amaro bitters on the finish. 500ml. Screw cap. | 16.9% alc. | Drink 2022–2022 | $15 | JP

Mt Pilot Estate ★★★★☆

208 Shannons Road, Byawatha, Vic 3678 **T** 0419 243 225 **www**.mtpilotestatewines.com.au **OPEN** By appt
WINEMAKER Marc Scalzo **EST.** 1996 **DOZENS** 600 **VYDS** 13ha

Lachlan and Penny Campbell have planted shiraz (7ha), cabernet sauvignon (3ha), viognier (2ha) and durif (1ha). The vineyard is planted on deep, well-drained granitic soils at an altitude of 250m near Eldorado, 20km from Wangaratta and 35km from Beechworth. (JH)

---

95   **Durif 2019, North East Victoria** Another salutary lesson in never underestimating the degree of elegance that can be achieved with durif. The grape is very much misunderstood and it's wines like these, with poise and beauty defining the grape's more medium-bodied and spiced side, that will bring a deeper appreciation. And the grape's so-called big tannins are pure silk here. Screw cap. | 14.1% alc. | Drink 2021–2028 | $30 | JP

94   **Cabernet Sauvignon 2018, North East Victoria** Displays elegance in bright plum, cherry and blackberry aromas with a varietal leafiness. A sweet core of fruit holds the palate. Ripe, dense tannins and a long tail of juicy flavour combine to bring this lovely wine to a neat finish. Screw cap. | 14.2% alc. | Drink 2021–2030 | $30 | JP

Alpine Valleys

Anderson & Marsh ★★★★

6815 Great Alpine Road, Porepunkah, Vic 3740 **T** 0419 984 982 **OPEN** By appt **WINEMAKER** Eleana Anderson, Jo Marsh **EST.** 2014 **DOZENS** 60

A joint project between Alpine Valleys winemakers Eleana Anderson (of Mayford Wines) and Jo Marsh (of Billy Button). The first vintage of Catani Blanc de Blanc was made in '14 and was joined by Parell Albariño in '18 and Parell Tempranillo in '19 (Parell is Spanish for pair). Close friends and neighbours, they set out to produce the style of sparkling wines they love to drink. A local parcel of albariño became available in '18 which they were both very interested in, so they decided to make it together under their new label. (JH)

95 **Parell Albariño 2021, Alpine Valleys** With each release, these 2 talented winemakers work hard to unravel the Spanish grape's great mystery, not to mention suitability to our soils. They come mighty close in 2021, delivering a complex and aromatic wine of some beauty. Honeysuckle, lemon, pithy grapefruit, honeydew melon and a touch of preserved lemon savouriness join a fleshy, mealy texture and spiced palate. Utterly attention grabbing, not to mention, delicious. Screw cap. | 13% alc. | Drink 2022-2025 | \$35 | JP

Billy Button Wines

★★★★★

11 Camp Street, Bright, Vic 3741 and 61 Myrtle St, Myrtleford, Vic 3737 **T** (03) 5755 1569 **WWW**.billybuttonwines.com.au **OPEN** 7 days 12-6 **WINEMAKER** Jo Marsh, Glenn James **EST**. 2014 **DOZENS** 6000

Jo Marsh makes light of the numerous awards she won during her studies for her degree in agricultural science (oenology) at the University of Adelaide. She was appointed assistant winemaker at Seppelt Great Western in '03. By '08 she had been promoted to acting senior winemaker. After Seppelt, she became winemaker at Feathertop, and after 2 happy years decided to step out on her own in '14. Billy Button also shares a cellar door with Bush Track Wines in the heart of Myrtleford. (JH)

95 **The Affable Barbera 2021, Alpine Valleys** Lifted perfume in sour cherry, blackberry, licorice and lavender. Masses of fruit flavour fills the mouth with a good, firm cut of acidity bringing home a clean finish. Screw cap. | 14% alc. | Drink 2022-2027 | \$32 | JP

The Alluring Tempranillo 2021, Alpine Valleys The use of Flexcube, i.e. no oak, ensures some powerfully persuasive fruit is elevated and totally engaging in this utterly delicious wine. Captures the grape and its perfect suitability to the Alpine Valleys in a fine display of juicy, dark fruits and lively spice, red licorice and supple tannins. Screw cap. | 14.5% alc. | Drink 2022-2029 | \$32 | JP

The Groovy Grüner Veltliner 2021, Alpine Valleys Grüner loves a cool climate and responds accordingly. Crisp, elegant and oh, so delicate in aromas of apple blossom, green apple, lime and white peach. Maintains an even demeanour, lightly textural, with nectarine, peach, spiced apple and impressive length of flavour. So good. Screw cap. | 13% alc. | Drink 2022-2026 | \$27 | JP

The Clandestine Schioppettino 2021, Alpine Valleys This northern Italian variety has to be considered a future star variety of the Alpine Valleys if the last few releases are anything to go by. It's a meal-in-itself kind of wine, a rolling, fragrant mix of bramble, black pepper, wild berries, anise, chocolate, briar and earthiness in one. Finely etched acid and tannin shape the palate ripe in fruit and with real presence in the glass. Screw cap. | 14% alc. | Drink 2022-2027 | \$32 | JP | ♥

The Beloved Shiraz 2020, Bendigo Fruit sourced from Bendigo due to smoke taint in the Alpine Valleys. Well, this is an eye opener! Jo Marsh dives right in and delivers a stunning wine. Vibrant purple hues. Upbeat, fragrant aromas of red fruits, blackberry, plum, sweet vanillin oak and a fleck of signature Bendigo eucalyptus. Energy to burn on the palate, nicely promoted by supple tannins and balanced oak. Screw cap. | 14.5% alc. | Drink 2021-2032 | \$32 | JP

94 **Rosso 2021, Alpine Valleys King Valley** A blend of 5 Mediterranean red grapes, 37/23/18/13/9% barbera/tempranillo/dolcetto/refosco/sangiovese. Demonstrates why blends matter, and even more so why Mediterranean grape varieties are so well suited to this part of the world. Vivid, deep purple hues. Red cherry, wild raspberry, fennel seed, earth and spice aromas are welcoming, fresh and vital. The palate is supple and even with a brisk acid crunch. Screw cap. | 13.5% alc. | Drink 2021-2025 | \$22 | JP

Gapsted Wines

★★★★

3897 Great Alpine Road, Gapsted, Vic 3737 **T** (03) 5751 9100 **WWW**.gapstedwines.com.au **OPEN** Thurs-Mon 10-5 **WINEMAKER** Andrew Santarossa, Michael Cope-Williams, Toni Pla Bou, Greg Bennet **EST**. 1997 **DOZENS** 250000 **VYDS** 256.1ha

Gapsted is the major brand of the Victorian Alps Winery, which started life (and continues) as a large-scale contract winemaking facility. The quality of the wines made for its own brand has led to the expansion of production not only under that label, but also under a raft of subsidiary labels. As well as the substantial estate plantings, Gapsted sources traditional and alternative grape varieties from the King and Alpine valleys. (JH)

92 **Limited Release Fiano 2021, King Valley** There's a lot of drinking joy to be had with this wine, celebrating ripe tropical fruits, pear skin, citrus and spiced apple, all smoothly rolled out across the palate. A soft, textural landing brings with it plenty of scope for food matching. Screw cap. | 14% alc. | Drink 2022-2024 | $25 | JP

Beechworth

Eldorado Road ★★★★★

46-48 Ford Street, Beechworth, Vic 3747 **T** (03) 5725 1698 **www.**eldoradoroad.com.au **OPEN** Fri–Sat 11–6, Sun–Mon 11–4 **WINEMAKER** Paul Dahlenburg, Ben Dahlenburg, Laurie Schulz **EST.** 2010 **DOZENS** 1500 **VYDS** 4ha

Paul Dahlenburg (nicknamed Bear), Lauretta Schulz (Laurie) and their children leased a 2ha block of shiraz planted in the 1890s with rootlings supplied from France (doubtless grafted) in the wake of phylloxera's devastation of the Glenrowan and Rutherglen plantings. Bear and Laurie knew about the origins of the vineyard, which was in a state of serious decline after years of neglect. Years of tireless work reconstructing the old vines has resulted in tiny amounts of exceptionally good shiraz. (JH)

97 **Perseverance Old Vine Shiraz 2019, Beechworth** The concentration of fruit is truly extraordinary. Seductive in deep purple, gloriously complex and in total harmony, Perseverance is a wonderful celebration of old vines. Dark violet aromas meet a groundswell of black fruits, plum, anise, sage and tilled earth. Unfolds gently, seamlessly, elegantly and so long. Only 118 dozen produced. Screw cap. | 14.6% alc. | Drink 2022-2033 | $85 | JP | ♥

96 **Onyx Durif 2019, North East Victoria** Durif re-imagined, courtesy of cool-climate elegance (Beechworth) mixed with a dose of generosity (Rutherglen) that needs to be tasted by every drinker who was ever scared witless by the grape. This is not scary, rather it's brilliantly delivered as a serious wine of some beauty: aromatic, blueberry, plum, dark chocolate and spice all lifted, fresh and plush. Bravo. Screw cap. | 14.3% alc. | Drink 2022-2034 | $37 | JP | ♥

95 **Quasimodo Nero d'Avola Durif Shiraz 2019, Beechworth** Each grape was treated separately to make this beaut wine. The price belies the work and the wow factor achieved. Vibrant blueberry, black cherry, plum, anise, earth and spice take the lead, to be enhanced by sweet, vanillin oak. Finishes long and supple with an ongoing thread of rosemary. Screw cap. | 13.5% alc. | Drink 2022-2027 | $29 | JP

Fighting Gully Road ★★★★★

Kurrajong Way, Mayday Hill, Beechworth, Vic 3747 **T** 0407 261 373 **www.**fightinggullyroadwines.com.au **OPEN** By appt **WINEMAKER** Mark Walpole **VITICULTURIST** Mark Walpole **EST.** 1997 **DOZENS** 3500 **VYDS** 10.5ha

Mark Walpole and his partner Carolyn De Poi found their elevated north-facing site south of Beechworth in '95. They commenced planting the Aquila Audax Vineyard in '97. In '09 they were fortunate to lease the oldest vineyard in the region, planted by the Smith family in 1978. Mark says, 'We are now making wine in a building in the old and historic Mayday Hills Lunatic Asylum – a place that should be full of winemakers!' (JH)

97 **Black Label Smith's Vineyard Chardonnay 2019, Beechworth** The Smith's Vineyard's chardonnay vines were planted in 1978, the fruit of very high quality. The light touch of winemaker Mark Walpole results in a wine which is at once delicate and precise, yet complex and harmonious, akin to a top-quality chablis. Age shall not weary it. Screw cap. | 13.5% alc. | Drink 2024-2040 | $85 | JH

Giaconda ★★★★★

30 McClay Road, Beechworth, Vic 3747 **T** (03) 5727 0246 **www.**giaconda.com.au **OPEN** By appt **WINEMAKER** Rick Kinzbrunner, Nathan Kinzbrunner **VITICULTURIST** Casey White **EST.** 1982 **DOZENS** 2500 **VYDS** 4ha

These wines have a super-cult status and, given the small production, are extremely difficult to find; they are sold chiefly through restaurants and via their website. The Chardonnay is one of Australia's greatest and is made and matured in the underground wine cellar hewn out of granite. This permits gravity flow and a year-round temperature range of 14–15°C, promising even more for the future. (JH)

97 **Estate Vineyard Chardonnay 2019, Beechworth** The secret – if there is one – to Giaconda chardonnay is the depth of complexity achieved. It is a thing of wonder to get lost in, as you wander through layer upon layer of stone fruits, citrus and grilled nuts, almond cream, spice and then gently embedded oak. Screw cap. | 13.5% alc. | Drink 2022-2036 | $129 | JP | ♥

CENTRAL VICTORIA

GIPPSLAND

NORTH EAST VICTORIA

NORTH WEST VICTORIA

PORT PHILLIP

WESTERN VICTORIA

Savaterre ⓟ ★★★★★

929 Beechworth-Wangaratta Road, Everton Upper, Vic 3678 **T** (03) 5727 0551 **www**.savaterre.com
OPEN By appt **WINEMAKER** Keppell Smith **EST.** 1996 **DOZENS** 2500 **VYDS** 8ha

Keppell Smith embarked on a career in wine in 1996, studying winemaking at CSU and (at a practical level) with Phillip Jones at Bass Phillip. Organic principles govern the viticulture and the winemaking techniques look to the Old World rather than the New. Smith's stated aim is to produce outstanding individualistic wines far removed from the mainstream. (JH)

97   **Pinot Noir 2018, Beechworth** Take a deep breath, inhale; the scent of mountain wildflowers, violet, crushed raspberry and cherry is enthralling, addictive even. Intense and tight on the palate, it opens to layers of clean, bright red and black fruits, enhanced by savoury spice, warm background oak and ripe, textural tannins. A savoury ferrous, mineral finish offers yet another layer on this most complex pinot. Outstanding.   Screw cap. | 13.5% alc. | Drink 2022-2030 | $75 | JP | ♥

Serengale Vineyard ⓟⓐ ★★★★★

1168 Beechworth-Wangaratta Road, Everton Upper, Vic 3678 **T** 0428 585 348
www.serengalebeechworth.com.au **OPEN** By appt **WINEMAKER** Gayle Taylor **VITICULTURIST** Serena Abbinga, Gayle Taylor **EST.** 1999 **DOZENS** 1000 **VYDS** 7ha

Gayle Taylor and Serena Abbinga established their business in 1999. Gayle had worked in the wine industry for over 20 years, while Serena was seeking to return to North East Victoria after many years living and working in inner city Melbourne. A 3-year search culminated in the acquisition of a 24ha property in the Everton Hills. In '15 the winery was completed, and the first vintage made. (JH)

96   **Row 16 Chardonnay 2019, Beechworth** More structured, with a clean and linear mouthfeel, than the standard chardonnay, Row 16 embraces a mineral, flinty interpretation of the grape with almost chablis-like precision. Nougat, spiced apple, white peach and grapefruit concentrated flavours. Pure, fresh acidity is nicely integrated.   Screw cap. | 13.8% alc. | Drink 2021-2029 | $62 | JP

Vignerons Schmölzer & Brown ★★★★★

39 Thorley Road, Stanley, Vic 3747 **T** 0411 053 487 **www**.vsandb.com.au **WINEMAKER** Tessa Brown, Jeremy Scholzer **VITICULTURIST** Tessa Brown **EST.** 2014 **DOZENS** 1800 **VYDS** 2ha

Winemaker and viticulturist Tessa Brown graduated from CSU with a degree in viticulture in the late '90s and undertook postgraduate winemaking studies at the University of Adelaide in the mid '00s. In '09, Mark Walpole showed Tessa and partner Jeremy Schmölzer a property that he described as 'the jewel in the crown of Beechworth'. When it came onto the market unexpectedly in '12, they were in a position to jump. By sheer chance, just across the road from Thorley was a tiny vineyard, a bit over 0.4ha, with dry-grown pinot and chardonnay around 20 years old. When they realised it was not being managed for production, they struck up a working relationship with the owners, getting the vineyard into shape and making their first Brunnen wines in '14. (JH)

95   **Obstgarten T Riesling 2021, King Valley** T stands for trocken, meaning dry in the German riesling classification. With 6–8g/L RS, this is not necessarily as dry as Australians would consider it, but the high acidity is definitely softened and the result is quite a stunning display of precision with clear, bright lemon zest, grapefruit, green apple and white flowers with sherbety, bright acidity. Screw cap. | 11.5% alc. | Drink 2021-2032 | $35 | JP

Weathercraft Wine ⓟ ★★★★☆

1241 Beechworth-Wangaratta Road, Everton Upper, Vic 3678 **T** (03) 5727 0518
www.weathercraft.com.au **OPEN** By appt **WINEMAKER** Raquel Jones **VITICULTURIST** Raquel Jones **EST.** 1998 **DOZENS** 1800 **VYDS** 4ha

In 2016, Raquel and Hugh Jones discovered a vineyard 10min out of Beechworth, neighbouring the likes of Giaconda and Castanga. It had an immaculate 20yo of shiraz, planted in 1998, with fruit sold to Yalumba as well as to smaller producers. Biological farming and soil health is a priority for them and the preference is for traditional, low-intervention winemaking, including the use of amphora. (JH)

96   **Amphora Blanco 2021, Beechworth** Albariño/chardonnay blend. A revelation! The use of amphora opens up not only complexity and the textural possibilities of albariño and chardonnay, but performs

it with a streamlined, seamless beauty. Grapefruit, lemon zest, tangerine, white nectarine and saline aromas. Time in amphora has knitted the whole piece together. Screw cap. | 12% alc. | Drink 2021-2026 | $38 | JP | ♥

94   **Pinot Gris 2021, Alpine Valleys** Striking exotic, complex aromas: spiced apple, white peach, mango, talc and musk. The soft, gentle mouthfeel is a feature, together with a delicious spiciness before finishing clean. Easy to love. Screw cap. | 13% alc. | Drink 2021-2025 | $25 | JP

CENTRAL VICTORIA

GIPPSLAND

NORTH EAST VICTORIA

NORTH WEST VICTORIA

PORT PHILLIP

WESTERN VICTORIA

REGION

King Valley

Brown Brothers ★★★★★

239 Milawa-Bobinawarrah Road, Milawa, Vic 3678 **T** (03) 5720 5500 **www**.brownbrothers.com.au **OPEN** 7 days 9-5 **WINEMAKER** Joel Tilbrook, Cate Looney, Geoff Alexander, Katherine Brown, Tom Canning, Simon McMillan **VITICULTURIST** Brett McClen, Sean Dean **EST.** 1889 **DOZENS** 1 million **VYDS** 570ha

Brown Brothers draws upon a considerable number of vineyards spread throughout a range of site climates – from very warm to very cool. An expansion into Heathcote added significantly to its armoury. In '10 Brown Brothers acquired Tasmania's Tamar Ridge. In May '16 it acquired Innocent Bystander, and with it a physical presence in the Yarra Valley. A founding member of Australia's First Families of Wine. (JH)

96   **Patricia Cabernet Sauvignon 2017, King Valley** Always a strength in the Patricia range, this cabernet style is effortless and all class. Quality of fruit is the star, with oak bringing a layer of nuance and complexity to a solid core of cassis and plum fruits with bracken, earth, violets, cassia bark and a dusting of powdery cocoa. Brings both cabernet leafiness and spiced-filled liveliness to the finish. A joy to drink. Screw cap. | 14.5% alc. | Drink 2022-2030 | $62 | JP | ♥

Chrismont ★★★★☆

251 Upper King River Road, Cheshunt, Vic 3678 **T** (03) 5729 8220 **www**.chrismont.com.au **OPEN** 7 days 10-5 **WINEMAKER** Warren Proft, Prasad Patil **VITICULTURIST** Arnie Pizzini, Warren Proft **EST.** 1980 **DOZENS** 25000 **VYDS** 100ha

Arnie and Jo Pizzini's substantial vineyards in the Cheshunt and Whitfield areas of the upper King Valley have been planted to riesling, chardonnay, pinot gris, merlot, barbera, sagrantino, marzemino, arneis, prosecco, fiano, petit manseng, tempranillo, sangiovese and nebbiolo. The La Zona range ties in the Italian heritage of the Pizzinis and is part of the intense interest in all things Italian. (JH)

96   **Pinot Gris 2021, King Valley** The winemaker aims for a luscious style and delivers a little treasure. The grape is in its happy place here, with a striking, fully ripened, complex wine with a touch of the exotic. Talc, musk, citrus, spiced apple and peach aromas unfurl. While luscious with supple texture, it keeps its freshness all the while as you discover layer after layer of quince, citrus, apple, grilled nuts and the most captivating spice. Screw cap. | 13.5% alc. | Drink 2021-2026 | $26 | JP

Dal Zotto Wines ★★★★★

Main Road, Whitfield, Vic 3733 **T** (03) 5729 8321 **www**.dalzotto.com.au **OPEN** 7 days 10-5 **WINEMAKER** Michael Dal Zotto, Daniel Bettio **EST.** 1987 **DOZENS** 60000 **VYDS** 46ha

The Dal Zotto family is a King Valley institution; ex-tobacco growers, then contract grapegrowers, they are now 100% focused on their Dal Zotto wine range. Founded by Otto and Elena, ownership has now passed to sons Michael and Christian and their partners Lynne and Simone, who handle winemaking, sales and marketing respectively. Dal Zotto is producing increasing amounts of Italian varieties of consistent quality from its substantial estate vineyard. (JH)

95   **Pucino VP Prosecco 2021, King Valley** A different look for the popular Pucino, with a vintage release that brings added complexity and introduces a touch of savouriness. Aromas embrace a core of citrus and apple and then explore baked quince, white peach, orange peel and acacia. The '21 vintage was a ripper in the King Valley, and there's good natural balance and texture here, together with a concentrated flavour that finishes with a thread of intriguing preserved lemon. Crown. | 10.5% alc. | $27 | JP

94   **Fiano 2021, King Valley** The fiano grape continues its takeover of our hearts and minds, with another strong performance. Pear skin, stone fruits, quince jelly and spice offer an attractive introduction to a wine that retains a strong presence in the glass, while at the same time appearing deliciously easy to get to know. Look to the texture, the spice and the downright ease with which it bewitches. Screw cap. | 13.8% alc. | Drink 2022-2026 | $27 | JP

Pizzini ⓨⓦⓐ ★★★★★

175 King Valley Road, Whitfield, Vic 3768 **T** (03) 5729 8278 **www**.pizzini.com.au **OPEN** 7 days 10–5 **WINEMAKER** Joel Pizzini **VITICULTURIST** David Morgan **EST.** 1980 **DOZENS** 30 000 **VYDS** 75ha

The Pizzini family have been grapegrowers in the King Valley for over 40 years. Originally, much of the then riesling, chardonnay and cabernet sauvignon grape production was sold, but since the late '90s the focus has been on winemaking, particularly from Italian varieties. Pizzini's success has enabled an increase vineyard in holdings to 75ha. (JH)

94 **Pietra Rossa Sangiovese 2019, King Valley** Celebrates what we love about the sangiovese grape from an immediate red-fruit and spice intensity through to a warm, textural mouthfeel and light savouriness. That's a lot to pack into the price. Black cherry, raspberry, pomegranate, potpourri, thyme aromas and flavours aplenty. Flavours envelop the tastebuds, moving in time with gentle oak. Savoury tannins bring added character to this impressive, well-priced sangiovese. Screw cap. | 13.8% alc. | Drink 2021-2029 | $28 | JP

REGION

Rutherglen

All Saints Estate ⓨⓦ⊜ⓐ ★★★★★

205 All Saints Road, Wahgunyah, Vic 3687 **T** 1800 021 621 **www**.allsaintswine.com.au **OPEN** 7 days 10–5 & public hols 11–5 **WINEMAKER** Nick Brown **EST.** 1864 **DOZENS** 22 000 **VYDS** 47.9ha

The winery rating reflects the fortified wines, including the unique releases of Museum Muscat and Muscadelle, each with an average age of more than 100 years (and table wines). All Saints and St Leonards are owned and managed by fourth-generation Brown family members Eliza, Angela and Nick. Eliza is an energetic and highly intelligent leader, wise beyond her years, and highly regarded by the wine industry. (JH)

97 **Grand Muscat NV, Rutherglen** All Saints Estate has a fineness of touch across all of its fortifieds, a real elegance which is here in spades. An intense tasting experience awaits, wrapped in bright neutral spirit, rich and layered in treacle, chocolate-covered coffee beans, fruitcake, fig and golden walnuts. 375ml. Vinolok. | 18% alc. | $75 | JP

Rare Muscat NV, Rutherglen The official Rare Muscat classification is for fortifieds with an average 30+ years. All Saints' Rare averages 45 years, testament to the astonishing breadth and depth of stocks in its possession. How those stocks are managed, how neutral spirit is used to brighten and freshen them is the secret to a great muscat. It's here in a luscious core of dried fruit, fruitcake, soused raisins, honey and treacle-drenched walnut. Then comes the clean, driving spirit elevating everything into sheer decadence. 375ml. Vinolok. | 18% alc. | $120 | JP

Campbells ⓨⓦⓐ ★★★★★

4603 Murray Valley Highway, Rutherglen, Vic 3685 **T** (02) 6033 6000 **www**.campbellswines.com.au **OPEN** 7 days 10–5 **WINEMAKER** Julie Campbell **EST.** 1870 **DOZENS** 36 000 **VYDS** 72ha

Campbells has a long and rich history, with 5 generations of wine making. There have been spectacular successes in unexpected quarters (white table wines, especially riesling) and expected success with muscat and topaque. Following the death of Colin Campbell in '19, daughters Jane and Julie Campbell are now at the helm, as managing director and head winemaker respectively. A founding member of Australia's First Families of Wine. (JH)

99 **Merchant Prince Rare Muscat NV, Rutherglen** The oldest base wine is more than 70 years old. Definitely a once-in-a-lifetime experience. It is both luscious and multi-faceted in flavours. The house style brings deep pockets of the most delicious spice to enliven plum pudding, burnt fig, salted caramel, nougat with a chocolate-covered almond nuttiness. 375ml. Screw cap. | 17.5% alc. | $126 | JP

97 **Isabella Rare Topaque NV, Rutherglen** One look and you know you are in Rare territory: dark walnut brown with olive tinge. Moves slowly in the glass and asks the drinker to pause and contemplate its astounding richness and concentration of aromas and flavours gathered over decades. Boiled fruitcake, malt biscuits, soused raisins, caramel, treacle and chocolate aromas gather pace on the palate. A wine to get lost in, with its layers of complexity, dense and deep. Count the minutes the taste remains alive in the mouth. 375ml. Screw cap. | 17.5% alc. | $140 | JP

96 **The Barkly Durif 2017, Rutherglen** First impression? This is one serious, structured red wine. And the second? Make mine a medium-rare steak. The Barkly affords durif the status it deserves, celebrating its bold ways and its much under-rated elegant herbal/floral detail and savoury tannins. A masterful winemaking performance. Screw cap. | 14.5% alc. | Drink 2022-2033 | $70 | JP

Grand Muscat NV, Rutherglen Grand is a step up in average age in the classification and everything else follows. There is seamless beauty here. Deep walnut hue. Complexity rises dramatically with dark chocolate, licorice, treacle, raisin, plum pudding and baking spice. Intense. Runs smoothly across the palate, so naturally warm and sweet and fresh. Memorable. 375ml. Screw cap. | 17.5% alc. | $70 | JP

Grand Topaque NV, Rutherglen Topaque is about elegance and poise. Here it is multiplied by age and winemaker skill to reveal both delicacy and concentration. It's a fine tightrope walked and mastered here, with its lifted aromatics, freshness and utter deliciousness in dark malt biscuit, dried dates, fruit cake, butterscotch and nutty rancio qualities. And so, so smooth. Very special. 375ml. Screw cap. | 17.5% alc. | $70 | JP

95   **Bobbie Burns Shiraz 2019, Rutherglen** This release celebrates 50 vintages of Bobbie Burns. The wine is symbolic of the generosity and enduring style of Rutherglen shiraz, not to mention an upfront, honest approach to winemaking that lets the fruit sing. Incredibly consistent performer in ripe, spicy black fruits, dusty cocoa powder, earth and spice. Strong yet measured on the palate with fine, lithe tannins guaranteeing longevity. Brilliant wine for the price. Screw cap. | 14.8% alc. | Drink 2022-2030 | $25 | JP

Chambers Rosewood ⓘ   ★★★★★

Barkly Street, Rutherglen, Vic 3685 **T** (02) 6032 8641 **www**.chambersrosewood.com.au **OPEN** 7 days 10-4 **WINEMAKER** Stephen Chambers **EST.** 1858 **DOZENS** 5000 **VYDS** 50ha

Chambers' Rare Muscat and Rare Muscadelle (previously Topaque or Tokay) are the greatest of all in the Rutherglen firmament and should be treated as national treasures; the other wines in the hierarchy also magnificent. Stephen Chambers (6th generation) is winemaker, but father Bill is seldom far away. (JH)

96   **Grand Muscat NV, Rutherglen** The solera for this fortified was started in the 1930s. You read that correctly, 1930s! Winemaker Stephen Chambers looks to a higher level of wood-derived flavour and greater lusciousness in his Grand Muscat, which comes, in big part, from the depth of his astonishing solera system. Should this be the start of a great fortified love affair for many, such is its sweet abandon into rich raisiny Christmas cake, dried fruit, butterscotch, roasted coffee and alluring rancio nuttiness. And so fresh. Bravo! 375ml bottle. Screw cap. | 18.5% alc. | $60 | JP

95   **Classic Tawny NV, Rutherglen** A fortified blend of shiraz, grenache, touriga nacional, grand noir and graciano. A glorious tawny that is both fresh and divinely rich in rancio nuttiness, walnuts drenched in toffee and dried fruits. 750ml. Screw cap. | 18% alc. | $25 | JP

Old Vine Muscat NV, Rutherglen Equivalent to the Classic Muscat classification. A beauty of a fortified, displaying all of the seductive allure of the grape in honeyed fruitcake, dried figs and chocolate raisins, fuelled by lingering rose oil aromatics. And so fresh. An intriguing wine to start a fortified obsession. 375ml. Screw cap. | 18% alc. | $30 | JP

Morris ⓘ @   ★★★★★

Mia Mia Road, Rutherglen, Vic 3685 **T** (02) 6026 7303 **www**.morriswines.com **OPEN** Mon-Sun 10-4 **WINEMAKER** David Morris **EST.** 1859 **DOZENS** 100000 **VYDS** 96ha

One of the greatest of the fortified winemakers, ranking an eyelash behind Chambers Rosewood. Morris has changed the labelling system for its sublime fortified wines with a higher-than-average entry point for the (Classic) Liqueur Muscat; Topaque and the ultra-premium wines are being released under the Old Premium Liqueur (Rare) label. These Rutherglen fortified wines have no equivalent in any other part of the world. In July 2016 Casella Family Brands acquired Morris after decades of ownership by Pernod Ricard. (JH)

98   **Old Premium Rare Topaque NV, Rutherglen** The perpetual understudy to Rutherglen's more celebrated and vivacious muscat, Morris lifts Topaque – aka muscadelle – up to where it belongs, as an equal. The perfume envelops the drinker, the palate astounds in waves of dried fruit, toffee, honey cake, caramel and roasted nuts, luscious but nicely kept trim and clean in neutral spirit. The work of a master. 500ml bottle. Screw cap. | 17.5% alc. | $90 | JP

97   **Old Premium Rare Muscat NV, Rutherglen** Each year I reach for superlatives, each year I give up: imagine your favourite dessert and then multiply it tenfold: plum pudding, dark chocolate, sticky date, panforte with fruit peel, caramel sauce, all smoothly honed and lifted by neutral spirit. And the best part is, for all of its lusciousness, it remains attainable. 500ml bottle. Screw cap. | 17% alc. | $90 | JP

95   **Classic Topaque NV, Rutherglen** A well-priced masterpiece. The perfume is both fresh, sweet and savoury. The palate sets the tastebuds alight in honeyed walnuts, butterscotch, malt biscuits and golden raisins, with a nutty rancio lift. Finishes with a clean, tannic splash of muscadelle's signature cold tea. Great value. 500ml. Screw cap. | 17.5% alc. | $25 | JP

94   **VP Vintage 2009, Rutherglen** Compared to its sibling, the '08 VP, this wine seems markedly younger, fresher and the brandy spirit more obvious. What a difference a year makes. It is still in building mode, but I suspect it will be a more elegant VP, more aromatic, floral and a wine to remember. Screw cap. | 19% alc. | $25 | JP

Classic Muscat, Rutherglen Meets the pricepoint and smashes it with complexity and vibrancy. So much life and energy in this aged muscat, from the lifted aromatics and lusciousness of raisin, orange peel, caramel, mocha-coffee and gentle rancio nuttiness, to the freshness of younger material and clean, neutral spirit. Works a treat. 500ml. Screw cap. | 17.5% alc. | $25 | JP

Pfeiffer Wines ⓎⓃⒻ ★★★★★

167 Distillery Road, Wahgunyah, Vic 3687 **T** (02) 6033 2805 **www**.pfeifferwines.com.au **OPEN** Mon-Sat 9-5, Sun 10-5 **WINEMAKER** Jen Pfeiffer, Chris Pfeiffer **VITICULTURIST** Paul Heard, Mick Patford **EST.** 1984 **DOZENS** 20000 **VYDS** 33ha

Family-owned and run, Pfeiffer Wines occupies one of the historic wineries (built in 1885) that abound in North East Victoria. In 2012, Chris Pfeiffer was awarded an Order of Australia Medal (OAM) for his services to the wine industry. Pfeiffer's Muscats, Topaques and other fortified wines are a key part of the business. The arrival of daughter Jen, has dramatically lifted the quality of the table wines. Chris Pfeiffer celebrated his 40th vintage in '13, having well and truly set the scene for supremely gifted daughter Jen to assume the chief winemaking role. (JH)

97   **Rare Muscat NV, Rutherglen** Few winemakers can enter into the rarefied Rare classification of muscat. Pfeiffer Wines, here boasting an average of 25 years, brings a fresh, fruity and floral input on what remains a luscious, concentrated fortified. Dark amber in hue. Walnut kernel, toasted hazelnut, blackstrap licorice, fig, treacle and rose petal bring a luxurious richness in aroma and taste, enhanced and brought to life with energy by the blender's art. Lives long. 500ml. Screw cap. | 17.5% alc. | $130 | JP

Rare Topaque NV, Rutherglen The Pfeiffer style is quite distinctive, the cold-brew-coffee aromas so characteristic, joined by almond nougat, Christmas cake, prune, burnt butter and Saunders' malt extract. Winds and glides its way through the mouth, intensely sweet but also cleanly delivered. Lovely. 500ml. Screw cap. | 17.5% alc. | $130 | JP

95   **Seriously Fine Pale Dry Apera NV, Rutherglen** Jen Pfeiffer practises a dying winemaking art with gusto. More power to her, as she delivers one super-refreshing, dry and sultry apera. One whiff of the almond, orange peel, salted butter and nutty flor aromas gets the saliva working. A touch of lime-rich marmalade and salted nuts on the palate with plenty of tang, and it's an irresistible force. 500ml bottle. Screw cap. | 16% alc. | $29 | JP

Classic Muscat NV, Rutherglen Classic sets the standard, the house style for most Rutherglen makers, and this sets it very high indeed. Aromas of wet rose petal, orange peel, dried fruit and butterscotch. Sets the scene for a sweet (261g/L), clean and fresh fortified that offers amazing quality for the price. 500ml. Screw cap. | 17.5% alc. | $35 | JP

Classic Rutherglen Topaque NV, Marginally drier (248g/L) than the Classic Muscat and gives the strong impression of being younger and fresher than its sibling. It isn't. Average age remains 12-13 years. Golden syrup, salted caramel and orange peel are the trademarks for this house's Topaque, together with a bright freshness and long finish. Another winner from master fortified makers Chris and Jen Pfeiffer. 500ml. Screw cap. | 17.5% alc. | $35 | JP

St Leonards Vineyard ⓎⓃⒻ ★★★★

St Leonards Road, Wahgunyah, Vic 3687 **T** 1800 021 621 **www**.stleonardswine.com.au **OPEN** Thurs-Sun 10-5 **WINEMAKER** Nick Brown, Chloe Earl **EST.** 1860 **DOZENS** 3500 **VYDS** 12ha

An old favourite, with a range of premium wines cleverly marketed through an attractive cellar door and bistro at the historic winery on the banks of the Murray. It is run by Eliza Brown (CEO), sister Angela (online communications manager) and brother Nick (vineyard and winery manager). They are perhaps better known as the trio who fulfil the same roles at All Saints Estate. (JH)

92   **Hip Sip Muscat NV, Rutherglen** A timely reflection on the beauty of the style with an abiding floral charm. Rose oil infiltrates every space with dried fruit, fig and orange peel with a sweet golden syrup harmony. 350ml. Screw cap. | 17.5% alc. | $22 | JP

Hip Sip Tawny NV, Rutherglen This amber-coloured tawny carries both freshness and richness in flavour: prune, dried fruit, walnut and burnt toffee. Smooth palate texture follows with bright, clean spirit leading the way. 350ml bottle. Vinolok. | 17.5% alc. | $22 | JP

Stanton & Killeen Wines Ⓨ ★★★★★

440 Jacks Road, Murray Valley Highway, Rutherglen, Vic 3685 **T** (02) 6032 9457 **www**.stantonandkilleen.com.au **OPEN** Mon-Sat 9-5, Sun & public hols 10-5 **WINEMAKER** Faustine Ropars **EST.** 1875 **DOZENS** 10000 **VYDS** 34ha

In 2020, Stanton & Killeen celebrated its 145th anniversary. The business is owned and run by 7th-generation vigneron Natasha Killeen and her mother and CEO, Wendy Killeen. Fortifieds are a strong focus for the winery with around half of its production dedicated to this style. A vineyard rejuvenation program has been implemented since '14, focusing on sustainable and environmentally friendly practices. (JH)

95   **Vintage Fortified 2018, Rutherglen** A mix of 5 Portuguese traditional port varieties and durif (a Rutherglen favourite), brings a certain distinctive North East Victorian feel to this vintage fortified. It carries on the fine tradition set by generations of Stanton & Killeen winemakers. A brilliant and well-judged blend. Arrives with speed, a rush of sweet, nutty, savoury scents of anise, woodsy spices, blackberry, black cherry, licorice and chocolate panforte. Gathers pace on the palate, sped along with bright, brisk neutral spirit. Still feeling its way. Do not disturb for 10 years, at least!!   Cork. | 18% alc. | $22 | JP

94   **Arinto 2021, Rutherglen** S&K are making a name for their promotion of Iberian grape varieties. Here, Portugal's arinto speaks loudly, without the presence of oak, in citrus, green apple, orange peel with musk. Shows a clean, dry pair of heels.   Screw cap. | 13% alc. | Drink 2022-2025 | $30 | JP

North West Victoria

Murray Darling

Chalmers ★★★★★

118 Third Street, Merbein, Vic 3505 **T** 0400 261 932 **www**.chalmers.com.au **WINEMAKER** Bart van Olphen, Tennille and Kim Chalmers **VITICULTURIST** Bruce Chalmers, Troy McInnes **EST.** 1989 **DOZENS** 10000 **VYDS** 27ha

The Australian wine industry owes a debt of gratitude to the Chalmers family. For more than a decade, the family, led by Bruce and Jenni Chalmers, have led the way in importing new, 'alternative' grape varieties to this country through their Merbein nursery and vineyard. With vineyards in the Murray Darling (established in the 1980s) and Heathcote regions (2011), and under the second generation Kim and Tennille Chalmers, the family produces cutting-edge wines. The family excels as both growers and producers, never content with the status quo. (JP)

95   **Pecorino 2021, Heathcote** It shows its class here with the lifted scent of honeysuckle, citrus and baked apple. Rich and textural, it fills the mouth with delicious flavour that goes and goes, replete in peach, nectarine and dried herbs wrapped in a light blanket of honey. Acidity balances everything very nicely.   Screw cap. | 13.5% alc. | Drink 2022-2027 | $31 | JP

MDI Wines ★★★★

198 Gertrude St, Fitzroy, Vic 3065 **T** www.mdi.wine **OPEN** By appt **WINEMAKER** Kevin McCarthy **EST.** 2022 **DOZENS** 4000

MDI Wines is a celebration of winemaker Kevin McCarthy's enduring love affair with the people, land and wines of the Murray Darling. His first up-close, hands-on grapes experience occurred in 2002 when he bought Murray Darling sangiovese to fill otherwise empty tanks after a disastrously small vintage on the Peninsula at his then winery, T'Gallant. With MDI he embraces the alternative grape varieties of the region to create approachable skin-contact wines. (JP)

93   **Sangiovese 2020, Murray Darling** A summer fruit bowl of the freshest red cherries, raspberries, anise and dusty cacao. The fragrance is mesmerising. Takes a savoury turn on the palate with an undercurrent of cherry kirsch, salty capers and earth, against black fruits and a smoky nuttiness. Chalky tannins drive through to the finish.   Diam. | 13% alc. | Drink 2022-2025 | $25 | JP

Zilzie Wines ★★★★★

544 Kulkyne Way, Karadoc, Vic 3496 **T** (03) 5025 8100 **www**.zilziewines.com **OPEN** By appt **WINEMAKER** Jonathan Creek **VITICULTURIST** Andrew Forbes, Steven Forbes **EST.** 1999 **VYDS** 700ha

The Forbes family has been farming since the early 1900s. Zilzie is currently run by Roslyn Forbes and sons Steven and Andrew. Having established a dominant position as a

CENTRAL VICTORIA

GIPPSLAND

NORTH EAST · VICTORIA

NORTH WEST VICTORIA

PORT PHILLIP

WESTERN VICTORIA

supplier of grapes to Southcorp, Zilzie formed a wine company in '99 and built a winery in 2000, expanding it to its current capacity of 60000t. The wines consistently far exceed expectations, that consistency driving the substantial production volume in an extremely competitive market. The winery is certified organic. (JH)

95 **Platinum Edition Arinto 2021, Riverland** A mild summer in the Riverland has delivered a beauty of a wine. Arinto, the Portuguese white grape, brings forth its lemon citrus tang in spades here with pear, spice and apple. Acidity is keen, delicious and super-dry. Screw cap. | 12.5% alc. | Drink 2021-2025 | $35 | JP

REGION

Swan Hill

Andrew Peace Wines ★★★★

Murray Valley Highway, Piangil, Vic 3597 **T** (03) 5030 5291 **www**.apwines.com **OPEN** Mon-Fri 9-5, Sat 12-4 **WINEMAKER** Andrew Peace, David King **EST**. 1995 **DOZENS** 180000 **VYDS** 270ha

The Peace family has been a major Swan Hill grapegrower since '80, moving into winemaking with the opening of a $3 million winery in '96. The planting of sagrantino is the largest of only a few such plantings in Australia. (JH)

91 **Full Moon Durif 2020, Swan Hill** Combines all the things we love about durif – power and beauty, all within a medium-bodied frame. Deep, inky purple-black cherry hues. Aromatic of blueberry, black cherry, dark chocolate and smokey lapsang souchong tea. For all its abundant complex fruit, it remains finely edged in sapid, fine tannins. Great value here. Screw cap. | 13.5% alc. | Drink 2022-2027 | $22 | JP

ZONE

Port Phillip

Dinny Goonan ★★★★☆

880 Winchelsea-Deans Marsh Road, Bambra, Vic 3241 **T** 0438 408 420 **www**.dinnygoonan.com.au **OPEN** 7 days Jan, w'ends & public hols Nov-Jun **WINEMAKER** Dinny Goonan, Angus Goonan **EST**. 1990 **DOZENS** 1500 **VYDS** 5.5ha

The genesis of Dinny Goonan dates back to 1988, when Dinny bought a 20ha property near Bambra, in the hinterland of the Otway Coast. Dinny had recently completed a viticulture diploma at CSU and initially a wide range of varieties was planted in what is now known as the Nursery Block, to establish those best suited to the area. As these came into production Dinny headed back to CSU, where he completed a wine science degree. (JH)

95 **Single Vineyard Riesling 2021, Port Phillip** Another winning riesling from the maker sourcing single-vineyard fruit from the Otway Hinterland, giving ever-increasing credence to the grape in this part of the world. So enticingly fragrant in white flowers, citrus blossom, lime, lemon drop and orange peel. Clean, with a delicious purity of fruit, well supported by brisk acidity. Screw cap. | 13% alc. | Drink 2021-2032 | $30 | JP

Shadowfax Winery ★★★★★

K Road, Werribee, Vic 3030 **T** (03) 9731 4420 **www**.shadowfax.com.au **OPEN** Wed-Mon 11-5 **WINEMAKER** Alister Timms **VITICULTURIST** Ko Hironaka **EST**. 2000 **DOZENS** 10000 **VYDS** 28ha

Once an offspring of Werribee Park and its grand mansion, Shadowfax is now very much its own master. Alister Timms, with degrees in science (University of Melbourne) and oenology (University of Adelaide) became chief winemaker in '17 (replacing long-serving winemaker Matt Harrop). (JH)

95 **Minnow Roussanne 2021, Port Phillip** Heady aromas of ginger flower and honeysuckle, mandarin, white stone fruit and pear, all in perfect proportion. A drizzle of honey and ginger, plus some cinnamon with fluffy creamy lees filling out the finely tuned palate. The lemon acidity takes it to a long finish. Screw cap. | 13% alc. | Drink 2022-2025 | $28 | JF

Pinot Gris 2021, Macedon Ranges Gosh, I'd swear there's gewürztraminer in the mix given the lychee aroma and flavour – most unusual yet appealing, too. That adds to delicious flavours of baked apple and pear crumble, ginger cream and tangy lemon sauce. The palate is luscious without being heavy. It finishes convincingly. Screw cap. | 13% alc. | Drink 2021-2025 | $30 | JF

Chardonnay 2021, Geelong A wave of white nectarine, grapefruit and lemon layered with zest, ginger cream, woodsy spices plus vanillin toasty oak, not too much, set the richer scene. However, the saline-like acidity is pure, long and reins everything back into a svelte shape. Screw cap. | 13% alc. | Drink 2022-2029 | $35 | JF

Pinot Noir 2020, Macedon Ranges A light, bright, enticing ruby hue and so aromatic: florals, damp forest floor, spiced macerated cherries and a pepperiness too, with a hint of meaty reduction. Lighter framed with fine tannins and while this is overall savoury, it's led more by refreshing acidity, rendering it a vivacious wine. Made from a blend of fruit off 4 single-vineyard sites and in this vintage, very much the sum of its parts – and shining as a result. Screw cap. | 13% alc. | Drink 2021-2028 | $35 | JF

94   **Minnow Grenache Mataro 2021, Port Phillip** An even split between the varieties and they are good friends as each complements the other, resulting in a balanced, complete wine in the drink-me-now category. It's such a great mix because it's floral and spicy, full of juicy, red berries, sarsaparilla, cherry cola and meaty charcuterie characters. Plenty of refreshing perky acidity and grainy, light tannins to guide across the mid-weighted palate. Screw cap. | 13% alc. | Drink 2022-2028 | $28 | JF

Studley Park Vineyard   ★★★☆

5 Garden Terrace, Kew, Vic 3101 (postal) **T** (03) 9852 8483 **www.studleypark.com.au** **WINEMAKER** Llew Knight (Contract) **EST.** 1994 **DOZENS** 500 **VYDS** 0.5ha

Geoff Pryor's Studley Park Vineyard is one of Melbourne's best kept secrets. It is on a bend of the Yarra River barely 4km from the Melbourne CBD, on a 0.5ha block once planted to vines, but for a century used for market gardening, then replanted with cabernet sauvignon. (JH)

90   **Rosé 2020, Port Phillip** A bright, light orange. Cherry, blood orange and gentle spice aromas lead onto the dry and well-balanced palate, before closing with gently grippy tannins which should make this a treat with grilled lamb cutlets and barbecued salmon or tuna this summer. Screw cap. | 12.5% alc. | Drink 2021-2022 | $20 | PR

REGION
Geelong

Banks Road   ★★★★★

600 Banks Road, Marcus Hill, Vic 3222 **T** 0455 594 391 **www.banksroad.com.au** **OPEN** Fri–Sun 11–5 **WINEMAKER** William Derham **EST.** 2001 **DOZENS** 2000 **VYDS** 6ha

Banks Road is a family-owned and operated winery on the Bellarine Peninsula. The estate vineyard is adopting biodynamic principles, eliminating the use of insecticides and moving to eliminate the use of all chemicals on the land. The winery not only processes the Banks Road grapes, but also makes wine for other small producers in the area. (JH)

94   **CS Wine Co Shiraz 2019, Heathcote** Sourced from the Greenstone Vineyard and arrives in typical Heathcote deep purple hues. There's an elegance here, real poise with a touch of whole-bunch-driven lifted aromas of dried herbs and violet mingling with black fruits, anise and cassia bark. The palate is fully integrated, framed in background vanillin oak. Finishes clean, long. A stunner for the price. Screw cap. | 13.5% alc. | Drink 2021-2032 | $28 | JP

Bannockburn Vineyards    ★★★★★

92 Kelly Lane, Bannockburn, Vic 3331 **T** (03) 5281 1363 **www.bannockburnvineyards.com** **OPEN** By appt **WINEMAKER** Matthew Holmes **VITICULTURIST** Lucas Grigsby **EST.** 1974 **DOZENS** 6000 **VYDS** 21.2ha

The late Stuart Hooper had a deep love for the wines of Burgundy, and was able to drink the best. When he established Bannockburn, it was inevitable that pinot noir and chardonnay would form the major part of the plantings. Bannockburn is still owned by members of the Hooper family, who continue to respect Stuart's strong belief in making wines that reflect the flavours of the certified organic vineyard. (JH)

98   **S.R.H. 2019, Geelong** A superbly balanced wine, the fruit foremost, effortlessly holding its graceful line and length, and perfect to drink tonight or in a decade. Screw cap. | 13.8% alc. | Drink 2022-2034 | $77 | JH

CENTRAL VICTORIA

GIPPSLAND

NORTH EAST VICTORIA

NORTH WEST VICTORIA

PORT PHILLIP

WESTERN VICTORIA

97   **De La Terre 2019, Geelong** Typically powerful and complex, with dark fruits that have made light work of the oak, but haven't moved out of primary mode. Will cruise along the next 15–20 years, as the savoury, forest floor and spice notes develop in a leisurely fashion.   Screw cap. | 13.3% alc. | Drink 2022-2034 | $67 | JH

Serré 2019, Geelong Serré is French for 'tightly packed' and refers to the close-planted block of pinot noir, planted in '84 and certified organic. Love the delicacy on display here, the slow creep of florals, red berries, leaf, sage and spice that work their way deep into the senses. And so smooth. Textbook tannin integration and a long, floating finish caps off this most complete wine. Screw cap. | 12.9% alc. | Drink 2021-2029 | $95 | JP | ♥

96   **Sauvignon Blanc 2018, Geelong** Made in 3 batches of equal size: the first fermented on skins, the second in French oak, the last fermented in tank. Unsurprisingly providing a wine of power and length. Grapefruit hits a high note on the finish and aftertaste, the texture is also very important. Screw cap. | 13% alc. | Drink 2021-2028 | $30 | JH

Bellarine Estate ★★★★☆

2270 Portarlington Road, Bellarine, Vic 3222 **T** (03) 5259 3310 **WWW**.bellarineestate.com.au **OPEN** Saturday 11–4 **WINEMAKER** Julian Kenny **VITICULTURIST** Julian Kenny **EST**. 1995 **DOZENS** 1500 **VYDS** 10.5ha

Established in 1996 by Peter and Lizette Kenny, Bellarine Estate is family run from the ground up. Every stage of the winemaking process, all the way to the final bottling, occurs on-site. This business runs parallel with the Bellarine Brewing Company, also situated in the winery, and the extended operating hours of Julian's Restaurant. (JH)

95   **First Blush Rosé 2021, Geelong** 70/20/7/3% merlot/pinot noir/ shiraz/viognier. A co-ferment with ageing in French oak (5% new) brings a rich dimension to this coral-hued rosé. Expressive summer berry scents mix with musk and woodsy spice. Opens warmly with a strong textural bent and keeps on going. Screw cap. | 12% alc. | Drink 2022-2026 | $28 | JP

Marcus Hill Vineyard ★★★★☆

560 Banks Road, Marcus Hill, Vic 3222 (postal) **T** 0421 728 437 **WWW**.marcushillvineyard.com.au **OPEN** By appt **WINEMAKER** Chip Harrison **EST**. 2000 **DOZENS** 1000 **VYDS** 3ha

In 2000, Richard and Margot Harrison, together with 'gang-pressed friends', planted 2ha of pinot noir overlooking Point Lonsdale, Queenscliff and Ocean Grove, a few kilometres from Bass Strait and Port Phillip. The vineyard is run with minimal sprays, and the aim is to produce elegant wines that truly express the maritime site. (JH)

95   **Bellarine Peninsula Pinot Meunier 2019, Geelong** Heady scent of florals – violet, lilac – with briar, dusty leafiness, dark berries and spice with a touch of musk. It has everything, including firm but fine tannins for some future down time. Screw cap. | 13.5% alc. | Drink 2022-2028 | $35 | JP

Mulline ★★★★★

131 Lumbs Road, Sutherlands Creek, Vic 3331 (postal) **T** 0402 409 292 **WWW**.mulline.com **WINEMAKER** Ben Mullen **EST**. 2019 **DOZENS** 1000

This is the venture of Ben Mullen and business partner Ben Hine. Mullen grew up in the Barossa Valley and studied oenology. His journey thereafter was in the purple, working at Yarra Yering, Oakridge, Torbreck and Leeuwin Estate, Domaine Dujac in Burgundy in '13, Craggy Range in NZ ('15), coming back to Geelong as winemaker for Clyde Park in '17–18. Ben Hine also came from SA, and worked in hospitality for many years before obtaining his law degree; he is working full-time as a lawyer. When they met, it was he who took the running in creating the brand and the business structure behind it. (JH)

96   **Single Vineyard Sutherlands Creek Shiraz Viognier 2021, Geelong** The fragrant perfume rocks in blackberries, plum, lifted baking spices, pepper and bush herbs. Explores real depth on the palate in black fruits, blueberries and lasting red licorice, spice and pepper notes. And it goes and goes. Holds something for now and a lot for later. Screw cap. | 13.5% alc. | Drink 2022-2030 | $50 | JP

Oakdene ★★★★★

255 Grubb Road, Wallington, Vic 3221 **T** (03) 5256 3886 **WWW**.oakdene.com.au **OPEN** 7 days 10-4
WINEMAKER Robin Brockett, Marcus Holt **VITICULTURIST** Sally Enders, Sally Powell **EST.** 2001 **DOZENS** 8000
VYDS 32ha

Bernard and Elizabeth Hooley purchased Oakdene in 2001. Bernard focused on planting the vineyard while Elizabeth worked to restore the 1920s homestead. Much of the wine is sold through the award-winning Oakdene Restaurant and cellar door. The quality is exemplary, as is the consistency of that quality; Robin Brockett's skills are on full display. (JH)

95   **Liz's Single Vineyard Bellarine Peninsula Chardonnay 2020, Geelong** Quieter and more fine-boned than the '19 vintage, Liz nevertheless maintains her usual high level of chardonnay poise and class. Bright and fresh in shades of citrus – lemon, grapefruit, lime zest – with signature honeysuckle aromas. Walks a firm, tight line in racy acidity, all the while the citrus, saline, mandarin skin and gentle oak qualities of the wine are gathering their forces quietly, firmly and resolutely. This wine intends to be around for a while.   Screw cap. | 13% alc. | Drink 2021-2032 | $35 | JP

Scotchmans Hill ★★★★★

190 Scotchmans Road, Drysdale, Vic 3222 **T** (03) 5251 3176 **WWW**.scotchmans.com.au **OPEN** 7 days
11.30-4 **WINEMAKER** Robin Brockett, Marcus Holt **EST.** 1982 **DOZENS** 50000 **VYDS** 80ha

Established in 1982, Scotchmans Hill has been a consistent producer of well-made wines under the stewardship of long-term winemaker Robin Brockett and assistant Marcus Holt. The wines are released under the Scotchmans Hill, Cornelius, Jack & Jill and Swan Bay labels. A change of ownership in '14 resulted in significant vineyard investment. (JH)

98   **Bellarine Peninsula Shiraz 2019, Geelong** Spectacularly deep colour with a crimson rim. Typical Scotchmans Hill vinification: whole bunches and whole berries, cold soak, wild ferment, new and used French oak. The wonder of cool-grown shiraz with attention to detail from start to finish, part the mouth-watering spice and black pepper, licorice and blackberry flavours, part the texture and structure. Irresistible Australian shiraz.   Screw cap. | 14.5% alc. | Drink 2022-2049 | ♥

96   **Bellarine Peninsula Pinot Noir 2020, Geelong** Bright colour sets the tone for a deliciously scented bouquet of cherry blossom, wafts of red berry fruits and gentle but persistent spices. The palate is lively and juicy, the aftertaste fresh.   Screw cap. | 13% alc. | Drink 2022-2030 | $42 | JH

REGION
Macedon Ranges

Bindi Wines ★★★★★

343 Melton Road, Gisborne, Vic 3437 (postal) **T** (03) 5428 2564 **WWW**.bindiwines.com.au
WINEMAKER Michael Dhillon, Stuart Anderson (Consultant) **EST.** 1988 **DOZENS** 2000 **VYDS** 6ha

One of the icons of Macedon. The chardonnay is top-shelf, the pinot noir as remarkable (albeit in a very different idiom) as Bass Phillip, Giaconda or any of the other tiny-production, icon wines. The addition of Heathcote-sourced shiraz under the Pyrette label confirms Bindi as one of the greatest small producers in Australia. Michael Dhillon was the Companion's inaugural Winemaker of the Year in 2022. (JH)

96   **Dhillon Col Mountain Vineyard Rosé Grenache 2021, Heathcote** I adore everything about this rosé, from its pastel pink-bronze hue, its cherry blossom and rose aroma to its flavour profile – watermelon, alpine strawberries and cinnamon. It has texture, length and is delightfully dry and crisp.   Screw cap. | 13% alc. | Drink 2022-2024 | $32 | JF

Kostas Rind Chardonnay 2020, Macedon Ranges While Quartz gets the bow for its complexity and depth, Kostas Rind is no slouch. A lovely balance of citrus, white stone fruit, ginger spice and a touch of nutty lees that are more like seasoning, same with the oak influence. There's a lightness and purity with some complex sulphides and ultra-refreshing acidity. Very satisfying. Utterly enticing.   Screw cap. | 13% alc. | Drink 2022-2032 | $65 | JF

CENTRAL VICTORIA

GIPPSLAND

NORTH EAST VICTORIA

NORTH WEST VICTORIA

PORT PHILLIP

WESTERN VICTORIA

Cobaw Ridge ★★★★★

31 Perc Boyers Lane, Pastoria, Vic 3444 **T** (03) 5423 5227 **WWW**.cobawridge.com.au **OPEN** W'ends 12-5 **WINEMAKER** Nelly Cooper, Alan Cooper **VITICULTURIST** Alan Cooper **EST.** 1985 **DOZENS** 1000 **VYDS** 5ha

When the Coopers started planting in the early '80s there was scant knowledge of the best varieties for the region, let alone the Cobaw Ridge site. Cobaw Ridge is fully certified biodynamic, and all winery operations are carried out according to the biodynamic calendar. (JH)

96   **Il Pinko Rosé 2020, Macedon Ranges** Could there be a more perfect rosé? A classy, savoury wine with a seamless balance of aromas and flavours – think Angostura bitters, potpourri, blood orange and its peel. But what sets this apart from so many other examples is its texture, akin to raw silk and talc-like, giving the wine more shape. Superfine acidity guides and glides to a long finish. Stunning. My favourite rosé from vintage '20.   Diam. | 13.1% alc. | Drink 2021-2025 | $42 | JF | ♥

      Syrah 2019, Macedon Ranges A wine that's so alive it pulses with energy and vitality. It comes up all savoury and spicy at first, with a damp-forest fragrance, red roses, licorice root, mint chocolate and cedary oak. The fruit within is excellent. It's elegant across its more mid-weighted palate, the tannins superfine and the finish long. Totally seductive syrah.   Diam. | 13.8% alc. | Drink 2022-2034 | $65 | JF | ♥

      Syrah 2018, Macedon Ranges Sit back, relax and take in the beauty of this wine. It politely introduces itself with a heady fragrance of florals, wood smoke, autumn leaves and alpine herbs. Then it reveals its true savoury personality across the supple palate with fine, textural tannins, quality oak, umami, vegemite and dark chocolate infusing the core of perfect fruit.   Diam. | 13.7% alc. | Drink 2021-2033 | $62 | JF

Curly Flat ★★★★★

263 Collivers Road, Lancefield, Vic 3435 **T** (03) 5429 1956 **WWW**.curlyflat.com **OPEN** Fri-Sun 12-5 **WINEMAKER** Matt Harrop, Ben Kimmorley **EST.** 1991 **DOZENS** 6000 **VYDS** 13ha

Founded by Phillip Moraghan and Jenifer Kolkka in '91, Jenifer has been the sole owner of Curly Flat since '17. The focus has always been on the vineyard, a dedicated team ensuring quality is never compromised. Matt Harrop is now overseeing production. (JH)

96   **Western Pinot Noir 2020, Macedon Ranges** My pick of the 3 Curly Flat '20 pinots, for its completeness and balance. This is composed, moreish and fabulous now, with its heady aromas of florals, forest floor and earthiness, to flavours of red cherries enmeshed in a light mix of baking spices. There's a brightness within and while there's plenty of tannin, this is more medium weighted, with a long persistent finish.   Screw cap. | 13.2% alc. | Drink 2021-2033 | $57 | JF

95   **Pinot Gris 2021, Macedon Ranges** This is a beauty. Flavoursome with nashi pear, lemon drops, a decent smattering of ginger spice and a creaminess throughout. Texture abounds but not at all weighty, as it feels effortless.   Screw cap. | 13.6% alc. | Drink 2021-2025 | $30 | JF

      White Pinot 2021, Macedon Ranges Gosh this is good: complex, savoury yet equally refreshing. Tantalising pinot characters of cherries and wild strawberries, warm earth and forest-floor aromas. The palate comes alive with a richness, a plumpness of fruit, yet finishes dry and oh, so satisfying.   Screw cap. | 14% alc. | Drink 2021-2024 | $30 | JF

Granite Hills ★★★★★

1481 Burke and Wills Track, Baynton, Vic 3444 **T** (03) 5423 7273 **WWW**.granitehills.com.au **OPEN** By appt **WINEMAKER** Llew Knight, Rowen Anstis **VITICULTURIST** Andrew Conforti **EST.** 1970 **DOZENS** 5000 **VYDS** 11.5ha

Granite Hills is one of the enduring classics, having pioneered the successful growing of riesling and shiraz in an uncompromisingly cool climate. The Rieslings age superbly, and the Shiraz was the forerunner of the cool-climate school in Australia. (JH)

96   **Knight 1971 Block Riesling 2021, Macedon Ranges** It's meant to be significantly different and more complex, as the fruit comes off the 1971 plantings. It's special with such precision, clarity and length. A burst of lime and lemon freshness and a flutter of spice to follow as it builds across the tightly held palate. A hint of ginger cream, lemon verbena and while the acidity is perky, there's just a softness on the finish.   Screw cap. | 13% alc. | Drink 2022-2035 | $38 | JF

95   **Knight Riesling 2021, Macedon Ranges** Granite Hills has long held the riesling mantle in this region. It's an ever-reliable drink thanks to its vitality, crunchy acidity, length plus all the citrus, tangy and juicy flavours. It's also stylish and pure.   Screw cap. | 13% alc. | Drink 2022-2033 | $28 | JF

Hanging Rock Winery ⑨⑭⑱ ★★★★★

88 Jim Road, Newham, Vic 3442 **T** (03) 5427 0542 **www**.hangingrock.com.au **OPEN** 7 days 10–5
WINEMAKER Robert Ellis **EST.** 1983 **DOZENS** 20000 **VYDS** 14.5ha

The Macedon area has proved marginal in spots and the Hanging Rock vineyards, with their lovely vista towards the rock, are no exception. In '11 John's children Ruth and Robert returned to the fold: Robert has an oenology degree from the University of Adelaide, after that working as a Flying Winemaker in Champagne, Burgundy, Oregon and Stellenbosch. Ruth has a degree in wine marketing from the University of Adelaide. (JH)

95   **Jim Jim Sauvignon Blanc 2021, Macedon Ranges** An altogether refreshing and satisfying wine, delivering some varietal punch with a bit more complexity across the palate. Succulent and juicy citrus aromas and flavours alongside fresh basil, just-mown grass and pea shoots with a dash of passionfruit juice and pith. It also is finely tuned, finishes tight and you'll be pouring another glass quick smart.   Screw cap. | 13% alc. | Drink 2022-2023 | $35 | JF

Passing Clouds ⑨⑭⑱ ★★★★★

30 Roddas Lane, Musk, Vic 3461 **T** (03) 5348 5550 **www**.passingclouds.com.au **OPEN** 7 days 10–5
WINEMAKER Cameron Leith **EST.** 1974 **DOZENS** 5500 **VYDS** 5ha

Graeme Leith and son Cameron undertook a monumental change when they moved the entire operation that started way back in 1974 in the Bendigo region to its new location at Musk, near Daylesford. Graeme has now left the winemaking in the hands of Cameron and Marion, who have made a coup with the establishment of a new train stop (and dedicated platform) at the Passing Clouds cellar door and winery at Musk. (JH)

95   **Riesling 2021, Macedon Ranges** This wine should come with a warning: take the rest of the day off and enjoy, for it instils a carefree attitude in the imbiber. Well, it happened to me, all thanks to the racy acidity dashing across the palate alongside a balance of florals, citrus and spice with some talc-like texture. Top-notch, cool and cooling rizza.   Screw cap. | 11.8% alc. | Drink 2022-2031 | $34 | JF

    Macedon Pinot Noir 2020, Macedon Ranges A refreshingly pure and unadulterated wine that's such a delight to drink. Unencumbered by winemaking artefact, especially oaky flavour as this goes into used French hogsheads, so the fruit and the cool site are the stars. Heady aromas lead the way as a whorl of dark and red cherries lead off on the mid-weighted palate with some forest-floor complexity and exotic spices. The tannins are savoury, the superfine natural acidity is refreshing and ensures the finish is long. In context of the price and quality, this is spot on.   Screw cap. | 12% alc. | Drink 2022-2026 | $28 | JF

REGION

Mornington Peninsula

Crittenden Estate ⑨⑭⑯ ★★★★★

25 Harrisons Road, Dromana, Vic 3936 **T** (03) 5981 8322 **www**.crittendenwines.com.au **OPEN** 7 days 10.30–4.30 **WINEMAKER** Rollo Crittenden, Matt Campbell **EST.** 1984 **DOZENS** 10000 **VYDS** 4.8ha

Garry Crittenden was a pioneer on the Mornington Peninsula, establishing the family vineyard over almost 40 years and introducing a number of avant-garde pruning and canopy management techniques. Much has changed – and continues to change – in cool-climate vineyard management. Crittenden has abandoned the use of synthetic fertilisers in the vineyard, focusing on biological soil health using natural tools such as compost and cover crops. In 2015, winemaking returned to the family vineyard on the Mornington Peninsula in a newly built facility, with son Rollo in charge of the winemaking and general management and daughter Zoe overseeing marketing. (JH)

97   **Cri de Coeur Sous Voile Savagnin 2017, Mornington Peninsula** Bearing witness to a wine's creation – as in tasting all since its inception in '11 and understanding the story behind sous voile – allows a picture to form. Winemaker Matt Campbell is credited with kickstarting the revolution à la Jura at Crittenden Estate and all I can say is, thank you. Oh and '17, the finest to date. Spending nearly 4 years under flor and matched to an excellent vintage has created a complex, savoury and utterly compelling wine. Expect a harmony of grilled almonds, toffee praline, salted lemons, poached quince with mouth-watering, heady aldehydes. The palate is incredibly silky and long, yet has lots of tangy acidity too; it's elegant and importantly, ultra-fresh and alive. What a wine. Alas, just 800 bottles made.   Diam. | 14.5% alc. | Drink 2022-2030 | $85 | JF | ♥

CENTRAL VICTORIA

GIPPSLAND

NORTH EAST VICTORIA

NORTH WEST VICTORIA

PORT PHILLIP

WESTERN VICTORIA

95 **Pinot Gris 2021, Mornington Peninsula** It's always a go-to gris, because aside from the varietal inputs, it's a terrific drink. Honeysuckle, ginger spice, nashi pear and lemon-cream tart. Luscious across the palate, yet finishes with a gentle acid freshness. Screw cap. | 13% alc. | Drink 2022-2025 | $34 | JF

Oggi 2021, Mornington Peninsula 62/38% pinot grigio/white muscat. A coppery orange colour and so fragrant (via the muscat) with honeysuckle, musk, lychee and a burst of spices. The palate has plenty of grip, a sway of phenolics adding texture and intrigue, plus flavours of blood orange and Angostura bitters. It's super-dry. A fabulous aperitif style. Screw cap. | 12% alc. | Drink 2022-2024 | $35 | JF

Eldridge Estate of Red Hill ⓥ

120 Arthurs Seat Road, Red Hill, Vic 3937 **T** 0414 758 960 **www**.eldridge-estate.com.au **OPEN** Fri-Mon 11–5 **WINEMAKER** David Lloyd **EST.** 1985 **DOZENS** 1000 **VYDS** 3ha

Wine has been a constant throughout David Lloyd's life and career. His father, a church minister, baptised and married many members of the Hardy winemaking clan. While studying for a BSc at Monash Uni, David joined the wine club and 'fell in love with the mix of science and art that is winemaking.' With his wife, Wendy, he bought a vineyard on the Mornington Peninsula in '95 and planted chardonnay, pinot noir and gamay. Later, friends in Oregon alerted him to the qualities of 20 different clones of pinot noir, setting him off on a complex clonal journey that earned him the moniker 'the clone ranger'. In '12, Wendy was diagnosed with stage 4 cancer and sadly died 2 years later; David has fought and won his own cancer battles since. In early '22, he placed Eldridge Estate on the market. (JP)

95 **PTG 2021, Mornington Peninsula** Such a cheery wine, with enchanting aromas of violets, baking spices and red fruit. The mid-weighted palate leads with tangy, ultra-refreshing acidity, a pop of cherries and raspberries, finishing with a gentle radicchio bitterness and fine, sandy tannins. 100% refreshment, 100% enjoyment guaranteed. Screw cap. | 14% alc. | Drink 2022-2026 | $35 | JF

Foxeys Hangout ⓥⓜ

795 White Hill Road, Red Hill, Vic 3937 **T** (03) 5989 2022 **www**.foxeys-hangout.com.au **OPEN** 7 days 11–5 **WINEMAKER** Tony and Michael Lee **EST.** 1997 **DOZENS** 14000 **VYDS** 3.4ha

After 20 successful years in hospitality operating several cafes and restaurants, brothers Michael and Tony Lee planted their first vineyard in '97 at Merricks North. The venture takes its name from the tale of 2 fox hunters in the '30s hanging the results of their day's shooting in opposite branches of an ancient eucalypt, using the tree as their scorecard. Michael makes the sparkling wines, Tony (a qualified chef) makes the table wines and also cooks for the cellar door kitchen. (JH)

95 **Rosé 2021, Mornington Peninsula** A 3-way blend of pinot noir, pinot gris and shiraz and a delicious, delightful and refreshing drink. A stream of spices comes sluicing through the watermelon, Packham pear and raspberry flavours, making it all juicy and tangy across the palate. It has texture though, as it's not a one-trick pony. Refreshing acidity and a twist of blood orange on the finish make it all the more appealing. Screw cap. | 13% alc. | Drink 2022-2024 | $28 | JF

Garagiste

72 Blaxland Ave, Frankston South, Vic 3199 **T** 0439 370 530 **www**.garagiste.com.au **WINEMAKER** Barnaby Flanders **EST.** 2006 **DOZENS** 2200 **VYDS** 6ha

Barnaby Flanders was a co-founder of Allies Wines in 2003, with some of the wines made under the Garagiste label. Allies has since gone its own way and Barnaby has a controlling interest in the Garagiste brand. The grapes are hand-sorted in the vineyard and again in the winery. Chardonnay is whole-bunch pressed, barrel-fermented with wild yeast in new and used French oak, mlf variably used, 8–9 months on lees. Seldom fined or filtered. (JH)

96 **Le Stagiaire Chardonnay 2021, Mornington Peninsula** This has to be the best value chardonnay from the peninsula matched to quality but also, this vintage has delivered the finest to date. It's superbly balanced with pristine fruit, the right amount of flinty sulphides, savouriness, texture and definition. There's some tension on the palate, a purity to the acidity and excellent length. Screw cap. | 13% alc. | Drink 2022-2030 | $30 | JF

Merricks Chardonnay 2021, Mornington Peninsula Made the same as its Tuerong sibling, so site trumps everything. This is sublime. Flinty, spicy, citrusy and intense, in a good and satisfying way. The palate glides with such precision thanks to minerally fresh acidity. Mornington Peninsula chardonnay, but perhaps not as you know it. Screw cap. | 13% alc. | Drink 2022-2031 | $45 | JF

Tuerong Chardonnay 2021, Mornington Peninsula Plenty of flavour and succulence across the palate, yet it remains taut thanks to its acidity. Grapefruit, dried fig, oak spice, lemon curd and creamy lees come together on the flavour spectrum. Screw cap. | 13% alc. | Drink 2022-2028 | $45 | JF | ♥

Terre de Feu Pinot Noir 2019, Mornington Peninsula There's attention to detail with all the Garagiste wines, none more so than Terre de Feu. Beautifully harnessed flavours of cherry and pips, Middle Eastern spices, wood smoke, twigs and a grind of pepper. Furry tannins shapely across the fuller-bodied palate and mouth-watering acidity to close. Stamped with savouriness and serious intent. Screw cap. | 13.5% alc. | Drink 2022-2034 | $75 | JF

95　**Le Stagiaire Pinot Gris 2021, Mornington Peninsula** While this offers restrained PG flavours – pears, apple pie, spiced up with ginger and musk – 7 months in barrel on lees has added more complexity and depth. The citrussy acidity lights up the finish and extends the length. Screw cap. | 13% alc. | Drink 2022-2026 | $30 | JF

Tuerong Aligoté 2021, Mornington Peninsula Barnaby Flanders can only source a small amount of aligoté, but he weaves magic with the fruit anyway. Layers of flavour and depth: lemon, tart apple and stone fruit dance along with savoury, smoky notes. A whisper of sulphides and a smidge of nutty lees is teasing out the otherwise tight palate, led by a line of excellent acidity. Screw cap. | 13% alc. | Drink 2022-2028 | $35 | JF

94　**Le Stagiaire Pinot Noir 2021, Mornington Peninsula** While there's a flutter of cherries and spice with plum fruit sweetness across the palate, this is a much more savoury offering than usual. Lighter framed, with peach-fuzz tannins, raspberry-sorbet acidity and freshness throughout. Good to pour now. Screw cap. | 13.5% alc. | Drink 2022-2028 | $30 | JF

Kerri Greens ★★★★★

38 Paringa Road, Red Hill South, Vic 3937 **T** (03) 5989 2572 **www**.kerrigreens.com **OPEN** Sat 11-5, Fri, Sun 12-5 **WINEMAKER** Tom McCarthy, Lucas Blanck **VITICULTURIST** Lucas Blanck, Tom McCarthy **EST.** 2015 **DOZENS** 1000

Kerri Greens (named after a local surf break) offers excellent and energising wines. Tom McCarthy (son of local Peninsula producers, Kathleen Quealy and Kevin McCarthy) is the lead winemaker at Quealy Wines these days and Lucas Blanck (son of winemaker Frederic, from Domaine Paul Blanck in Alsace) is viticulturist. Since it began in 2013, Tom and Paul have worked tirelessly to bring life back to the various vineyards they manage. Organics, sustainability and treading gently are important considerations. It's also a family business strengthened by their wives, Alyce Blanck and Sarah Saxton, who are very much at the forefront of the business. (JF)

95　**Ohne Gewürztraminer 2021, Mornington Peninsula** Such a contrast to the tighter rendition in '20, yet this is no less fabulous. It's just richer, fleshier and riper, but not heavy. Lychees and musk, poached quinces topped with cinnamon and drizzled with rosewater syrup. Tannins add a slippery, textural coating and grip across the full-bodied palate. Screw cap. | 12.5% alc. | Drink 2022-2026 | $30 | JF

Kooyong ★★★★★

263 Red Hill Road, Red Hill **T** (03) 5989 4444 **www**.kooyongwines.com.au **OPEN** Mon-Sun 11-5 **WINEMAKER** Glen Hayley **VITICULTURIST** Stuart Marshall **EST.** 1996 **DOZENS** 13000 **VYDS** 41.11ha

Kooyong, owned by Giorgio and Dianne Gjergja, released its first wines in 2001. In July '15, following the departure of Sandro Mosele, his assistant of 6 years, Glen Hayley, was appointed to take his place. The Kooyong wines are made at the state-of-the-art winery of Port Phillip Estate, also owned by the Gjergjas. (JH)

96　**Farrago Single Block Chardonnay 2020, Mornington Peninsula** Both single-vineyard chardonnays are on song, as Farrago opens up to a reveal layers of flavour from stone fruit, citrus to creamy lees with tight yet refreshing acidity reining everything in. It's luscious without being heavy, with plenty of energy and drive. This is a touch racier than Faultline, yet both are moreish and satisfying. Screw cap. | 13.5% alc. | Drink 2022-2026 | $60 | JF

Faultline Single Block Chardonnay 2020, Mornington Peninsula Oh yeah. This is in a good spot. Tight and linear. It kick starts with a waft of florals, white stone fruit and no shortage of citrus tones. Superb line and length as the acidity joins the lees and oak in perfect balance. Screw cap. | 13% alc. | Drink 2022-2030 | $60 | JF

Montalto ★★★★★

33 Shoreham Road, Red Hill South, Vic 3937 **T** (03) 5989 8412 **www**.montalto.com.au **OPEN** 7 days 11-5 **WINEMAKER** Simon Black **VITICULTURIST** Dan Prior **EST.** 1998 **DOZENS** 12000 **VYDS** 47ha

John Mitchell and family established Montalto in '98, but the core of the vineyard goes back to '86. Intensive vineyard work opens up the canopy, with yields of 3.7–6.1t/ha. Wines are released in 3 ranges: the flagship Single Vineyard, Montalto estate wines and Pennon Hill. Montalto leases several external vineyards that span the peninsula, giving vastly greater diversity of pinot noir sources and greater insurance against weather extremes. Montalto has hit new heights with its wines from these blocks. (JH)

97   **Single Vineyard Merricks Block Pinot Noir 2020, Mornington Peninsula** By some distance, the deepest colour of the quartet in this tasting, and the most powerful, with savoury, foresty texture and structure. Will live long.   Screw cap. | 13.5% alc. | Drink 2022-2035 | $70 | JH

96   **Single Vineyard Main Ridge Block Pinot Noir 2020, Mornington Peninsula** Among the lightest of colours, but – as with all the Montalto pinots – bright and clear, the perfumed red cherry and plum bouquet a striking foreplay to the palate.   Screw cap. | 13.5% alc. | Drink 2022-2030 | $70 | JH

      Single Vineyard Tuerong Pinot Noir 2020, Mornington Peninsula Splitting hairs, the colour is the most developed – and lightest – of the 4 Montalto pinots in this tasting, ex whole bunch, and has a highly fragrant fruit expression, spanning the cherry family, and complexed by whole bunch a la Simon Black.   Screw cap. | 13.5% alc. | Drink 2022-2032 | $70 | JH

Moorooduc Estate ★★★★★

501 Derril Road, Moorooduc, Vic 3936 **T** (03) 5971 8506 **www.**moorooducestate.com.au **OPEN** 7 days 11–5 **WINEMAKER** Dr Richard McIntyre, Jeremy Magyar **VITICULTURIST** Peninsula Vine Care **EST.** 1983 **DOZENS** 6000 **VYDS** 14ha

Richard McIntyre has taken Moorooduc Estate to new heights, having completely mastered the difficult art of gaining maximum results from wild-yeast fermentation. Starting with the 2010 vintage, there was a complete revamp of grape sources and hence changes to the tiered structure of the releases. These changes were driven by the simple fact that the McIntyre vineyard could only yield 1500 dozens, and by leasing additional Mornington Peninsula vineyards the business was able to expand to the 5000-6000 dozen produced annually. Daughter Kate McIntyre MW joined the business full-time after attaining her master of wine in '10. (JH)

96   **Robinson Vineyard Chardonnay 2020, Mornington Peninsula** Such a pristine wine with its definition, purity and superfine acid line. Balanced flavours of grapefruit and nougat. Tangy, flinty and moreish, with terrific length. Impossible to hold back pouring another glass. So don't.   Screw cap. | 13% alc. | Drink 2022-2028 | $60 | JF

Port Phillip Estate ★★★★★

263 Red Hill Road, Red Hill, Vic 3937 **T** (03) 5989 4444 **www.**portphillipestate.com.au **OPEN** 7 days 11–5 **WINEMAKER** Glen Hayley **EST.** 1987 **DOZENS** 7000 **VYDS** 21.04ha

Port Phillip Estate has been owned by Giorgio and Dianne Gjergja since 2000. In July '15, following the departure of winemaker Sandro Mosele, his assistant of 6 years, Glen Hayley, was appointed to take his place. The futuristic, multi-million-dollar restaurant, cellar door and winery complex, designed by award-winning Wood/Marsh Architecture, overlooks the vineyards and Westernport Bay. (JH)

95   **Sauvignon 2021, Mornington Peninsula** The fruit is gently whole-bunch pressed to old French barriques, fermented wild and left on lees for a couple of months, which explains the excellent texture, complexity and even flow of this wine. It's subtle and savoury, with flinty sulphides but includes grapefruit and pith, white stone fruit and rocket. This is a sauvignon I'd gladly drink anytime.   Screw cap. | 13.5% alc. | Drink 2022-2025 | $27 | JF

      Salasso Rosé 2021, Mornington Peninsula A light and enticing copper hue. When slightly chilled, this rosé means summer in a glass. Really lovely aromatics; all florals and red berries, quite spicy too. Starts fruit-sweet on the palate then savouriness takes over all the way to a dry, fresh finish. Excellent rosé in anyone's book.   Screw cap. | 13% alc. | Drink 2021-2023 | $27 | JF

      Amber Pinot Gris 2021, Mornington Peninsula I'm not sure if winemaker Glen Hayley is turning into a hipster or if there's another reason for this terrific wine. Its pale cherry-terracotta hue entices immediately; roseships, poached quince, chinotto and blood orange – lots going on aroma and flavour-wise. The palate is composed with delicate phenolics, with just some chew and shape to the finish. Fresh all the way through. Bravo.   Screw cap. | 12.5% alc. | Drink 2022-2024 | $32 | JF

      Pinot Noir Shiraz 2021, Mornington Peninsula This rendition is exactly what the style should be about, which is a vibrancy of fruit and freshness. Spiced plums and cherries with lots of savoury inputs some woodsy spices, herbs and a succulence across the light- to mid-weighted palate. Textural tannins and juicy acidity to close.   Screw cap. | 13% alc. | Drink 2022-2026 | $34 | JF

Quealy Winemakers ⚲⑭

62 Bittern-Dromana Road, Balnarring, Vic 3926 **T** (03) 5983 2483 **www**.quealy.com.au **OPEN** 7 days 9-5 **WINEMAKER** Kathleen Quealy, Tom McCarthy **VITICULTURIST** Lucas Blanck, Kevin McCarthy **EST.** 1982 **DOZENS** 8000 **VYDS** 8ha

★★★★★

Kathleen Quealy and Kevin McCarthy were among the early waves of winemakers on the Mornington Peninsula. They successfully challenged the status quo – most publicly by introducing Mornington Peninsula pinot gris/grigio. Behind this was improvement and diversification in site selection, plus viticulture and winemaking techniques. Son Tom stepped up as head winemaker in '19. Lucas Blanck manages the certified organic estate vineyards; the leased vineyards are moving towards 100% organic management. (JH)

95   **Balnarring Vineyard Pinot Grigio 2021, Mornington Peninsula** There's great tension between the acidity and the restrained flavours racing through this delicious wine. Loads of citrus, juice and zest, with some lemon thyme and a thirst-quenching saline sensation across the palate. Screw cap. | 12.8% alc. | Drink 2022-2025 | $35 | JF

Scorpo Wines ⚲

23 Old Bittern-Dromana Road, Merricks North, Vic 3926 **T** (03) 5989 7697 **www**.scorpowines.com.au **OPEN** first w'end each month or by appt **WINEMAKER** Paul Scorpo **EST.** 1997 **DOZENS** 6000 **VYDS** 17.3ha

★★★★★

Paul Scorpo has a background as a horticulturist and landscape architect, working on major projects ranging from private gardens to golf courses in Australia, Europe and Asia. His family has a love of food, wine and gardens, all of which led to them buying a derelict apple and cherry orchard on gentle rolling hills between Port Phillip and Western Port bays. (JH)

96   **Eocene Single Vineyard Chardonnay 2020, Mornington Peninsula** While there are layers of flavour and a depth to this, it doesn't come across as too big or too much of a good thing, but just right. Citrus and stone fruit, spice and a subtle oak influence, long and pure across the palate, coming out rather savoury. Screw cap. | 13% alc. | Drink 2022-2030 | $75 | JF

95   **Rosé 2021, Mornington Peninsula** Is it the aroma or texture that make this such a compelling drink? Well, probably both. It's an attractive pale coppery pink for starters. Wafts of black pepper, aniseed and red cherries with watermelon and rind which set things rolling. It's juicy, tangy and vibrant, yet there's texture too, and lithe, light tannins. This is a top-notch, totally delicious rosé. Screw cap. | 13.4% alc. | Drink 2021-2023 | $28 | JF

Aubaine Chardonnay 2021, Mornington Peninsula Oh yeah. Rock solid chardonnay from a lovely vintage. Everything just so – the citrus flavours, spice, a dash of quality oak, the layer of creamy lees – not too much – and finishes with fine acidity. This glides across the palate leaving a desire for another glass. Screw cap. | 13.2% alc. | Drink 2022-2028 | $32 | JF

Noirien Pinot Noir 2021, Mornington Peninsula A very classy Noirien that perfectly matches savoury attributes to the excellent fruit within. Dark cherries, all spiced up with some tart rhubarb and blood orange, fresh herbs and chinotto. Unencumbered by new oak, but the palate is shapely, the tannins persuasive and the acidity humming. Screw cap. | 13.6% alc. | Drink 2022-2021 | $32 | JF

Stonier Wines ⚲⑭

Cnr Thompson's Lane/Frankston-Flinders Road, Merricks, Vic 3916 **T** (03) 5989 8300 **www**.stonier.com.au **OPEN** 7 days 11-5 **WINEMAKER** Michael Symons, Will Byron **VITICULTURIST** Luke Buckley **EST.** 1978 **DOZENS** 35000 **VYDS** 17ha

★★★★★

Stonier has embarked on a serious sustainability program that touches on all aspects of its operations. It has created a balanced ecosystem in the vineyard by strategic planting of cover crops and reduction of sprays; and its need to irrigate. All wines are estate-grown and made with a mix of wild yeast and cultured yeast, and almost all are destemmed to open fermenters. All have a 2-stage maturation – always French oak and variable use of barriques and puncheons for the first stage. Justin Purser takes over as head winemaker from '22. (JH)

97   **W-WB Pinot Noir 2021, Mornington Peninsula** Smoky, twiggy, bitter herbs, rhubarb liqueur and all the complexity that comes from whole bunches are complementary to the dark cherries, spice and woodsy flavours. A structured palate with textural, furry tannins and a fragrant lift throughout. Screw cap. | 13.8% alc. | Drink 2022-2035 | $90 | JF | ♥

96   **Gainsborough Park Vineyard Chardonnay 2021, Mornington Peninsula** I can't recall a better, more focused Gainsborough Park Vineyard Chardonnay. This is smokin'. Tight and linear with excellent fruit clarity; the lemon flavours enhanced by creamy lees and moreish sulphides. Superfine acidity guides it to a long finish. Screw cap. | 13.5% alc. | Drink 2022-2031 | $45 | JF

KBS Vineyard Chardonnay 2021, Mornington Peninsula Comes packed with flavour, complexity and depth, yet fantastic acidity to drive this. Grapefruit, Meyer lemon and lemon balm to the fore, building on the fine palate before meeting up with a touch of delicate oak spice, nutty lees and a flourish of savouriness. Moreish and impossible to resist a second glass. Screw cap. | 13.5% alc. | Drink 2022-2031 | \$50 | JF

Reserve Chardonnay 2021, Mornington Peninsula The Reserve is always a blend of the best vineyards. It's not necessarily better than the single-site wines – although it can be – it's a different expression. In this excellent vintage, it's complex and pure. Certainly a core of citrus and stone fruit, but the layering effect from oak, lees and a touch of flint give this a distinct savoury outlook. It is a great shame the '21 wines are winemakers Michael Symons and Will Byron's last, although they can leave on a high. Screw cap. | 13.5% alc. | Drink 2022-2031 | \$50 | JF

Georgica Vineyard Pinot Noir 2021, Mornington Peninsula Merron's vineyard was recently sold and renamed Georgica. As usual, no new oak used and the fruit clarity shines through. A heady fragrance delights, so too, sweet cherries, a dash of kirsch, some pips and woodsy spices, yet all glossy and detailed across the medium-bodied palate. Superfine tannins and acidity to close. Beautiful wine. Screw cap. | 13.8% alc. | Drink 2022-2031 | \$55 | JF

Reserve Pinot Noir 2021, Mornington Peninsula Fragrant, lightly stemmy and herbal (but not green), with flavours of red cherries, chinotto, blood orange and sandalwood. Fleshy fruit across the fuller-bodied palate with raw silk tannins holding sway. Incredibly refreshing now, but will garner even more complexity in time. Screw cap. | 13.8% alc. | Drink 2022-2035 | \$60 | JF

KBS Vineyard Pinot Noir 2021, Mornington Peninsula A composed yet charming drink. Plenty of savoury fruit-derived tannin and refreshing acidity, so there's a depth and structure within plus sweet, ripe black cherries, kirsch and baking spices. It's a mouth-watering style and approachable now, but will reward the patient, too. Screw cap. | 13.5% alc. | Drink 2022-2033 | \$65 | JF

Trofeo Estate

85 Harrisons Road, Dromana, Vic 3936 **T** (03) 5981 8688 **www**.trofeoestate.com **OPEN** 7 days 10-5 **WINEMAKER** Richard Darby **EST**. 2012 **DOZENS** 7500 **VYDS** 18.5ha

This property has had a chequered history. In the 1930s Passiflora Plantations Company was set up to become Australia's leading exporter of passionfruit and associated products. By '37, 120ha was covered with 70 000 passionfruit vines and a processing factory was in operation. The following year a disease devastated the passionfruit and the company went into receivership. In '48 a member of the Seppelt family planted a vineyard on the exact site of Trofeo Estate and it was thereafter acquired by the late Doug Seabrook, who maintained the vineyard and made the wine until the vines were destroyed in a bushfire in '67. In '98 it was replanted but passed through several hands and fell into and out of neglect until the latest owner, Jim Manolios, developed the property as a restaurant, vineyard and winery. (JH)

95   **Aged in Terracotta Shiraz 2019, Mornington Peninsula** This comes dripping in dark fruits and spice with an attractive meaty reduction adding to the savoury profile. Full-bodied, juicy and tangy with fine sandpaper tannins creating more texture. Screw cap. | 14% alc. | Drink 2022-2029 | \$34 | JF

Yabby Lake Vineyard

86-112 Tuerong Road, Tuerong, Vic 3937 **T** (03) 5974 3729 **www**.yabbylake.com **OPEN** 7 days 10-4 **WINEMAKER** Tom Carson, Chris Forge, Luke Lomax **EST**. 1998 **DOZENS** 3350 **VYDS** 50ha

This high-profile wine business was established in 1998 by Robert and Mem Kirby of Village Roadshow. The vineyard enjoys a north-facing slope, capturing maximum sunshine while also receiving sea breezes. The arrival of the hugely talented Tom Carson as group winemaker in '08 added lustre to the winery and its wines, making the first Jimmy Watson Trophy–winning pinot noir in '14 and continuing to blitz the Australian wine show circuit with single-block pinot noirs. (JH)

95   **Single Vineyard Pinot Noir Rosé 2021, Mornington Peninsula** There's a coppery tinge to the light ruby hue; a joyous mix of raspberries, chinotto, cranberry tartness, watermelon and a touch of spice yet savoury through and through. The palate is refreshing with red apple and juicy acidity, plus the right amount of feathery tannins to give it shape. Screw cap. | 12.5% alc. | Drink 2021-2023 | \$30 | JF

Sunbury

Craiglee ⑨ ★★★★★

785 Sunbury Road, Sunbury, Vic 3429 **T** (03) 9744 4489 **WWW**.craigleevineyard.com **OPEN** first Sun each month **WINEMAKER** Patrick Carmody **EST**. 1976 **DOZENS** 2000 **VYDS** 9.5ha

A winery with a proud 19th-century record, Craiglee recommenced winemaking in '76 after a prolonged hiatus. Produces one of the finest cool-climate shiraz wines in Australia, redolent of cherry, licorice and spice in the better (warmer) vintages; lighter bodied in the cooler ones. Mature vines and improved viticulture have made the wines more consistent over the past 10 years or so. (JH)

96   **Shiraz 2018, Sunbury** There are some wines that are special and unique because they not dictated to by fashion or shareholders and more importantly, they have a strong sense of place. That's Craiglee. Expect a taste of dark plums, cedary oak, pepper and spice, licorice and gum leaf. The palate is full bodied, with ripe, silky tannins hugging all the way through to a resounding finish. Screw cap. | 14% alc. | Drink 2022-2038 | $60 | JF

Yarra Valley

Bird on a Wire Wines ★★★★★

51 Symons Street, Healesville, Vic 3777 (postal) **T** 0439 045 000 **WWW**.birdonawirewines.com.au **WINEMAKER** Caroline Mooney **EST**. 2008 **DOZENS** 850

This is the full-time business of winemaker Caroline Mooney. She grew up in the Yarra Valley and has had other full-time winemaking jobs in the valley for over 10 years. The focus is on small, single-vineyard sites owned by growers committed to producing outstanding grapes. Having worked at the legendary Domaine Jean-Louis Chave in the '06 vintage, she has a special interest in shiraz and marsanne, both grown from distinct sites on a single vineyard in the Yarra Glen area. (JH)

96   **Chardonnay 2018, Yarra Valley** Quite a deep but bright green gold. White nectarines, a little struck match, lemon curd and toasted hazelnuts can all be found on the nose of this very well-constructed wine. Quite rich by the standards of some Yarra chardonnay, this is textured and flavourful, but it's also fine and very well balanced. Finishes subtle and long and is drinking superbly now. Screw cap. | 13.1% alc. | Drink 2021-2025 | $50 | PR

Chandon Australia ⑨⑪ ★★★★★

727 Maroondah Highway, Coldstream, Vic 3770 **T** (03) 9738 9200 **WWW**.chandon.com.au **OPEN** 7 days 10.30-4.30 **WINEMAKER** Dan Buckle, Glenn Thompson, Adam Keath **EST**. 1986 **VYDS** 184ha

Established by Möet & Chandon, this is one of the 2 most important wine facilities in the Yarra Valley; the tasting room has a national and international reputation, having won a number of major tourism awards in recent years. The sparkling wine product range evolved with the '94 acquisition of a substantial vineyard in the cool Strathbogie Ranges and the '14 purchase of the high-altitude vineyard established by Brown Brothers, supplementing the large intake from the Yarra Valley at various altitudes. Under the leadership of chief winemaker Dan Buckle the high-quality standards have been maintained. (JH)

96   **Blanc de Blancs 2016, Victoria** All estate-grown fruit from Whitlands, Strathbogie and Greenpoint in the Yarra. Disgorged after 4 and a half years on lees, dosage 5g/L. Bright gold with green tinges. Honeyed with grilled hazelnuts, white peaches, a hint of orange oil and aromas of freshly baked gougères. Both vinous and fine boned, this accomplished and complex wine finishes dry and long. A great New World sparkling. Diam. | 12.5% alc. | $39 | PR | ♥

95   **Blanc de Blancs NV, Victoria** 90% from '17 vintage, 24 months on lees, 6g/L dosage. A bright, green gold. Aromas of struck match, toast, freshly fried crêpes as well as white stone fruits. The mousse is fine and delicate. An elegant, persistent and very well-put together wine and a ridiculously good Australian sparkling at this price. Diam. | 12.5% alc. | $25 | PR

Coldstream Hills ★★★★★

29-31 Maddens Lane, Coldstream, Vic 3770 **T** (03) 5960 7000 **www**.coldstreamhills.com.au
OPEN Fri-Mon 10-5 **WINEMAKER** Andrew Fleming, Greg Jarratt, James Halliday AM (Consultant)
EST. 1985 **VYDS** 100ha

Founded by James Halliday AM, Coldstream Hills has 100ha of estate vineyards as its base,
3 in the Lower Yarra Valley and 2 in the Upper Yarra Valley. Vintage conditions permitting,
Chardonnay and Pinot Noir are made in Reserve, Single Vineyard and varietal forms. In
addition, Amphitheatre Pinot Noir was made in tiny quantities in '06 and '13. A winery was
erected in '10 with a capacity of 1500t. (JH)

97 **Reserve Pinot Noir 2020, Yarra Valley** A medium, deep, crimson purple. Crushed strawberries,
Asian spices, coriander seeds, rose petals and a gentle char can all be found in this superb pinot.
Sappy and silky, with good flow and persistent, structured, but satiny tannins. The balance here is
spot-on and while you can enjoy this now, it will only become more complex over the next ten years.
Screw cap. | 13% alc. | Drink 2021-2031 | $85 | PR

Coombe Yarra Valley ★★★★★

673-675 Maroondah Highway, Coldstream, Vic 3770 **T** (03) 9739 0173 **www**.coombeyarravalley.com.au
OPEN Mon, Wed-Sun 10-5 **WINEMAKER** Travis Bush **VITICULTURIST** Xavier Mende **EST.** 1999 **DOZENS** 10000
VYDS 60ha

Coombe Yarra Valley is one of the largest and oldest family estates in the Yarra Valley.
Once home to world famous opera singer Dame Nellie Melba, it continues to be owned
and operated by her descendants, the Vestey family. Coombe's wines come from 60ha of
vineyards planted in '98 on the site of some of the original vineyards planted in the 1850s. The
renovated motor house and stable block now contain the cellar door, providore, gallery and
restaurant which overlook the gardens. (JH)

96 **Tribute Series Lady Celia Pinot Noir 2021, Yarra Valley** A medium, very bright crimson. Fragrant, with
lifted, freshly picked red cherries, raspberries, some floral notes and a little cinnamon and nutmeg
spice. Medium bodied, this is very composed and I really like the balance between the fruit, the
use of whole bunches, oak and tannins, which are superfine and long. Screw cap. | 12.5% alc. |
Drink 2023-2028 | $65 | PR

Dappled Wines ★★★★★

1 Sewell Road, Steels Creek, Vic 3775 **T** 0407 675 994 **www**.dappledwines.com.au **OPEN** By appt
WINEMAKER Shaun Crinion **EST.** 2009 **DOZENS** 800

Owner and winemaker Shaun Crinion was introduced to wine in '99, working for his
winemaker uncle at Laetitia Winery & Vineyards on the central coast of California. His career
since then has been so impressive I (James) can't cut it short: 2000 Devil's Lair, Margaret
River and Corbett Canyon Vineyard, California; '02 Houghton, Middle Swan; '03 De Bortoli,
Hunter Valley; '04-06 Pipers Brook, Tasmania; '06 Bay of Fires, Tasmania; '06-07 Williams
Selyem, California; '08 Domaine Chandon, Yarra Valley; '10 Domaine de Montille, Burgundy;
'09- present Dappled Wines (plus part-time for Rob Dolan). His longer-term ambition is to buy
or establish his own vineyard. (JH)

96 **Champs de Cerises Single Vineyard Chardonnay 2020, Yarra Valley** A high-quality wine, making its
mark from the first whiff with fragrant pink grapefruit, white peach and nectarine to the fore, toasted
almonds and a whisper of French oak, all playing the same song on the palate through to the finish.
Screw cap. | 13% alc. | Drink 2022-2035 | $45 | JH

95 **Limited Release Tradition Cabernets 2019, Yarra Valley** An 84/16% blend of cabernet sauvignon and
cabernet franc. The wine is, as one expects from owner and winemaker Shaun Crinion, all about
elegance, finesse and attention to detail, with fruit, tannins and oak all on duty. Gentle cassis is the
heartbeat of the cabernet sauvignon, a leafy, cedary whisper from the cabernet franc, and structure
from the tannins. Diam. | 13% alc. | Drink 2022-2035 | $35 | JH

DCB Wine ★★★★

505 Gembrook Road, Hoddles Creek, Vic 3139 **T** 0419 545 544 **www**.dcbwine.com.au **WINEMAKER** Chris
Bendle **EST.** 2013 **DOZENS** 1300

DCB is a busman's holiday for Chris Bendle, currently a winemaker at Hoddles Creek Estate,
where he has been since 2010. He previously made wine in Tasmania, NZ and Oregon, so he

is the right person to provide wines that are elegant, affordable and reward the pleasure of drinking (Chris's aim); the wines also offer excellent value. (JH)

92   **Chardonnay 2021, Yarra Valley** A bright green gold. Stone fruits intermingle with more savoury, charcuterie notes and a little grilled cashew. Taut, with good persistence, this very well-priced modern Yarra chardonnay should fill out nicely over next 6–12 months. Screw cap. | 13.1% alc. | Drink 2022-2025 | $25 | PR

     Pinot Noir 2021, Yarra Valley A light bright crimson. With its aromas of cherries and brown spice, this bright, light-to medium-bodied and savoury wine flows nicely across the palate. Fine, powdery tannins round out wine that will provide both value and enjoyment in the short–medium term. Screw cap. | 13% alc. | Drink 2022-2026 | $25 | PR

De Bortoli ★★★★★

Pinnacle Lane, Dixons Creek, Vic 3775 **T** (03) 5965 2271 **www**.debortoli.com.au **OPEN** 7 days 10-5 **WINEMAKER** Stephen Webber, Sarah Fagan, Andrew Bretherton **VITICULTURIST** Rob Sutherland, Andrew Ray, Brian Dwyer **EST**. 1987 **DOZENS** 350000 **VYDS** 520ha

Arguably the most successful of all Yarra Valley wineries, not only in terms of the sheer volume of production but also the quality of its wines. It is run by the husband-and-wife team of Leanne De Bortoli and Steve Webber, but owned by the De Bortoli family. The wines are released in 3 quality (and price) groups: at the top Single Vineyard, then Estate Grown and in third place Villages. Small-volume labels increase the offer with Riorret Single Vineyard Pinot Noir, Melba, La Bohème, an aromatic range of Yarra Valley wines and Vinoque, enabling trials (at the commercial level) of new varieties and interesting blends in the Yarra. (JH)

97   **PHI Gamay Noir 2021, Yarra Valley** Vibrant crimson. Reminiscent of cru Beaujolais with its aromas of dark cherries, satsuma plums, violets and spice. Medium bodied and very nicely weighted, this has excellent depth while remaining light on its feet at the same time. Finishes long with crunchy, perfectly judged chalky tannins. A joy to drink. Screw cap. | 13.3% alc. | Drink 2022-2028 | $35 | PR | ♥

96   **PHI Single Vineyard Pinot Noir 2021, Yarra Valley** A light, very bright crimson. Perfumed and bright as a button with its aromas of pomegranate, cranberries and strawberries along with a dusting of Asian spices. Equally bright on the palate, it's not a big wine, but it's got good depth. It finishes with crisp acidity and fine, supple tannins, giving this lovely wine structure and focus. Screw cap. | 13.5% alc. | Drink 2022-2028 | $33 | PR

95   **Estate Grown Cabernet Sauvignon 2019, Yarra Valley** An impressive deep crimson purple. Textbook Yarra cabernet, redolent of perfectly ripened blackberry and cranberry fruits intermingled with gentle cedary oak and a touch of blackberry leaf. Medium bodied, with excellent concentration and structure, this extremely well priced wine is delicious now but, equally, will still be looking good 10 years from now. Screw cap. | 13% alc. | Drink 2023-2030 | $28 | PR

Denton ★★★★★

Viewhill Vineyard, 160 Old Healesville Road, Yarra Glen, Vic 3775 **T** 0402 346 686 **www**.dentonwine.com **OPEN** By appt **WINEMAKER** Luke Lambert **VITICULTURIST** Julian Parrott **EST**. 1997 **DOZENS** 2500 **VYDS** 31.3ha

Leading Melbourne architect John Denton and son Simon began the establishment of the vineyard with a first stage planting in '97, completing the plantings in '04. The name Viewhill derives from the fact that a granite plug 'was created 370 million years ago, sitting above the surrounding softer sandstones and silt of the valley'. This granite base is most unusual in the Yarra Valley, and, together with the natural amphitheatre that the plug created, has consistently produced exceptional grapes. (JH)

96   **Nebbiolo 2019, Yarra Valley** A bright, medium, ruby red. There's lots going on here. Aromas of dark cherries, cherry and sandalwood, dried roses, orange peel and botanicals such as quinine and juniper. The palate is ripe and beautifully brought back into focus by the wine's refreshing acidity and grippy yet fine tannins. Finishes ferrous and long. Screw cap. | 14% alc. | Drink 2023-2029 | $70 | PR

Dominique Portet ★★★★★

870 Maroondah Highway, Coldstream, Vic 3770 **T** (03) 5962 5760 **www**.dominiqueportet.com **OPEN** 7 days 10-5 **WINEMAKER** Ben Portet, Tim Dexter **EST**. 2000 **DOZENS** 15000 **VYDS** 9ha

Dominique Portet spent his early years at Château Lafite and was one of the first Flying Winemakers, commuting to Clos du Val in the Napa Valley where his brother was also a winemaker. He then spent over 20 years as managing director of Taltarni and Clover Hill.

CENTRAL VICTORIA

GIPPSLAND

NORTH EAST VICTORIA

NORTH WEST VICTORIA

PORT PHILLIP

WESTERN VICTORIA

He then moved to the Yarra Valley where in '00 built his winery and cellar door. Son Ben is now executive winemaker, Dominique consultant and brand marketer. Ben himself has a winemaking CV of awesome scope, covering all parts of France, South Africa, California and 4 vintages at Petaluma. (JH)

96   **Cabernet Sauvignon 2019, Yarra Valley** With 2/1% merlot/petit verdot. A gorgeous, bright, medium crimson-purple hue. A supremely fragrant wine, with aromas of blackcurrant, currant leaf, chocolate powder and a hint of cedar and spice. On the palate, this thoughtfully put-together wine marries intensity and elegance in equal measure, with focused cassis fruit and superfine tannins that make this a wine to be enjoyed now and over the next 10 or so years. Cork. | 13.5% alc. |
Drink 2022-2032 | $70 | PR

First Foot Forward ★★★★

6 Maddens Lane, Coldstream, Vic 3770 **T** 0402 575 818 **WWW**.firstfootforward.com.au **OPEN** By appt **WINEMAKER** Martin Siebert **VITICULTURIST** Robin Wood **EST.** 2013 **DOZENS** 800

With an impressive CV that includes Yarra Yering and Coldstream Hills in the Yarra as well as Benjamin Leroux (Burgundy) and Pegasus Bay (NZ), Martin Siebert landed at Tokar Estate as chief winemaker in time for the cracking 2012 vintage, starting his own First Foot Forward a year later. He likens himself to a classically minded musician dabbling in punk music, using terracotta amphorae and eggs as well as some skin contact on the whites. (PR)

93   **Amphora Ferment Single Vineyard Sauvignon Blanc 2021, Yarra Valley** Fermentation began on skins before being pressed to 800L amphorae. The result is a slightly different and excellent take on sauvignon blanc. Bright green gold, this leaps out of the glass with its aromas of fresh guava, passionfruit, kiwi and snow pea tendrils. The flavour-packed palate is bright, gently textured and balanced and the finish is crisp and long. Screw cap. | 13% alc. | Drink 2022-2025 | $25 | PR

Gembrook Hill ★★★★★

Launching Place Road, Gembrook, Vic 3783 **T** (03) 5968 1622 **WWW**.gembrookhill.com.au **OPEN** By appt **WINEMAKER** Andrew Marks **EST.** 1983 **DOZENS** 1500 **VYDS** 5ha

Ian and June Marks established Gembrook Hill, one of the oldest vineyards in the southernmost part of the Upper Yarra Valley. The northeast-facing vineyard is in a natural amphitheatre; the low-yielding sauvignon blanc, chardonnay and pinot noir are not irrigated. The unexpected death of Ian in Mar '17, and the decision of former winemaker Timo Mayer to concentrate on his own label, left son Andrew Marks in charge of winemaking at Gembrook Hill. (JH)

96   **Blanc de Blancs 2015, Yarra Valley** Traditional method, on tirage 6 years, 5.5g/L dosage – brave, but I'm ok with it; disgorged May '21. Well made, doubtless whole-bunch pressed, no pressings. Diam. | 11.5% alc. | $58 | JH

95   **Sauvignon Blanc 2020, Yarra Valley** A pale, bright green gold. Consistently good, this restrained sauvignon blanc has aromas of green apple, lemongrass and just a hint of fresh peas. Gently textured, fresh, clean and crisp with a long lemon-curd finish. A serious wine in an oversaturated sauvignon blanc market. Screw cap. | 12% alc. | Drink 2021-2025 | $32 | PR | ♥

Giant Steps ★★★★★

314 Maroondah Highway, Healesville, Vic 3777 **T** (03) 5962 6111 **WWW**.giantstepswine.com.au **OPEN** 7 days 11–4 **WINEMAKER** Melanie Chester, Steve Flamsteed, Jess Clark **VITICULTURIST** Ashley Wood **EST.** 1997 **DOZENS** 30000 **VYDS** 60ha

Since the sale of Innocent Bystander in '16, the focus has been on the high-quality, single-vineyard, single-variety wines in what is demonstrably a very distinguished portfolio. Giant Steps was purchased by Jackson Family Wines in Aug '20. (JH)

98   **Applejack Vineyard Pinot Noir 2021, Yarra Valley** A deep, bright, crimson purple. Maraschino cherry into plum, there's an exotic and riotous amalgam of Asian five-spice and a gentle savoury, umami character. What elevates this vintage is the concentration, along with Applejack's trademark perfume and spice. Just so vibrant and fresh on the palate, the tannins are both silky and plentiful. You will have no problems opening and enjoying this now, but the wine's track record suggests you'll have some to drink 7–10 years from now, if not longer. Screw cap. | 13.5% alc. | Drink 2022-2032 | $70 | PR | ♥

97   **Rosé 2021, Yarra Valley** 100% pinot noir, hand picked specifically for this rosé, wild-yeast fermented. Vibrantly fresh aromas and flavours; rose petals, violets and delicate spices on the bouquet, wild strawberries and raspberries on the mouth-watering palate. Great wine, not just great rosé. And it will repay cellaring. Screw cap. | 12% alc. | Drink 2021-2025 | $30 | JH | ♥

CENTRAL VICTORIA

GIPPSLAND

NORTH EAST VICTORIA

NORTH WEST VICTORIA

PORT PHILLIP

WESTERN VICTORIA

Sexton Vineyard Chardonnay 2021, Yarra Valley Smells tightly wound and concentrated with aromas of ripe peach and nectarine, together with just a hint of lanolin and apple custard. Equally powerful and punchy on the palate. This has more of everything, including sprightly acid and some phenolic grip on the very long, stone-fruit pithy finish. Today, this is my pick of the 4 single-vineyard '21 chardonnays, but who knows what will come out on top in 5 or even 10 years from now! Screw cap. | 13% alc. | Drink 2022-2028 | $65 | PR

Primavera Vineyard Pinot Noir 2021, Yarra Valley A very bright crimson purple. So pure and perfumed with briary cherries, ripe redcurrants and freshly cut roses. Poised, juicy and energetic, the wine has so much tang and crunch, you barely notice that this is also structured finishing with long, gently puckering tannins. A wine with immediate appeal, but also one that will reward at least another 7-10 years in the cellar. Screw cap. | 13% alc. | Drink 2022-2031 | $70 | PR

96   **Pinot Noir 2021, Yarra Valley** A very bright, light–medium crimson red. A gentle waft of fresh raspberries and cranberries, with just the right amount of spice-rack spices. Delicious right out of the gate, this medium-bodied and refreshing wine will age well too. The perfect introduction to modern Yarra pinot. Screw cap. | 13.5% alc. | Drink 2021-2026 | $38 | PR

Applejack Vineyard Chardonnay 2021, Yarra Valley A very bright green gold. Very bright and pure fruited, with its aromas of freshly poached apples, just-picked white peach and a little spice. The oak is already perfectly integrated. The flow and texture on the palate is seamless and I love that bit of 'chew' on the finish. Screw cap. | 12.5% alc. | Drink 2022-2028 | $65 | PR

Sexton Vineyard Pinot Noir 2021, Yarra Valley A dark, deep crimson. A more robust Yarra Valley pinot with its aromas of dark cherries, black plum and a dried-earth character that makes it quite different to the other Giant Step single-vineyard pinots. Sweetly fruited, concentrated and structured on the palate, what this impressive wine doesn't have in finesse, it makes up for in power and grunt. This should still be looking good 10, if not 15, years from now. Screw cap. | 13.5% alc. | Drink 2023-2032 | $70 | PR

Fatal Shore Pinot Noir 2021, Southern Tasmania A gorgeous, bright, crimson. Perfumed and seductive, this leaps out of the glass with an array of aromas including red and black fruits, peony, Asian spices, orange peel and a hint of fresh vanilla bean. More sweet fruited and textured on the mid palate compared to the more fine-boned and linear Yarra single-vineyard pinots. Concentrated but not heavy, with ripe, gently chewy and persistent tannins rounding out an impressive and still quite tightly wound wine that will need another year or 2 to relax and really hit its straps. Screw cap. | 13.5% alc. | Drink 2023-2029 | $75 | PR

Clay Ferment Ocarina Chardonnay 2020, Yarra Valley It's quite astonishing how these vessels shape the feel and taste of the final blend. This chardonnay is tight, linear and superfine with its acid profile. Yet it has plenty of flavour with hints of citrus, lemon salts and a smidge of creamed honey. It's refreshing and pulsating with energy. Screw cap. | 12.5% alc. | Drink 2021-2030 | $60 | JF

Wombat Creek Vineyard Chardonnay 2020, Yarra Valley Giant Steps' higher-elevation sites, as in this and Applejack Vineyard, have turned out racy, long and superfine wines – it's the moreish, mouth-watering acidity. Of course, there's more: the complex flavours and heady aromas. Smoky, slinky and talc-like texture to the acidity, with a dab of creamed honey and citrus on the palate. There's a lot of precision and it's a pure wine in a way that evolves superbly in the glass. Screw cap. | 13% alc. | Drink 2021-2029 | $60 | JF

Applejack Vineyard Pinot Noir 2020, Yarra Valley Pinot purity right here, folks. There's a certain precision and definition, too. A delightful combo of joy and complexity: rhubarb and freshly grated beetroot, sweet red cherries, florals and warm spices, with the oak neatly tucked in. Superfine tannins, laser-like acidity and terrific length seal the deal. Screw cap. | 13.5% alc. | Drink 2021-2031 | $65 | JF

Helen's Hill Estate ★★★★★

16 Ingram Road, Lilydale, Vic 3140 **T** (03) 9739 1573 **www**.helenshill.com.au **OPEN** Thurs-Mon 10-5 **WINEMAKER** Scott McCarthy **EST.** 1984 **DOZENS** 15000 **VYDS** 53ha

Helen's Hill Estate is named after the previous owner of the property, Helen Fraser. Venture partners Andrew and Robyn McIntosh and Roma and Allan Nalder combined childhood farming experience with more recent careers in medicine and finance to establish and manage the day-to-day operations of the estate. Scott McCarthy started his career early by working vintages during school holidays before gaining diverse and extensive experience in the Barossa and Yarra valleys, Napa Valley, Languedoc, the Loire Valley and Marlborough. (JH)

97   **The Smuggler Single Clone Pinot Noir 2019, Yarra Valley** This is a striking and delicious wine, with fluid drive and line to its mix of dark cherries, spices and pomegranate. The balance between fruit, oak and tannin is perfect, as is its length. Diam. | 12.8% alc. | Drink 2023-2035 | $60 | JH

95   **Hill Top Single Vineyard Syrah 2020, Yarra Valley** A high-toned, intensely focused shiraz, the syrah soubriquet spot on. Black and blue berry fruits are moulded together with a splash of spice and peremptory tannins. Screw cap. | 14.8% alc. | Drink 2025-2040 | $35 | JH

Hoddles Creek Estate ⑨ ★★★★★

505 Gembrook Road, Hoddles Creek, Vic 3139 **T** (03) 5967 4692 **www**.hoddlescreekestate.com.au **OPEN** By appt **WINEMAKER** Franco D'Anna, Chris Bendle **VITICULTURIST** Franco D'Anna **EST**. 1997 **DOZENS** 30000 **VYDS** 33.3ha

The D'Anna family established their vineyard on a property that had been in the family since 1960. The vines are hand pruned and hand harvested. A 300t, split-level winery was built in 2003. Son Franco is the viticulturist and inspired winemaker; he graduated to chief wine buyer by the time he was 21. He completed a bachelor of commerce before studying viticulture at CSU. A vintage at Coldstream Hills, then 2 years' vintage experience with Peter Dredge at Witchmount and, with Mario Marson (ex-Mount Mary) as mentor in '03, has put an old head on young shoulders. (JH)

97   **1er Chardonnay 2020, Yarra Valley** Draws you in within a split second of the first sniff of the bouquet; wild ferment in French oak and lees contact create a wine that is very complex, on the edge of funk, but not letting it dominate the white peach, melon and grapefruit flavours. Gentle acidity carrys the very long finish and lingering aftertaste.   Screw cap. | 13.2% alc. | Drink 2022-2032 | $55 | JH

96   **Wickhams Road Chardonnay 2021, Yarra Valley** It sidles up to you, and it's only on the second taste that its sheer intensity and class drops its guard. The price of the wine should be doubled, to reflect this perfect rendition of the varietal array of pink grapefruit and blood orange.   Screw cap. | 13% alc. | Drink 2022-2036 | $19 | JH

      DML Pinot Noir 2020, Yarra Valley More bright red-hued than its 1er Pinot sibling, a sign of a wine built around the beautifully delineated fruit aromas and flavours. Cherry, strawberry and plum all in the game, spontaneously giving it pleasure; long and refined.   Screw cap. | 13% alc. | Drink 2022-2032 | $60 | JH

95   **Wickhams Road Pinot Noir 2021, Gippsland** The ravishingly fragrant bouquet of flowers and red and purple fruits, morphing into fruits of the forest. Spice and dried berries share 50% of the palate, rose petals et al. the other half. The fruit attack on the tip of the tongue is of surgical precision.   Screw cap. | 13.5% alc. | Drink 2022-2031 | $20 | JH

      Wickhams Road Pinot Noir 2021, Yarra Valley Like its siblings, a light but brilliantly clear colour. A highly perfumed bouquet of strawberries leads into a palate with the precision and clarity of a Dutch painter 300 or so years ago. There's no other producer in the Yarra Valley to even come close to the value offered by this wine.   Screw cap. | 13% alc. | Drink 2022-2036 | $20 | JH

      Skins Pinot Gris 2021, Yarra Valley A bright, medium-deep amber terracotta. Complex with pear skin, red currants, savoury fennel-seed notes and a little Turkish delight. Equally good on the palate, this delicious non-binary wine is textured and saline and the digestif-like grippy tannins are begging for a plate of charcuterie to accompany it. 500ml bottle.   Screw cap. | 12.5% alc. | Drink 2021-2024 | $25 | PR

      Pinot Noir 2020, Yarra Valley Don't be alarmed by the pale ruby colour – this is not at all wimpy. Instead, it's a refined and lighter-framed rendition with layers of flavour. It has an almost whole-bunch character, but winemaker Franco d'Anna destems the fruit. Still, expect flavours of earthy rhubarb and grated raw beetroot with a sappy freshness. Tangy, spritely acidity and fine tannins add to the pleasure of drinking.   Screw cap. | 13.2% alc. | Drink 2023-2030 | $25 | JF

      Pinot Gris 2020, Yarra Valley A pale copper hue, with wafts of almond meal, pears in puff pastry and poached quinces lightly spiced with ginger. The palate is surprisingly delicate and laden with citrus. Refreshing, lively and the acidity more pronounced than usual. It has texture, with some phenolic grip and decent length, too.   Screw cap. | 12% alc. | Drink 2021-2024 | $22 | JF

94   **Chardonnay 2020, Yarra Valley** Another terrific well-priced chardy that consistently punches above its weight. A balance of flavours from stone fruit and lemon zest to savoury spices and neat phenolics. It has texture, even a plumpness, but the wine is well contained, thanks to mouth-watering acidity. It's moreish and lingers long. Smart now, and will unfurl in the next few years.   Screw cap. | 13.2% alc. | Drink 2022-2029 | $22 | JF

Lone Star Creek Vineyard ★★★★

75 Owens Rd, Woori Yallock, Vic, 3139 **T** 0414 282 629 **www**.lonestarcreekwines.com.au **WINEMAKER** Franco D'Anna **VITICULTURIST** Steve Sadlier **EST**. 1997 **DOZENS** 800 **VYDS** 22ha

The Lone Star Creek vineyard was established in 1997 by Robin Wood and Gillian Bowers, who are primarily contract growers; 2017 was the first vintage under their own label. Situated on the border of Woori Yallock and Hoddle's Creek, the cool-climate upper Yarra fruit was sold to wineries including Hoddle's Creek Estate, so when the time came to start producing wine under the Lone Star Creek Vineyard label, enlisting Hoddle's Creek's own Franco D'Anna as winemaker must have seemed an obvious choice. (JH)

94   **Pinot Noir 2021, Yarra Valley** A bright crimson purple. Fragrant and immediately appealing with its aromas of strawberry puree, raspberries and gentle spice. The bright, light to medium-bodied palate is well weighted with crunchy and refreshing tannins, rounding out a wine that will continue to improve over the next 2-3 years if not longer. A single-vineyard Upper Yarra pinot at this price is a steal. Screw cap. | 12.5% alc. | Drink 2022-2027 | $28 | PR

Mandala ★★★★☆

1568 Melba Highway, Dixons Creek, Vic 3775 **T** (03) 5965 2016 **www**.mandalawines.com.au **OPEN** Mon-Fri 11-4, w'ends 10-5 **WINEMAKER** Charles Smedley, Don Pope **EST**. 2007 **DOZENS** 10 500 **VYDS** 29ha

Mandala is owned by Charles Smedley, who acquired the established vineyard in '07. The vineyard has vines up to 25 years old, but the spectacular restaurant and cellar door complex is a more recent addition. The vineyards are primarily at the home base in Dixons Creek and there is a separate 4.4ha vineyard at Yarra Junction planted entirely to pinot noir with an impressive clonal mix. (JH)

92 **Rosé 2021, Yarra Valley** Blend of 75/25% merlot/pinot noir. A pale, bright salmon skin. Attractive raspberry, redcurrant and herb aromas. Lively and packed with red berry, tangerine and orange pith flavours. Finishes, dry and gently grippy. I imagine it would be an excellent food wine. Screw cap. | 13.5% alc. | Drink 2022-2025 | $25 | PR

Mayer ★★★★★

66 Miller Road, Healesville, Vic 3777 **T** (03) 5967 3779 **www**.timomayer.com.au **OPEN** By appt **WINEMAKER** Timo Mayer **EST**. 1999 **DOZENS** 2000 **VYDS** 3ha

Timo Mayer teamed with partner Rhonda Ferguson to establish Mayer on the slopes of Mount Toolebewong, 8km south of Healesville. The steepness of those slopes is presumably 'celebrated' in the name given to the vineyard (Bloody Hill). Mayer's winemaking credo is minimal interference and handling, and no filtration. (JH)

97 **Syrah 2021, Yarra Valley** A wonderful, deep, purple crimson. Smells fabulous – reminiscent of good Cornas, with its aromas of dark fruits, crushed granite, brined black olives, red peppercorns and bay leaf. Backwards and structured on the palate, I'd suggest decanting this if you're going to open a bottle or any time soon, but you'd really want to have some in the cellar to enjoy in 5–10 years, if not longer. Screw cap. | 13% alc. | Drink 2023-2032 | $55 | PR

96 **Dr Mayer Pinot Noir 2021, Yarra Valley** A medium, bright crimson red. Raspberries, mountain herbs from 100% whole bunches, and sweet spices as it opens up, all found in this youthful and concentrated wine. You will find pomegranate and blood oranges on the palate, which is also saline and structured. The tannins are fine, yet tightly wound and this will only get better over the next 5–8 years. Diam. | 12.5% alc. | Drink 2022-2030 | $60 | PR

95 **Bloody Hill Villages Shiraz 2021, Yarra Valley** Bright, crimson purple. Redolent of dark cherries, blood plums, a hint of pomegranate, black peppercorns, olives and some floral notes. Medium bodied and delicious straight off the bat, with its dark fruits and chalky, fine tannins. Drink now and over the next 5–8 years. Diam. | 13.5% alc. | Drink 2022-2029 | $32 | PR

Medhurst ★★★★★

24-26 Medhurst Road, Gruyere, Vic 3770 **T** (03) 5964 9022 **www**.medhurstwines.com.au **OPEN** Thurs-Mon & public hols 11-5 **WINEMAKER** Simon Steele **EST**. 2000 **DOZENS** 6000 **VYDS** 12ha

The wheel has come full circle for Ross and Robyn Wilson. Ross was CEO of Southcorp when it brought the Penfolds, Lindemans and Wynns businesses under its banner. Robyn spent her childhood in the Yarra Valley, her parents living less than a kilometre away from Medhurst. The visual impact of the winery has been minimised by recessing the building into the slope of land and locating the barrel room underground. The building was recognised for its architectural excellence at the Victorian Architecture Awards. The arrival of Simon Steele has enhanced the already considerable reputation of Medhurst. (JH)

97 **Estate Vineyard Chardonnay 2021, Yarra Valley** A very bright green gold. Beautifully crafted, you'll find white nectarines, grapefruit pith, orange blossom, jasmine, subtle peony and very subtle struck match. An essay in chardonnay purity, this taut, powerful and beautifully balanced wine tapers into a long, satisfying and saline finish. Screw cap. | 13.1% alc. | Drink 2022-2028 | $44 | PR

Reserve Cabernet 2019, Yarra Valley Only 30 dozen made of this supremely good Yarra Valley cabernet. A deep, plummy crimson purple. Densely packed with dark fruits, spice-rack spices, and already beautifully integrated and well-handled cedary oak. Compact and precise on the palate with dark currants, boysenberry and blood plums. Gently textured, with layered, bright and crunchy tannins, this beauty will still be looking good, in 10, if not 20, years from now. Screw cap. | 13.1% alc. | Drink 2023-2036 | $90 | PR

CENTRAL VICTORIA

GIPPSLAND

NORTH EAST VICTORIA

NORTH WEST VICTORIA

PORT PHILLIP

WESTERN VICTORIA

95 **Estate Vineyard Rosé 2021, Yarra Valley** The pale salmon hue reflects whole-bunch pressed cabernet sauvignon and shiraz, fermented off skins. Wafts of perfume float in the air, rose petals to the fore. The unexpectedly intense fruits span spices, light and dark, and small forest berries. Typical Medhurst class. Screw cap. | 13% alc. | Drink 2021-2023 | $27 | JH

Mount Mary

Coldstream West Road, Lilydale, Vic 3140 **T** (03) 9739 1761 **www**.mountmary.com.au **WINEMAKER** Sam Middleton **EST**. 1971 **DOZENS** 4500 **VYDS** 18ha

Mount Mary was one of the foremost pioneers of the rebirth of the Yarra Valley after 50 years without viticultural activity. From the outset they produced wines of rare finesse and purity. The late founder, Dr John Middleton, practised near-obsessive attention to detail long before that phrase slid into oenological vernacular. Charming grandson Sam Middleton is equally dedicated. In '08, Mount Mary commenced a detailed program of vine improvement, in particular assessing the implications of progressively moving towards a 100% grafted vineyard to provide immunity from phylloxera. Winery of the Year in the Halliday Wine Companion 2018. (JH)

98 **Quintet 2020, Yarra Valley** Winner of 2 awards in the Wine Companion 2023 Red Wine of the Year and Cabernet & Family of the Year. A blend of 44/30/18/4/4% cabernet sauvignon/merlot/cabernet franc/malbec/petit verdot. An essay in elegance and understatement. A medium, bright and translucent ruby red, this is beautifully perfumed with aromas of just-ripened blackcurrants, red cherries, rose petals and gentle cedar notes from the oak. The palate is exceptionally pure-fruited and gently textured. The wine finishes with these incredibly silky, long tannins that are in perfect harmony with the fruit and acid. This majestic wine is gorgeous to drink even now but those that still have some in their cellar in 10-15 years (if not longer) will be grateful. Screw cap. | 13.2% alc. | Drink 2023-2035 | $165 | PR | ♥

97 **Chardonnay 2020, Yarra Valley** Typically refined and elegant, but isn't stand-offish. The Yarra Valley's calling card of chardonnay is its extreme length, built around natural acidity and citrus zest. Oak is part of the upbringing, but discreet, and the wine has a very long plateau ahead. Screw cap. | 13.3% alc. | Drink 2025-2040 | $120 | JH

Oakridge Wines ⑨⑪

864 Maroondah Highway, Coldstream, Vic 3770 **T** (03) 9738 9900 **www**.oakridgewines.com.au **OPEN** 7 days 10-5 **WINEMAKER** David Bicknell, Tim Perrin **EST**. 1978 **DOZENS** 35 **VYDS** 61ha

Winemaker David Bicknell has proved his worth time and again as an extremely talented winemaker. At the top of the Oakridge brand tier is 864, all Yarra Valley vineyard selections, only released in the best years; next is the Vineyard Series; and the Over the Shoulder range, drawn from all of the sources available to Oakridge. The estate vineyards are Oakridge Vineyard, Hazeldene Vineyard and Henk Vineyard. (JH)

98 **864 Single Block Release Drive Block Funder & Diamond Vineyard Chardonnay 2020, Yarra Valley** A bright green gold, expect aromas of lemon and pink grapefruit pith, freshly baked ginger-spice biscuits from the beautifully handled and integrated oak as well as jasmine, freshly laundered linen, wet stone and a hint of gunflint. Like many great wines, this balances power and delicacy in equal measure. There's a refreshing limoncello bitterness on the long, super-satisfying finish. Screw cap. | 13.5% alc. | Drink 2022-2028 | $95 | PR | ♥

97 **Horst Riesling 2021, Yarra Valley** A pale, lemon gold, this simply beautiful riesling opens with delicate lychee, tangerine and a little fresh, lemon sherbet. Even better on the palate. Bright and energetic, there's subtle orange blossom and feijoa fruit. I love the finely judged tension between the wine's gentle 18g/L RS of sugar and the fine vein of acidity that courses seamlessly through the wine. Screw cap. | 11.5% alc. | Drink 2022-2028 | $45 | PR | ♥

Vineyard Series Henk Chardonnay 2020, Yarra Valley A bright green gold, this is immediately engaging and open with its aromas of white peach, white flowers and preserved lemons. With its superb purity of fruit, I love the way the acidity cuts through the wine, giving it backbone and length. All the 2020 Vineyard Series chardonnays are subtle variations on a theme, with the Henk being my pick today.. Screw cap. | 12.7% alc. | Drink 2022-2026 | $45 | PR

Vineyard Series Willowlake Pinot Noir 2020, Yarra Valley Bright ruby. Subtle aromas of cranberries, quince, blood orange, fennel, lavender together with a little vanilla bean. Gently fleshy and compact, this also has excellent depth and concentration. This is deceptive, in that while it's delicious now, the tension between the core of fine tannins and bright acidity gives the wine considerable structure and will reward your patience should you have the necessary restraint. Screw cap. | 13.1% alc. | Drink 2022-2026 | $45 | PR

864 Single Block Release Winery Block Oakridge Vineyard Cabernet Sauvignon 2019, Yarra Valley Made virtually identically to the Original Vineyard Cabernet, this is a totally different, yet equally impressive, beast. A brilliant and bright medium crimson purple. Still a baby, this has a core of concentrated, perfectly pitched cassis fruit, together with some cedar and cigar box and a whiff of gravel and lavender. A touch closed at present, this has terrific purity and depth of fruit on the palate, with everything in place for this to improve for at least the next decade or 2, if not longer! Screw cap. | 13% alc. | Drink 2023-2039 | $95 | PR

96 **Vineyard Series Hazeldene Chardonnay 2021, Yarra Valley** A superb Hazeldene with white peach, wet stone, fresh mint, white flowers and a hint of macadamia nut. Pure fruited, concentrated and beautifully balanced, this will provide a lot of pleasure now and for years to come. Screw cap. | 13.5% alc. | Drink 2022-2029 | $45 | PR

Vineyard Series Hazeldene Pinot Noir 2020, Yarra Valley A bright ruby red. A very complex and fragrant nose redolent of dark cherry, musk sticks and potpourri. The palate is layered and delicate and I like the tension between the sinewy, long tannins and moreish acidity. Screw cap. | 13.4% alc. | Drink 2022-2026 | $45 | PR

Vineyard Series Willowlake Chardonnay 2020, Yarra Valley A very bright green gold. Excites from the first, with its aromas of white cut pears, stone fruits and an intriguing, perfectly handled flinty, freshly torched brûlée-top reduction. This has terrific drive and persistence on the palate, and the textured and layered mouth feel is balanced by the wine's perfectly integrated acidity. Screw cap. | 13.2% alc. | Drink 2022-2027 | $45 | PR

Original Vineyard Cabernet Sauvignon 2019, Yarra Valley A wine of medium-deep crimson colour, with gorgeous aromatics including dark cherries, satsuma plums, violets and a gentle waft of cedar from the oak. Classic, medium-bodied and beautifully poised cabernet, with silky long tannins. This should age effortlessly over the next 10–15 years. Screw cap. | 13% alc. | Drink 2022-2035 | $95 | PR

95 **Vineyard Series Willowlake Sauvignon 2020, Yarra Valley** Sauvignon blanc. A wine that speaks of its location as much as its variety, with its cool aromas of lemon pith, lemongrass and greengage. Taut, chalky and linear on the palate. Screw cap. | 11.3% alc. | Drink 2022-2027 | $30 | PR

94 **Chardonnay 2021, Yarra Valley** A bright green gold. A terrific introduction to Oakridge chardonnays, showing just how good they can be. Classic Bicknell struck match and flint to go with the apple, yellow nectarine and white peach fruit aromas. Tightly wound, this has good depth and will be even better in another six months or so. Excellent value. Screw cap. | 12.8% alc. | Drink 2022-2026 | $30 | PR

Payne's Rise

★★★★

10 Paynes Road, Seville, Vic 3139 **T** (03) 5964 2504 **www**.paynesrise.com.au **OPEN** Thurs–Sun 11–5 **WINEMAKER** Franco D'Anna (Contract) **VITICULTURIST** Tim Cullen **EST.** 1998 **DOZENS** 2000 **VYDS** 5ha

Tim and Narelle Cullen have progressively established 5ha of cabernet sauvignon, shiraz, pinot noir, chardonnay and pinot gris since '99. They carry out all the vineyard work (Tim is also a viticulturist for a local agribusiness) and are planting new clones and rootstocks with an eye to the future. Narelle is responsible for sales and marketing. The contract-made wines have won both gold medals and trophies at the Yarra Valley Wine Show and the Victorian Wines Show. (JH)

95 **Anniversary Cabernet Sauvignon 2019, Yarra Valley** Fruit planted in Seville in the Upper Yarra in 1999, hence the anniversary bottling. An impressive bright deep purple colour. Dense, with dark fruit, dark chocolate and a moreish, savoury, meaty edge. Concentrated on the palate, this well-made and -priced medium-bodied wine finishes with classic chewy, gravelly tannins. Screw cap. | 13.5% alc. | Drink 2022-2032 | $35 | PR

94 **Chardonnay 2021, Yarra Valley** A very bright green gold. Terrific cool-climate chardonnay from a cool year, with aromas of quince, pear and stone fruits, sitting alongside a little spice from the oak and well-handled gunflint reduction. Elegant and tightly wound, this needs another 3–6 months to fill out and reveal it's full potential. Screw cap. | 12.5% alc. | Drink 2021-2027 | $30 | PR

Punt Road

★★★★★

10 St Huberts Road, Coldstream, Vic 3770 **T** (03) 9739 0666 **www**.puntroadwines.com.au **OPEN** 7 days 10–5 **WINEMAKER** Tim Shand, Travis Bush **EST.** 2000 **DOZENS** 20000 **VYDS** 65.61ha

Punt Road is owned by the Napoleone family, third-generation fruit growers in the Yarra Valley. Their vineyard in Coldstream is one of the most historic sites in Victoria, first planted to vines by Swiss immigrant Hubert De Castella in 1860. The Napoleone Vineyard was established on the property in 1987. Chief winemaker Tim Shand joined the winery in 2014 and has established a reputation for consistent quality of all the Punt Road wines. The 2 main ranges are Punt Road and Airlie Bank, plus a small production of single-vineyard 'Block' wines, only available at cellar door, made only in the best vintages. (JH)

92 **Airlie Bank Sauvignon Blanc 2021, Yarra Valley** A light green gold. Aromas of passionfruit and lemon pith, nashi pear and fresh guava are all present in this subtle and beautifully put together Yarra

CENTRAL VICTORIA

GIPPSLAND

NORTH EAST VICTORIA

NORTH WEST VICTORIA

PORT PHILLIP

WESTERN VICTORIA

sauvignon blanc. Dry, chalky textured and refreshing, this will be at peak now and over the next 12–24 months. Screw cap. | 11% alc. | Drink 2021-2021 | $22 | PR

91 **Airlie Bank Gris Fermented On Skins 2021, Yarra Valley** A bright copper colour. Attractive aromas of apricot kernel, strawberries, musk sticks and rose petals, while the palate is dry with a reasonably long, chalky finish. Screw cap. | 12% alc. | Drink 2021-2023 | $22 | PR

Garden Red 2021, Yarra Valley Equal parts grenache, gamay and cabernet franc. A really bright crimson purple. Dark fruits, mountain herbs and violets pervade this new and interesting blend. Medium–full bodied, this richly fruited wine has good depth and structure, with chalky tannins rounding out and good each-way bet between drinking now or watching it soften and mature over the next 5 years. Screw cap. | 12.5% alc. | Drink 2021-2025 | $22 | PR

Salo Wines

28 Dorothy Street, Healesville, Vic 3777 (postal) **T** (03) 5962 5331 **www**.salowines.com.au **WINEMAKER** Steve Flamsteed, Dave Mackintosh **EST.** 2008 **DOZENS** 250

Business partners Steve Flamsteed and Dave Mackintosh say that Salo means dirty and a little uncouth, which with the Australian sense of humour, can be used as a term of endearment. They wish to keep their wines a little dirty by using hands-off, minimal winemaking to make more gritty, textured wines. (JH)

96 **Chardonnay 2021, Yarra Valley** A really vibrant green gold. Pure fruited with seductive nashi pear, almond skin and subtle wet rock and gun flint. Gently creamy but with racy, fresh acidity too. It's an excellent combination, making it delicious as a young wine but with the potential to age well too. **Tops.** Screw cap. | 13% alc. | Drink 2022-2028 | $40 | PR

Santolin Wines

c/- 21-23 Delaneys Road, South Warrandyte, Vic 3134 **T** 0402 278 464 **www**.santolinwines.com.au **WINEMAKER** Adrian Santolin **EST.** 2012 **DOZENS** 1000

Adrian Santolin grew up in Griffith, NSW, and has worked in the wine industry since he was 15. His wife Rebecca has worked in marketing roles at various wineries. Together, they moved to the Yarra Valley in '07. Adrian's love of pinot noir led him to work at wineries such as Wedgetail Estate, Rochford, De Bortoli, Sticks and Rob Dolan Wines. In '12 his dream came true when he was able to buy 2t of pinot noir from the Syme-on-Yarra Vineyard, increasing production in '13 to 4t. (JH)

96 **Gladysdale Chardonnay 2020, Yarra Valley** An impressive wine from the first, with its aromas of stone fruits, grilled nuts and discreet, well-judged struck match. There are white nectarines and grapefruit pith on the mouth-watering palate, and I like the touch of grip on the long finish, derived, most probably, from one barrel that was a whole-berry ferment. A lovely effort. Screw cap. | 12.9% alc. | Drink 2022-2027 | $45 | PR

Serrat

115 Simpsons Lane, Yarra Glen, Vic 3775 **T** (03) 9730 1439 **www**.serrat.com.au **WINEMAKER** Tom Carson, Kate Thurgood **VITICULTURIST** Tom Carson, Kate Thurgood **EST.** 2001 **DOZENS** 1000 **VYDS** 3.5ha

Serrat is the family business of Tom Carson (after a 12-year reign at Yering Station, now running Yabby Lake and Heathcote Estate for the Kirby family) and wife Nadège. The vineyards are undergoing organic conversion. As well as being a consummate winemaker, Tom has one of the best palates in Australia and a deep understanding of the fine wines of the world, which he and Nadège drink at every opportunity (when they aren't drinking Serrat). Tom Carson is the Halliday Wine Companion 2023 Viticulturist of the Year. (JH)

98 **Shiraz Viognier 2021, Yarra Valley** A vibrant crimson purple. A truly wonderful set of wines from Tom Carson in '21, cementing (not that it's needed) his place as one of Australia's best winemakers and the Serrat vineyard as a great, modern-day site. Seductive aromas of cherry plums, dark cherries and raspberries, graphite, sandalwood incense and star anise. Even better on the palate, which is creamy textured, bright, crunchy and perfectly balanced. The tannins are silken and long. This seriously good and gorgeous wine can be enjoyed now and over the next 10–15 years, if not longer. Screw cap. | 13.5% alc. | Drink 2022-2033 | $48 | PR | ♥

97 **Grenache Noir 2021, Yarra Valley** A light, bright crimson purple. Pretty and perfumed with aromas of black cherries, raspberries, strawberries, lilacs, thyme and just a hint of bay leaf. Perfectly weighted, this is simultaneously intense, silky and light on the palate. A gorgeous wine that finishes with bright acidity and very fine, gently chalky tannins. Remarkable to think that a grenache of this quality can be made in the Yarra. Screw cap. | 14% alc. | Drink 2022-2031 | $45 | PR | ♥

Pinot Noir 2021, Yarra Valley A brilliant, medium-deep crimson. There's a lot going on here from the outset, with its wild, briary, red fruits, a ferrous character, violets, rose petals and a hint of sweet spice. Medium bodied, the palate is multi layered with fine, persistent and chalky tannins providing considerable backbone and structure. Tightly coiled at the moment, but bear in mind it has just recently been bottled. This will look even better in just a few months and will continue to improve for years to come. Screw cap. | 13% alc. | Drink 2022-2031 | $45 | PR

96   **Fourre-Tout 2021, Yarra Valley** Fourre-Tout is a French word meaning 'catch-all' and the '21 is a blend of 80/15% barbera/nebbiolo, with a little grenache and pinot noir making up the remainder. A deep, vibrant, crimson purple. Opens up with unctuous blueberries, satsuma plums, violets and mountain herbs. Smells super. And it tastes as good as it smells, with its core of densely packed red and black fruits, plum skins, refreshing acidity and very fine, chalky tannins. Delicious now, I've got no doubt this also has the potential to become more complex over at least the next 5 years. Screw cap. | 13% alc. | Drink 2022-2029 | $45 | PR

Chardonnay 2021, Yarra Valley A very bright green gold. Restrained, with aromas of pink grapefruit, Beurre Bosc pears, jasmine and wet stone. Concentrated and intense but not remotely heavy, there's a steeliness here that's in total harmony with the fruit. Excellent now, this will only open up and become more complex over the next 3–5 years, if not longer. Screw cap. | 13.5% alc. | Drink 2022-2028 | $45 | PR

Seville Estate 🍷🍴 ★★★★★

65 Linwood Road, Seville, Vic 3139 **T** (03) 5964 2622 **www**.sevilleestate.com.au **OPEN** 7 days 10-5 **WINEMAKER** Dylan McMahon **EST.** 1972 **DOZENS** 8000 **VYDS** 12ha

Seville Estate was founded by Dr Peter and Margaret McMahon in 1972. After several changes of ownership, Yiping Wang purchased the property in early '17. Yiping's supportive yet hands-off approach has allowed winemaker and general manager Dylan McMahon (grandson of founder Peter McMahon) to steer the ship. The estate has expanded to encompass the neighbouring vineyard and property (formerly Ainsworth Estate). (JH)

97   **Old Vine Reserve Pinot Noir 2021, Yarra Valley** A bright, medium, crimson purple. A special wine from the first whiff, there are aromas of red and black fruits, floral notes, spice-rack spices together with complex ferrous notes. Concentrated but pure, structured and balanced. A special wine in the making and one of the very best '21 Yarra pinots I tasted for this year's Companion. So long. Drink a bottle now but worth putting some away to enjoy 10–15 years from now. Screw cap. | 13% alc. | Drink 2022-2035 | $90 | PR

Reserve Chardonnay 2021, Yarra Valley A deepish bright green gold. A superb Yarra chardonnay – power without weight. Lemon oil, melon, spices, a nougat nuttiness and ginger. A rich, complex, yet focused and structured mouthful, becoming fleshier and more open the longer it sits in the glass. Worth decanting or giving it some air in the glass, but know that this will continue to improve and become more complex in the bottle over the next 5–10 years. Screw cap. | 12.6% alc. | Drink 2022-2028 | $90 | PR

Old Vine Reserve Shiraz 2020, Yarra Valley A brilliant crimson magenta. Beautifully perfumed and pure. Redolent of raspberry coulis, peony, Asian spices and potpourri. Supremely elegant and structured, there's a gentle meatiness to go with the pure red fruits. The tannins are silky and persistent. Finishes very long and too good to spit! Screw cap. | 13% alc. | Drink 2023-2029 | $90 | PR

96   **Chardonnay 2021, Yarra Valley** An effortless wine that has power but doesn't feel as if it's been 'made' or forced in any way. Subtle stone fruits, spice and a mineral note that follows onto the palate, which is simultaneously generous yet restrained; the acidity in total harmony with the fruit. In a word – lovely. Screw cap. | 12.8% alc. | Drink 2022-2029 | $55 | PR

Stefani Estate 🍷🍴🚪 ★★★★☆

735 Old Healesville Road, Healesville, Vic 3777 **T** 0492 993 446 **www**.stefaniwines.com.au **OPEN** Thurs-Fri by appt, Sat-Sun 11-5 **WINEMAKER** Peter Mackey **EST.** 1998 **DOZENS** 5730 **VYDS** 18ha

Stefano Stefani came to Australia in '85. Business success has allowed him and his wife Rina to follow in the footsteps of his grandfather, who had a vineyard and was an avid wine collector. The first property they acquired was at Long Gully Road in the Yarra Valley. The next was in Heathcote, where they acquired a property adjoining that of Mario Marson and built a winery. In '03 a second Yarra Valley property was acquired and dijon clones of chardonnay and pinot noir were planted; that vineyard is currently undergoing organic conversion. (JH)

96   **The Gate Shiraz 2018, Yarra Valley** A very youthful and deep crimson purple. Aromas of ripe, juicy cranberries. fresh red plum and well-handled cedar oak that will settle down in time. Medium–full bodied, this has a core of concentrated, dark, briary fruits and there are enough ripe and persistent tannins to suggest this will age well over the next decade. Diam. | 14.2% alc. | Drink 2022-2028 | $65 | PR

CENTRAL VICTORIA

GIPPSLAND

NORTH EAST VICTORIA

NORTH WEST VICTORIA

PORT PHILLIP

WESTERN VICTORIA

Sticks ★★★☆

3/436 Johnston St, Abbotsford, Vic 3067 **T** (03) 9224 1911 **WWW**.sticks.com.au **WINEMAKER** Anthony Fikkers **EST.** 2000 **DOZENS** 15000

One of many labels under the Joval Wine Group, headed by John Valmorbida, with a strong link to the Australian food-and-wine scene thanks to his Italian family heritage. The Sticks brand is all about offering entry-level yet fresh and simple everyday wines sourced from Yarra Valley floor sites at Coldstream, Dixon's Creek and Yarra Glen. In 2019, Anthony Fikkers took over as chief winemaker. (JF)

92 **Rosé 2021, Yarra Valley** A bright salmon colour. Cherry, tangerine and a touch of florals make for an attractive nose that follows through onto the palate which is dry, well weighted, refreshing and long. Good stuff. Screw cap. | 12.5% alc. | Drink 2021-2023 | $24 | PR

TarraWarra Estate ⓟⓦ ★★★★★

311 Healesville-Yarra Glen Road, Yarra Glen, Vic 3775 **T** (03) 5957 3510 **WWW**.tarrawarra.com.au **OPEN** Tues-Sun 11-5 **WINEMAKER** Clare Halloran, Adam McCallum **VITICULTURIST** Stuart Sissins **EST.** 1983 **DOZENS** 9000 **VYDS** 28ha

TarraWarra is, and always has been, one of the top-tier wineries in the Yarra Valley. Founded by Marc Besen AC and wife Eva Besen AO, it has operated on the basis that quality is paramount, cost a secondary concern. Changes in the vineyard include the planting of shiraz and merlot, and in the winery, the creation of a 4-tier range: a deluxe MDB label made in tiny quantities and only when the vintage permits; the single-vineyard range; a Reserve range; and the 100% estate-grown varietal range. (JH)

97 **Cellar Release Reserve Chardonnay 2012, Yarra Valley** This lovely self-possessed wine is on its plateau of perfection, and will hold its form for years (5+) to come. The freshness of its finish and lingering aftertaste is its ace in the hole. Screw cap. | 12.8% alc. | Drink 2021-2027 | $60 | JH

96 **Late Disgorged Vintage Reserve Blanc de Blanc 2010, Yarra Valley** Traditional method; disgorged May '21. This is a remarkable wine, a one-off that has handsomely repaid the decision to defer disgorgement for a decade. The bright straw-green colour signals an elegant, finely strung array of white flowers on the bouquet, moving to white peach, citrus and brioche on the palate. The overall balance and length are perfect. Diam. | 12.8% alc. | $70 | JH

Reserve Chardonnay 2020, Yarra Valley A bright and medium-deep green gold. Aromas of yellow stone fruits, acacia, orange blossom and fresh vanilla bean are all present on the nose of this complex and powerful wine. The palate is rich and textured, yet equally refined and balanced. Finishes long and satisfying. Screw cap. | 13% alc. | Drink 2021-2026 | $65 | PR

J Block Shiraz 2019, Yarra Valley A deep, almost opaque purple red. A slightly atypical but nonetheless super-impressive and accomplished Yarra shiraz with its Crozes-Hermitage-like aromas of dark fruits, freshly hung meat, black olive, and both white and black pepper. The viognier provides just the right amount of lifted violets. Medium bodied and seductively textured, with superfine tannins in support, this is a wine that can be enjoyed now and over the next 5-10 years. Screw cap. | 13.6% alc. | Drink 2022-2031 | $40 | PR

95 **Barbera 2020, Yarra Valley** A deep, crimson plummy red. A convincing and appealing barbera from the start, with its aromas of dark morello cherry, fresh plum, sage and thyme. Totally delicious on the palate too. Ripe and rich, but not heavy, with fine-grained tannins rounding out a wine that can be enjoyed now and over the next 3-5 years. Would be fantastic with a bowl of pasta! Screw cap. | 14% alc. | Drink 2022-2027 | $35 | PR

Thick as Thieves Wines ⓟ ★★★★☆

355 Healesville-Koowerup Road, Badger Creek, Vic 3777 **T** 0417 184 690 **WWW**.tatwines.com.au **OPEN** By appt **WINEMAKER** Syd Bradford **VITICULTURIST** Syd Bradford **EST.** 2009 **DOZENS** 2000 **VYDS** 1.5ha

Syd Bradford is living proof that small can be beautiful and, equally, that an old dog can learn new tricks. A growing interest in good food and wine might have come to nothing had it not been for Pfeiffer Wines giving him a vintage job in 2003. In that year he enrolled in the wine science course at CSU; he then moved to the Yarra Valley in '05, gaining experience at a number of wineries including Coldstream Hills. In '09 he came across a small parcel of arneis from the Hoddles Creek area, and Thick as Thieves was born. These days Syd farms 1.5ha of his own pinot noir (MV6 and Abel clones) and purchases other varieties from both the Yarra and King Valleys. The techniques used could only come from someone who has spent a long time observing and thinking about what he might do if he were calling the shots. (JH)

96   **Another Bloody Chardonnay 2021, Yarra Valley** Leaps out of the glass with attractive aromas of pink grapefruit pith, lemon oil, white peaches and an undercurrent of cashew and flint. Loads of flavour, but equally this is poised and very well balanced, finishing minerally and long. A very accomplished wine.   Screw cap. | 12.7% alc. | Drink 2022-2027 | $37 | PR

94   **The Aloof Alpaca Arneis 2021, Yarra Valley** Used 24-hour pre-fermentation skin contact (old is new), wild-yeast barrel fermentation and lees contact. Every bit as powerful and complex as the variety – and its vinification – suggests. Difficult to be dogmatic about the outcome, but at $25 there's room for debate and little or no downside.   Screw cap. | 12.5% alc. | Drink 2022-2026 | JH

Yarra Burn ★★★★

60 Settlement Road, Yarra Junction, Vic 3797 **T** 131 492 **WWW**.yarraburn.com.au **WINEMAKER** Ed Carr, Ella Hoban **EST**. 1975

At least in terms of name, this is the focal point of Accolade's Yarra Valley operations. However, the winery was sold and the wines are now made elsewhere. The Upper Yarra vineyard largely remains. (JH)

93   **Prosecco 2021, King Valley** The Charmat method and 5% 'other' grapes produce this attractive young prosecco. Fresh and vibrant on the bouquet in fresh-cut free apple, pear, lemon zest. Fills out on the palate cushioned by a splash of sugar (9.7g/L) and gentle creaminess. Good balance and length here.   Cork. | 12% alc. | $26 | JP

Yarra Yering ★★★★★

4 Briarty Road, Gruyere, Vic 3770 **T** (03) 5964 9267 **WWW**.yarrayering.com **OPEN** 7 days 10-5 **WINEMAKER** Sarah Crowe **EST**. 1969 **DOZENS** 5000 **VYDS** 40ha

In September 2008, founder Bailey Carrodus died and in April '09 Yarra Yering was on the market. It was Bailey Carrodus's clear wish and expectation that any purchaser would continue to manage the vineyard and winery, and hence the wine style, in much the same way as he had done for the previous 40 years. Sarah Crowe was appointed winemaker after the '13 vintage. She has made red wines of the highest imaginable quality right from her first vintage in '14 and, to the delight of many, myself (James) included, has offered all the wines with screwcaps. Her exceptional talent was recognised by her being named Winemaker of the Year in the Wine Companion 2017. The Halliday Wine Companion 2022 named Yarra Yering the Winery of the Year, and the Yarra Yering Dry Red No. 1 2019 the Wine of the Year. (JH)

97   **Dry Red No. 1 2020, Yarra Valley** 60/20/15/5% cabernet sauvignon/merlot/malbec/petit verdot. A deep, bright crimson-purple hue. Essence of great cabernet with its core of blackcurrant and boysenberry fruit, as well as a complex assortment of cardamom, coriander seed, black tea and gentle, fresh tobacco leaf. Just as good on the detailed, layered and persistent palate. There is a coolness and restraint to the cassis fruit that builds, culminating in a long, chalky tannin finish. A complete and beautiful wine.   Screw cap. | 13.5% alc. | Drink 2022-2035 | $120 | PR

     Underhill 2020, Yarra Valley A very bright, medium crimson purple. A riotous amalgam of aromas including blueberries, potpourri, licorice root, Szechuan pepper and caraway seeds. Medium bodied and elegant, this has terrific viscosity and the tannins are oh, so powdery and fine. Gorgeous now and over the next 10 years or longer.   Screw cap. | 13.5% alc. | Drink 2022-2035 | $120 | PR

Yeringberg ★★★★★

810 Maroondah Highway, Coldstream, Vic 3770 **T** (03) 9739 0240 **WWW**.yeringberg.com.au **OPEN** By appt **WINEMAKER** Sandra de Pury **VITICULTURIST** David de Pury **EST**. 1863 **DOZENS** 1500 **VYDS** 12ha

A 19th century Yarra Valley pioneer, Yeringberg's renaissance began when the third generation wine grower, Guill and Katherine de Pury began replanting vines in 1969, making their first commercial wine in '74. Since '08, the wines have been made by daughter Sandra while her brother, David, who has a PhD in plant physiology, manages the vineyards and Yeringberg's grass-fed lamb and cattle. Committed to the future, a new winery is in design phase and a new vine program began in '20 to mitigate against climate change and phylloxera. (PR)

97   **Yeringberg 2020, Yarra Valley** A blend of 61/10/10/10/9% cabernet sauvignon/cabernet franc// merlot/petit verdot/malbec. A medium and bright ruby red. Aromas of subtle cranberry, blackberries and brambly blackberry leaf, together with a little clove and fresh vanilla bean from the well-handled oak. Medium bodied and beautifully poised, this has fine, elegant tannins contributing to a wine that, as delicious as it is now, boasts a track record that means you can cellar it for as long as you have the patience to do so. An under-priced icon wine.   Screw cap. | 13% alc. | Drink 2022-2035 | $95 | PR

CENTRAL VICTORIA

GIPPSLAND

NORTH EAST VICTORIA

NORTH WEST VICTORIA

PORT PHILLIP

WESTERN VICTORIA

96 **Chardonnay 2020, Yarra Valley** A bright, medium green gold. Lovely aromatics with yellow peach and nectarine fruit as well as subtle oatmeal and grilled nuts. Orange blossom and a hint of matchstick too. Textured and bright in the mouth, I like the touch of grip on the long and satisfying finish. Screw cap. | 12.5% alc. | Drink 2022-2028 | $65 | PR

ATR Wines ⓘ ⑭ ⓐ ★★★★★

103 Hard Hill Road, Armstrong, Vic 3377 **T** 0457 922 400 **WWW**.atrwines.com.au **OPEN** Thurs-Sun & public hols 1-5 **WINEMAKER** Adam Richardson **EST**. 2005 **DOZENS** 4000 **VYDS** 7.6ha

Perth-born Adam Richardson began his winemaking career in '95, working for Normans, d'Arenberg and Oakridge along the way. He has held senior winemaking roles, ultimately with TWE America before moving back to Australia with his wife Eva and children in late '15. In '05 he had put down roots in the Grampians region, establishing a vineyard with old shiraz clones from the 19th century and riesling, extending the plantings with tannat, nebbiolo, durif and viognier. (JH)

96 **Chockstone Riesling 2021, Grampians** You could drown in the aromatic beauty of the scent: white flowers, lime, green apple, lemon zest, spice and musk. Dry and stylish acidity (it's the only word to describe the combination of bright and soft acidity) caress the palate, mouth-wateringly so. A touch of barely there sugar helps amplify the depth of fruit. A delight. Screw cap. | 12% alc. | Drink 2022-2033 | $24 | JP | ♥

Hard Hill Road Writer's Block Riesling 2020, Great Western Excitingly fragrant in jasmine florals, citrus, baked apple, bergamot and orange peel. Builds and builds in the mouth, creamy and bright, the intensity of flavour assisted by hints of pear and almond. A wine of some depth, and it's only just revealing the tip of the iceberg. Screw cap. | 12% alc. | Drink 2022-2033 | $38 | JP

95 **Chockstone Shiraz 2020, Grampians** The wildness of the Grampians just seems to effortlessly bring a high level of attractive herbals and spice to its shiraz. This is one example, where the scent alone offers a walk through country: acacia, bracken, anise, pepper and sage. Well supported by blackberries and dark chocolate, with woodsy oak tannins. Another Chockstone shiraz to enjoy now or cellar and forget. Screw cap. | 14.5% alc. | Drink 2022-2045 | $28 | JP

94 **Chockstone Rosé 2021, Grampians** The winemaker deliberately selected each of these strange vinous bedfellows – nebbiolo, durif, shiraz, tannat and a 'touch' of riesling – for this rosé. It's a standout in the glass in ruddy pink. Nebbiolo brings some attractive florals to add to the aroma of red berries and musk. Concentrated and creamy on the palate with a whisper of sweetness. Screw cap. | 13.5% alc. | Drink 2022-2025 | $22 | JP

Best's Wines ⓘ ⑭ ⊜ ⓐ ★★★★★

111 Best's Road, Great Western, Vic 3377 **T** (03) 5356 2250 **WWW**.bestswines.com **OPEN** Mon-Sat 10-5, Sun 11-4 **WINEMAKER** Justin Purser, Jacob Parton **VITICULTURIST** Ben Thomson **EST**. 1866 **DOZENS** 25000 **VYDS** 147ha

Best's winery and vineyards date back to 1866. One of the vines planted in the Nursery Block has defied identification and is thought to exist nowhere else in the world. The Thomson family has owned the property since 1920. Best's consistently produces elegant, supple wines; the Bin No. 0 is a classic, the Thomson Family Shiraz is magnificent. Very occasionally a unique pinot meunier (with 15% pinot noir) is made solely from 1868 plantings of those 2 varieties. Best's were awarded Wine of the Year '17 and Best Value Winery '21; in '23 they win Wine of the Year once more. (JH)

96 **Riesling 2021, Great Western** As ever, a very distinguished riesling, its fluid power and the insistence of the palate results in exceptional length, crackling minerally acidity married with lemon and lime fruit. Bargain. Screw cap. | 11% alc. | Drink 2021-2036 | $25 | JH

Foudre Ferment Riesling 2021, Great Western Winner of 3 awards in the Wine Companion 2023 Wine of the Year, White Wine of the Year and one of two joint winners for the Riesling of the Year. Each vintage it tingles and impresses and in a good year like '21, it excels. Jasmine florals, bergamot, lime cordial, lemon curd and peach-skin aromas. A wine of some complexity and nuance, featuring bright, vibrant fruits, soft mealy texture with a hint of savouriness. Seamless and sustained. Screw cap. | 11.5% alc. | Drink 2022-2030 | $35 | JP | ♥

95 **Young Vine Pinot Meunier 2021, Great Western** Young is always a relative term at Best's – these 'young vines' were planted in '71. An English garden of arresting aromatic scents, of violets, cranberry, cherry, plum, anise and sage. As always, quietly complex and fleshy, finishing firm in the embrace of fine tannins. Welcomes more time in bottle, as long as you might have. Screw cap. | 12% alc. | Drink 2022-2033 | $35 | JP

LSV Shiraz Viognier 2020, Great Western A co-ferment with a small amount of viognier brings forth a complex and fragrant wine. Viognier helps lift the bouquet in violet, anise, pepper and briar with black fruits and blueberry. The palate stretches out across the palate in fine, lithe tannins. Fabulous flavour concentration and deliciousness for the price. Screw cap. | 14% alc. | Drink 2022-2033 | $35 | JP

Cabernet Sauvignon 2020, Great Western Delivers a nuanced interpretation of the grape, proving once again that cabernet is right at home in the Grampians. Briar, bush mint, bay leaf, bracken and earth here, a dollop of vanillin oak and concentrated black fruits there, with taut tannins laying the groundwork for a long, brilliant future. Screw cap. | 14% alc. | Drink 2022-2035 | $25 | JP

Black & Ginger

563 Sugarloaf Road, Rhymney, Vic 3374 **T** 0409 964 855 **WWW**.blackandginger.com.au **WINEMAKER** Hadyn Black **EST.** 2015 **DOZENS** 500

This is the venture of 2 friends who met in '02 after attending the same high school. Hadyn Black is cellar hand and winemaker, working in the Great Western region. Darcy Naunton (Ginger) is an entrepreneur in Melbourne. Their common interest in wine saw them take a great leap in '15 and buy 1t of shiraz from the renowned Malakoff Vineyard in the Pyrenees, with further vintages following. Hadyn and partner Lucy Joyce purchased a rundown vineyard in Great Western in late '16, naming the wine Lily's Block after Hadyn's mother, who did much of the pruning and picking but unfortunately passed away before tasting the wine. (JH)

94 **Miss Piggy Muscat & Riesling 2021, Great Western** 70/30% orange muscat/riesling. Ok, a readjustment is needed here. Set those muscat expectations aside, this is definitely not sweet, spicy or grapey. This is quietly elegant, textural and dry, with impressive apple blossom, white peach, citrus and pear notes. The riesling is strong in this relationship and orange muscat is a willing, attentive partner, never overpowering. Screw cap. | 13% alc. | Drink 2021-2025 | $18 | JP

Clarnette

270 Westgate Road, Armstrong, Vic 3377 **T** 0409 083 833 **WWW**.clarnette-ludvigsen.com.au **OPEN** By appt **WINEMAKER** Leigh Clarnette **VITICULTURIST** Andrew Toomey **EST.** 2022 **DOZENS** 400 **VYDS** 15.5ha

With the death of his great friend, viticulturist and business partner, Kym Ludvigsen, in 2013, winemaker Leigh Clarnette has taken the plunge and retired their long-running wine business, Clarnette & Ludvigsen. He will now operate under Clarnette. Under the new Clarnette brand, Leigh has also begun sourcing from other vineyards in the region, including the Portuguese clone of tempranillo (tinta roriz). In '21, he added pinot noir from the Pyrenees and is also keen to source grapes closer to his home in Ballarat. He says 'I feel Kym on my shoulder every day. It's reality, though, and to excite current and emerging customers I must re-shape to survive and thrive.' (JP)

95 **Riesling 2021, Grampians** Riesling lovers will rejoice in the fineness of detail, the subtle beauty of apple-blossom scents mixing with lemon sorbet, grapefruit and talc. Brisk acidity provides admirable line and length but it is the absolute zing, the sherbety brightness that so engages. That's a wow and still so young. Can only get better. Screw cap. | 11% alc. | Drink 2021-2030 | $28 | JP

92 **C&L Rosé 2021, Grampians** Blend of 40/25/17/11/7% shiraz/sangiovese/grenache/riesling/viognier. Winemaker Leigh Clarnette pursues texture and body in rosé. Here, he delivers. Rose gold meets ruddy pink in hue, it presents a subtle picture of dried herbs, acacia, cranberry, spice and florals. When you consider that 5 grapes contributed to this rosé, that's a lot of personality. It runs smooth, long and super-fresh. Screw cap. | 12.5% alc. | Drink 2021-2024 | $25 | JP

Fallen Giants

4113 Ararat-Halls Gap Road, Halls Gap, Vic 3381 **T** (03) 5356 4252 **WWW**.fallengiants.com.au **OPEN** By appt **WINEMAKER** Justin Purser **VITICULTURIST** Rebecca Drummond **EST.** 1969 **DOZENS** 3000 **VYDS** 10.5ha

The first time some drinkers may have heard of Fallen Giants was in 2021 when the Fallen Giants Shiraz 2019 took home the Jimmy Watson Memorial Trophy at the Melbourne Royal Wine Awards. It took out Best Victorian Shiraz and the well-regarded Trevor Mast Trophy for Best Shiraz. Originally planted in 1969, the (now) Fallen Giants vineyard had once been part of the Grampians' well-regarded Mount Langi Ghiran, before being bought by the late Trevor

CENTRAL VICTORIA

GIPPSLAND

NORTH EAST VICTORIA

NORTH WEST VICTORIA

PORT PHILLIP

WESTERN VICTORIA

Mast. Following his death, it was purchased by siblings Aaron and Rebecca Drummond and renamed Fallen Giants in '13. The Drummonds grew up on the Mornington Peninsula; Aaron went on to work for the Rathbone Wine Group, while Rebecca headed into global financial market trading. (JP)

NSW

95   **Cabernet Sauvignon 2020, Grampians** A striking wine from the get-go, so fragrant in regional Aussie bush characters. A lovely gentle complexity awaits the drinker with concentrated black fruits, cassis, licorice, spice, a splash of mocha oak and layers of dense tannins.   Screw cap. | 14.5% alc. | Drink 2021-2031 | $35 | JP

   Shiraz 2020, Grampians The follow-up vintage to the '19 winner of the Jimmy Watson Trophy at the '21 Melbourne Royal Wine Awards. The '20 is similarly blessed with great elegance and poise. A sheer, fragrant lift to the perfume in peppery red fruits, baking spices and plum with convincing, concentrated flavours. Tannins run fine through to the finish with a gentle grip.   Screw cap. | 14.5% alc. | Drink 2021-2033 | $35 | JP

94   **Riesling 2021, Grampians** Sweet herbal notes and lifted florals introduce a steely, lemon, lime-cordial and white-nectarine-perfumed riesling that shows the full appeal of the Grampians' most underrated white grape. Great focus and drive, not to mention longevity, thanks to brisk acidity.   Screw cap. | 12.5% alc. | Drink 2021-2028 | $30 | JP

Kimbarra Wines   ★★★★

422 Barkly Street, Ararat, Vic 3377 T 0428 519 195 WWW.kimbarrawines.com.au OPEN By appt
WINEMAKER Peter Leeke, Justin Purser, Adam Richardson EST. 1990 DOZENS 180 VYDS 11ha

SA

Peter Leeke has 8.5ha of shiraz, 1.5ha of riesling and 1ha of cabernet sauvignon – varieties that have proven best suited to the Grampians region. The particularly well-made, estate-grown wines deserve a wider audience. (JH)

94   **Riesling 2021, Great Western** Kimbarra captures the singular purity of Great Western riesling from vintage to vintage. Yet again in '21, it's all about the region's beautiful florals enhanced delicately, perceptively, in intense lime cordial, lemon rind, kaffir lime and green apple. And bringing it all together is bright acidity, piquant and zesty.   Screw cap. | 11.8% alc. | Drink 2022-2031 | $30 | JP

Miners Ridge   ★★★★☆

135 Westgate Rd, Armstrong, Vic 3377 T 0438 039 727 WWW.minersridge.com.au OPEN By appt
WINEMAKER Adam Richardson VITICULTURIST Andrew Toomey EST. 2000 DOZENS 450 VYDS 17ha

VIC

Andrew and Katrina Toomey established Miners Ridge Wines in 2000 after many years growing grapes in the Great Western region for other wineries. They decided to take small parcels of their finest fruit and craft a range of wines to reflect their 17ha vineyard site at Armstrong, enlisting experienced local winemaker Adam Richardson (ATR Wines) as their contract winemaker. (JP)

95   **Riesling 2021, Grampians** Once again, Grampians riesling rises to the heights many of us know it is capable of. So fine, so delicately floral, in white flowers and in citrus, lime zest, green apple and light spice. Clean, lemon sherbet acidity and crunch through a long, linear finish. Delightful. Trophy Western Victorian Wine Challenge '21 and trophy Ballarat Wine Show '21.   Screw cap. | 12% alc. | Drink 2022-2028 | $25 | JP

Mount Langi Ghiran Vineyards   ★★★★★

80 Vine Road, Bayindeen, Vic 3375 T (03) 5359 4400 WWW.langi.com.au OPEN 7 days 10-5
WINEMAKER Adam Louder, Darren Rathbone VITICULTURIST Damien Sheehan EST. 1969 DOZENS 45000 VYDS 65ha

WA

A maker of outstanding cool-climate peppery shiraz, crammed with flavour and vinosity, and very good cabernet sauvignon. The shiraz has long pointed the way for cool-climate examples of the variety. The business was acquired by the Rathbone family group in 2002. The marketing is integrated with the Yering Station and Xanadu Estate wines, a synergistic mix with no overlap. (JH)

TAS

96   **Cliff Edge Shiraz 2020, Grampians** Often cited as a benchmark cool-climate shiraz. There's no denying this is yet another impressive, elegant shiraz from a strong vintage. Boasts refined richness and a depth of flavour that is well-matched to a vivacious personality. Fruit is the star, with flecks of pepper and spice assisted by plump tannins. That's a WOW!   Screw cap. | 14.5% alc. | Drink 2021-2033 | $35 | JC

95   **Cliff Edge Cabernet Merlot 2020, Grampians** A wine guaranteed to make you smile, highlighting the beauty of Grampians cabernet with a little help from some friendly merlot. Deeply coloured and concentrated in the glass, it launches into a beautifully balanced display of plum, mulberry and cassis, all ripe and warmly spiced with a hint of leafiness. Nicely measured tannins to the finish. Screw cap. | 13.5% alc. | Drink 2021-2033 | $35 | JP

The Story Wines ★★★★★

170 Riverend Road, Hangholme, Vic 3175 T 0411 697 912 www.thestory.com.au OPEN By appt WINEMAKER Rory Lane EST. 2004 DOZENS 2500

Over the years I have come across winemakers with degrees in atomic science, doctors with specialties spanning every human condition, town-planners, sculptors and painters; Rory Lane adds yet another to the list: a degree in ancient Greek literature. Vintages in Australia and Oregon germinated the seed and he zeroed in on the Grampians, where he purchases small parcels of high-quality grapes. He makes the wines in a small factory where he has assembled a basket press, a few open fermenters, a mono pump and some decent French oak. (JH)

97 **Syrah 2019, Grampians** Has built on its layers of savoury and spicy cool-grown shiraz flavours over the past year, adding weight and depth but without compromising its freshness. The lingering aftertaste is special, throwing up sparklets of blackberry and blackcurrant. Screw cap. | 13.5% alc. | Drink 2023-2040 | $30 | JH

96 **Westgate Vineyard Shiraz 2020, Grampians** Intense, deep purple-red colour, a good indication of what follows. Lane has worked ripeness and richness into a smooth result: blood plum, black fruits, chocolate, licorice and signature Grampians pepperiness. Tannins are firm and free flowing. Finishes with a touch of amaro bitters. Complex and still so very young. Screw cap. | 13.5% alc. | Drink 2022-2035 | $75 | JP

95 **Super G Grenache Syrah Mourvèdre 2021, Grampians** Delightfully open, honest and plush in lifted violet, red licorice, ripe dark fruits, bracken and tilled earth. The star is the spice that binds: the peppery, clove and cinnamon with a dash of menthol that sends it – together with firm tannins – off into a world of its own. Screw cap. | 14% alc. | Drink 2022-2031 | $30 | JP

Seppelt ★★★★★

36 Cemetery Road, Great Western, Vic 3377 T (03) 5361 2239 www.seppelt.com.au OPEN 7 days 10-5 WINEMAKER Clare Dry EST. 1851 VYDS 648ha

Seppelt once had dual, and very different, claims to fame. The first was as Australia's foremost producer of both white and red sparkling wine, the former led by Salinger, the latter by Show Sparkling and Original Sparkling Shiraz. The second claim, even more relevant to the Seppelt of today, was based on the small-volume superb red wines made by Colin Preece from the 1930s through to the early '60s. These were ostensibly Great Western–sourced but – as the laws of the time allowed – were often region, variety and vintage blends. Two of his labels (also of high quality) were Moyston and Chalambar. Ararat businessman Danial Ahchow has leased the cellar door and surrounds, including the underground drives. Winemaker Clare Dry took over from Adam Carnaby from the '21 vintage. (JH)

97 **Drumborg Vineyard Pinot Noir 2020, Henty** Deeper hue than the Pinot Meunier, with more purple. This is a ravishing wine, the bouquet expressive, the palate explosive, with a profusion of red and blue berries, rhubarb and spice, given texture and structure by savoury tannins and a nudge of oak. Screw cap. | 13% alc. | Drink 2022-2032 | $45 | JH

96 **Drumborg Vineyard Riesling 2021, Henty** A new senior winemaker (Clare Dry) and a top vintage combine to produce a fully formed classic Drumborg Riesling. Tasted just 10 days after bottling and it was already in scintillating form. Can't wait to see how this progresses over the decade. Palest lemon in colour and a mere 11% alcohol belies the depth and beauty of this wine; its alluring florals of white flowers and spring blossom, of fresh-cut citrus, lime zest and musk. It all rolls into a textural, juicy, lemony-fresh, lightly spiced wonder with life assured for a decade and more. Screw cap. | Drink 2021-2034 | $40 | JP

REGION

Henty

Crawford River Wines ★★★★★

741 Hotspur Upper Road, Condah, Vic 3303 T (03) 5578 2267 www.crawfordriverwines.com OPEN By appt WINEMAKER Belinda Thomson VITICULTURIST Belinda Thomson EST. 1975 DOZENS 3000 VYDS 11ha

CENTRAL VICTORIA

GIPPSLAND

NORTH EAST VICTORIA

NORTH WEST VICTORIA

PORT PHILLIP

WESTERN VICTORIA

Once a tiny outpost in a little-known wine region, Crawford River is now a foremost producer of riesling (and other excellent wines), originally thanks to the unremitting attention to detail and skill of its founder and winemaker, John Thomson. His elder daughter Belinda has worked alongside her father part-time from '04–11 (full-time between June '05–08) and has been chief winemaker since '12. She obtained her viticulture and oenology degree in '02 and has experience in Marlborough, Bordeaux, Tuscany and the Nahe. Between '08 and '16 she was a senior winemaker and technical director of a winery in Rueda, Spain. Younger daughter Fiona is in charge of sales and marketing. (JH)

97   **Reserve Riesling 2015, Henty** Still incredibly youthful and fine, with little or no colour development. The delicately scented bouquet is matched with a tightly furled palate, with grapefruit zest and acidity made to precise measure. Deserves a cheer for bravery in pricing. Screw cap. |
13.5% alc. | Drink 2021-2040 | $120 | JH

96   **Riesling 2021, Henty** A marvel! So fully formed in its youth and delivering outstanding deliciousness. The maker balances ripe riesling fruit – white nectarine, grapefruit, Delicious apple, lime – with racy, cool-climate acidity to deliver a wine complex in flavour, warm in texture and lively in personality. It's quite a feat. Screw cap. | 13.5% alc. | Drink 2022-2031 | $50 | JP

Jackson Brooke

126 Beaconsfield Parade, Northcote, Vic 3070 (postal) **T** 0466 652 485
WWW. jacksonbrookewine.com.au **WINEMAKER** Jackson Brooke **EST**. 2013 **DOZENS** 500

Jackson Brooke graduated from the University of Melbourne in 2004 with a science degree and, having spent a summer working at Tarrington Vineyards, went on to study oenology at Lincoln University in NZ. A vintage at Wedgetail Estate in the Yarra Valley was followed by stints in Japan, Southern California and then 3 years as assistant winemaker to Ben Portet. With his accumulated knowledge of boutique winemaking, he has abandoned any idea of building a winery for the foreseeable future, currently renting space at Witchmount Estate. (JH)

94   **Chardonnay 2020, Henty** A strong follow-up to the '19 vintage with similarly fine features and precise cool-climate detail. Citrus-drenched aromas and flavours join in unison with white peach, Pink Lady apple, pear and just-baked bread. Bright quince-like acidity runs away with the wine. All's right for a rewarding future. Screw cap. | 12.5% alc. | Drink 2021-2028 | $28 | JP

Pyrenees

DogRock Winery

114 Degraves Road, Crowlands, Vic 3377 **T** 0409 280 317 **WWW**.dogrock.com.au **OPEN** By appt
WINEMAKER Allen Hart **VITICULTURIST** Andrea Hart **EST**. 1998 **DOZENS** 1000 **VYDS** 6.2ha

This is the venture of Allen (now full-time winemaker) and Andrea (viticulturist) Hart. Having purchased the property in '98, the planting of shiraz, riesling, tempranillo, grenache, chardonnay and marsanne began in '00. Given Allen's former post as research scientist and winemaker with Foster's, the attitude taken to winemaking is unexpected. The estate-grown wines are made in a low-tech fashion, without gas cover or filtration. DogRock installed the first solar-powered irrigation system in Australia, capable of supplying water 365 days a year, even at night or in cloudy conditions. (JH)

95   **Shiraz 2020, Pyrenees** Great value here with another excellent display of just how good Pyrenees shiraz can be at this pricepoint. Over-delivers in lifted, fragrant aromas and flavours that fill the mouth with intense black cherry, blueberry, bramble, baking spice, earth and bitter chocolate. Attractive freshness throughout, juicy, vibrant tannins to close. Screw cap. | 14% alc. |
Drink 2022-2030 | $30 | JP

Degraves Road Single Vineyard Arinto 2021, Pyrenees Arinto is a Portuguese variety from north of Lisbon, known for its retention of acidity. It otherwise has similarities to Hunter Valley semillon, with lemony fruit and cleansing acidity. Its length and aftertaste, coupled with fresh but not sharp acidity, suggest it will cellar well. One to watch. Screw cap. | 11.5% alc. | Drink 2021-2031 | $30 | JH

Mitchell Harris Wines ⑨⑪ ★★★★★

38 Doveton Street North, Ballarat, Vic 3350 **T** (03) 5331 8931 **www**.mitchellharris.com.au
OPEN Sun-Mon 11-5, Tues-Thurs 11-9, Fri-Sat 11-11 **WINEMAKER** John Harris **EST.** 2008 **DOZENS** 2300

Mitchell Harris Wines is a partnership between Alicia and Craig Mitchell and Shannyn and John Harris. John, the winemaker, began his career at Brown Brothers, then spent 8 years as winemaker at Domaine Chandon in the Yarra Valley, cramming in Northern Hemisphere vintages in California and Oregon. The Mitchell and Harris families grew up in the Ballarat area and have an affinity for the Macedon and Pyrenees regions. While the total make is not large, a lot of thought has gone into the creation of each of the wines, which are sourced from the Pyrenees, Ballarat and Macedon regions. (JH)

96   **Sabre 2018, Victoria** 78/22% chardonnay/pinot noir. The chardonnay hails from the Macedon Ranges, the pinot noir is a blend of Henty and Pyrenees. Natural acidity brings real drive and a strong linear focus. Flinty on the nose with chalky lemon, apple, stone fruits and nougat, it moves into a complex whole on the palate. Three years on yeast lees release a lovely nutty intricacy of flavours, spice and texture. A top Aussie sparkling.   Cork. | 12% alc. | $50 | JP | ♥

Taltarni ⑨⑪ ★★★★★

339 Taltarni Road, Moonambel, Vic 3478 **T** (03) 5459 7900 **www**.taltarni.com.au **OPEN** Wed-Sun 11-5
WINEMAKER Robert Heywood, Peter Warr, Ben Howell **EST.** 1969 **DOZENS** 80000 **VYDS** 78.5ha

The American owner and founder of Clos du Val (Napa Valley), Taltarni and Clover Hill (see separate entry) has brought the management of these 3 businesses and Domaine de Nizas (Languedoc) under the one roof, the group known as Goelet Wine Estates. Insectariums are established in permanent vegetation corridors, each containing around 2000 native plants that provide a pollen and nectar source for the beneficial insects, reducing the need for chemicals. Taltarni celebrates 45 years of winemaking in 2022. (JH)

96   **Old Vine Estate Cabernet Sauvignon 2020, Pyrenees** Sourced from the original cabernet sauvignon vines planted in the late '60s and, once again, doesn't disappoint. One sip and you're in, seduced by the grace and beauty. Cassis, dark plums, bay leaf, spice and a gentle dusting of vanillin oak prevail, ably assisted by fine, lithe tannins. Elegance in the glass.   Screw cap. | 14% alc. | Drink 2022-2033 | $45 | JP

CENTRAL VICTORIA

GIPPSLAND

NORTH EAST VICTORIA

NORTH WEST VICTORIA

PORT PHILLIP

WESTERN VICTORIA

Technically Western Australia has five zones, but only two have vineyards: Greater Perth and South West Australia. The Greater Perth zone has three regions. **Peel** has shiraz as the leader, cabernet sauvignon next, then verdelho and chardonnay, all wines that are medium-bodied and immediately approachable. The **Swan District** has a very unusual split between red and white varieties. Instead of the usual more than 65% reds, less than 35% whites, here the varieties that made Houghton Blue Stripe White Burgundy the largest-selling white wine in the early 1980s see chenin blanc in pole position, followed by verdelho, chardonnay and semillon. The slopes of **Perth Hills** have been scattered with vineyards since the 1880s, today home to chardonnay, shiraz, cabernet sauvignon and merlot, and most notably our 2023 Shiraz of the Year!

The South West Australia zone accounts for the remainder of Western Australia's output. It has six regions, with one, **Great Southern**, having five subregions: Albany, Denmark, Frankland River, Mount Barker and Porongurup. Tony Smith, founder of Plantagenet and a long leading figure in WA's fine-wine scene, makes no secret in regretting that these subregions are responsible for more fine wine than the other five regions.

Great Southern has shiraz way out in front, reflecting its nigh-on magical blend of intense varietal fruit expression, tannin-derived texture and structure, balance and length, all within medium-bodied freshness. What is bewildering is riesling, equal fifth with semillon, both representing just a small proportion of plantings. Porongurup, Frankland River and Mount Barker make lissom riesling of world class. Cabernet sauvignon shares the purity that is also part of riesling's character. Albany and Denmark complete the mosaic.

Margaret River produced just under two-thirds of the state's 2021 crush, thanks first to majestic cabernet sauvignon, then sauvignon blanc, semillon, sumptuous chardonnay and shiraz, merlot and chenin blanc. **Geographe** has as its neighbours Peel to the northeast, **Blackwood Valley** to the southeast, the northern tip of Margaret River on its southeastern corner, and the Indian Ocean as its entire eastern boundary. Diminutive **Manjimup** is dominated by pinot gris/grigio (making up more than half the plantings), the remainder split between pinot noir

CENTRAL WA

EASTERN PLAINS/
INLAND/NORTH

GREATER PERTH

SOUTH WEST
AUSTRALIA

SOUTH EAST
COASTAL

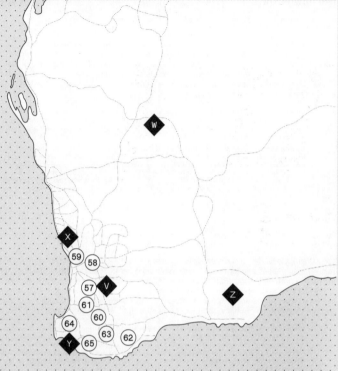

and chardonnay. Nearby **Pemberton** is a two-horse race with sauvignon blanc and chardonnay.

ZONE	REGION
V Central Western Australia	
W Eastern Plains, Inland and North of Western Australia	
X Greater Perth	57 Peel
	58 Perth Hills
	59 Swan District
Y South West Australia	60 Blackwood Valley
	61 Geographe
	62 Great Southern
	63 Manjimup
	64 Margaret River
	65 Pemberton
Z West Australian South East Coastal	

Battles Wine

★★★★★

77 Aitken Drive, Winthrop, WA 6150 (postal) **T** 0434 399 964 **www**.battleswine.com.au
WINEMAKER Lance Parkin **EST.** 2018 **DOZENS** 850

Battles Wine was started by friends Lance Parkin (winemaker) and Kris Ambrozkiewicz (sommelier, sales) in 2019. Parkin was a winemaker at Houghton in the Swan Valley before the sale to the Yukich family in '19, at which point the Swan Valley-based component of the Houghton team disbanded and formed their own ventures. Ambrozkiewicz (aka Ambro) has a longstanding and intense love of wine, paired with an impressively honed bank of wine knowledge and years of sales experience. (EL)

96   **Chardonnay 2021, Margaret River** This is pure and viscous. The flavour is palate staining, yet delicate – a feat in itself. Yellow peach, saline acidity, red apple skins, preserved lemons and white nectarine are packaged in a glassy, polished and crystalline casing of phenolics; the fruit and oak so seamlessly entwined as to be one. Superb. Screw cap. | 13.3% alc. | Drink 2021-2036 | $45 | EL

   Granitis Shiraz 2020, Perth Hills Halliday Wine Companion Shiraz of the Year 2023. The power of suggestion is strong – this is granitic, mineral, shaley and cooling. The fruit is pungently inky and intense, speaking of mulberries, raspberries, blood plums and vanilla pod. The tannins are like fine-grit sandpaper, they shape and impact the voluminous fruit and keep it all hemmed in. This is bloody and raw, like a mainline into the dirt. It's wild ... but it's also compact, controlled, restrained, flowing and sleek. A svelte wine of circumstance and presence. Screw cap. | 13.8% alc. | Drink 2021-2036 | $40 | EL | ♥

Cherubino

★★★★★

3462 Caves Road, Wilyabrup, WA 6280 **T** (08) 9382 2379 **www**.larrycherubino.com **OPEN** 7 days 10-5
WINEMAKER Larry Cherubino, Andrew Siddell, Matt Buchan **EST.** 2005 **DOZENS** 8000 **VYDS** 120ha

Larry Cherubino has had a particularly distinguished winemaking career, first at Hardys Tintara, then Houghton and thereafter as consultant and Flying Winemaker in Australia, NZ, South Africa, the US and Italy. He has developed numerous ranges, including Cherubino, single-vineyard range The Yard, and the single-region Ad Hoc label. The runaway success of the business has seen the accumulation of 120ha of vineyards, the appointment of additional winemakers and Larry's own appointment as director of winemaking for Robert Oatley Vineyards. (JH)

97   **Cherubino Chardonnay 2020, Margaret River** This wine amassed 8 trophies at shows in '21 and was made in such tiny quantities that sales are now limited to a bottle a customer. If you can still get it. Distinctive for its custard powder nose, this is an opulent, luxurious chardonnay of voluminous depth and power. Salted peach, kiwi-fruit acidity and long, undulating layers of flavour. Immediately, obviously, a gold-pointed wine in the chardonnay class I judged at Margaret River Wine Show '21. One for the ages. Screw cap. | 13.5% alc. | Drink 2022-2037 | $95 | EL

96   **Cherubino Riesling 2021, Porongurup** This has jasmine, green apples, lemon zest and limestone on the nose and palate. Poised and super-pretty, this has all the length to indicate that the fruit has the horsepower required for ageing, but as with all Porongurup rieslings, it is beautiful to drink in its youth, too. Choose your weapon. Screw cap. | 11.5% alc. | Drink 2021-2036 | $45 | EL

   The Yard Acacia Shiraz 2020, Frankland River This wine is sensational. Oh my goodness. It's saturated, earthy and polished, laden with ferrous, blood, raspberries and licorice. The tannins are firm, fine and yet pliable. The whole affair is just, well, sensational. What a wine. Frankland River is here and this is what it does best. Eat your heart out. Screw cap. | 14.5% alc. | Drink 2021-2031 | $35 | EL

   Cherubino Gingin Wilyabrup Chardonnay 2020, Margaret River Expansive flavours of yellow peach, nectarine, red apple skins and brine are tumbled together to create a voluminous experience – the fruit billows in the mouth and spills out over a long finish. Lush and evocative. The acid is high (7.47g/L), but it is countersunk into the fruit so it is structuring, rather than intrusive. Not to be missed. Screw cap. | 13.1% alc. | Drink 2022-2037 | $55 | EL

   Cherubino Chardonnay 2020, Pemberton Pemberton has an uncanny knack for concentrated flavour in white wines particularly, and the Dijon clones express so beautifully here. It tastes like malo has been blocked (although no mention), which makes for mouth-puckering drinking right now. Having said that, the fruit is so intense that there is a strange balance achieved here. Saline, fine, taut and pure ... a classy wine to the very end. Screw cap. | 13.9% alc. | Drink 2022-2037 | $65 | EL | ♥

   Cherubino Riversdale Vineyard Shiraz Mataro 2020, Frankland River The nose here has everything you could both want and expect from a blend of these 2 varieties: the shiraz brings the blackberries, the licorice and the spice, while the mataro is responsible for the purple berries, earth and cocoa dust. There is deli meat, with salted plums alongside. The inimitable Frankland River DNA of red earth, ferrous ironstone and blood is laced through the finish ... A very (very) smart wine. Screw cap. | 14.9% alc. | Drink 2022-2032 | $65 | EL

   Cherubino Caves Road Vineyard Chardonnay 2020, Margaret River The selection of parcels linked by Caves Road, from the (comparative) warmth of Wilyabrup, then south through Wallcliffe, thence to the (comparative) cool of Karridale, has pre-ordained the magic of the generosity of the white stone-fruit mid palate and the precision of the citrusy acidity on the finish. While it's a truly lovely chardonnay now, it will gain more complexity and richness through to the end of the decade. Screw cap. | 13.5% alc. | Drink 2022-2029 | $75 | JH

95 **The Yard Riversdale Shiraz 2020, Frankland River** This is seriously good. It is earthy and textured, slightly more grounded than the Acacia shiraz from '20 (which I also loved, it's just different to this), and loaded with red berries, earthy spice and shaped by oak. The tannins are a real highlight, they're slightly gravelly, slightly chewy, and add an extra dimension of pleasure to the wine. A standout. Screw cap. | 14.5% alc. | Drink 2021-2031 | $35 | EL

The Yard Justin Shiraz 2020, Frankland River Another utterly sensational wine here. It shares many similarities with The Yard Acacia Shiraz 2020, yet this seems the more structured, the firmer of the 2. They both carry the regional DNA of ferrous, ironstone, red dirt, blood and raspberry, however this is framed by more pronounced tannins and slightly lighter/more delicate fruit weight. A wildly impressive wine. Frankland River is an absolute marvel. Screw cap. | 14.5% alc. | Drink 2021-2031 | $35 | EL

94 **Pedestal Semillon Sauvignon Blanc 2021, Margaret River** Juniper, jalapeño, lime cordial, green apples and green table grapes. Bright and lithe and endowed with a slippery texture in the mouth, no doubt aided by the short time spent in oak. Balanced and supple – a joyous wine of poise and grace. Screw cap. | 12.4% alc. | Drink 2021-2031 | $27 | EL

The Yard Riversdale Riesling 2021, Frankland River The vines are grown in red dirt, and the rocky soils are responsible for the region's DNA. This is a plum expression: salted preserved lemons, apples, citrus zest, graphite, tightly coiled acidity and spring. Screw cap. | 12.6% alc. | Drink 2021-2031 | $29 | EL

Clandestine ★★★★

PO Box 501 Mount Lawley, WA 6050 **T** 0427 482 903 **www**.clandestinevineyards.com.au **WINEMAKER** Andrew Vessey (WA), Ben Riggs and Daniel Zuzolo **EST.** 2020 **DOZENS** 2000

Owners Nick and Trudy Stacy source fruit and winemaking in the key regions of Margaret River, Mount Barker, Adelaide Hills and McLaren Vale. The new range of Clandestine wines are vegan-friendly and use minimal sulphites and/or preservatives. (EL)

94 **Shiraz 2020, Mount Barker** Brawn and muscle define the fruit here – the palate is propped by firm tannins and propelled by pert acidity. If the fruit were not so concentrated and intense, it would have a hard time carrying the other components, however as it stands, it is an impressive rendition of shiraz from Mount Barker, especially for the price. Screw cap. | 14.5% alc. | Drink 2021-2028 | $30 | EL

PLAN B! WINES ★★★★

Freshwater Drive, Margaret River, WA 6285 **T** 0413 759 030 **www**.planbwines.com **WINEMAKER** Vanessa Carson **EST.** 2003 **DOZENS** 35000 **VYDS** 40ha

Plan B is owned and run by wine consultant Terry Chellappah 'between rocking the bass guitar and researching bars'. He says he is better at one than the other. Plan B has been notably successful, with significant increases in production. Winemaker Vanessa Carson has made wine in Margaret River and Frankland Valley, as well as in Italy and France. (JH)

92 **Mental Blanc 2021, Frankland River** Despite all the hoo-hah on the back label of the bottle about Mental Blancs and pearly whites, the wine in the glass is very good. Structural and chalky with taut acidity that shapes the citrus fruit. Long and reminiscent of crushed shells and brine. Smart. Screw cap. | 13.5% alc. | Drink 2021-2025 | $25 | EL

Risky Business Wines ★★★★

PO Box 6015, East Perth, WA 6892 **T** 0457 482 957 **www**.riskybusinesswines.com.au **WINEMAKER** Andrew Vesey **VITICULTURIST** Rob Quenby **EST.** 2013 **DOZENS** 8900

The name Risky Business is decidedly tongue-in-cheek because the partnership headed by Rob Quenby has neatly side-stepped any semblance of risk. The grapes come from vineyards in Great Southern and Margaret River that are managed by Quenby Viticultural Services. Since the batches of wine are small, the partnership is able to select grapes specifically suited to the wine style and price. So there is no capital tied up in vineyards, nor in a winery – the wines are contract-made. (JH)

95 **Prosecco NV, King Valley** Stays true to its award-winning style which celebrates the grape's laser-like purity of flavour. Citrus blossom, lemon sorbet, mandarin peel and green apple aromas. Super-clean sherbety acidity – it positively tingles – with citrus and green apple intensity. Does the grape proud. Crown. | 10.5% alc. | $25 | JP

Greater Perth

Perth Hills

Millbrook Winery ⚥🍴🎨 ★★★★★

Old Chestnut Lane, Jarrahdale, WA 6124 **T** (08) 9525 5796 **www.millbrook.wine OPEN** Wed–Mon 10–5 **WINEMAKER** Julian Langworthy **VITICULTURIST** John Fogarty **EST**. 1996 **DOZENS** 10000 **VYDS** 8ha

Located at the picturesque Chestnut Farm, Millbrook backs on to the Serpentine River and is nestled among jarrah forests. Chestnut Farm dates back to the 19th century, when the original owner planted an orchard and grapevines in 1865, providing fruit to the local timber-millers in Jarrahdale. In 1996 Chestnut Farm and Millbrook Winery were bought by Peter and Lee Fogarty, marking the family's first entry into the wine business. In 2001 a state-of-the-art winery was completed, including a restaurant. (JH)

95 **Single Vineyard Shiraz 2020, Frankland River** Frankland River delivers characters and textures that you don't get in other parts of WA (or Australia). The shiraz wines are laden with ferrous, blood, rust, red gravel, and they are evocative of the vast, open blue skies down there. This wine shows us those parts of itself; the tannins support the weight of the fruit, the oak imperceptible save for the texture … testament to the muscle, brawn and might of the fruit. Very smart indeed. Screw cap. | 14.5% alc. | Drink 2021-2031 | $35 | EL

MyattsField Vineyards ⚥ ★★★★

Union Road, Carmel Valley, WA 6076 **T** (08) 9293 5567 **www.myattsfield.com.au OPEN** Fri–Sun and public hols 11–5 **WINEMAKER** Josh Davenport, Rachael Davenport, Josh Uren **EST**. 1997 **DOZENS** 4000 **VYDS** 4.5ha

MyattsField Vineyards is owned by Josh and Rachael Davenport. Both have oenology degrees and domestic and Flying Winemaker experience, especially Rachael. In 2006 they decided they would prefer to work for themselves. They left their employment, building a winery in time for the '07 vintage. (JH)

94 **Vermentino 2021, Perth Hills** Pithy, salted lemons and white nectarine – plenty of flavour here. Savoury, spicy and impressive. A really smart wine. Screw cap. | 12.6% alc. | Drink 2021-2028 | $24 | EL

Swan District

Corymbia ⚥ ★★★★★

7046 Caves Road, Redgate WA 6286 **T** 0439 973 195 **www.corymbiawine.com.au OPEN** By appt **WINEMAKER** Robert Mann, Genevieve Mann **VITICULTURIST** Robert Mann, Genevieve Mann **EST**. 2013 **DOZENS** 900 **VYDS** 3.5ha

Rob Mann is a 6th-generation winemaker from the second-oldest wine region in Australia. He was chief winemaker at Cape Mentelle in Margaret River, where he and wife Genevieve lived. Rob's father had established a family vineyard in the Swan Valley more than 25 years ago, where they both worked together in Rob's early years as a winemaker. Genevieve worked as a winemaker in her native South Africa, as well as France, California and South Australia before meeting Rob and moving to Margaret River in '07 to be winemaker for Howard Park. (JH)

95 **Chenin Blanc 2021, Swan Valley** Delicate, as usual, with a flood of green apple, white flowers, Turkish apricots, cheesecloth and beeswax. This has Australian bush, and wide open summer air, and saltbush, too. The phenolics have a bitter little kick in them through the finish … but that's ok, I was waiting for it. The waxy, lanolin character is exactly en pointe for the variety. Screw cap. | 12.7% alc. | Drink 2022-2030 | $32 | EL

Chenin Blanc 2020, Swan Valley Despite all the international chaos, '20 was a great vintage in WA. Warm, low yielding and with plenty of structure and power. That shows in the intensity of white summer apricot, green apple skin, lanolin and crushed cashew that spools out over the very long, neat finish. Saline acid laces all of these characters together. Another brilliant release. Screw cap. | 12.5% alc. | Drink 2021-2036 | $32 | EL

Faber Vineyard ★★★★★

233 Haddrill Road, Baskerville, WA 6056 **T** (08) 9296 0209 **www**.fabervineyard.com.au **OPEN** Fri–Sun 11–4 **WINEMAKER** John Griffiths **EST.** 1997 **DOZENS** 4000 **VYDS** 4.5ha

John Griffiths, former Houghton winemaker, teamed with wife Jane Micallef to found Faber Vineyard. John says, 'It may be somewhat quixotic, but I'm a great fan of traditional warm-area Australian wine styles, wines made in a relatively simple manner that reflect the concentrated ripe flavours one expects in these regions. And when one searches, some of these gems can be found from the Swan Valley.' (JH)

97   **Liqueur Muscat NV, Swan Valley** This is sensational. It is both fresh and aged; vibrant and brooding. It is like liquid velvet in the mouth and has silken toffee, jersey caramels, fresh honeycomb, morning coffee, dark fruitcake, summer figs, date, and a plethora of other flavours in the same vein. Pure, complex and astounding. 500ml.   Screw cap. | 18% alc. | $60 | EL | ♥

Mandoon Estate ★★★★★

10 Harris Road, Caversham, WA 6055 **T** (08) 6279 0500 **www**.mandoonestate.com.au **OPEN** 7 days 10–5 by appt **WINEMAKER** Ryan Sudano, Lauren Pileggi **EST.** 2009 **DOZENS** 10000 **VYDS** 50ha

Mandoon Estate, headed by Allan Erceg, made a considerable impression with its wines in a very short time. In '08 the family purchased a site in Caversham in the Swan Valley. Construction of the winery was completed in time for the first vintage in '10. They have also purchased 20ha in Margaret River. Winemaker Ryan Sudano has metaphorically laid waste to Australian wine shows with the quality of the wines he has made from the Swan Valley, Frankland River and Margaret River. (JH)

97   **Reserve Chardonnay 2020, Margaret River** Has it both ways: elegance and richness (with intensity and length), and a citrus-blossom fragrance. All of these characters come together, along with white peach and Granny Smith apple, to make magic.   Screw cap. | 13% alc. | Drink 2022–2032 | $59 | JH

    Reserve Research Station Cabernet Sauvignon 2017, Margaret River The hyper-fragrant bouquet of cassis and spice plays out in leisurely fashion on the palate, as bay leaf and earth notes join hands with the core of the fruit. It's Margaret River's ability to grow cabernet and fully ripen it as 14% alcohol that is so wonderful.   Screw cap. | 14% alc. | Drink 2025–2042 | $84 | JH

Nikola Estate ★★★★★

148 Dale Road, Middle Swan, WA 6056 **T** (08) 9374 8050 **www**.nikolaestate.com.au **OPEN** Thurs–Sun 10–5 **WINEMAKER** Damian Hutton, Marcello Fabretti **VITICULTURIST** Matty Trent **EST.** 2019 **VYDS** 56ha

While the Nikola brand may be new to the Swan Valley, the Yukich family behind it is anything but. In late '19, Houghton Estate in the Swan Valley (vineyards, historic cellar door, est 1836, and the winemaking facility) was purchased by brothers Graeme and third generation Kim Yukich. Winemaker Damian Hutton has moved from a long history at Millbrook (Fogarty Group) to assume the mantle at Nikola. (EL)

96   **Gallery Range: The Surrealist 2021, Swan Valley Geographe** 38/24/16/10/7/5% montepulciano/ mencia/barbera/grenache/nero d'Avola/arinto. This is really smart. There's a lot going on, but by virtue of co-fermentation, the varieties are absolutely and seamlessly integrated. It is bloody, gritty, savoury, salty and yet fresh. The lush purple and red fruit is only half the story; the tobacco leaf, saltbush, brine, clove, nutmeg, star anise and mountain herbs are the other half. Awesome. Screw cap. | 15.2% alc. | Drink 2022–2032 | $50 | EL

94   **Regional Rosé 2021, Geographe** 100% tempranillo. It is pure and plump, dominated by cherry, pomegranate, finely ground pepper, fennel flower and red apples. It's spicy too, a star anise, za'atar character through the finish. Smart wine, smart packaging. All good! Screw cap. | 13.4% alc. | Drink 2021–2024 | $30 | EL

    Regional Shiraz 2020, Frankland River French oak (16 months in 30% new) is impactful here, lending the fruit a savoury edge, however nothing is going to smother that dense, muscular and concentrated fruit. Slow ripples of blackberry, raspberry, licorice, red dirt and ferrous notes all coalesce on the palate. Bloody smart for $30. Screw cap. | 14.5% alc. | Drink 2021–2031 | $30 | EL

Oakover Wines ★★★★

14 Yukich Close, Middle Swan, WA 6056 **T** (08) 9374 8000 **www**.oakoverwines.com.au **OPEN** Wed–Sun 11–4 **WINEMAKER** Daniel Charter **EST.** 1929 **DOZENS** 15000 **VYDS** 27ha

Oakover Wines is a family-operated winery located in the Swan Valley. Formerly part of Houghton, it came under the Yukich family's control as Oakover Estate in 1990. Prominent Perth funds manager Graeme Yukich and his family have been involved in the region since Nicholas Yukich purchased his first block of land in 1929. In 2002 Oakover Estate became Oakover Wines and is now the third-largest winery in the Swan Valley. (JH)

93   **Chenin Blanc 2021, Western Australia** Fermented entirely in stainless steel, this is soft, round, plush, pretty, and chalky. With aromas of nashi pear, honeysuckle, honey, beeswax and green apples, it has it all going on. Is there any RS in there? If not, the fruit has such concentration as to appear so. Anyway, chenin always gets better with age, so this one will likely accelerate over the next year or more. A flaming bargain. Screw cap. | 10.9% alc. | Drink 2022-2028 | $14 | EL

90   **Shiraz 2020, Western Australia** Fruit from the Swan Valley. It's high-octane alcohol, and high-octane flavour, but for $14 it's very impressive indeed. It is concentrated, vibrant and brooding at once. There's blood, there's a bit of hung deli meat, there's blackberry and there's licorice. Bonza. Fantastic value. Screw cap. | 15% alc. | Drink 2022-2027 | $14 | EL

Pinelli Wines

30 Bennett Street, Caversham, WA 6055 **T** (08) 9279 6818 **www**.pinelliwines.com.au **OPEN** Mon-Sat 9-5, Sun & public hols 10-5 **WINEMAKER** Robert Pinelli, Daniel Pinelli **EST**. 1980 **DOZENS** 17000 **VYDS** 9.78ha

Domenic and Iolanda Pinelli emigrated from Italy in the mid '50s. With the benefit of 20 years' experience gained with Waldeck Wines he purchased a 2.8ha vineyard in '80. It became the site of the Pinelli family winery, cellar door and home vineyard. Son Robert, has been the winemaker at Pinelli for over 20 years. His brother Daniel obtained his oenology degree from CSU in '07. He graduated with distinction, and was awarded the Domaine Chandon Sparkling Wine Award for best sparkling wine production student. (JH)

91   **La Tavola Shiraz 2020, Western Australia** As one of Australia's oldest wine regions, the Swan Valley has plenty to be proud of. Not the least of which, is its ability to produce ripe, concentrated shiraz in a style very different to that of other regions. This is uncomplicated, littered with blackberries, mulberries, star anise, some warm spice (think cinnamon, cardamom and the like) and cloves. Screw cap. | 14% alc. | Drink 2021-2027 | $20 | EL

RiverBank Estate

126 Hamersley Road, Caversham, WA 6055 **T** (08) 9377 1805 **www**.riverbankestate.com.au **OPEN** Wed-Sun & public hols 10-4 **WINEMAKER** Troy Overstone **EST**. 1982 **DOZENS** 4500 **VYDS** 12ha

RiverBank Estate was first planted on the fertile banks of the Swan River in 1982 and has grown to encompass 12ha of mature, low-yielding vines (18 varieties), the wines made onsite. The property was purchased by the Lembo family in 2017 and has been rebranded into 3 wine ranges: On The Run, Rebellious and Eric Anthony. RiverBank was named Best Small Wine Producer of the Year '19 by Ray Jordan and Best Small Cellar Door in the Swan Valley '19 by Peter Forrestal of Gourmet Traveller. (JH)

94   **Rebellious Tempranillo 2021, Swan Valley** With 5% malbec; the tempranillo co-fermented with 8% vermentino (skins), co-planted in the vineyard. Bacon fat, maple and violets are the introduction while the palate is saturated in red licorice, raspberries and black cherries. It's juicy and bright and delicious. The tannins are ever present, but not overbearing. Screw cap. | 14% alc. | Drink 2022-2027 | $25 | EL

Sittella Wines

100 Barrett Street, Herne Hill, WA 6056 **T** (08) 9296 2600 **www**.sittella.com.au **OPEN** Tues-Sun & public hols 11-4 **WINEMAKER** Colby Quirk, Yuri Berns **EST**. 1998 **DOZENS** 15000 **VYDS** 25ha

Simon and Maaike Berns acquired a 7ha block (with 5ha of vines) at Herne Hill, making the first wine in 1998 and opening a most attractive cellar door facility. They also own the Wildberry Estate Vineyard in Margaret River. Plantings in Margaret River have increased with new clones of cabernet sauvignon, cabernet franc, P95 chardonnay and malbec. New clones of tempranillo and touriga nacional have also been added to the Swan Valley plantings. (JH)

96   **Pedro Ximénez NV, Swan Valley** This is gorgeous. The old material enriches the foundations, while the top notes remain fresh and vibrant. Quince, fig, loquat, cumquat, date and star anise are the stars here. The length of flavour lingers and curls in the mouth, while all components are beautifully integrated. Coffee grounds, toffee and caramel. Smooth to the very last drop. 350ml. Screw cap. | 18.5% alc. | $50 | EL

95 | **Museum Release Silk 2015, Swan Valley** Verdelho, chenin blanc and chardonnay. The nose is an amalgam of cheesecloth, lanolin, summer apricots, kiwifruit, poached green apples and white peeper. In the mouth the wine is texturally creamy and complex ... a really engaging and kaleidoscopic wine that has both poise and volume. Verdelho is a variety in use far less often than it once was, which is a damn shame when you see it like this. Glorious. Screw cap. | 13.5% alc. | Drink 2022-2037 | $35 | EL

94 | **Avant-Garde Dry Rosé 2021, Swan Valley** Old vine Swan Valley grenache for rosé feels decadent or excessive, not sure which. Regardless; raspberries, bramble, spice, red licorice and briny acidity course through the wine, tumbling over themselves for dominance in the mouth. Rose petals, crushed pistachios, red apples and more. The varietal characters of the grenache really shine here, the heat of the Swan has imbued it with concentration and life. Super-smart first release. Screw cap. | 13% alc. | Drink 2021-2025 | $25 | EL

South West Australia

Kerrigan + Berry ⚲⑭ ★★★★★

PO Box 221, Cowaramup, WA 6284 **T** (08) 9755 6046 **WWW**.kerriganandberry.com.au **OPEN** 7 days 10–5 **WINEMAKER** Michael Kerrigan, Gavin Berry **EST**. 2007 **DOZENS** 1500

Owners Michael Kerrigan and Gavin Berry have been making wine in WA for a combined period of over 50 years and say they have been most closely associated with the 2 varieties that in their opinion define WA: riesling and cabernet sauvignon. This is strictly a weekend and after-hours venture, separate from their respective roles as chief winemakers at Hay Shed Hill (Michael) and West Cape Howe (Gavin). (JH)

95 | **Riesling 2021, Mount Barker** What a brilliant wine. Structured, staunch, brawny, powerfully concentrated and very long – this shows the strength of Mount Barker for this style of riesling. It is no shrinking violet. Neither restrained nor delicate; driven by acid. All things in place – a masterstroke. Better for cellaring than drinking now, although it will of course bend to either will. Screw cap. | 12% alc. | Drink 2021-2036 | $30 | EL

Geographe

Aylesbury Estate ★★★★★

72 Ratcliffe Road, Ferguson, WA 6236 **T** 0427 922 755 **WWW**.aylesburyestate.com.au **WINEMAKER** Luke Eckersley, Damian Hutton **VITICULTURIST** Ryan Gibbs **EST**. 2015 **DOZENS** 6500 **VYDS** 9ha

Ryan and Narelle Gibbs are the 6th generation of the pioneering Gibbs family in the Ferguson Valley. For generations the family ran cattle on the 200ha property, but in 1998 they decided to plant 4.2ha of cabernet sauvignon to diversify the business. Merlot (2.5ha) followed in '01, and sauvignon blanc (1.6ha) in '04. In '08 Ryan and Narelle took over the business from Ryan's father, selling the grapes until '15, when they made the first Aylesbury Estate wines. Three years later, they purchased the nearby 52 Stones vineyard, adding cooler-climate varieties chardonnay, arneis and gamay to the Aylesbury range. (JH)

95 | **QO5 Ferguson Valley Tempranillo 2020, Geographe** Beautiful wine, here. Salted black licorice, mulberries, raspberries, lashings of blackberry and a waft of violets through the finish. I want to say pretty, but it has bigger muscles and more density than that – although elements of it are undoubtedly pretty. Very smart wine. Screw cap. | 14.5% alc. | Drink 2021-2028 | $35 | EL

bakkheia ⚲ ★★★★★

2718 Ferguson Road, Lowden, WA 6240 **T** (08) 9732 1394 **WWW**.bakkheia.com.au **OPEN** By appt **WINEMAKER** Michael Edwards **EST**. 2006 **DOZENS** 1000 **VYDS** 3ha

This is the retirement venture of Michael and Ilonka Edwards. Michael had a career in the navy and marine industry while Ilonka enjoyed a career in the fashion and lifestyle industry. They moved to the Preston Valley in WA in '05 and purchased a property that had a patch of cabernet sauvignon planted in '99. They have an unusual approach to marketing, starting with the winery name linked to the Roman words for Bacchus and bacchanalian frenzies induced by wine, lots of wine. (JH)

97 **The Wonderful Miss Gerry Preston Valley Grenache 2020, Geographe** This has incredible intensity of flavour. There is blood and plum (distinct from blood plums), graphite and rocks. Star anise, licorice and aniseed, with bacon fat, maple and raspberry humbugs. A touch of stewed rhubarb, red apples and black tea. There's nori and black sesame in there too. It's all there. The concentration is a marvel, actually. The first thing I said when I put this in my mouth was 'wow'. Screw cap. | 15.1% alc. | Drink 2022-2032 | $21 | EL | ♥

95 **Monsieur Lapena Merlot 2016, Geographe** Wears its age well. It is savoury and natural (unpretentious), with mulberry, tobacco, coffee grounds and salted licorice. A string of rhubarb tart acidity slowly curls its way through the fruit. Leather strap and granular tannins are a highlight. It is long and precise and medium weighted at best. An intriguing wine of layers and earth. Screw cap. | 14.5% alc. | Drink 2022-2032 | $35 | EL

Ironcloud Wines

Suite 16, 18 Stirling Highway, Nedlands, WA 6009 (postal) **T** 0401 860 891 **WWW**.ironcloudwines.com.au **WINEMAKER** Michael Ng **EST.** 1999 **DOZENS** 2500 **VYDS** 11ha

In 2003 owners Warwick Lavis and Geoff and Karyn Cross purchased the then-named Pepperilly Estate, which had been planted in 1999 on red gravelly loam soils. Peppermint trees line the Henty Brook, the natural water source for the vineyard. In 2017 Michael Ng, formerly chief winemaker for Rockcliffe, succeeded Coby Ladwig. (JH)

95 **Rock of Solitude Ferguson Valley Touriga 2020, Geographe** As has become habit for this wine, Ironcloud has nailed the balance of savoury spice and pure fruit here, all of it teetering on a fulcrum of tannin. Campfire, blackberry, licorice, a kick of red dirt, sandalwood and black tea ... it floats on the tongue, while the tannins are chewy and textural. Tangible. It's awesome. Another touriga triumph. Screw cap. | 14.5% alc. | Drink 2022-2029 | $35 | EL

Talisman Wines ⓨ

Wheelman Road, Wellington Mill, WA 6236 **T** 0401 559 266 **WWW**.talismanwines.com.au **OPEN** By appt **WINEMAKER** Peter Stanlake **VITICULTURIST** Victor Bertola **EST.** 2009 **DOZENS** 3000 **VYDS** 9ha

Kim and Jenny Robinson began the development of their vineyard in 2000. Kim says that 'after 8 frustrating years of selling grapes to Evans & Tate and Wolf Blass, we decided to optimise the vineyard and attempt to make quality wines'. The measure of their success has been consistent gold-medal performance (and some trophies) at the Geographe Wine Show. They say this could not have been achieved without the assistance of vineyard manager Victor Bertola and winemaker Peter Stanlake. (JH)

93 **Ferguson Valley Riesling 2021, Geographe** '21 was a cool season in WA, and that is immediately evident on the nose here. Finely crushed white pepper, juniper, hints of star anise, lemon zest, apple skin and lychee (if you really look hard enough). In the mouth the wine goes lightly, tiptoeing across the tongue through to a delicate finish. Very pretty, very fine, very quiet. Screw cap. | 11.7% alc. | Drink 2021-2028 | $25 | EL

Willow Bridge Estate ⓨ

178 Gardin Court Drive, Dardanup, WA 6236 **T** (08) 9728 0055 **WWW**.willowbridge.com.au **OPEN** 7 days 10.30-4.30 **WINEMAKER** Kim Horton **EST.** 1997 **DOZENS** 25000 **VYDS** 59ha

Jeff and Vicky Dewar have followed a fast track in developing Willow Bridge Estate since acquiring the spectacular 180ha hillside property in the Ferguson Valley. Kim Horton, with 25 years of winemaking in WA, believes that wines are made in the vineyard; the better the understanding of the vineyard and its unique characteristics, the better the wines reflect the soil and the climate. (JH)

96 **Gravel Pit Shiraz 2020, Geographe** From the site of gravel once excavated from local roads, its deep colour and full-bodied palate replete with firm tannins typical of this site. 12 months' maturation in French oak (35% new) has added its weight to an altogether compelling wine, with a very long life ahead. Screw cap. | 14.2% alc. | Drink 2025-2045 | $30 | JH

Black Dog Shiraz 2018, Geographe Meaty, dense, savoury and full bodied, this is more in balance than it used to be and is all the better for it. It is a proud display of the intensity and concentration that Geographe is so capable of. The ripe, malleable, chewy tannins are the final indicator of quality. Cigar box, tobacco leaf, black tea, salted licorice, resin, char, blackberry compote and even cassis. Super good stuff here. Screw cap. | 14% alc. | Drink 2022-2037 | $65 | EL

95 **GSM 2021, Geographe** Willow Bridge are the masters of plush, pliable, supple wines that are fresh and affordable. Fruit rides the chariot and lashes the horses (tannins) ... it forges a path across the tongue leaving a trail of berries, spice and exotic flavours in its wake. This is, and always was, about the fruit. Long live the fruit. Hyah. Screw cap. | 14.5% alc. | Drink 2022–2028 | $25 | EL

REGION
Great Southern

Alkoomi ★★★★★

1411 Wingebellup Road, Frankland River, WA 6396 **T** (08) 9855 2229 www.alkoomiwines.com.au **OPEN** 7 days 10–4.30 Frankland River Mon–Sat 11–5 Albany **WINEMAKER** Andrew Cherry **VITICULTURIST** Tim Penniment **EST.** 1971 **DOZENS** 80000 **VYDS** 164ha

Established in 1971 by Merv and Judy Lange, Alkoomi has grown from 1ha to one of WA's largest family-owned and -operated wineries. Now owned by daughter Sandy Hallett and her husband Rod, Alkoomi is continuing the tradition of producing high-quality wines which showcase the Frankland River region. Alkoomi is actively reducing its environmental footprint; future plans will see the introduction of new varietals. A second cellar door is located in Albany. (JH)

95 **Alkoomi Collection Shiraz 2020, Frankland River** Co-fermented with 'a bit' of viognier. Silky, floral, velvety, robust, dusty, ripe and spiced. All very good things here, and unbelievably wrapped up in $28 and smart packaging. The Alkoomi Collection range is a bit of a marvel. Blood plum, mulberry, blackberry and raspberry with lashings of salted licorice, ferrous and lavender. Another ripping wine here – bravo team Cherry. Screw cap. | 14.5% alc. | Drink 2021–2031 | $28 | EL

Melaleuca 2018, Frankland River The extremely complex bouquet of this riesling sends the nasal receptors scurrying in all directions: juice, pith, zest and spice; the palate rolling all these up into a profoundly satisfying bundle of lemon and lime flavours. Screw cap. | 12.5% alc. | Drink 2021–2033 | $35 | JH

Wandoo 2016, Frankland River At 5 years old, this is a revelation in terms of its freshness, liveliness and intensity. Check, check and check. On the nose: lemongrass, preserved lemons, honey, hay and beeswax. The palate is where this really has the opportunity to project: apples, salted citrus, walnuts, cheesecloth and white pepper. Texturally, it is expansive and cushioned. Brilliant. Years left in the tank. Screw cap. | 11.5% alc. | Drink 2021–2031 | $35 | EL | ♥

Castelli Estate ★★★★★

380 Mount Shadforth Road, Denmark, WA 6333 **T** (08) 9364 0400 www.castelliestate.com.au **OPEN** By appt **WINEMAKER** Mike Garland **EST.** 2007 **DOZENS** 20000

Castelli Estate will cause many small winery owners to go green with envy. When Sam Castelli purchased the property in late '04, he was intending simply to use it as a family holiday destination. But because there was a partly constructed winery he decided to complete the building work and simply lock the doors. However, wine was in his blood courtesy of his father, who owned a small vineyard in Italy's south. The temptation was too much and in '07 the winery was commissioned. (JH)

94 **Silver Series Shiraz Malbec 2019, Frankland River** Super-swish new packaging for a wine that routinely outdoes itself in the value-for-money stakes. 51/49% shiraz/malbec. Inky, intense and concentrated with brilliantly dense tannins on the palate. Frankland does the ferrous/ironstone/rust/blood/dirt characters so well – and they are all here in spades. If you like saturated fruit flavours and robust shape then this is unequivocally for you. Delish. Screw cap. | 14.5% alc. | Drink 2021–2028 | $25 | EL

Castle Rock Estate ★★★★★

2660 Porongurup Road, Porongurup, WA 6324 **T** (08) 9853 1035 www.castlerockestate.com.au **OPEN** 7 days 10–4.30 **WINEMAKER** Robert Diletti **EST.** 1983 **DOZENS** 4500 **VYDS** 11.2ha

An exceptionally beautifully sited vineyard, winery and cellar door on a 55ha property with sweeping vistas of the Porongurup Range, operated by the Diletti family. The standard of viticulture is very high, and the vineyard itself is ideally situated. The 2-level winery, set on a natural slope, maximises gravity flow. The rieslings have always been elegant and have handsomely repaid time in bottle; the pinot noir is the most consistent performer in the region; the shiraz is a great cool-climate example; and chardonnay has joined a thoroughly impressive quartet, elegance the common link. (JH)

97 **Pinot Noir 2020, Porongurup** Perfect colour; a great pinot at the dawn of its life; plum and cherry riddled with spice, char, violets and forest floor. Sophisticated and confident. Screw cap. | 13.5% alc. | Drink 2022–2035 | $38 | JH

96   **Shiraz 2019, Great Southern** The grapes come from Mount Barker. The 28 April harvest underlines the very cool climate and resultant vibrantly fresh and elegant array of red, blue and black fruits, resting on a bed of fine tannins. Screw cap. | 13.5% alc. | Drink 2022-2035 | $34 | JH

95   **Shiraz 2020, Porongurup** Aromas of cool-climate shiraz fruit on show, paraded across the top of the wine in a procession of blackcurrant pastille, blue fruits, anise, fennel flower and graphite. In the mouth the wine is precisely as expected: detailed, super-pretty, elegant, chalky and supple. The endlessly attractive mineral tannins are a highlight. What a gloriously fine wine for the price. Screw cap. | 13.8% alc. | Drink 2021-2031 | $34 | EL

94   **Sauvignon Blanc 2021, Porongurup** The Porongurup Range is a place of great beauty. If you haven't been, you really must add it to the list. Castle Rock Estate is a great place to start: not only are the wines sensational, but the positioning of the vineyard on top of the hill ... well that's pretty impressive, too. As for this wine; cool, elegant, and clearly made by a riesling maker, such is its purity and finesse. '21 was responsible for delicate wines and this is a wonderful example. Screw cap. | 12.8% alc. | Drink 2021-2024 | $23 | EL

     Riesling 2021, Porongurup Just like '20, this is a sensational wine. Typified by quietly searing flavour intensity that really creeps up on you. Salty, pithy and fine, this has an understated volume that emerges mid palate onwards. Super-restrained, minerally and very pretty. Screw cap. | 11% alc. | Drink 2021-2031 | $26 | EL

Duke's Vineyard ⓎⒿ   ★★★★★

Porongurup Road, Porongurup, WA 6324 **T** (08) 9853 1107 **www**.dukesvineyard.com **OPEN** 7 days 10-4.30 **WINEMAKER** Robert Diletti **EST.** 1998 **DOZENS** 3500 **VYDS** 10ha

When Hilde and Ian (Duke) Ranson sold their clothing manufacturing business in '98, they were able to fulfil a long-held dream of establishing a vineyard in the Porongurup subregion of Great Southern with the acquisition of a 65ha farm at the foot of the Porongurup Range. Hilde, a successful artist, designed the beautiful, scalloped, glass-walled cellar door sales area, with its mountain blue cladding. (JH)

97   **Magpie Hill Reserve Riesling 2021, Porongurup** A super-floral nose leads into a tense and citrus-driven palate. The acidity is saline and omnipresent, curling and flicking around the fruit, shaping it all through the long finish. This has already developed and grown so much in the bottle between this glass and the last (a couple of months ago), that it surely has a very long road ahead of it. White pepper, lime flesh and laser-like precision through the finish. Layered and dappled – gorgeous. Screw cap. | 11.8% alc. | Drink 2021-2041 | $42 | EL

96   **Magpie Hill Reserve Shiraz 2020, Porongurup** Another startlingly impressive cuvée from this vineyard. Silky texture in the mouth, plump, concentrated black fruit and layers of sweet spice. It's a marvel. Love the plum through the finish ... Screw cap. | 14.1% alc. | Drink 2021-2031 | $42 | EL

94   **Single Vineyard Riesling 2021, Porongurup** Pristine, pure and precise. Laser-like acidity coils around and around on the palate, creating a vortex of energy and life in which the fruit can float. Long and saline; what a beautiful wine. The thing about Porongurup riesling is the floral aromatics coupled with austere acidity; the best have both in spades, one sometimes disguising the other, but never stepping out alone. Screw cap. | 11.5% alc. | Drink 2021-2031 | $26 | EL

Ferngrove Ⓨ⊜   ★★★★☆

276 Ferngrove Road, Frankland River, WA 6396 **T** (08) 9363 1300 **www**.ferngrove.com.au **WINEMAKER** Craig Grafton, Andrew Foot **VITICULTURIST** Chris Zur **EST.** 1998 **VYDS** 220ha

For over 20 years, Ferngrove has been producing consistent examples of cool-climate wines across multiple price brackets. The Ferngrove stable includes the flagship Orchid wines, Black Label, White Label and Independence ranges. Ferngrove Vineyards Pty Ltd enjoys the benefits of majority international ownership. (JH)

94   **Independence Shiraz 2020, Great Southern** 95/5% shiraz/viognier, co-fermented. Red fruits and flowers on the nose; 5% viognier is a noticeable hit, but it's well judged in this case. Potent midnight fruits mingle with the daytime vibes of raspberries and pink peppercorn. Lots to like, and all the while retaining the thing that makes it great: that Frankland River DNA of ferrous, ironstone, red dirt and blood plum. Distinctive, delicious and shapely. Unbelievable value for money. Screw cap. | 14% alc. | Drink 2021-2028 | $26 | EL

Forest Hill Vineyard Ⓨ⑪Ⓙ   ★★★★★

Cnr South Coast Highway/Myers Road, Denmark, WA 6333 **T** (08) 9848 2399 **www**.foresthillwines.com.au **OPEN** 7 days 10.30-5 **WINEMAKER** Liam Carmody, Guy Lyons **VITICULTURIST** Ross Pike **EST.** 1965 **DOZENS** 12000 **VYDS** 36ha

This family-owned business is one of the oldest 'new' winemaking operations in WA and was the site of the first grape plantings in Great Southern in 1965. The Forest Hill brand became well known, aided by the fact that a '75 Riesling made by Sandalford from Forest Hill grapes won 9 trophies. (JH)

96 **Riesling 2021, Mount Barker** An entrancing riesling with a perfumed bouquet of white flowers, lime blossom and more, the palate a ringmaster playing off the pure lime and passionfruit flavours with a rivulet of acidity that dances through to the aftertaste. Screw cap. | 12.5% alc. | Drink 2021-2036 | $29 | JH

Block 2 Riesling 2021, Mount Barker Fermented in a combination of stainless steel and oak. Kept on lees until bottling in Oct. 3g/L RS. Textural, dense and super-long; even without the prior knowledge of RS, it is evident in a little glycerol slick through the finish, perfectly in sync with the plump fruit that precedes it. Similarly, the oak component is invisible, save for the texture in the mouth. Not only is it awesome now, but this is going to age with interest and grace. Stock up. Screw cap. | 12.5% alc. | Drink 2021-2036 | $38 | EL

Block 1 Riesling 2021, Mount Barker 1.4g/L RS. This is long, with palate-staining intensity of flavour. The lack of oak or bâtonnage means this is pure fruit horsepower. The drive and composition of this wine illustrates both the brawn of Mount Barker and the grace of the old vines of Block 1. The cool '21 season delivers a finer expression of this wine. Screw cap. | 12.5% alc. | Drink 2021-2036 | $55 | EL

Block 9 Shiraz 2020, Mount Barker Savoury, spicy, and laden with intrigue, this wine carries across the palate and through to the extraordinarily long finish with grace and ease. Hung deli meat, black and red fruits and sprinklings of Chinese five-spice and licorice root. Very smart. Very long. Powerful. The tannins shape the wine in the mouth and cup the fruit as it makes its journey through time. Lovely. Screw cap. | 14% alc. | Drink 2021-2031 | $60 | EL

Block 5 Cabernet Sauvignon 2020, Mount Barker Svelte, concentrated and muscular in the most wonderful of ways. Mount Barker can give that salivating, bloody character of ferrous and red dirt (like Frankland River can) and it fills me with satisfaction to taste wine laced in this way. Inchoate as this wine is, all of the hallmarks required for ageing are here in spades. Just 840 bottles made. Screw cap. | 14% alc. | Drink 2022-2039 | $65 | EL

95 **Gewürztraminer 2021, Mount Barker** I routinely love this wine. It combines the power, might and muscle that comes so easily in Mount Barker, with the floral, exotic, lifted, gypsy vibes of the gewürztraminer to stunning effect. Caravans of rose petals, crushed pistachios and granite, combined with nashi pears, lychee, star anise, jasmine tea and Granny Smith apples roll across the palate. A distinct quartz-like minerality flows through it, all of it laced together within a fine and glassy structure. It's light as a feather, and cleansing and mineral through the finish. Stunning. Screw cap. | 13% alc. | Drink 2022-2027 | $30 | EL

Shiraz 2020, Mount Barker An attractive bouquet, and a purple-crimson hue. Warm spices and a modicum of oak quickly gain traction on a medium-bodied palate, riding high on juicy red and black cherries, licorice and perfectly pitched tannins. There's freshness, too, on the finish. Screw cap. | 14% alc. | Drink 2023-2039 | $30 | JH

94 **Highbury Fields Riesling 2021, Great Southern** Progressively unfolds its charms, the lime and apple blossom bouquet pleasing, the well-balanced palate bringing ripe, tangy citrus flavours to the table. Screw cap. | 12.5% alc. | Drink 2021-2036 | $24 | JH

Frankland Estate ⓥ ★★★★★

Frankland Road, Frankland, WA 6396 **T** (08) 9855 1544 **www.**franklandestate.com.au **OPEN** Mon-Fri 10-4, public hols & w'ends by appt **WINEMAKER** Hunter Smith, Brian Kent **EST.** 1988 **DOZENS** 20000 **VYDS** 34.5ha

A significant operation, situated on a large sheep property owned by Barrie Smith and Judi Cullam. The vineyard has been established progressively since 1988. The introduction of an array of single-vineyard rieslings has been a highlight, driven by Judi's conviction that terroir is of utmost importance, and the soils are indeed different; the Isolation Ridge Vineyard is organically grown. Frankland Estate has held important International Riesling tastings and seminars for more than a decade. (JH)

97 **Isolation Ridge Riesling 2021, Frankland River** Sandalwood, preserved citrus, black tea leaves and jasmine seamlessly merge into the more expected Frankland River riesling characters of lemon zest, green apple skins and chalk. In the mouth, the acidity is like a coiled spring, cushioned by voluminous fruit padding on all sides. This is generous, but it's tense and taut too … disguised austerity. Slatey. Screw cap. | 13.5% alc. | Drink 2022-2042 | $52 | EL | ♥

Smith Cullam Riesling 2021, Frankland River Supreme balance. This wine is silky and lush (thanks to the RS, as this is the off-dry style for the house), but it is carried on linear tracks of steel-like acidity … they crest the horizon, which seems never-ending. White flowers, black tea, nashi pear skin, mandarin pith, lemon zest, nutmeg, even oud … tea tree … it's a seriously good wine. Spectacular. In terms of vintage context, this cool (and sometimes wet!) year has imbued this with detail and poise. Screw cap. | 11.5% alc. | Drink 2022-2042 | $75 | EL

Smith Cullam Syrah 2020, Frankland River The nose is so fragrant that it takes some time to unpick it all. Winter mandarin, pink peppercorn, citrus blossom, blackberry, plum, licorice, clove, star anise, lavender and fennel flower. In the mouth, the graphite and black-tea tannins are a masterclass in svelte. It is the tannins that reveal to us how inchoate this wine truly is. It needs time. It will be superlative. For now, it is tightly wound, coiled even and needs time to unfurl and show its potential. What a profound wine. Wow. Owns the Syrah moniker. Screw cap. | 14.5% alc. | Drink 2022-2037 | $120 | EL | ♥

95   **Riesling 2021, Frankland River** Takes only a millisecond, once you taste the wine, for the mouth to flood with juicy lime flavours plus splashes of tropical fruits. Totally delicious now, but has the structure to develop well into the next decade. Screw cap. | 12.5% alc. | Drink 2021-2035 | $30 | JH

      Shiraz 2018, Frankland River The crimson-rimmed deep purple sets the scene for a powerful yet fragrant wine, with poached spiced plum fruit, ripe tannins and French oak beating a delicate tattoo on the finish. Screw cap. | 12.5% alc. | Drink 2022-2033 | $32 | JH

Harewood Estate ★★★★★

1570 Scotsdale Road, Denmark, WA 6333 **T** (08) 9840 9078 **www.**harewood.com.au **OPEN** Fri-Mon 11-5 (school hols 7 days) **WINEMAKER** James Kellie **EST.** 1988 **DOZENS** 15000 **VYDS** 19.2ha

In 2003 James and Careena Kellie, responsible for the contract making of Harewood's wines since '98, purchased the Harewood Estate. They constructed a 300t winery, offering both contract winemaking services and the ability to expand the Harewood range to include subregional wines from across the Great Southern region. (JH)

94   **Riesling 2021, Denmark** There is a character here that is not present in the Tunney or Porongurup riesling – like toasted saffron or turmeric, cashew. The fruit strays to the sugar snap pea end of the spectrum. It's a lovely, textural and layered wine with faceted fruit and spice characters. Screw cap. | 12% alc. | Drink 2021-2036 | $30 | EL

Mount Trio Vineyard ★★★★

2534 Porongurup Road, Mount Barker WA 6324 **T** (08) 9853 1136 **www.**mounttriowines.com.au **OPEN** By appt **WINEMAKER** Gavin Berry, Andrew Vesey, Caitlin Gazey **EST.** 1989 **DOZENS** 3500 **VYDS** 8.5ha

Mount Trio was established by Gavin Berry, Gill Graham and their business partners shortly after they moved to the Mount Barker area in late '88. Gavin took up the position of chief winemaker at Plantagenet, which he held until '04, when he and partners acquired the now very successful and much larger West Cape Howe. (JH)

94   **Shiraz 2019, Great Southern** Fresh and peppery cool-climate syrah. Layers of black fruit flavours are shaped by fine tannins and a distinct licorice character that cools everything down. Remarkably elegant drinking for $23. Bravo. Screw cap. | 13.5% alc. | Drink 2028 | $23 | EL

Paul Nelson Wines ★★★★★

14 Roberts Road, Denmark, WA 6333 (postal) **T** 0406 495 066 **www.**paulnelsonwines.com.au **OPEN** School hols 11-5 **WINEMAKER** Paul Nelson **EST.** 2009 **DOZENS** 1500 **VYDS** 2ha

Paul Nelson started making wine with one foot in the Swan Valley, the other in the Great Southern, while completing a bachelor's degree in viticulture and oenology at Curtin University. He then worked successively at Houghton in the Swan Valley, Goundrey in Mount Barker, Santa Ynez in California, South Africa (for 4 vintages), hemisphere-hopping to the Rheinhessen, 3 vintages in Cyprus, then moving to a large Indian winemaker in Mumbai before returning to work for Houghton. He has since moved on from Houghton and makes small quantities of table wines in partnership with his wife Bianca. (JH)

97   **Karriview Vineyard Chardonnay 2019, Denmark** There's a lot going on here, and like the brilliant '18 that came before it, this makes a compelling case for cool-climate chardonnay from Denmark. Complex, endlessly layered, rich and worked, but with a nuance and finesse that speaks volumes about the vineyard from whence it came. Curry leaf, crushed nuts, grilled peach, lemon zest, brine, jasmine tea, aniseed, crushed quartz and fennel flower. Dense, powerful, long. Yes. Screw cap. | 13% alc. | Drink 2021-2036 | $65 | EL

96   **Karriview Vineyard Pinot Noir 2019, Denmark** Super-elegant lacy tannins shape the sweet cherry and cranberry fruit. Counterpoint to the pretty characters here, there is also olive tapenade and salted heirloom tomato. This layers of fine spice; the mineral saline acidity curls and weaves its way across the palate. Another supreme release. Screw cap. | 13.4% alc. | Drink 2021-2036 | $65 | EL | ♥

Singlefile Wines ★★★★★

90 Walter Road, Denmark, WA 6333 **T** 1300 885 807 **www.**singlefilewines.com **OPEN** 7 days 11-5 **WINEMAKER** Mike Garland, Coby Ladwig, Patrick Corbett **EST.** 2007 **DOZENS** 10000 **VYDS** 3.75ha

In 1986, Phil Snowden and his wife Viv moved from South Africa to Perth, where they developed their successful multinational mining and resource services company, Snowden Resources. Following the sale of the company in 2004, they turned their attention to their long-held desire to make and enjoy fine wine. In '07 they bought an established vineyard (planted in '89) in the beautiful Denmark subregion. They pulled out the old shiraz and merlot vines, kept and planted more chardonnay and retained Larry Cherubino to set up partnerships with established vineyards in Frankland River, Porongurup, Denmark, Pemberton and Margaret River. (JH)

95 **Riesling 2021, Great Southern** Fresh and lively; a delicious array of lime, lemon and passionfruit to open proceedings on the palate and bouquet; steely acidity runs throughout, but does so without disturbing the peace. Changes will emerge down the track, but don't hesitate to drink it tonight. Screw cap. | 11.9% alc. | Drink 2021-2031 | $25 | JH

Swinney ★★★★★

325 Frankland-Kojonup Road, Frankland River, WA 6396 **T** (08) 9200 4483 **www**.swinney.com.au **WINEMAKER** Rob Mann **VITICULTURIST** Rhys Thomas **EST.** 1998 **DOZENS** 2500 **VYDS** 160ha

The Swinney family (currently parents Graham and Kaye, and son and daughter Matt and Janelle) has been resident on their 2500ha property since it was settled by George Swinney in 1922. In the '90s they decided to diversify and now have 160ha of vines across 4 vineyards, including the Powderbark Ridge Vineyard in Frankland River (planted in '98, purchased in partnership with former Hardys winemaker Peter Dawson). (JH)

97 **Farvie Syrah 2020, Frankland River** An utterly gorgeous nose awaits. Ferrous, blood plum, rust, pastrami, blackberries in summer, black cherries and mulberries too. '20 was warm and yields were low. Across the board, berries were small. An odd observation perhaps, until you encounter the tannins. It insists on a decant as it's tight as a drum currently – you will miss the complete spectrum of texture if you decide to wade right in. This is a monumental wine of gravitas and poise, the flavour all clustered on the back palate. I suspect we haven't seen the best of it yet. Screw cap. | 14% alc. | Drink 2022-2042 | $150 | EL

96 **Mourvèdre Syrah Grenache 2020, Frankland River** The mourvèdre just has such beautiful tannins and shape. Gloriously earthy, gravelly yet fine, it underpins the success of the other varieties and lends a real chew to the overall. Beautiful, supple, vibrant. With muscle. Screw cap. | 14% alc. | Drink 2021-2031 | $42 | EL | ♥

3 Drops ★★★★★

PO Box 1828, Applecross, WA 6953 **T** 0417 172 603 **www**.3drops.com **WINEMAKER** Robert Diletti (Contract) **EST.** 1998 **DOZENS** 3500 **VYDS** 21.5ha

3 Drops is the name given to the Bradbury family vineyard at Mount Barker. The name reflects 3 elements: wine, olive oil and water – all of which come from the substantial property. 3 Drops also owns the 14.7ha Patterson's Vineyard, planted in 1982. (JH)

96 **Riesling 2021, Great Southern** A pale quartz green hue foretells a wine of unbridled intensity; aromas of white flowers, passionfruit and Granny Smith apple open proceedings on a palate of vibrant drive and intensity. Rose's lime juice with soaring acidity drive the seemingly endless flavours demanding an extra glass (or 2). Screw cap. | 12% alc. | Drink 2021-2031 | $26 | JH

95 **Shiraz 2019, Great Southern** Bright crimson-purple hue. A lively, fresh and juicy medium-bodied wine, its spicy red and black cherry fruits and fine tannins holding hands as they dance along the palate without a care in the world. There's every reason to drink it forthwith, but it will wait patiently for those wishing to cellar it for 5 or so years. Screw cap. | 14.5% alc. | Drink 2022-2030 | $28 | JH

94 **Merlot 2020, Great Southern** A fragrant and pure expression of a good merlot clone, grown in a climate that is perfect for it. An armful of red fruits and roses fill this medium-bodied wine, sufficient tannins also contributing (not distracting). Screw cap. | 14% alc. | Drink 2022-2035 | $27 | JH

West Cape Howe Wines ★★★★★

Lot 14923 Muir Highway, Mount Barker, WA 6324 **T** (08) 9892 1444 **www**.westcapehowewines.com.au **OPEN** Mon-Fri 10-5, w'ends 11-4 **WINEMAKER** Gavin Berry, Caitlin Gazey **VITICULTURIST** Rob Quenby **EST.** 1997 **DOZENS** 60000 **VYDS** 310ha

West Cape Howe is owned by a partnership of 4 WA families, including those of Gavin Berry and Rob Quenby. Grapes are sourced from estate vineyards in Mount Barker and Frankland River. The Langton Vineyard (Mount Barker) has 100ha planted to cabernet sauvignon, shiraz, riesling, sauvignon blanc, chardonnay and semillon; the Russell Road Vineyard (Frankland

River) has 210ha. West Cape Howe also sources select parcels of fruit from valued contract growers. Best Value Winery Wine Companion 2016. (JH)

95   **Riesling 2021, Mount Barker** Ticks each and every box along the journey, starting with the quartz-green colour, then the flowery and fragrant aromas telling of the citrus-accented palate gathering drive as it explores lime and passionfruit. All throughout the line of acidity provides cohesion. Screw cap. | 12.5% alc. | Drink 2021-2032 | $22 | JH

94   **Sauvignon Blanc 2021, Mount Barker** First up are juicy tutti-frutti aromas, flavours and feel until the crisp finish. Screw cap. | 12.5% alc. | Drink 2021-2023 | $22 | JH

        Shiraz 2019, Frankland River A small portion finishes its ferment in new oak barriques; matured in new and used French oak. You have to wonder how any new-oak expenditure could be justified by the giveaway price. Unbeatable now or for later consumption, with its spicy black fruits and precise tannin control. Screw cap. | 14.5% alc. | Drink 2022-2037 | $22 | JH

Wignalls Wines ★★★☆

448 Chester Pass Road (Highway 1), Albany, WA 6330 **T** (08) 9841 2848 **www**.wignallswines.com.au **OPEN** Thurs-Mon 11-4 **WINEMAKER** Rob Wignall, Michael Perkins **EST.** 1982 **DOZENS** 7000 **VYDS** 18.5ha

Founder Bill Wignall was one of the early movers with pinot noir, producing wines that, by the standards of their time, were well in front of anything else coming out of WA. The establishment of an onsite winery and the assumption of the winemaking role by son Rob, with significant input from Michael Perkins, saw the quality and range of wines increase. (JH)

89   **Cabernet Merlot 2020, Great Southern** The difference that 30 minutes in the glass has made, tells us a lot about this wine. On opening, the oak presented a varnishy and metallic ring, which distracted from the display of fruit beneath. As it was the last on the bench, it had the chance to open up – and it needed it. Uncomplicated, bright fruit, perfectly in line with the pricepoint. The oak is still assertive, but it's manageable. Screw cap. | 14% alc. | Drink 2021-2028 | $19 | EL

REGION
Margaret River

Abbey Vale ★★★★☆

1071 Wildwood Road, Yallingup Hills, WA 6282 **T** (08) 9755 2121 **www**.abbeyvalewines.com.au **OPEN** Wed-Sun 10-5 **WINEMAKER** Ben Roodhouse, Julian Langworthy **EST.** 2016 **DOZENS** 2000 **VYDS** 17ha

Situated in the north of the Margaret River region, the Abbey Vale vineyards were established in '85 by the McKay family. The highest quality fruit comes from the original plantings of chardonnay, shiraz and cabernet sauvignon. The picturesque cellar door offers a range of local produce and artisan cheeses to accompany the wines, and overlooks a large dam that provides visitors with one of the most sublime views in the region. (JH)

94   **Premium RSV Chenin Blanc 2021, Margaret River** I've seen this wine a number of times and the acidity is truly a standout highlight – pithy and titillating. The fruit around it is purely apricots, apples, honeydew melon, spring blossoms and brine. Generally all-round delicious. Highly recommended. Yum. Screw cap. | 12.5% alc. | Drink 2021-2031 | $25 | EL

Amelia Park Wines ★★★★★

3857 Caves Road, Wilyabrup, WA 6280 **T** (08) 9755 6747 **www**.ameliaparkwines.com.au **OPEN** 7 days 10-5 **WINEMAKER** Jeremy Gordon **EST.** 2009 **DOZENS** 25000 **VYDS** 9.6ha

Jeremy Gordon's winemaking career started with Evans & Tate, and Houghton thereafter, before moving to the eastern states to broaden his experience. He eventually returned to Margaret River, and after several years founded Amelia Park Wines with his wife Daniela Gordon and business partner Peter Walsh. Amelia Park initially relied on contract-grown grapes, but in '13 purchased the Moss Brothers site in Wilyabrup, allowing the construction of a new winery and cellar door. (JH)

95   **Semillon Sauvignon Blanc 2021, Margaret River** A 60/40% blend. Citrus, lemon blossom and cut-grass aromas set the scene for the complex palate, with both texture and structure achieved without the use of oak. Impressive at any price, let alone this. Screw cap. | 12.5% alc. | Drink 2021-2025 | $23 | JH

        Shiraz 2020, Frankland River Vivid crimson purple. Vibrant black cherry, cracked pepper, multiple spice aromas and a tightly focused palate, with acidity driving its freshness. Oak and tannins are very much the junior partners. Screw cap. | 14.5% alc. | Drink 2023-2035 | $33 | JH

Ashbrook Estate  ★★★★☆

379 Tom Cullity Drive, Wilyabrup, WA 6280 **T** (08) 9755 6262 **WWW**.ashbrookwines.com.au **OPEN** 7 days 10-5 **WINEMAKER** Catherine Edwards, Brian Devitt **VITICULTURIST** Richard Devitt, Brian Devitt **EST.** 1975 **DOZENS** 12500 **VYDS** 17.4ha

This fastidious producer of consistently excellent estate-grown table wines shuns publicity and is less known than is deserved, selling much of its wine through the cellar door and to a loyal mailing list clientele. It is very much a family affair: Brian Devitt is at the helm, winemaking is by his daughter Catherine, and viticulture by son Richard who is also a qualified winemaker. (JH)

96 **Reserve Chardonnay 2018, Margaret River** Crushed salted pistachios and walnuts on the nose. This is creamy, satisfying, saline and layered with orchard fruit. In the mouth, the wine is complex, plump and deeply satisfying. Classically structured and totally beautiful. The collision of the 2 is surely the most fortuitous intersect possible, producing one of the greatest Ashbrook Reserve chardonnay in years. Screw cap. | 13.5% alc. | Drink 2022-2037 | $65 | EL

CENTRAL WA

Cape Mentelle ★★★★★

331 Wallcliffe Road, Margaret River, WA 6285 **T** (08) 9757 0888 **WWW**.capementelle.com.au **OPEN** 7 days 10-5 **WINEMAKER** Coralie Lewis **EST.** 1970 **DOZENS** 80000 **VYDS** 145ha

Part of the LVMH (Louis Vuitton Möet Hennessy) group. Cape Mentelle is firing on all cylinders, with the winemaking team fully capitalising on the extensive and largely mature vineyards, which obviate the need for contract-grown fruit. Sauvignon blanc semillon, chardonnay, shiraz and cabernet sauvignon lead the portfolio. (JH)

96 **Shiraz 2017, Margaret River** With 3/2% grenache/viognier. Sophisticated and detailed vinification has paid big dividends, from bunch thinning and hand picking through to the finished wine. Medium bodied, but richly textured, black and blue fruits, the oak positive but integrated, the tannins likewise. Margaret River shiraz has come of age. Screw cap. | 14.5% alc. | Drink 2022-2037 | $49 | JH

EASTERN PLAINS/ INLAND/NORTH

Clairault Streicker Wines ★★★★★

3277 Caves Road, Wilyabrup, WA 6280 **T** (08) 9755 6225 **WWW**.clairaultstreicker.com.au **OPEN** Wed-Sun 10-5 **WINEMAKER** Bruce Dukes **VITICULTURIST** Christopher Gillmore **EST.** 1976 **DOZENS** 12000 **VYDS** 113ha

This multifaceted business is owned by New York resident John Streicker. It began in '02 when he purchased the Yallingup Protea Farm and vineyards. This was followed by the purchase of the Ironstone Vineyard in '03 and then the Bridgeland Vineyard. The Ironstone Vineyard is one of the oldest vineyards in Wilyabrup. In Apr '12, Streicker acquired Clairault, bringing a further 40ha of estate vines, including 12ha now over 40 years old. The 2 brands are effectively run as one venture. (JH)

96 **Streicker Ironstone Block Chenin Blanc 2019, Margaret River** Green mango, apple skins, brine, lanolin and apricots. All classic chenin things. There is also capgun, flint, garden mint and elderflower. On the palate the phenolics really create a plump, pillowy shape in the mouth. The phenolics are absolutely countersunk into the fruit in a very sleek way, the spices are flinty and savoury, but in no way cloud the purity of the fruit. A wonderful, nuanced wine. Very long. Screw cap. | 12.5% alc. | Drink 2021-2036 | $28 | EL

GREATER PERTH

SOUTH-WEST AUSTRALIA

Credaro Family Estate ★★★★★

2175 Caves Road, Yallingup, WA 6282 **T** (08) 9756 6520 **WWW**.credarowines.com.au **OPEN** 7 days 10.30-5 **WINEMAKER** Trent Kelly, Paul Callaghan **VITICULTURIST** Chris Credaro **EST.** 1988 **DOZENS** 25000 **VYDS** 110ha

The Credaro family first settled in Margaret River in 1922, migrating from northern Italy. Initially a few small plots of vines were planted to provide the family with wine in the European tradition. The most recent vineyard acquisition was a 40ha property, with 18ha of vineyard, in Wilyabrup (now called the Summus Vineyard) and the winery has been expanded to 1200t with 300000L of additional tank space. Credaro now has 7 separate vineyards (150ha in production), spread throughout Margaret River. (JH)

97 **1000 Crowns Chardonnay 2020, Margaret River** Elegance takes the pulpit from the word go, and doesn't relinquish it. The fruit aromas are grapefruit, nectarine and white peach, braced by zesty acidity that drives the wine into the longest finish I've encountered for some time. Oak is merely a vehicle. Screw cap. | 12.5% alc. | Drink 2022-2038 | $75 | JH

SOUTH EAST COASTAL

Cullen Wines ⑨⑪⊖ ★★★★★

4323 Caves Road, Wilyabrup, WA 6280 **T** (08) 9755 5277 **WWW**.cullenwines.com.au **OPEN** 7 days 10-4.30 **WINEMAKER** Vanya Cullen, Andy Barrett-Lennard **VITICULTURIST** Vanya Cullen **EST**. 1971 **DOZENS** 20000 **VYDS** 49ha

A pioneer of Margaret River, Cullen Wines has always produced long-lived wines of highly individual style from the mature estate vineyard. The vineyard has progressed beyond organic to biodynamic certification and, subsequently, has become the first vineyard and winery in Australia to be certified carbon positive. Winemaking is in the hands of Vanya Cullen, daughter of founders Kevin and Diana Cullen. Vanya is a pioneer of biodynamic viticulture in Australia and was awarded the Companion's inaugural Viticulturist of the Year in 2022, Cullen's 50th anniversary year. (JH)

98 **Diana Madeline 2020, Margaret River** The perfumed bouquet has already soaked up the 13 months in 50% new oak, the purity of the fruit in a cassis-redcurrant-blueberry spectrum. The small berries of a quasi-drought summer might have imposed awkward tannins, but the medium-bodied palate is so perfectly balanced it has a drinking span of 30 years and counting. Screw cap. | 13% alc. | Drink 2025-2055 | $150 | JH | ♥

Kevin John 2020, Margaret River 2020 was a fast and short vintage with heartbreakingly low yields in Margaret River, yet it produced wines of effortless grace and poise. This is most certainly one of those. Like a rhythmic pulse of flavour in the mouth … steady, like a heartbeat. All elements are in harmony: fruit, acid, phenolics; they gently seesaw between each other, spooling out a seemingly never-ending trail of flavour. Breathtakingly beautiful, again. Screw cap. | 13.9% alc. | Drink 2021-2035 | $150 | EL | ♥

94 **Mangan Vineyard Sauvignon Blanc Semillon 2021, Margaret River** A blend of 59/35/6% sauvignon blanc/semillon/verdelho. The verdelho provides distinct chalky structure on the palate and through the finish, adding to the complexity of the wine. An interesting observation and lesson in the significance of the blend. This, like all the others, is very good. Screw cap. | 12.5% alc. | Drink 2021-2031 | $29 | EL

Deep Woods Estate ⑨ Best Value Winery 2023 ★★★★★

889 Commonage Road, Yallingup, WA 6282 **T** (08) 9756 6066 **WWW**.deepwoods.wine **OPEN** Mon, Wed-Sun 10-5 **WINEMAKER** Julian Langworthy, Emma Gillespie, Andrew Bretherton **VITICULTURIST** John Fogarty **EST**. 1987 **DOZENS** 50000 **VYDS** 14ha

Deep Woods Estate is a key part of the dynamic wine business of Peter Fogarty that includes Millbrook in the Perth Hills, Evans & Tate, Margaret River Vintners and extensive vineyard holdings in Wilyabrup and elsewhere in Margaret River, plus in Smithbrook in Pemberton. The Fogarty business is the largest producer in WA with 600000 dozen. Deep Woods is the Wine Companion 2023 Best Value Winery. (JH)

97 **Single Vineyard G5 Cabernet Sauvignon 2020, Margaret River** Rose petals, raspberry leaf tea, red snakes, Szechuan and pink peppercorns and red apple skins. This is gorgeous. Utterly, utterly beautiful. The fruit is ripe and rippling, the tannins poised and totally in cahoots, working together to spiral across the palate and fly through the finish. Arm in arm, they spool out flavour as they go, all of it caught in the web of fine, saline acidity. Screw cap. | 14% alc. | Drink 2022-2037 | $50 | EL

Reserve Chardonnay 2020, Margaret River To say the wine is elegant does it no justice. It's way more than that; line, length and balance likewise. This is a barrel-by-barrel selection from a large number, ex a specific vineyard source. White peach and pink grapefruit play off against each other, oak a means to an end. Screw cap. | 13% alc. | Drink 2022-2042 | $65 | JH

Reserve Cabernet Sauvignon 2019, Margaret River Deep, vivid crimson purple. Fascinating bouquet that has the bay leaf I often find on the back palate/finish of quality cabernet sauvignon; also cassis (no surprise) wrapped in a fine gauze of oak and pliable tannins. Line, length and balance are all attributes of a classic Margaret River cabernet. Screw cap. | 14% alc. | Drink 2024-2049 | $85 | JH

96 **Single Vineyard Cabernet Malbec 2020, Margaret River** This is a sensational wine, impossibly intense and saturated with flavour, and the volume is boosted in 2020. Decant it, because the frisky malbec needs the oxygen to calm it down. It'll live an age, though. Screw cap. | 14% alc. | Drink 2022-2037 | $50 | EL

Reserve Shiraz 2020, Margaret River This is as powerful as any of its breed, with the blackest of black fruits and tannins normally the confines of cabernet sauvignon, French oak lost in the wash. Screw cap. | 14% alc. | Drink 2030-2045 | $65 | JH

95 **Sauvignon Blanc 2021, Margaret River** Much richer – and more complex – than the vast majority, with the precision brought by the cool Karridale district in the far south of Margaret River, the busts of passionfruit and snow peas, and the smoky notes ex barrel ferment that all play hide and seek on the bouquet and palate alike. Impossible to beat the value offered here. Screw cap. | 13% alc. | Drink 2021-2023 | $20 | EL

94 **Hillside Cabernet Sauvignon 2020, Margaret River** Just $25, and you know it's going to be good. Fine, shapely, powdery tannins (slightly chewy, too) back up the concentrated ripe red and black

berry fruit. With a sprinkling of ground star anise, peppercorns and laced together with briny acidity, this is a cracking little wine. Super-smart. Screw cap. | 14% alc. | Drink 2021-2031 | $25 | EL

Shiraz et al 2020, Margaret River Vivid colour. $20 beggars belief. It's the real deal – a wine with layer upon layer of red and black fruits and serious tannins, and then given that time in French oak. Screw cap. | 14.5% alc. | Drink 2023-2033 | $20 | JH

Domaine Naturaliste ★★★★★

160 Johnson Road, Wilyabrup, WA 6280 **T** (08) 9755 6776 **www**.domainenaturaliste.com.au **OPEN** 7 days 10–5 **WINEMAKER** Bruce Dukes **EST.** 2012 **DOZENS** 12000 **VYDS** 21ha

Bruce Dukes is wholly talented, and while he makes high-quality acclaimed wines for his own estate – Domaine Naturaliste – he also does this for a raft of other, smaller producers in Margaret River and Geographe. His winemaking style is one of fresh, pure fruit over obvious or intrusive winemaking artifact, and the wines routinely possess a polish and eminent drinkability. (EL)

97   **Rebus Cabernet Sauvignon 2018, Margaret River** The bouquet is a fragrant mix of cassis, cedar, cigar box and bay leaf, the intense palate with a tapestry of flavours. Yet it has the lightest of tannin touches encouraging a quick return to the glass. Screw cap. | 14% alc. | Drink 2023-2038 | $36 | JH

    Morus Cabernet Sauvignon 2018, Margaret River This swings into action from the first whiff, with a cavalcade of dark berry fruits of all persuasions, the precisely delineated palate that follows with cassis, redcurrant, a sombre edge of earth and dried olive, joining mouth-watering tannins. Cork. | 14% alc. | Drink 2023-2043 | $89 | JH

96   **Sauvage Sauvignon Blanc 2020, Margaret River** A great white wine vintage. Bright straw green, barrel fermented in French puncheons (33% new), but that's not the only winemaking input, some enriching use of solids also in play. It's complex, with a lineage that will ensure the wine has a very healthy life ahead. Screw cap. | 13% alc. | Drink 2022-2025 | $33 | JH | ♥

94   **Discovery Syrah 2020, Margaret River** Pink berries and raspberry dust adorn the nose and palate. Typically spicy and plump, this is a cracking wine for the price, delivering both reliable satisfaction and something simply sexy. The fruit has a distinct Beaujolais character. Gorgeous. Screw cap. | 14% alc. | Drink 2021-2027 | $25 | EL

Driftwood Estate ★★★★★

3314 Caves Road, Wilyabrup, WA 6282 **T** (08) 9755 6323 **www**.driftwoodwines.com.au **OPEN** 7 days 11–4 **WINEMAKER** Kane Grove **EST.** 1989 **DOZENS** 18000 **VYDS** 22ha

Driftwood Estate is a well-established landmark on the Margaret River scene. Quite apart from offering a casual dining restaurant capable of seating 200 people and a mock Greek open-air theatre, its wines feature striking and stylish packaging and opulent flavours. Its wines are released in 4 ranges: Single Site, Artifacts, The Collection and Oceania. (JH)

97   **Single Site Chardonnay 2020, Margaret River** I have seen this wine, blind, 3 times in '21, and it is so firmly imprinted on my memory that I hardly needed to taste it again today, save but for the context it could bring to the surrounding wines. It is pure, fine, lingering and spicy. The fruit is woven into the very fabric of the wine, threaded in place by fine strands of briny acidity that is pronounced, but sings, rather than intrudes. The spicy, toasty oak holds it together and is perfectly matched to the fruit. Succulent and streamlined. Several previous vintages have been as impressive. Get on board. Screw cap. | 13% alc. | Drink 2022-2037 | $70 | EL

95   **Artifacts Meritage 2020, Margaret River** 41/36/20/3% petit verdot/malbec/cabernet sauvignon/ other. Delicious, in a word. There is plentiful tannin – fine, soft and shapely – and loads of fresh fruit: blackberries, raspberries, pomegranate, blood plums and red apples; with spice and additional flavours galore (dark chocolate, nutmeg, star anise, a strap or 2 of red licorice, fresh tobacco leaves and fennel). This is very good. Screw cap. | 14% alc. | Drink 2022-2032 | $35 | EL

Evans & Tate ★★★★★

Cnr Metricup Road/Caves Road, Wilyabrup, WA 6280 **T** (08) 9755 6244 **www**.evansandtate.wine **OPEN** By appt **WINEMAKER** Matthew Byrne, Feleasha Prendergast **EST.** 1970 **VYDS** 12.3ha

The history of Evans & Tate has a distinct wild-west feel to its ownership changes since 1970, when it started life as a small 2-family-owned business centred on the Swan District. Suffice it to say, it was part of a corporate chess game between McWilliam's Wines and the Fogarty Wine Group. It is now 100% owned by Fogarty, who previously held 70%. (JH)

96   **Redbrook Reserve Cabernet Sauvignon 2018, Margaret River** Potently intense fruit here – the wine enters the mouth with fanfare and pomp; the fruit that gathers here is riddled with cassis, raspberry leaf, black tea, pepper, exotic spice and more. Classical cabernet from Margaret River, from a great vintage. Exactly what we have come to expect from the Redbrook Reserve range. Screw cap. | 14.5% alc. | Drink 2022-2037 | $65 | EL

Evoi Wines

529 Osmington Road, Bramley, WA 6285 **T** 0437 905 100 **www**.evoiwines.com **OPEN** 7 days 10-5
WINEMAKER Nigel Ludlow **EST**. 2006 **DOZENS** 10000

NZ-born Nigel Ludlow has a graduate diploma in oenology and viticulture from Lincoln University, NZ. It took time for Evoi to take shape, the first vintage of chardonnay being made in the lounge room of Nigel's house. By 2010 the barrels had been evicted to more conventional storage and since '14 the wines have been made in leased space at a commercial winery. (JH)

95   **Chardonnay 2019, Margaret River** Trying to unpick the characters in this wine is no simple thing. The concentration of flavour is impressive; this tells a story of curry leaf, white peach, brine, hazelnuts and exotic white spice. The palate has all of these, with the addition of dragon fruit, pink grapefruit, sourdough and crushed-shell minerality woven through the very (very) long finish. Astounding wine for the money. Ridiculous, in fact.   Screw cap. | 13.5% alc. | Drink 2020-2035 | $32 | EL

Fermoy Estate

838 Metricup Road, Wilyabrup, WA 6280 **T** (08) 9755 6285 **www**.fermoy.com.au **OPEN** 7 days 11-5
WINEMAKER Jeremy Hodgson **VITICULTURIST** Andrew Keig **EST**. 1985 **DOZENS** 25000 **VYDS** 27.28ha

The Young family acquired Fermoy Estate in '10 and built a larger cellar door which opened in '13, signalling the drive to increase domestic sales. Jeremy Hodgson brings with him a first-class honours degree in oenology and viticulture, and a CV encompassing winemaking roles with Wise Wines, Cherubino Consultancy and, earlier, Plantagenet, Houghton and Goundrey Wines. (JH)

96   **Reserve Chardonnay 2020, Margaret River** Of all the Fermoy wines, the Reserve Chardonnay was the wine I was holding out to see. My memory of previous vintages is of acidity so finely woven into the fruit that the affair becomes succulent and juicy … chewy and satisfying. It brings a smile to the face. As this does. Concentrated, classical, a little bit creamy, a little bit nutty, definitely spicy and voluminous in its powerful fruit explosion in the mouth. It won't always be just $65, though we can hope it will.   Screw cap. | 13.5% alc. | Drink 2022-2037 | $65 | EL

95   **Coldfire Fumé Blanc 2021, Margaret River** The 50% skin-contact component is really clear here and it is glorious. There is orange zest, soft orange blossom, nougat, cardamom, cumin, brine, white peach, turmeric, toasty oak and poached apples and rhubarb. 'Clementine, lavender, kernel' says the back of the bottle: apt. This is ethereal and fully integrated … totally awesome. Brilliant.   Screw cap. | 13% alc. | Drink 2022-2028 | $30 | EL

94   **Cabernet Sauvignon Merlot 2019, Margaret River** If Fermoy isn't edging onto your radar, you need to perk up. The wines have refreshed packaging, which reiterates the value found inside the bottles. This is very smart. Succulent, pure fruit is shaped by fine, chalky tannins that help the flavour sail over the palate and off into the distance. Really impressive for the price, it looks the part too.   Screw cap. | 14.5% alc. | Drink 2021-2031 | $27 | EL

Flametree

Cnr Caves Road/Chain Avenue, Dunsborough, WA 6281 **T** (08) 9756 8577 **www**.flametreewines.com
OPEN 7 days 10-5 **WINEMAKER** Cliff Royle, Julian Scott **EST**. 2007 **DOZENS** 20

Flametree, owned by the Towner family (John, Liz, Rob and Annie), has had extraordinary success since its first vintage in 2007. The usual practice of planting a vineyard and then finding someone to make the wine was turned on its head: a state-of-the-art winery was built, and grape purchase agreements signed with growers in the region. Show success was topped by the winning of the Jimmy Watson Trophy with its '07 Cabernet Merlot. If all this were not enough, Flametree has secured the services of winemaker Cliff Royle. (JH)

96   **S.R.S. Wallcliffe Chardonnay 2020, Margaret River** As usual, this is an absolute mouthful of saline acid, powerful peachy fruit and a whole lot of oak/spice and funk. Delish. The '20 vintage was big (in terms of flavour, not yields) and this is clearly evident in the glass; marzipan, crushed nuts and a little bit of nougat in the background. The vintage suits the style, making this an exceptional iteration of S.R.S. Chardonnay. It will keep – the acid and the fruit say so – but it is so delicious now, the question is, why would you wait?   Screw cap. | 13.3% alc. | Drink 2021-2031 | $65 | EL

Flowstone Wines ★★★★★

11298 Bussell Highway, Forest Grove, WA 6286 **T** 0487 010 275 **www**.flowstonewines.com **OPEN** By appt
WINEMAKER Stuart Pym **VITICULTURIST** Stuart Pym **EST**. 2013 **DOZENS** 1500 **VYDS** 3ha

CENTRAL WA

EASTERN PLAINS/
INLAND/NORTH

GREATER PERTH

SOUTH-WEST
AUSTRALIA

SOUTH EAST
COASTAL

Veteran Margaret River winemaker Stuart Pym's career constituted long-term successive roles: beginning with Voyager Estate in '91, thereafter with Devil's Lair, and finishing with Stella Bella in '13, the year he and Perth-based wine tragic Phil Giglia established Flowstone Wines. In '03 Stuart purchased a small property on the edge of the Margaret River Plateau in the beautiful Forest Grove area. From '17, Flowstone leased a vineyard at Karridale, planted to long-established sauvignon blanc and chardonnay. The lease puts the vineyard on par with the estate plantings; the best fruit is retained, the balance sold. (JH)

| 96 | **Queen of the Earth Sauvignon Blanc 2020, Margaret River** Halliday Wine Companion Sauvignon Blanc of the Year 2023. Intense, sweaty, concentrated ... this is a rippling pool of flavour. The oak impact is significant (as usual), meaning it is built to last. So: here we have quenching wine, stuffed to the gills with salted pineapple, crunchy, ripe Granny Smith apples, saline acidity ... and lots of other good green things. Delicious. Screw cap. | 12.8% alc. | Drink 2022-2037 | $55 | EL | ♥ |

| 95 | **Moonmilk Shiraz Grenache 2020, Margaret River** With 3% viognier. A delicious fresh and juicy blend of red cherry and raspberry fruit on the bouquet, the palate adding feathery tannins on the lingering finish. Screw cap. | 14% alc. | Drink 2021-2028 | $25 | JH |

Sauvignon Blanc 2020, Margaret River The '20 vintage will be remembered for wines of grace, power and effortlessness. Stuart Pym at Flowstone makes sauvignon blanc of concentration, liquidity (the silky, mellifluous mouthfeel of the wines), poise and intensity. This is all of that and more. Made in tiny quantities, and sold for far less than they should be. Don't tell Pym we said that. Screw cap. | 13% alc. | Drink 2021-2030 | $32 | EL

| 94 | **Moonmilk White 2021, Margaret River** Viognier, pinot gris, gewürztraminer, sauvignon blanc. Turkish dried apricots, crushed pistachios, rose petals, red apple skins and lashings of fine white spice. This is saline, silky and succulent verging on opulent; all the while, desperately interesting. Another sensational Moonmilk release, although at $22, one wonders how Stuart Pym can afford to feed his dogs. Screw cap. | 12% alc. | Drink 2022-2026 | $22 | EL |

Forester Estate ★★★★

1064 Wildwood Road, Yallingup, WA 6282 **T** (08) 9755 2000 **www**.foresterestate.com.au **OPEN** By appt **WINEMAKER** Kevin McKay, Todd Payne **EST.** 2001 **DOZENS** 52000 **VYDS** 33.5ha

Forester Estate is owned by Kevin and Jenny McKay. Winemaker Todd Payne has had a distinguished career, starting in the Great Southern, thereafter the Napa Valley, back to Plantagenet, then Esk Valley in Hawke's Bay, plus 2 vintages in the Northern Rhône Valley, one with esteemed producer Yves Cuilleron in '08. His move back to WA completed the circle. The tasting room is housed in a French Renaissance-style castle, built in 2007. (JH)

| 93 | **Lifestyle Cabernet Sauvignon 2020, Margaret River** Another beautiful, approachable and ready-now release from the Lifestyle range. Plump, supple and moving to floral, with fine structure and decent length. There's a little hint of crushed ant and gravel/ferrous on the nose that elevates the drinking experience here. Unmissable at the price. Screw cap. | 13.5% alc. | Drink 2021-2028 | $25 | EL |

Lifestyle Shiraz 2019, Margaret River Vibrant, spicy, juicy and delicious. Uncomplicated drinking here, all things kept in check, the fruit riding out in front. Screw cap. | 13.7% alc. | Drink 2021-2031 | $25 | EL

| 92 | **Lifestyle Cabernet Merlot 2019, Margaret River** A super-pretty, plump, floral, uncomplicated cabernet with a fine smudge of chalky tannins through the finish. Very, very lovely. Screw cap. | 13.4% alc. | Drink 2021-2027 | $25 | EL |

Fraser Gallop Estate ★★★★★

493 Metricup Road, Wilyabrup, WA 6280 **T** (08) 9755 7553 **www**.frasergallopestate.com.au **OPEN** 7 days 11-4 **WINEMAKER** Clive Otto, Ellin Tritt **VITICULTURIST** Mike Bolas **EST.** 1999 **DOZENS** 10000 **VYDS** 20ha

Nigel Gallop began the development of the vineyard in 1999, planting what is now just over 20ha of cabernet sauvignon and chardonnay (6.8ha each) as well as semillon, petit verdot, cabernet franc, malbec, merlot and sauvignon blanc. The wines have been made by Clive Otto since '07, and in that time have amassed an impressive array of domestic and international acclaim. (EL)

| 97 | **Palladian Chardonnay 2020, Margaret River** We must all follow different houses for their different styles. Here, Fraser Gallop's chardonnay style is on show: lower alcohol, pristine, crystalline fruit, shaped by fine saline acid and curving in a quartz-like, delicate manner through the finish. This '20 Palladian is the best, finest, most magical, most alluring Palladian release I have ever tried. It is off the charts. Screw cap. | 12.5% alc. | Drink 2022-2037 | $140 | EL |

| 96 | **Parterre Cabernet Sauvignon 2019, Margaret River** Houghton clone in Wilyabrup expresses itself as supple, succulent, red fruited and powerful; it imbues the wines with grace and ease. So too, this release. This has all these attributes, layers of pomegranate, raspberry, red licorice, saltbush, cassis and peppercorn. A beautiful wine, with a proven track record for graceful ageing. This vintage will be no exception. Screw cap. | 14% alc. | Drink 2021-2036 | $50 | EL |

Hamelin Bay ★★★★

McDonald Road, Karridale, WA 6288 **T** 0417 954168 **WWW.**hbwines.com.au **OPEN** 7 days 10.30–4.30
WINEMAKER Richard Drake-Brockman **EST.** 1992 **DOZENS** 5000 **VYDS** 23.5ha

The Hamelin Bay vineyard was established by the Drake-Brockman family, pioneers of the region. Richard Drake-Brockman's great-grandmother, Grace Bussell, was famous for her courage when, in 1876, aged 16, she rescued survivors of a shipwreck not far from the mouth of the Margaret River. Richard's great-grandfather Frederick, known for his exploration of the Kimberley, read about the feat in Perth's press and rode 300km on horseback to meet her – they married in 1882. Hamelin Bay's vineyard and winery is located within a few kilometres of Karridale, at the intersection of the Brockman and Bussell Highways, which were named in honour of these pioneering families. (JH)

94   **Five Ashes Vineyard Sauvignon Blanc 2021, Margaret River** Sandalwood, saffron curls, hints of lychee, nashi pear and jasmine florals. Pretty, bright and fresh, with saline acidity that whirls through the mouth. Lovely, delicate, oyster shell wine. Persistent, lingering finish. A beautiful wine. Classy. Screw cap. | 12.5% alc. | Drink 2021-2023 | $26 | EL

Happs ★★★★

575 Commonage Road, Dunsborough, WA 6281 **T** (08) 9755 3300 **WWW.**happs.com.au **OPEN** 7 days 10–5
WINEMAKER Erl Happ, Mark Warren **EST.** 1978 **DOZENS** 15000 **VYDS** 35.2ha

One-time schoolteacher, potter and winemaker Erl Happ is the patriarch of a 3-generation family. More than anything, Erl has been a creator and experimenter: building the self-designed winery from mudbrick, concrete form and timber; and making the first crusher. In '94 he planted a new 30ha vineyard at Karridale to no less than 28 varieties. The Three Hills label is made from varieties grown at this vineyard. (JH)

94   **Sauvignon Blanc Semillon 2020, Margaret River** Super-pretty talcy fruit laid out on a smorgasbord of cassis, red apples, juniper, musk sticks, lemon flesh, lime zest and slices of pink grapefruit. Loads of flavour. Spot on texturally, too. Very smart. Screw cap. | 13.4% alc. | Drink 2021-2025 | $24 | EL

Hay Shed Hill Wines ★★★★★

511 Harmans Mill Road, Wilyabrup, WA 6280 **T** (08) 9755 6046 **WWW.**hayshedhill.com.au **OPEN** 7 days 10–5 **WINEMAKER** Michael Kerrigan **EST.** 1987 **DOZENS** 24000 **VYDS** 18.55ha

Mike Kerrigan, former winemaker at Howard Park, acquired Hay Shed Hill in late 2006 (with co-ownership with the West Cape Howe syndicate) and is now the full-time winemaker. He had every confidence that he could dramatically lift the quality of the wines and has done precisely that. The estate-grown wines are made under the Vineyard and Block series. The KP Wines label is a collaboration between Michael and his daughter Katie Priscilla Kerrigan. (JH)

95   **Tempranillo 2020, Margaret River** Dr John Gladstones long ago – before much was grown in Australia – placed tempranillo alongside pinot noir as an early ripening variety. Deep crimson purple, it is only medium bodied but has exceptional texture and structure, its red (cherry) and blue fruits coalescing with a fine tannin mesh. Screw cap. | 14% alc. | Drink 2022-2037 | $30 | JH

94   **Block 1 Semillon Sauvignon Blanc 2020, Margaret River** From some of the oldest semillon and sauvignon blanc vines in the Margaret River, and involves some barrel ferment that increases complexity, depth and length. Moves it into a place all of its own. Screw cap. | 12% alc. | Drink 2022-2026 | $30 | JH

Higher Plane ⑨ ★★★★☆

98 Tom Cullity Drive, Cowaramup, WA 6284 **T** (08) 9755 9000 **WWW.**higherplanewines.com.au **OPEN** 7 days 10–5 **WINEMAKER** Mark Messenger, Luc Fitzgerald **VITICULTURIST** Ianto Ward **EST.** 1996 **DOZENS** 3000 **VYDS** 14.52ha

Higher Plane was purchased by Roger Hill and Gillian Anderson, owners of Juniper Estate, in 2006. The brand was retained with the intention of maintaining the unique and special aspects of the site in the south of Margaret River distinct from those of Wilyabrup in the north. The close-planted vineyard is sustainably farmed using organic principles. Sons Nick and Tom (with winemaking experience in the Yarra Valley) run the business. (JH)

95 **Cabernet Malbec 2020, Margaret River** The '20 vintage was beautiful: ripe and graceful, glossy and polished. This wine is perfectly that; the combination of cabernet and malbec is the way of the future, surely. Both pure and structured – beautiful. There is enough licorice, ferrous, kelp, raspberry and cassis to balance the seesaw ... the fulcrum, brine. It's really good. Screw cap. | 14% alc. | Drink 2021-2031 | $28 | EL

94 **Fiano 2021, Margaret River** Comes through strongly with that illusion of oak on the bouquet, then a super-fresh palate with great energy and drive in a citrus skin, zest and juice theme. Screw cap. | 13.5% alc. | Drink 2022-2026 | $28 | JH

Howard Park ⓞⓐ ★★★★★

Miamup Road, Cowaramup, WA 6284 **T** (08) 9756 5200 **www**.burchfamilywines.com.au **OPEN** 7 days 10-5 **WINEMAKER** Nic Bowen, Mark Bailey **VITICULTURIST** David Botting, Steve Kirby **EST.** 1986 **VYDS** 183ha

Over the last 30 years, the Burch family has slowly acquired vineyards in Margaret River and Great Southern. The Margaret River vineyards range from Leston in Wilyabrup to Allingham in southern Karridale; Great Southern includes Mount Barrow and Abercrombie, with Houghton cabernet clones, planted in 1975, all in Mount Barker. At the top of the portfolio are the Howard Park Abercrombie Cabernet Sauvignon and the Allingham Chardonnay, followed by the rieslings, chardonnay and sauvignon blanc. The Miamup and the Flint Rock regional ranges were established in 2012. A founding member of Australian First Families of Wines. (JH)

95 **Sauvignon Blanc 2021, Western Australia** Complex, concentrated and utterly delicious. This is balanced and poised and so wonderful. The acidity is plump and juicy – like ripe lemons, or lime flesh. All things in place, backed by texture that can only come from a bit of barrel ferment, drawing out over a long finish. My word – what a wine. Screw cap. | 12.5% alc. | Drink 2021-2031 | $31 | EL

Jilyara ⓞ ★★★★★

2 Heath Road, Wilyabrup, WA 6280 **T** (08) 9755 6575 **www**.jilyara.com.au **OPEN** By appt **WINEMAKER** Kate Morgan, Laura Bowler **VITICULTURIST** Craig Cotterell **EST.** 2017 **DOZENS** 4000 **VYDS** 10ha

Craig Cotterell and Maria Bergstrom planted the 9.7ha Jilyara Vineyard in '95. Until '17 the crop was sold to other producers in the region, but the game changed that year. There are 3 tiers: at the top The Williams' Block duo of Chardonnay and Cabernet Sauvignon (incorporating small amounts of malbec and petit verdot); next comes the Heath Road banner with Chardonnay, Malbec and Cabernet Sauvignon; the last group is Honeycomb Corner with a Sauvignon Blanc and Cabernet Sauvignon. (JH)

96 **The Williams' Block Cabernet Sauvignon 2020, Margaret River** The '20 vintage was warm and short, producing red wines of lush fruit and firm tannins. Here, the fruit is almost spilling from the glass, such is the opulence and concentration of characters: red currants, pomegranates, blackberries and raspberries. The oak has a sweet biscuity flavour – Malt-O-Milk, or oatmeal or something similar – and the tannins are supremely awesome: chewy, dense, pliable, like cocoa and almost whippy. Epic wine. Really smart. Screw cap. | 14.5% alc. | Drink 2022-2042 | $75 | EL

95 **Heath Road Chardonnay 2021, Margaret River** This is surprisingly nutty, in a really great way. It's cashews, it's pine nuts, it's toasty sweet vanillin oak ... This is saline and slinky; the fruit, although present, is very much secondary to the work and it drinks beautifully for it. Creamy and sophisticated. Screw cap. | 12% alc. | Drink 2022-2032 | $35 | EL

Juniper ⓞ ★★★★★

98 Tom Cullity Drive, Cowaramup, WA 6284 **T** (08) 9755 9000 **www**.juniperestate.com.au **OPEN** 7 days 10-5 **WINEMAKER** Mark Messenger, Luc Fitzgerald **VITICULTURIST** Ianto Ward **EST.** 1973 **DOZENS** 12000 **VYDS** 19.5ha

Roger Hill and Gillian Anderson purchased the Wrights' Wilyabrup property in 1998, driven by the 25yo vineyard with dry-grown cabernet as the jewel in the crown. They also purchased complementary vineyards in Forest Grove (Higher Plane) and Wilyabrup; the vineyards are sustainably farmed using organic principles. Sons Nick and Tom (formerly a winemaker in the Yarra Valley) are now running the business. The Juniper Crossing and Small Batch wines are sourced from the 3 vineyards, while the Single Vineyard releases are made only from the original vineyard on Tom Cullity Drive. (JH)

90 **Crossing Original Red 2020, Margaret River** 80/10/4/3/3% cabernet sauvignon/merlot/cabernet franc/malbec/petit verdot. For a little cheapie – this packs a punch. Perfectly Margaret River, uncomplicated in its expression, and coloured by a bevy of bright fruits. Compelling! Screw cap. | 14% alc. | Drink 2021-2026 | $18 | EL

L.A.S. Vino Dark Horse 2023 ★★★★★

PO Box 361 Cowaramup, WA 6284 **T** www.lasvino.com **WINEMAKER** Nic Peterkin **EST.** 2013 **DOZENS** 800

Owner Nic Peterkin is the grandson of the late Diana Cullen (Cullen Wines) and the son of Mike Peterkin (Pierro). After graduating from the University of Adelaide with a master's degree in oenology and travelling the world as a Flying Winemaker, he came back to roost in Margaret River with the ambition of making wines that are a little bit different, but also within the bounds of conventional oenological science. Achieving 5 stars for the first time this edition, L.A.S. Vino wins the Wine Companion 2023 Dark Horse Award. (JH)

97 **Wildberry Springs Chardonnay 2020, Margaret River** Fresh curry leaf, white peach, crushed cashew, flat leaf parsley, red apple skins, a whack of pink grapefruit and layers of orchard flowers, gum leaf and licorice. What a cracking wine this is. A kaleidescopic array of fruit, a flinty, wild kind of countenance, and a long, sinuous line of flavour that gives a little 'come hither' at the final turn. Screw cap. | 14% alc. | Drink 2021-2036 | $75 | EL

96 **CBDB Chenin Blanc Dynamic Blend 2020, Margaret River** Taut, textural, tense and almost nervy, the classic waxiness of chenin emerges only on the mid palate and beyond. This speaks of Geraldton wax flower, lanolin, brine, green apples, cheesecloth, a touch of lantana and a sprinkle of grapefruit zest. Long, modern and exciting, it shows chenin in a new light, quite different from the greats of the Loire, but no less profound. Diam. | 14% alc. | Drink 2021-2036 | $50 | EL | ♥

Leeuwin Estate (?)(♯)(♫) ★★★★★

Stevens Road, Margaret River, WA 6285 **T** (08) 9759 0000 **www.**leeuwinestate.com.au **OPEN** 7 days 10-5 **WINEMAKER** Tim Lovett, Phil Hutchison, Breac Wheatley **VITICULTURIST** David Winstanley **EST.** 1974 **DOZENS** 50000 **VYDS** 160ha

This outstanding winery and vineyard is owned by the Horgan family, founded by Denis and Tricia, who continue their involvement, with son Justin Horgan and daughter Simone Furlong joint chief executives. The Art Series Chardonnay is, in my (James') opinion, Australia's finest example based on the wines of the last 30 vintages. The move to screw cap brought a large smile to the faces of those who understand just how superbly the wine ages. (JH)

98 **Art Series Chardonnay 2019, Margaret River** Leeuwin Art Series Chardonnay on release is an achingly painful thing to drink, because once you've known the utter pleasure these wines bring at 5 or more years of age, it becomes a mess of cognitive dissonance to drink them so young. So, all I can humbly do here, is place the vintage in context. Through the lens of the cool year, this glitters with a purity and finesse that is deeply attractive. Aligned in style with the '17. Screw cap. | 13.5% alc. | Drink 2022-2042 | $138 | EL

97 **Art Series Cabernet Sauvignon 2018, Margaret River** This was a freak vintage in the hands of many winemakers in WA, capable of power, balance, ripeness and glory. This has pomegranate, red licorice and peppered raspberry. The fruit flavours, while slinky and seductive, are not the major player here. And that is saying something. The key to the brilliance of this wine, like the '14, the '10 and to some extent the '05 before it, is the texture. The tannins. They are tightly woven, very fine and serve to support the fruit and the acid. This wine is built on a stable scaffold of tannin that both cushions the experience and defines it. What a wine. Screw cap. | 13.5% alc. | Drink 2022-2042 | $79 | EL

96 **Prelude Vineyards Chardonnay 2020, Margaret River** A second label for a wine of great distinction, and its usual sourcing of fruit from estate and contract-grown vines: purity, intensity and extreme length. Grapefruit speaks louder about the boys in the band. I suppose oak has played some part in shaping the wine, but it isn't obvious. Screw cap. | 13.5% alc. | Drink 2025-2040 | $38 | JH

95 **Prelude Vineyards Cabernet Sauvignon 2019, Margaret River** With 2% malbec. Cabernet and malbec are meant to be together. This is vibrant and intense, layered with cassis and pomegranate, licorice, clove, graphite and nori. The layers are sewn together with threads of saline acidity that create structure within the shape provided by the oak. All things in place here — yet another compelling Prelude release from the team at Leeuwin. Unbelievable value for money. Screw cap. | 13.5% alc. | Drink 2021-2036 | $32 | EL

MadFish Wines (?) ★★★☆

137 Fifty One Road, Cowaramup, WA 6284 **T** 08 9756 5200 **www.**madfishwines.com.au **OPEN** 7 days 10-5 **WINEMAKER** Nic Bowen **VITICULTURIST** Dave Botting **EST.** 1992

Named after a renowned bay in the Great Southern (near Denmark), MadFish was established in 1992 by Howard Park as a standalone brand with a focus on making expressive, affordable, drink-now wines. In its 30 years history it has grown to become a widely recognised and exported wine brand. In '07, Gold Turtle was established, projected as a regional (GI specific) tier of wines exclusively for Endeavour Drinks. In the past few years both Gold Turtle and MadFish have expanded to include sparkling wines. (EL)

91 **Gold Turtle Shiraz 2020, Margaret River** Maraschino cherry, blood plums, raspberries and pomegranate make up the core of this vibrant, fresh, delicious and uncomplicated wine. There is an impressive core of fruit that is quite moreish. Screw cap. | 14.5% alc. | Drink 2021-2027 | $22 | EL

Marq Wines ⓘ ★★★★☆

860 Commonage Road, Dunsborough, WA 6281 **T** (08) 9756 6227 **www**.marqwines.com.au **OPEN** Fri-Sun & public hols 10-5, Mon 10-4 **WINEMAKER** Mark Warren **EST.** 2011 **DOZENS** 2500 **VYDS** 1.5ha

Mark Warren has a degree in wine science from CSU and a science degree from the University of WA; to complete the circle, he is currently lecturing in wine science and wine sensory processes at Curtin University, Margaret River. He is responsible for 60 to 70 individual wines each year, now including wines under his own Marq Wines label. A quick look at the list – Vermentino, Fiano, Wild & Worked Sauvignon Blanc Semillon, Wild Ferment Chardonnay, Rose, Gamay, Tempranillo, Malbec, and Cut & Dry Shiraz (Amarone style) – points to the underlying philosophy: an exploration of the potential of alternative varieties and unusual winemaking methods. (JH)

94 **Cabernet Franq 2020, Margaret River** Pretty, spicy, leafy, plump and delicious cabernet franc. I could smell it all day long. Hard to fathom how this rolls out at just $25, but whatever it is – massive fan. Mark Warren manages a little crunch and grit in the tannins, alongside leafy, varietal fruit – all of it wrapped in a spicy blanket. Lots to like here. Screw cap. | 13.9% alc. | Drink 2021-2030 | $25 | EL

McHenry Hohnen Vintners ⓘ ★★★★★

10406 Bussell Hwy, Witchcliffe, WA 6286 **T** (08) 9757 9600 **www**.mchenryhohnen.com.au **OPEN** 7 days 10.30-4.30 **WINEMAKER** Jacopo Dalli Cani, Henry Wynn **VITICULTURIST** Mike Sleegers **EST.** 2004 **DOZENS** 7500 **VYDS** 50ha

The McHenry and Hohnen families have a long history of grapegrowing and winemaking in Margaret River. They joined forces in 2004 to create McHenry Hohnen with the aim of producing wines honest to region, site and variety. Vines have been established on the McHenry, Calgardup Brook and Rocky Road properties, all farmed biodynamically. (JH)

97 **Calgardup Brook Vineyard Chardonnay 2020, Margaret River** All single-vineyard chardonnays are made in the same way here, highlighting the differences in terroir. Where the Burnside is granitic, mineral and fine, this is pithy, saline and expansive, with layers of cheesecloth and lanolin among the ripe stone fruit. More volume and density of flavour than the Burnside (neither here nor there qualitatively, simply an observation), this is sensational. Utterly. Screw cap. | 13.5% alc. | Drink 2022-2037 | $65 | EL

Hazel's Vineyard Chardonnay 2020, Margaret River OK, context: I've tasted this wine blind in pretty esteemed company (several times), the likes of Bâtard-Montrachet, Chevalier-Montrachet, Genevrières etc, and while it has come just under those wines in ranking, it is more than stood its ground, and has earned my unwavering respect in doing so. Powerful, layered, fragrant, balanced, rippling and exciting. Back up the car – this is too cheap currently. Screw cap. | 13.7% alc. | Drink 2022-2037 | $65 | EL

Hazel's Vineyard Cabernet Sauvignon 2019, Margaret River In recent global blind tastings, the McHenry Hohnen Hazel's Vineyard Chardonnay and Cabernet have both come in the top 5 on my page, among eye-watering company: Château Lafite, Château Léoville Poyferré, Chevalier-Montrachet, Les Genevrières and others. The price, when you consider the ability to stand up alongside these wines is equal to but a penny, tuppence ... graphite, cassis, mulberry, briny acidity and layers of exotic spice. Screw cap. | 14% alc. | Drink 2022-2038 | $70 | EL

Rolling Stone 2018, Margaret River 78/16/3/3% cabernet sauvignon/malbec/merlot/petit verdot. This is closed, restrained and cooling, with layers of graphite tannins and salty mineral acidity ... the fruit is supple and elegant, defined wholly by blackberries, mulberries and raspberry coulis. This has eons left in the tank. It would be impatient of you to drink it earlier than '25 (we would forgive you if you did though, because it is already delicious). Screw cap. | 14.4% alc. | Drink 2022-2042 | $135 | EL

96 **Laterite Hills Chardonnay 2020, Margaret River** Wowsers. This is super-serious. Unbelievable value for money: scintillating citrus acid line, concentrated, mouth-staining fruit and complex layers of crushed nuts, creamy tannins ... all wrapped into a long and reverberating tail of flavour. $42: speechless. Screw cap. | 13.7% alc. | Drink 2021-2036 | $42 | EL

Burnside Vineyard Chardonnay 2020, Margaret River Mineral, crunchy acidity frames lush stone-fruit characters, both aromatically and in the mouth. This is svelte, classy and spicy, with a granitic backbone of acid structure. If you like this wine today, you'll be staggered (no hyperbole here) by it in several years' time. Buy them all by the boot load – they only get better. Screw cap. | 13.5% alc. | Drink 2022-2037 | $65 | EL

Miles from Nowhere ★★★★

PO Box 128, Burswood, WA 6100 **T** (08) 9264 7800 **www**.milesfromnowhere.com.au **WINEMAKER** Frederique Perrin, Gary Stokes **EST.** 2007 **DOZENS** 20000 **VYDS** 46.9ha

Miles from Nowhere is one of the 2 wineries owned by Franklin and Heather Tate. Franklin returned to Margaret River in 2007 after working with his parents establishing Evans & Tate from '87 to '05. The Miles from Nowhere name comes from the journey Franklin's ancestors made over 100 years ago from Eastern Europe to Australia: upon their arrival, they felt they had travelled 'miles from nowhere'. (JH)

92 **Best Blocks Cabernet Sauvignon 2019, Margaret River** Salted licorice and aniseed lace the blackberry fruit. The wine is soft and plump, the oak creates frame and shape around it in the mouth. There's a gravelly, ferrous character through the finish which elevates the experience. Screw cap. | 14.5% alc. | Drink 2021-2028 | $25 | EL

Moss Wood ★★★★★

926 Metricup Road, Wilyabrup, WA 6284 **T** (08) 9755 6266 **www**.mosswood.com.au **OPEN** By appt **WINEMAKER** Clare Mugford, Keith Mugford **EST.** 1969 **DOZENS** 11000 **VYDS** 18.14ha

Widely regarded as one of the best wineries in the region, producing glorious chardonnay, power-laden semillon and elegant cabernet sauvignon that lives for decades. Moss Wood also owns RibbonVale Estate, the wines treated as vineyard-designated within the Moss Wood umbrella. (JH)

97 **Chardonnay 2020, Margaret River** Last year I commented on the 2019 vintage, that it was 'an opulent, luxurious style of chardonnay ... tempered by the cool season'. Be careful what you wish for. Here, through the lens of the warm and ripe '20 vintage, a wine of unbridled, sybaritic luxury is revealed. It has rivulets of flavour tucked in at every possible place, and effortlessly displays the full spectrum of brine, toffee apples, yellow peach, apple skins, some curry leaves and plush, juicy acid. Don't hold it back, and don't wish for the restraint of a cool year – this wine needs to be itself, to be its best. Screw cap. | 14% alc. | Drink 2022-2037 | $93 | EL

96 **Ribbon Vale Cabernet Sauvignon 2019, Margaret River** The '18 Ribbon Vale Cabernet Sauvignon almost had me falling off my chair it was so good. This is no different. Like the '18, it is silky, sumptuous and very fine: red fruited, floral, spicy and shaped by fine, chalky tannins. It is a superstar, and at $72, a bargain for the quality you receive. If you're a fan of Moss Wood cabernet, this is the wine you should drink while you wait for the MW to come of age. Screw cap. | 14% alc. | Drink 2022-2037 | $72 | EL

Nocturne Wines ★★★★★

185 Sheoak Dr, Yallingup, WA 6282 **T** 0477 829 844 **www**.nocturnewines.com.au **WINEMAKER** Julian Langworthy **EST.** 2007 **DOZENS** 1300 **VYDS** 8ha

Nocturne Wines create consistently high-quality, limited-quantity wines, which explore Margaret River's subregions and vineyards. Nocturne started as the side hustle that has evolved into a fully fledged (and sought after) 'swan' brand. In '16, Julian Langworthy purchased the Sheoak Vineyard in Yallingup, with its 4ha of mature cabernet sauvignon vines. The 2019 SR Rosé (sangiovese/nebbiolo from Carbunup) was awarded the Halliday Wine Companion Best Rosé 2021. (EL)

97 **Sheoak Vineyard Cabernet Sauvignon 2020, Margaret River** Firmly placed on the midnight spectrum and twinkling with as many cabernet flavours as there are stars in the sky. Scintillating. Achingly intense. Totally delicious. Screw cap. | 14% alc. | Drink 2022-2042 | $55 | EL

Tassell Park Vineyard Chardonnay 2020, Margaret River Toasted curry leaves, yellow peach, supported by clean and salty minerality (the white sand of the vineyard is powerfully suggestive) and layers upon layers of rippling flavour. You should always get to know a wine that you love over a number of days, and this will show you many sides of its beautiful face over the course of 3 or 4, if you can stretch it out that long. Screw cap. | 13% alc. | Drink 2022-2037 | $55 | EL

96 **Treeton SR Chardonnay 2020, Margaret River** Super-juicy acidity punches deep into the ripe, concentrated orchard fruit. The texture is wild and shapely and curvy and fine. What a wine. I mean it. It's salivatingly good. Screw cap. | 13% alc. | Drink 2021-2036 | $36 | EL

CENTRAL WA

EASTERN PLAINS/
INLAND/NORTH

GREATER PERTH

SOUTH WEST
AUSTRALIA

SOUTH EAST
COASTAL

Oates Ends ★★★★☆

22 Carpenter Road, Wilyabrup, WA 6280 **T** 0401 303 144 **WWW** www.oatesends.com.au **OPEN** By appt **WINEMAKER** Cath Oates **VITICULTURIST** Russ Oates **EST.** 1999 **DOZENS** 2000 **VYDS** 11ha

Cath Oates returned home to Margaret River after an international winemaking career spanning 15 years. The wines are made from the family Wilagri Vineyard, planted in '99 and now owned and managed by viticulturist brother Russ Oates. The vineyard is run on sustainable farming principles (Cath is also chair of AGW's Sustainability Advisory Committee). The name comes from the shed wine made for family and friends in the early 2000s from the ends of the rows the harvesters missed and acknowledges the importance of family farming traditions. (JH)

94   **Tempranillo 2021, Margaret River** This is super-light in colour, compared with both the other tempranillos on the bench and the '20 vintage before it. This is spicy, herbaceous and also floral: we're talking fennel, licorice root, glacé ginger, raspberry, pomegranate and rose petals. In the mouth the wine is gorgeous – the tannins very fine and quite slinky. Drinks like a pinot. I like it.
Screw cap. | 13% alc. | Drink 2022-2029 | $30 | EL

Pierro ★★★★★

Caves Road, Wilyabrup via Cowaramup, WA 6284 **T** (08) 9755 6220 **WWW** www.pierro.com.au **OPEN** 7 days 10-5 **WINEMAKER** Dr Michael Peterkin **EST.** 1979 **DOZENS** 10000 **VYDS** 7.85ha

Dr Michael Peterkin is another of the legion of Margaret River medical practitioner-vignerons; for good measure, he married into the Cullen family. Pierro is renowned for its stylish white wines, which often exhibit tremendous complexity; the Chardonnay can be monumental in its weight and texture. That said, its red wines from good vintages can be every bit as good. (JH)

98   **Chardonnay VR 2018, Margaret River** This is a thundering wine of booming power and length. It is characteristic of the '18 vintage of course, but few people were able to extract this reverberating density of flavour. It is long. It is nuanced. It is not restrained. It is awesome. For all of the complexity and beauty of Pierro Chardonnay, it appears positively fine boned and delicate when tried alongside this VR. The length here is a tour de force ... it spools flavour, endlessly. It stains the mouth with it.
Screw cap. | 14% alc. | Drink 2022-2042 | $125 | EL

96   **Cabernet Sauvignon Merlot L.T.Cf. 2018, Margaret River** All things on paper here speak of restraint: the responsibly weighted glass, low percentage of new oak, time in oak, a balance of varieties ... and in the mouth all is confirmed. This is elegant and layered flavour in every part of the mouth. It creeps up on you, and lingers long after it has gone. This is a wonderful wine, and evidence that restraint was possible in the wonderful '18 vintage. Superb. Screw cap. | 14% alc. | Drink 2021-2036 | $48 | EL

Rosabrook Margaret River Wines ★★★★

1390 Rosa Brook Road, Rosabrook WA 6285 **T** (08) 9368 4555 **WWW** www.rosabrook.com.au **WINEMAKER** Severine Logan **VITICULTURIST** Murray Edmonds **EST.** 1980 **DOZENS** 12000 **VYDS** 25ha

The original Rosabrook estate vineyards were established between 1984 and '96. In later years Rosabrook relocated to a more eastern part of the Margaret River wine region. Warm days and cool nights, influenced by the ocean, result in slow, mild-ripening conditions. (JH)

94   **Lamarque Reserve Sauvignon Blanc 2020, Margaret River** If you've ever had the pleasure of meeting winemaker Severine Logan, you will encounter a feisty, uncompromising and whipcrack smart French woman – her way is evident in this wine. This is long, expertly constructed and complex, with a saline acid thread woven through every aspect of the fruit. Super-smart wine here.
Screw cap. | 13% alc. | Drink 2021-2030 | $28 | EL

Stella Bella Wines ★★★★★

205 Rosabrook Road, Margaret River, WA 6285 **T** (08) 9758 8611 **WWW** www.stellabella.com.au **OPEN** 7 days 10-5 **WINEMAKER** Luke Jolliffe, Jarrad Olsen **EST.** 1997 **DOZENS** 40000 **VYDS** 55.7ha

This enormously successful winemaking business produces wines of true regional expression with fruit sourced from the central and southern parts of Margaret River. The company owns and operates 6 vineyards, and also purchases fruit from small contract growers. (JH)

98   **Luminosa Chardonnay 2020, Margaret River** Halliday Wine Companion Chardonnay of the Year 2023. A very complex wine of immediate power, with a deliberately funky bouquet, then changing tack with the glorious purity and focus of the palate, white peach, grapefruit, cashew and almond combining in a single stream of joy. Screw cap. | 13.6% alc. | Drink 2021-2030 | $70 | JH | ♥

97 **Luminosa Cabernet Sauvignon 2019, Margaret River** You've got to love a premium cabernet at 13.9% – it's the sweet spot. Aromatically, the nose is laden with a sumptuous spread of forest fruits, star anise, fennel, maraschino cherry and even cocoa. In the mouth the wine is succulent and sleek, screaming past with the speed and slipstream of an F1 car – there's so much horsepower under the hood here that it's hard to compete. Screw cap. | 13.9% alc. | Drink 2022–2042 | $90 | EL

96 **Suckfizzle Cabernet Sauvignon 2019, Margaret River** A luminescent ruby hue all but shimmers in the light. The fruit in this glass is scintillatingly pure, the acidity threaded through is briny and enlivening. The tannins provide shape and support as the carriage of flavour makes its way over the tongue, hinting at the capability of this wine to age over the coming years. Quite gorgeous now though, I bet many don't make it past middle age. Screw cap. | 14.1% alc. | Drink 2022–2039 | $65 | EL

94 **Sauvignon Blanc 2021, Margaret River** Fruit from Karridale, and how we love Karridale. Cool and wet most of the time, grapes from this area often exhibit bright natural acid and plenty of delicacy and nuance; this is no exception. Like biting into a crunchy green apple with a few flakes of sea salt still on your lips, the texture on the palate is finely structured and chalky, and it drags the fruit out over the long finish. More mineral and spicy than it is punchy and obvious. Class act. Screw cap. | 12.6% alc. | Drink 2021–2026 | $25 | EL

Thompson Estate ★★★★★

Tom Cullity Drive, Wilyabrup, WA 6284 **T** (08) 9755 6406 **www.**thompsonestate.com **OPEN** 7 days 10.30–4.30 **WINEMAKER** Paul Dixon **EST.** 1994 **DOZENS** 10000 **VYDS** 38ha

Cardiologist Peter Thompson planted the first vines at Thompson Estate in '97, inspired by his and his family's shareholdings in the Pierro and Fire Gully vineyards and by visits to many of the world's premium wine regions. Thompson Estate wines are made onsite at its state-of-the-art winery. (JH)

97 **The Specialist Cabernet Sauvignon 2018, Margaret River** Bright crimson purple; the colour is indicative of the great vintage, but that's just the start. This is a perfect rendition of cabernet sauvignon à la Margaret River, with a full-bodied well of cassis and blackcurrant, tapenade with powerful – but appropriate and not grippy – tannins that underwrite the long-term future of this great cabernet. Screw cap. | 14.5% alc. | Drink 2025–2050 | $90 | JH

96 **Chardonnay 2020, Margaret River** Grapefruit is the leader of the fruit pack, though white peach and nectarine are also involved, along with some French oak spice. The overall line and length is very good. Screw cap. | 13.3% alc. | Drink 2023–2035 | $50 | JH

tripe.Iscariot ★★★★★

20 McDowell Road, Witchcliffe, WA 6286 **T** 0414 817 808 **www.**tripeiscariot.com **WINEMAKER** Remi Guise **EST.** 2013 **DOZENS** 800

This has to be the most way-out winery name of the century. It prompted me (James) to email South African–born and trained winemaker Remi Guise asking to explain its derivation. He courteously responded with a reference to Judas as 'the greatest black sheep of all time', and a non-specific explanation of 'tripe' as 'challenging in style'. The wines provide a better answer, managing to successfully harness highly unusual techniques at various points of their elevage. His day job as winemaker at Naturaliste Vintners provides the technical grounding, allowing him to throw the 'how to' manual out of the window when the urge arises. (JH)

95 **Absolution Wilyabrup Chenin Blanc 2020, Margaret River** The Absolution chenins are all made in the same fashion, but from different growing areas. This is the roundest and most obvious of the 3 chenins, but it is, at this stage, the most pleasurable. Apricots, tangelos, green apples and lemons. This has chalky phenolics that shape and caress the fruit, with a swathe of exotic spice through the finish. Drink it in a couple of years and your pleasure will be amplified. Screw cap. | 12.5% alc. | Drink 2022–2036 | $32 | EL

Vasse Felix ★★★★★

Cnr Tom Cullity Drive/Caves Road, Cowaramup, WA 6284 **T** (08) 9756 5000 **www.**vassefelix.com.au **OPEN** 7 days 10–5 **WINEMAKER** Virginia Willcock **VITICULTURIST** Bart Molony **EST.** 1967 **DOZENS** 150000 **VYDS** 330ha

Vasse Felix is Margaret River's founding wine estate, established in 1967 by regional pioneer Dr Tom Cullity. Owned and operated by the Holmes à Court family since '87, Paul Holmes à Court has brought the focus to Margaret River's key varieties of cabernet sauvignon and chardonnay. Chief Winemaker Virginia Willcock has energised the winemaking and viticultural team with her no-nonsense approach and fierce commitment to quality. Vasse Felix has 4 scrupulously managed vineyards throughout Margaret River that contribute all but a small part of the annual production. (JH)

99 **Tom Cullity Cabernet Sauvignon Malbec 2018, Margaret River** This wine is the benchmark of the latent power, grace and inherent balance of the '18 vintage in Margaret River. Texturally similar to the classically sophisticated '14 vintage, but with far greater density and weight. Waves of blood plum, cassis, blackberry, pomegranate, juniper, raspberries, saltbush, bay leaf and salted red licorice crash against the rocks, as kelp, nori, iodine, red gravel and brine ride the smaller sets out the back. Sensational. Astounding. A wine for the ages. Screw cap. | 13.5% alc. | Drink 2022-2052 | $190 | EL | ♥

97 **Heytesbury Chardonnay 2020, Margaret River** In warmer vintages like '20, the Heytesbury chardonnay has extension and flex on release, billowing with flavour and pleasure, with the oak seeming to be enveloped by it early on. So goes the story here: like the '18 (on release) this is a scintillating show of powerful fruit, juicy mineral acidity and layers of crushed rocks, petrichor, nori, summer fig and salted yellow peaches. A superstar wine – it's closed now though: patience or a decant is recommended. Screw cap. | 13.5% alc. | Drink 2022-2037 | $100 | EL

96 **Chardonnay 2020, Margaret River** The '20 vintage was made for the Vasse Felix chardonnay style. This is seamless, concentrated, floral, intense, so smart that it elicited a little chuckle upon tasting. Notes of peach and apple skin (of course) backed by jacaranda flowers, curry leaf, brine, crispy nori and pan fried nuts. What a wine. And what a bargain for this pedigree – so classy it's ridiculous. Screw cap. | 13% alc. | Drink 2021-2036 | $44 | EL

94 **Filius Chardonnay 2020, Margaret River** The immediacy of the complexity of the bouquet and the juicy white peach that floods the palate leave no room for discussion. This is a perfect rendition of a drink-now chardonnay of the highest quality within its station of life (and price). Screw cap. | 13% alc. | Drink 2021-2030 | $29 | JH

Filius Sauvignon Blanc Semillon 2020, Margaret River You can be assured that when Virginia Willcock turns her mind to something, it's going to be good. Sauvignon blanc here – a component has been fermented on skins, which layers the wine with an extra spicy sumthin sumthin. This is a serious, bordeaux blanc style, and at a very low price to match. So smart! Screw cap. | 13% alc. | Drink 2021-2026 | $29 | EL

Victory Point Wines ★★★★★

92 Holben Road, Cowaramup, WA 6284 **T** 0417 954 655 **www.**victorypointwines.com **OPEN** Wed-Sun 11-4 **WINEMAKER** Mark Messenger (Contract) **VITICULTURIST** Colin Bell **EST.** 1997 **DOZENS** 2500 **VYDS** 13.7ha

Judith and Gary Berson have set their sights high. They established their vineyard without irrigation, emulating those of the Margaret River pioneers (including Moss Wood). The cellar door overlooks the 20+yo vineyard. (JH)

95 **Rosé 2021, Margaret River** Slickly made, with a blend of pinot noir, cabernet franc and malbec. A luxuriantly rich rosé, but remains nimble on its feet as the bevy of red fruits roll along the tongue. Top-class match for Asian food. Screw cap. | 13.5% alc. | Drink 2021-2023 | $25 | JH

94 **The Mallee Root Cabernet Sauvignon Petit Verdot Cabernet Franc 2019, Margaret River** The heady aromatics of the petit verdot lend lashings of blueberries and potpourri to the nose here. On the palate this is silky, saturated in ripe fruit and layered with exotic market spices. Licorice, aniseed and fennel flowers linger through the finish, adorning the resplendent red fruit. Quite gorgeous. At this price, a steal. Screw cap. | 14% alc. | Drink 2021-2029 | $29 | EL

Wills Domain ★★★★★

Cnr Abbeys Farm Road/Brash Road, Yallingup, WA 6281 **T** (08) 9755 2327 **www.**willsdomain.com.au **OPEN** 7 days 10-5 **WINEMAKER** Richard Rowe **VITICULTURIST** Ernie Lepidi **EST.** 1985 **DOZENS** 20000 **VYDS** 20ha

When the Haunold family purchased the original Wills Domain Vineyard in '00, they were adding another chapter to a family history of winemaking stretching back to 1383 in what is now Austria. The onsite restaurant has won numerous accolades. (JH)

94 **Mystic Spring Cabernet Sauvignon 2020, Margaret River** Super-bright and delicious. This has supple redcurrant, wine gums, pomegranate and raspberry fruit, backed by salted licorice, a sheet of nori and crushed black pepper. Concentrated and lively, this is a compelling way to spend $25. Screw cap. | 13.8% alc. | Drink 2021-2031 | $25 | EL

Windance Wines ★★★★☆

2764 Caves Road, Yallingup, WA 6282 **T** (08) 9755 2293 **www.**windance.com.au **OPEN** 7 days 10-5 **WINEMAKER** Tyke Wheatley **VITICULTURIST** Tyke Wheatley **EST.** 1998 **DOZENS** 4500 **VYDS** 9ha

Drew and Rosemary Brent-White founded this family business, situated 5km south of Yallingup. The estate wines are all certified organic. Daughter Billie and husband Tyke Wheatley now own the business: Billie, a qualified accountant, was raised at Windance and manages the business and the cellar door; and Tyke (with winemaking experience at Picardy, Happs and Burgundy) has taken over the winemaking and manages the vineyard. (JH)

| 94 | **Cabernet Merlot 2020, Margaret River** An ultra-rich full-bodied blend that needs time to settle down, but has the balance to give confidence that it will happen for the patient drinker – and the price is decidedly right. Screw cap. | 14% alc. | Drink 2029-2039 | $29 | JH |

Windows Estate ★★★★★

4 Quininup Road, Yallingup, WA 6282 **T** (08) 9756 6655 **WWW**.windowsestate.com **OPEN** 7 days 10-5
WINEMAKER Chris Davies **VITICULTURIST** Chris Davies **EST**. 1999 **DOZENS** 2000 **VYDS** 7ha

Chris Davies planted the Windows Estate vineyard in 1996, at the tender age of 19. He has tended the vines ever since, gaining organic certifcation in '19. Initially selling the grapes, Chris moved into winemaking in '06 and has had considerable show success for the consistently outstanding wines. (JH)

| 97 | **La Fenêtre Chardonnay 2018, Margaret River** Through the lens of the ripe, powerful and graceful '18 vintage, one would expect that this wine would blow your socks off. Actually, it is incredibly restrained and fine, with a tension and line that carve a track across the tongue. This is saline, mineral, expansive and exciting. If you buy one chardonnay this year that isn't one of the 'big guys', this has to be it. Sadly only 600 bottles made – get on their mailing list. Utterly glorious. Screw cap. | 13.5% alc. | Drink 2021-2036 | $85 | EL |

| 96 | **Petit Lot Chenin Blanc 2020, Margaret River** This vintage in Margaret River was warm, short and low yielding, producing wines of intense concentration like this one: deeply flavoured, layered and very long. The juicy acid gives a lick of moreishness through the enduring finish. Very smart, again. Screw cap. | 12% alc. | Drink 2021-2036 | $39 | EL |

| | **Petit Lot Chardonnay 2020, Margaret River** Incredibly aromatic: pink grapefruit, lavender, fennel flower, white peach, musk stick, preserved lemon, crushed cashew and ocean spray all rise up as one from the glass. On the palate the acidity is taut and alive – it drags saliva from the back of the mouth and inundates the senses in a wave of saline, crushed rocks and shell. Screw cap. | 13.5% alc. | Drink 2021-2031 | $50 | EL |

Wise Wine ★★★★★

237 Eagle Bay Road, Eagle Bay, WA 6281 **T** (08) 9750 3100 **WWW**.wisewine.com.au **OPEN** Sun-Fri 9-5,
Sat 9-6 **WINEMAKER** Andrew Siddell, Matt Buchan, Larry Cherubino (Consultant) **EST**. 1986 **DOZENS** 10000
VYDS 2.5ha

Wise Wine, headed by Perth entrepreneur Ron Wise, has been a remarkably consistent producer of high-quality wine. The vineyard adjacent to the winery in the Margaret River is supplemented by contract-grown grapes from Pemberton, Manjimup and Frankland River. (JH)

| 96 | **Eagle Bay Chardonnay 2020, Margaret River** This is pristine, driven and pure, with a creamy, crushed-nut undertow beneath the fruit. It billows and undulates and it's awesome. This is a routinely great wine and the '20 continues form. You better get used to it. Screw cap. | 13.2% alc. | Drink 2022-2037 | $65 | EL |

Woodlands ★★★★★

3948 Caves Road, Wilyabrup, WA 6280 **T** (08) 9755 6226 **WWW**.woodlandswines.com **OPEN** 7 days 10-5
WINEMAKER Stuart Watson **VITICULTURIST** Jaden McLean **EST**. 1973 **DOZENS** 15000 **VYDS** 26.5ha

Founders David Watson and wife Heather had spectacular success with the cabernets he made in 1979 and the early '80s. With the advent of sons Stuart and Andrew (Stuart primarily responsible for winemaking), the estate has bounced back to pre-eminence. The wines come in 4 price bands, the bulk of the production under the Chardonnay and Cabernet Merlot varietals, then a series of Reserve and Special Reserves, then Reserve de la Cave and finally Cabernet Sauvignon. The top end wines primarily come from the original Woodlands Vineyard, where the vines are almost 50 years old. (JH)

| 98 | **Xavier Cabernet Sauvignon 2018, Margaret River** If you haven't had the pleasure of drinking one of these cabernets as an older wine, you may not get the full scope of the young wine on release. Here, today, it is tightly coiled, spicy and concentrated. The savoury, biscuity oak we often associate with good quality bordeaux is here in spades, and it encases the kaleidoscopic flavours that lie possible beyond. However, in 10 years, this wine transforms into a powerful and expansive wine of depth, grace and evocation. Screw cap. | 13.5% alc. | Drink 2022-2052 | $179 | EL | ♥ |

| 96 | **Margaret 2018, Margaret River** 80/10/10% cabernet sauvignon/merlot/malbec. Rooted in the very fabric of this wine is a savoury lining of spice. It is inescapable, and it's what makes this wine a wonder. Is it better than the great '14? Hard to say – the '14 was pretty amazing. But this has all the ripe power and concentration of the vintage. The pure 'cabernosity' of this wine is a thing to marvel at. I keep coming back to the savoury layers – they are a defining characteristic of the house style. Screw cap. | 13.5% alc. | Drink 2022-2042 | $70 | EL |

Xanadu Wines ★★★★★

316 Boodjidup Road, Margaret River, WA 6285 **T** (08) 9758 9500 **WWW**.xanaduwines.com **OPEN** 7 days 10–5 **WINEMAKER** Glenn Goodall, Brendan Carr, Steve Kyme, Darren Rathbone **VITICULTURIST** Suzie Muntz **EST**. 1977 **DOZENS** 45000 **VYDS** 82.8ha

Xanadu Wines was established in 1977 by Dr John Lagan and was purchased by the Rathbone family in 2005. Together with talented winemaker Glenn Goodall and his team, they have significantly improved the quality of the wines. The vineyard has been revamped via soil profiling, improved drainage, precision viticulture and reduced yields. The quality of the wines made since the acquisition of the Stevens Road Vineyard in '08 has been consistently outstanding. Glenn Goodall is the Wine Companion 2023 Winemaker of the Year. (JH)

97　**Stevens Road Chardonnay 2020, Margaret River** This wine is pristine, and routinely defined by acid on release. It is soft, pithy and lush (that acid), and it is met by white peach and nectarine, red apple and lime flesh. Brine, cheesecloth and little pockets of pop-rock vibrancy. This is a beautiful wine, but it is even better with some age. The temptation to drink them young however, is overwhelming. Screw cap. | 13% alc. | Drink 2022–2037 | $80 | EL

Reserve Chardonnay 2020, Margaret River The problem with Xanadu Reserve Chardonnay is that it is delicious on release. But that has nothing on what it morphs into, with age. This is a wine that is all too often overlooked (not in the show system, granted) by collectors, because too few people have been privy to the wines in their middle age. This is crystalline, pure – almost austere – toasty and spiced, with layers of undulating flavour through the fine, spooling finish. Screw cap. | 13% alc. | Drink 2022–2042 | $110 | EL

Stevens Road Cabernet Sauvignon 2019, Margaret River Scintillating, pure, creamy, salty and layered, this is every bit as impressive as I expected it to be. The cooler year is viewed here through perfectly ripe fruit, and has imparted a freshness to the acidity that only serves to highlight the pristine character of the wine. Hyperbole aside: it's very, very excellent. The tannins are like silk. Screw cap. | 14% alc. | Drink 2022–2042 | $80 | EL

Reserve Cabernet Sauvignon 2019, Margaret River Sometimes, you gotta start at the end of a wine, rather than the front. Usually it is because the wine is so long, that the first flavours are long forgotten. Such is life, here. The tannins, which are laced like a fine silky web through the finish, capture the pure fruit on the mid palate and coax it through the mouth. Caught also, like fine droplets of dew in a spider's web, are pockets of spice which add pop and thrill to the overall. Screw cap. | 14% alc. | Drink 2022–2042 | $110 | EL

95　**DJL Malbec 2020, Margaret River** This was a ripping little vintage. 'Little' is not intended in a pejorative – it was generally brutally low yielding, due to dry conditions at the end of '19 resulting in a small crop of small berries. This in turn lends a firmness to the tannins. This is no problem for a naturally tannic variety like malbec, that simply takes it in its stride. This wine is polished, glossy, ripe, saturated in black and purple fruit flavours and propped up by a fine mineral seam of saline acidity. Bring it on. Screw cap. | 14% alc. | Drink 2021–2031 | $28 | EL

DJL Shiraz 2020, Margaret River A supremely delicious and pure wine that unapologetically displays the finesse and slink that is possible with the variety, when handled this way. A lot of words to tell you: this is a wonderful wine, and ridiculous(ly good) value for money. Screw cap. | 14% alc. | Drink 2021–2028 | $28 | EL

REGION

Pemberton

Bellarmine Wines ⓨ ★★★★☆

1 Balyan Retreat, Pemberton, WA 6260 **T** 0409 687 772 **www**.bellarmine.com.au **OPEN** By appt **WINEMAKER** Dr Diane Miller **EST** 2000 **DOZENS** 5000 **VYDS** 20.2ha

This vineyard is owned by German residents Dr Willi and Gudrun Schumacher. Long-term wine lovers, the Schumachers decided to establish a vineyard and winery of their own, choosing Australia partly because of its stable political climate. The vineyard is planted to riesling, pinot noir, chardonnay, shiraz, sauvignon blanc and petit verdot. The flagship wines are 3 styles of riesling – dry, off-dry and sweet. (JH)

93　**Dry Riesling 2021, Pemberton** Super-floral, minerally nose; graphite and white pepper colour the edges of orange blossoms, fennel flower and green apple skins. On the palate the ever-present briny acidity encases the fruit and ushers it through the long, pithy finish. More powerful than it initially appears – the acidity really is the engine room in this cool vintage. Screw cap. | 11.5% alc. | Drink 2021–2031 | $27 | EL

Tasmania

1702ha | 1 zone | 3 regions

TAS

Whether your standpoint is grapegrower, winemaker or wine consumer, Tasmania is an enchanted island. The 2022 harvest is touted to be another stunner, particularly in Southern and Northern Tasmania, though in spite of significant new plantings in recent years, moderated yields will again fail to satiate an ever-increasing taste for these elegant and refreshing wines.

Pinot noir is Tasmania's pig's back, comprising the lion's share of the harvest. Chardonnay is its handmaiden, followed by sauvignon blanc, pinot gris, riesling and pinot meunier. An incredible 37% of all wine coming from the '22 vintage is sparkling. Moreover, the average price per tonne of grapes dedicated to this use rose to $3213, while table wine grape prices inflated to $3256 per tonne. The average of $3237 per tonne dwarfs the $630 per tonne for the overall Australian crop.

The Tamar Valley again took the lead in the size of its harvest (39%), followed by the Coal River Valley (22%), Pipers River (14%), the East Coast (13%), Derwent Valley (9%), North West (2%) and Huon Valley (1%), the latter the southernmost part of the island, with as yet tiny but exciting plantings.

All of the above raises the question whether Tasmania should seek official recognition of at least some areas by the Geographic Indications Committee. Since the island is a self-comprised zone, the relevant demarcations are regions and subregions.

The language used is vague and bureaucratic, and until the last years of the 20th century, it was of academic interest, as most potential regions lacked the basic size requirements. That has now changed, but the formal position of Wine Tasmania is to maintain the single GI for now, while continuing to 'explore, promote and discuss individual winegrowing areas and – perhaps more importantly in Tasmania given the incredible diversity over small distances – individual vineyard sites'. For this chapter, we have divided the island into three 'regions': **East Coast**, **Northern** and **Southern Tasmania**.

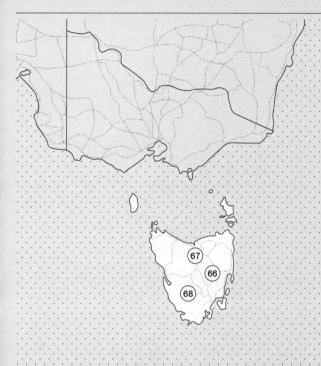

ZONE	REGION
Tasmania	66 East Coast Tasmania
	67 Northern Tasmania
	68 Southern Tasmania

Tasmania

East Coast Tasmania

Freycinet ★★★★★

15919 Tasman Highway via Bicheno, Tas 7215 **T** (03) 6257 8574 **WWW**.freycinetvineyard.com.au
OPEN 7 days 10-5 **WINEMAKER** Claudio Radenti, Lindy Bull, Keira O'Brian **EST**. 1979 **DOZENS** 9000
VYDS 15.9ha

The Freycinet vineyards are situated on the sloping hillsides of a small valley. The soils are brown dermosol on top of Jurassic dolerite; and the combination of aspect, slope, soil and heat summation produces red grapes with unusual depth of colour and ripe flavours. One of the foremost producers of pinot noir, with an enviable track record of consistency – rare in such a temperamental variety. In '12 Freycinet acquired part of the neighbouring Coombend property from Brown Brothers. (JH)

94 **Wineglass Bay Sauvignon Blanc 2020, Tasmania** Serious sauvignon of flesh and texture. A portion of French oak-barrel fermentation brings a compelling depth, richness, body and spicy overlay. Stone fruits, grapefruit and custard apple propagate long and full, impeccably freshened by the cool air of Freycinet. Screw cap. | 14% alc. | Drink 2022-2023 | $28 | TS

Ossa Wines ★★★★☆

100 Crossins Road, Swansea, Tas 7190 (postal) **T** 0447 404 469 **WWW**.ossa.wine **WINEMAKER** Liam McElhinney **VITICULTURIST** Jay Dillon **EST**. 2021 **DOZENS** 550 **VYDS** 20ha

Rod and Cecile Roberts retained the best consultants in the state when their 20ha Ossa vineyard was planted and the first wines made. Their desire for sustainability resulted in an entirely solar-powered structure; removing noxious plant species, fencing wildlife zones; and cleaning waterways. The vineyard wasn't in bearing in '20, so they sourced small parcels of chardonnay (175 dozen), pinot noir (250 dozen) and sparkling (35 dozen), and the first wine ex the estate Belbrook Vineyard was chardonnay '21 (85 dozen). All of which made the '20 Pinot Noir, winning Best Wine at the Australian Pinot Noir Challenge '21. (JH)

98 **Pinot Noir 2020, Tasmania** Stunning crimson-magenta colour sets the scene for a perfumed wine of exceptional quality, with ever-changing aromas and flavours encapsulated in an insistent heartbeat of purity. The mouthfeel, length and balance of the red and black cherry fruit underpins a wine that is great now, with spicy complexity just around the corner. Screw cap. | 13.5% alc. | Drink 2025-2035 | $120 | JH

Northern Tasmania

Holm Oak ★★★★

11 West Bay Road, Rowella, Tas 7270 **T** (03) 6394 7577 **WWW**.holmoakvineyards.com.au **OPEN** Thurs-Sun 11-5 **WINEMAKER** Rebecca Duffy **VITICULTURIST** Tim Duffy **EST**. 1983 **DOZENS** 15000 **VYDS** 15ha

Holm Oak takes its name from its grove of oak trees, planted around the beginning of the 20th century and originally intended for the making of tennis racquets. A boutique family affair, winemaker Rebecca Duffy has extensive winemaking experience in Australia and California; and husband Tim, a viticultural agronomist, manages the vineyard. Cellar door, winery, family home (and a pet pig named Pinot) all co-exist on the vineyard site. (JH)

95 **Pinot Noir 2020, Tasmania** Wonderful, crystal-clear crimson; the floral, red-fruit assemblage on the bouquet moves seamlessly into a complex palate in terms of the forest strawberry and cherry fruit, but a pure and tightly focused palate flowing effortlessly through to a long, fresh finish and lingering aftertaste. Screw cap. | 13% alc. | Drink 2023-2033 | $35 | JH

Josef Chromy Wines ★★★★★

370 Relbia Road, Relbia, Tas 7258 **T** (03) 6335 8700 **WWW**.josefchromy.com.au **OPEN** 7 days 10-5
WINEMAKER Jeremy Dineen, Ockie Myburgh **VITICULTURIST** Luciano Caravia **EST**. 2004 **DOZENS** 40000 **VYDS** 60ha

Josef Chromy escaped from Czechoslovakia in 1950, arriving in Tasmania 'with nothing but hope and ambition'. He went on to own or develop such well-known Tasmanian wine brands as Rochecombe (now Bay of Fires), Jansz, Heemskerk and Tamar Ridge. In '07, aged 76, Josef launched Josef Chromy wines. The foundation of the business is the Old Stornoway Vineyard, with 60ha of mature vines. Josef has won a string of awards for his services to the Tasmanian wine industry and his wines earn similar respect. Talented and hard-working winemaker Jeremy Dineen handed over the reins to his capable offsider Ockie Myburgh in January '21. (JH)

95 **Rosé 2021, Tasmania** Pale, bright salmon pink. Erupting with rose petals, morello cherries, strawberry hull and guava. Elegant yet concentrated. Grand line and length. Refreshing, enveloping Relbia acidity seals the deal. Already a strong contender for the rosé of the vintage! Screw cap. | 13.5% alc. | Drink 2021-2023 | $32 | TS | ♥

94 **Pinot Gris 2021, Tasmania** It upholds the mood of gris in its texture, spice and pear and stone-fruit flesh, yet tactically surfs the line of grigio in its elegant allure and lemon tang. Old oak has been skilfully deployed to build mouthfeel without in any way diminishing purity or tension. Screw cap. | 14% alc. | Drink 2021-2026 | $30 | TS

Pipers Brook Vineyard ★★★★★

1216 Pipers Brook Road, Pipers Brook, Tas 7254 **T** (03) 6382 7555 **www**.kreglingerwineestates.com **OPEN** By appt **WINEMAKER** Luke Whittle **VITICULTURIST** Kym Ayeliffe **EST.** 1974 **DOZENS** 70000 **VYDS** 176.51ha

The Pipers Brook empire has almost 200ha of vineyard supporting the Ninth Island, Pipers Brook and Kreglinger labels with the major focus, of course, being on Pipers Brook. Fastidious viticulture and a passionate winemaking team along with immaculate packaging and enterprising marketing create a potent and effective blend. (JH)

96 **Kreglinger Brut Rosé 2017, Tasmania** Halliday Wine Companion Sparkling Rosé of the Year 2023. Traditional method, aged 44 months on lees with 7.5g/L dosage. Delectable red cherry and wild-strawberry fruit seduces from the outset, graced with the signature Turkish delight of Pipers River, but it's the creamy, silky texture of barrel and lees work that really sets apart this sublime creation. Cork. | 12.5% alc. | $75 | TS | ♥

Tamar Ridge ★★★★★

1a Waldhorn Drive, Rosevears, Tas 7277 **T** (03) 6330 0300 **www**.tamarridge.com.au **OPEN** 7 days 10-5 **WINEMAKER** Tom Wallace, Anthony De Amicis **EST.** 1994 **VYDS** 130ha

Since the Brown Family Wine Group (then Brown Brothers) acquired Tamar Ridge and its sister brands of Pirie and Devil's Corner in '10, it has tactically honed each of the 3 labels to increasingly play to its strengths. For Tamar Ridge, this means a strategic focus on pinot noir, sourced from its magnificent and substantial Kayena Vineyard. Single Vineyard and experimental Research Series pinot noirs are exciting indicators of the direction of evolution of the brand under talented winemaker Tom Wallace. (JH)

95 **Tamar Ridge Pinot Noir 2019, Tasmania** Typical deep colour; a highly expressive and fragrant bouquet of spiced plum, forest floor and charcuterie lays down the path for the palate, with whole-bunch savoury notes alongside a rich core of juicy plum and berry flavours. Great value. Screw cap. | 13% alc. | Drink 2021-2029 | $34 | JH

REGION

Southern Tasmania

Chatto ★★★★★

68 Dillons Hill Road, Glaziers Bay, Tas 7109 **T** (03) 6114 2050 **www**.chattowines.com **WINEMAKER** Jim Chatto **VITICULTURIST** Paul Lipscombe **EST.** 2000 **DOZENS** 1000 **VYDS** 1.5ha

Jim Chatto is recognised as having one of the very best palates in Australia, and has proved to be an outstanding winemaker. He and wife Daisy long wanted to get a small Tasmanian pinot business up and running but, having moved to the Hunter Valley in '00, it took 6 years to find a site that satisfied all of the criteria they consider ideal. It is a warm, well-drained site in one of the coolest parts of Tasmania, looking out over Glaziers Bay. The '19 crop was lost to bushfire smoke taint, but the many Tasmanian vigneron friends of the Chatto family came to the rescue. (JH)

97 **Isle Black Label Pinot Noir 2020, Tasmania** A very arresting and complex bouquet of dark berries and forest floor, the palate with an infusion of savoury spices, the texture and structure perfect. Screw cap. | 13.5% alc. | Drink 2024-2035 | $90 | JH

96 **Intrigue Black Label Pinot Noir 2020, Tasmania** A stunning bouquet, with outright perfume sure to emerge in a year or 2; the palate already with spices alongside pure red and black cherry fruit. Screw cap. | 13% alc. | Drink 2023-2033 | $70 | JH

Merriworth

63 Merriworth Road, Tea Tree, Tas 7017 **T** 0406 657 774 **WWW.**merriworth.com.au **WINEMAKER** Anna Pooley and Justin Bubb **VITICULTURIST** Mark McNamara **EST.** 2017 **DOZENS** 600 **VYDS** 2ha

It was their love of pinot noir that lured Mark McNamara and Kirralee Hatch to Tasmania after several years studying viticulture and winemaking on the Australian mainland. In 2017 they purchased the 2ha Third Child vineyard and renamed it Merriworth. The site is home to 9 clones of pinot noir and 3 of riesling, planted on river flats of cracking clay soil and shallow, eroded slopes over dolerite rock. Vibrant, young wines are made with accuracy and precision by Anna Pooley and Justin Bubb.

93 **Estate Riesling 2021, Tasmania** A cool season, pristine fruit and acute winemaking make for a delightfully precise riesling. Nuances of rose petal dance over a spine of lemon, lime and Granny Smith apple. Energetic acid drive leads a long finish, brushed with just the right touch of residual sweetness. Screw cap. | 12.5% alc. | Drink 2022-2031 | $27 | TS

Pooley Wines Winery of the Year 2023

Butcher's Hill Vineyard, 1431 Richmond Road, Richmond, Tas 7025 **T** (03) 6260 2895 **WWW.**pooleywines.com.au **OPEN** 7 days 10-5 **WINEMAKER** Anna Pooley, Justin Bubb **VITICULTURIST** Hannah McKay **EST.** 1985 **DOZENS** 8500 **VYDS** 18ha

Pooley Wines is a glowing exemplar of a boutique Tasmanian family estate. Three generations of the family have been involved in its development, with the little hands of the fourth generation now starting to get involved. A cellar door was established in the heritage-listed sandstone barn and coach house of the distinguished 1830s convict-built Georgian home, standing in pride of place on the heritage property. Wine quality has risen to dramatic effect, no small feat while doubling production, since the return to Tasmania of Anna Pooley and husband Justin Bubb to establish the winemaking arm of the estate in 2012. Conversion to organic viticulture is currently underway, with a goal of achieving certification by the 2026 vintage. Pooley is the Wine Companion 2023 Winery of the Year. (TS)

99 **Jack Denis Pooley Pinot Noir 2020, Tasmania** This 33% whole-bunch pinot has depth beyond that of its siblings. It's full-on forest floor, full-on savoury spices, with tannins made to measure, but all bow down to the primacy of the dark berry fruit of the impossibly long finish. World class. Screw cap. | 13.1% alc. | Drink 2022-2037 | $140 | JH | ♥

97 **Butcher's Hill Pinot Noir 2020, Tasmania** Vivid crimson purple, slightly deeper than that of its siblings. The bouquet is extremely complex, with satsuma plum, dark cherry and a crescendo of spices, the palate as elegant as it is intense, and throwing in a pinch of savoury tannins. Screw cap. | 13.1% alc. | Drink 2022-2035 | $70 | JH

Cooinda Vale Pinot Noir 2020, Tasmania Although there's only 15% whole bunches, it makes its presence felt right from the first whiff, the first sip, like a Rubik's Cube in the hands of an expert. Satisfyingly elegant. Screw cap. | 13.2% alc. | Drink 2022-2035 | $70 | JH

96 **Cooinda Vale Chardonnay 2020, Tasmania** Identical vinification to Butcher's Hill except a 20-day (not 22) ferment. This has more intensity, more length, more grapefruit, but still has the finesse and balance of its Butcher's Hill sibling. Screw cap. | 13.2% alc. | Drink 2022-2035 | $65 | JH

Pressing Matters

665 Middle Tea Tree Road, Tea Tree, Tas 7017 **T** 0474 380 109 **WWW.**pressingmatters.com.au **OPEN** Thurs-Sun 10-4 by appt **WINEMAKER** Samantha Connew **VITICULTURIST** Mark Hoey **EST.** 2002 **DOZENS** 2600 **VYDS** 7.3ha

Greg Melick wears more hats than most people manage in a lifetime. He is a major general (the highest rank in the Australian Army Reserve) a top level barrister (senior counsel) and has presided over a number of headline special commissions and enquiries into subjects as diverse as cricket match-fixing and the Beaconsfield mine collapse. Yet, if asked, he would probably nominate wine as his major focus in life. Having built up an exceptional cellar of the great wines of Europe, he has turned his attention to grape growing and winemaking. (JH)

96　　R139 Riesling 2021, Tasmania Pale straw green; it leaps from the glass with brilliant purity of white lily fragrance, Granny Smith apple, lime and lemon. Not a molecule out of place. Sublime line and length. Irresistibly seductive right away, with decades of potential yet. 375mL.　Screw cap. | 7.5% alc. | Drink 2022-2051 | $39 | TS | ♥

Stargazer Wine ★★★★★

37 Rosewood Lane, Tea Tree, Tas 7017 **T** 0408 173 335 **WWW**.stargazerwine.com.au **OPEN** By appt
WINEMAKER Samantha Connew **VITICULTURIST** Samantha Connew, Bryn Williams **EST**. 2012 **DOZENS** 1800 **VYDS** 3ha

Samantha Connew obtained a postgraduate diploma of oenology and viticulture from Lincoln University, Canterbury, NZ, before moving to Australia. Here she undertook the Advanced Wine Assessment course at the Australian Wine Research Institute in 2000, was chosen as a scholar at the '02 Len Evans Tutorial, won the George Mackey Award for the best wine exported from Australia in '04 and was awarded International Red Winemaker of the Year at the International Wine Challenge, London in '07. After a highly successful and lengthy position as chief winemaker at Wirra Wirra, Sam moved to Tasmania to make the first wines for her own business. (JH)

97　　Coal River Valley Riesling 2021, Tasmania This is a glorious wine; the bouquet and fore palate are full of Rose's lime juice that has a siren allure, but it's the soaring finish and aftertaste that send all the senses into overdrive, with a quivering line of acidity within its fruit.　Screw cap. | 12% alc. | Drink 2022-2036 | $35 | JH

　　Palisander Vineyard Coal River Valley Riesling 2020, Tasmania The scented white flower and citrus blossom bouquet yields to a palate with mouth-watering grapefruit and lime, surrounded by endless crystalline acidity that creates balance now or in a decade or more.　Screw cap. | 13% alc. | Drink 2025-2040 | $42 | JH

　　Palisander Vineyard Coal River Valley Pinot Noir 2020, Tasmania Perfect clarity and colour; a vibrant pinot that caresses the mouth with its red cherry, wild strawberry, pomegranate flavours and gossamer tannins. Utterly delicious.　Screw cap. | 13.5% alc. | Drink 2024-2030 | $55 | JH

95　　Tupelo 2021, Tasmania A 51/34/15% blend of pinot gris, riesling and gewürztraminer. Eight hours of skin contact; wild-yeast ferment in used oak; 15% of the riesling component was fermented on skins; on lees for 3 months with lees stirring. A very good outcome for a daunting vinification of a daunting blend, that has avoided a phenolic trap.　Screw cap. | 12.5% alc. | Drink 2022-2030 | $35 | JH

Stefano Lubiana ★★★★★

60 Rowbottoms Road, Granton, Tas 7030 **T** (03) 6263 7457 **WWW**.slw.com.au **OPEN** Wed-Sun 11-4
WINEMAKER Steve Lubiana **EST**. 1990 **VYDS** 25ha

Monique and Steve Lubiana moved to the banks of the Derwent River in '90 to make high-quality sparkling wine. They built a gravity-fed winery and the winemaking approach has been based on attention to detail within a biodynamic environment. The Italian-inspired Osteria restaurant is based on their own biodynamically produced vegetables and herbs, the meats (all free-range) are from local farmers and the seafood is wild-caught. In '16, the Lubianas purchased the Panorama Vineyard, first planted in 1974. (JH)

96　　Chicane Malbec 2018, Tasmania An exceptional wine wherever grown and made – but Tasmania? Malbec? This is extraordinary, with depth, richness and ripeness plus black pepper, spice and fine-spun tannins for good measure.　Cork. | 13.5% alc. | Drink 2023-2028 | $55 | JH

Strelley Farm ★★★★

Level 1, 5 Ord Street, West Perth, WA 6872 (postal) **T** (08) 9282 5417 **WWW**.strelleyfarm.wine
WINEMAKER Liam McElhinney **VITICULTURIST** John Fogarty, Christian De Camps **EST**. 2021 **VYDS** 36ha

Strelley Farm is the commercial range of the Fogarty Group's significant Tasmanian development. Sourcing spans all the major growing areas of Tasmania, with a particular focus to date on the Tamar Valley, Coal River Valley and East Coast. The Strelley Farm vineyard itself comprises 36ha (and counting) on 170ha of land. A cellar door is scheduled to open near Richmond in the Coal River Valley in 2023. (TS)

96　　Strelley Farm Estate Pinot Noir 2019, Tasmania Bright, clear crimson; a fragrant, perfumed bouquet with red fruits and spices galore, the palate elegant and fine boned. Red fruits are again leading the band, with trumpets of spices providing a resounding finish and aftertaste.　Screw cap. | 13.5% alc. | Drink 2022-2031 | $40 | JH

Published in 2022 by Hardie Grant Books,
an imprint of Hardie Grant Publishing

Hardie Grant Books (Melbourne)
Wurundjeri Country
Building 1, 658 Church Street
Richmond, Victoria 3121

Hardie Grant Books (London)
5th & 6th Floors
52–54 Southwark Street
London SE1 1UN

hardiegrant.com/au/books

The *Halliday Wine Companion* is a joint venture between
James Halliday and HGX Pty Ltd.

The map in this publication incorporates data copyright
© Commonwealth of Australia (Geoscience Australia) 2004.
Geoscience Australia has not evaluated the data as altered
and incorporated within this publication and therefore gives
no warranty regarding accuracy, completeness, currency or
suitability for any particular purpose.

Australian wine zones and wine regions data copyright
© Wine Australia

Halliday Pocket Wine Companion 2023
ISBN 978 1 74379 920 8

Design: Pidgeon Ward
Typesetting: Megan Ellis
Photographs: pp. 7, 12, 13 Marie Pangaud and Sherpa; pp. 14, 17,
149, 179 Wine Australia
Printed by McPherson's Printing Group, Maryborough, Victoria

Hardie Grant acknowledges the Traditional Owners of the
country on which we work, the Wurundjeri people of the
Kulin nation and the Gadigal people of the Eora nation, and
recognises their continuing connection to the land, waters and
culture. We pay our respects to their Elders past and present.

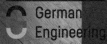

oak has been an integral part of winemaking for at least 1000 years. It is princ
viticulture is practised to a greater or lesser degree in all the major wine-produci
not been treated or processed to alter their state can be used, but manufacture
prohibited, as is any organism that has been genetically modified. **oxidation** occur
certain chemical changes in its composition. In broad terms, these changes resul
and palate. **palate** is the third leg of the colour, bouquet, palate trilogy used to ass
(or mouthfeel) of the wine once it is taken into the mouth, and after it is swallowed
described as the negative logarithm of hydrogen ion activity or concentration in v
wine, in the latter case having much to do with the potential longevity. **phylloxer**
While sprays were ultimately developed to control the mildews, effective and acc
remains the most devastating of all vine diseases. **pinot gris** is a white mutation
makes its appearance in European historical records earlier than any other variety
related varieties (pinot gris, pinot meunier and pinot blanc) is not clear. This tend
France alone), the choice of which has a profound influence on the quality and
winemaking texts the link is often discussed as the 'redox' potential of a wine. **resi**
and fructose that, either accidentally or deliberately, remains unconverted to alco
litre of wine, and can vary between 1 gram per litre and more than 500 grams per l
have been fine-tuned but not fundamentally changed since the 1960s, and encou
made for centuries. There are five ways to make roses, the most common in Au
macerate for between 12 and 48 hours before all or part of the juice is drawn off
grape variety, was identified in 1997 as one of the two parents of cabernet sauvig
sauvignon will know it offers a mix of crushed herbs, grass and asparagus, with a m
to seal glass jars, and in the 1930s the University of California, Davis, conducted
through the first decade of the 21st century repeatedly confirmed the superior
importantly, freedom from random oxidation. **semillon**, a white grape variety, was d
viticulture, during his extraordinary wine odyssey through Europe and back to Aust
country has shiraz as old as Australia's, nor plantings as large. As with many othe
become a major problem in parts of Australia, South Africa and California in the f
drought and associated extreme heat events have increased the risk of fires and a
Australian grapegrowers and consultants, the most significant soil attributes are
between free-draining capacity and waterholding capacity; pH (acid soils inhibit
amount of organic compounds present. **solids** is a non-technical term that is mair
fine particles of skin and pulp in suspension in the juice. Makers of chardonnay a
solids in the juice, thus gaining flavour complexity. **sour** is a term denoting a wine
itself on the back of the palate and in the aftertaste. **sparkling wine** can be mad
addition of a precise amount of sugar and yeast to a blend of still wines immedia
contains approximately 10 grams of pure alcohol. Because drinks conta
container will depend on the alcohol concentration of the drink. **supple** is a largel
describe a palate that is round and pliant, with no aggressive tannins. **tannins** ar
amount in the pulp of the grape is insignificant. If, as in the case of red wines, the s
be a greater extract of tannin in the resulting solution. By contrast, the skins, seed
in tear drops, also called 'legs') are especially obvious in white wines that have bee
adhering to the side of the glass and slowly moving down the side like tiny, slow-r
essentially turn on the difference in evaporation rates of alcohol and water. **terroir**
simply because it covers a multitude of environmental factors such as temperatur
mouthfeel and structure but does not concern itself with flavour elements, and is d
the finish and aftertaste. **total acidity** is one of the four most commonly used win
descriptive term for a wine named after the dominant grape variety from which
maturation of wine. Oak was the traditional medium, but in the late 19th and early 2
epoxy resin; mild steel with an enamel coating followed, and, in the second
material. **whole bunch** is, in part, self-explanatory. For white wines, whole bunches
skins and pips of the grapes; the result is very clear juice with pristine varietal frui
is very different. Here it refers to the practice of fermenting whole bunches, th
without which wine would not exist, nor food staples such as bread. **yield** is mo